Recipes for Immortality

Medicine, Religion, and Community in South India

RICHARD S. WEISS

OXFORD
UNIVERSITY PRESS
2009

OXFORD
UNIVERSITY PRESS

Oxford University Press, Inc., publishes works that further
Oxford University's objective of excellence
in research, scholarship, and education.

Oxford New York
Auckland Cape Town Dar es Salaam Hong Kong Karachi
Kuala Lumpur Madrid Melbourne Mexico City Nairobi
New Delhi Shanghai Taipei Toronto

With offices in
Argentina Austria Brazil Chile Czech Republic France Greece
Guatemala Hungary Italy Japan Poland Portugal Singapore
South Korea Switzerland Thailand Turkey Ukraine Vietnam

Published by Oxford University Press, Inc.
198 Madison Avenue, New York, New York 10016

www.oup.com

Library of Congress Cataloging-in-Publication Data
Weiss, Richard S.
Recipes for immortality : medicine, religion, and community in South India / Richard S. Weiss.
p. cm.
Includes bibliographical references and index.
ISBN 978-0-19-533523-1
1. Medicine, Siddha—Social aspects—India—Tamil Nadu. 2. Tamil (Indic people)—
Health and hygiene. 3. Group identity—India—Tamil Nadu. I. Title.
R607.T35W45 2009
610.89'9481105482—dc22 2008022066

9 8 7 6 5 4 3 2 1

Printed in the United States of America
on acid-free paper

For Mom and Dad,
and their unflagging support

Acknowledgments

The beginnings of this project, like siddha medicine, sometimes seem to disappear into the origins of time itself. There have been many who have provided support, teaching, and critique along the way.

Through his inspiring teaching, Douglas Brooks at the University of Rochester planted in my mind, at the time immersed in the minutiae of electromagnetic waves and density indexes, the practicality of pursuing an academic life in the humanities. Without his generous offer of time and encouragement, I might have gone on to produce lasers and weapons rather than this book. At the University of California at Berkeley, Sally Sutherland Goldman initiated me into the linguistic complexity of South Asian languages, and Robert Goldman instructed me in my early, awkward attempts to examine yogis and narratives.

My greatest intellectual debt is to my teachers at the University of Chicago, Wendy Doniger, Bruce Lincoln, and the late Norman Cutler. Wendy supported the project from start to finish with insight and warmth, and she consistently helped me to see how siddha medicine fit into broader South Asian contexts. Bruce has always challenged me to look at material critically, and this work has benefited immensely from his close reading and incisive comments. Norman was my primary Tamil teacher, and he saved me from many errors through his gentle criticisms and deep and wide-ranging knowledge. My study of Tamil began with Sam Sudanandha, whose remarkable teaching and love for the language made for a splendid summer of Tamil in Madison, Wisconsin. Indira Peterson has offered substantial input on the project, reading an earlier version in its entirety. My colleagues at Victoria University, and especially in religious studies, have provided a wonderful environment in which to work, write, and teach.

There have been many in India who have supported me and my research in numerous ways. S. Bharathy of the American Institute of Indian Studies in Madurai played a significant role in the development of my Tamil skills, and she introduced me to the topic of siddha medicine. In Thanjavur, V. R. Madhavan assisted me in the overall conception of the project and especially in its manuscript legacy. G. Bhaskaran led me in reading some of the poetry of the yogi siddhars, and C. Prema generously allowed me to be present in her consultations.

In Chennai, V. R. Jayalakshmi spent more than a year meeting with me to read early siddha medical texts, and her expertise and patience have contributed significantly to the project. The Institute of Asian Studies offered an institutional affiliation for my research. At the Mariamalai Adigal library in Georgetown, Mr. Sundaramurthy was always extremely helpful in tracking down items, and he led me to several sources that I would not have found otherwise. A number of siddha practitioners were particularly helpful: Kundrathur Ramamurthy, G. J. Parthasarathy, K. Venkatesan, K. V. Abirami, and Ajita Porkoti all generously offered their time, knowledge, publications, and invariably excellent food and drink. Jeyaram Soundrapandi deserves special recognition for his skill in orienting me to the landscape of contemporary siddha medical practice in Chennai.

Many others have played a role in shaping this project. Among them are Barney Bate, Joe Bulbulia, Maheswari Chidambaram, Whitney Cox, Don Davis, Deepali Dewan, Anna Gade, Lorena Garrido, Greg Grieve, Gary Hausman, Aliki Kalliabetsos, Srinivas Krishnamurthy, Layne Little, McKim Marriot, Cei Maslen, Paul Morris, Parimal Patil, Anushka Perinpanayagam, Sheldon Pollock, Michael Radich, T. N. Ramachandran, Ajay Rao, Frank Reynolds, Jon Schofer, Brigitte Sebastia, David Shulman, Jeyaram Soundrapandi, Will Sweetman, Peggy Trawick, Katherine Ulrich, A. R. Venkatachalapathy, R. Vijayalakshmy, Blake Wentworth, and two anonymous readers at Oxford University Press. I want to express my gratitude to Cynthia Read at OUP for enthusiastically taking on the project.

A number of grants supported this research. A Social Science Research Council Pre-Dissertation Fellowship (South Asia) provided funding for an exploratory trip to Thanjavur in 1997. Research in Chennai in 1998–2000 was supported by a Fulbright-Hays Doctoral Dissertation Research Abroad Fellowship and a Social Science Research Council/American Council of Learned Societies International Dissertation Field Research Fellowship. The Committee on South Asian Studies at the University of Chicago provided grants to support various stages of the project. The Martin Marty Center at the University of Chicago Divinity School supported a year of writing and provided a forum in which to present early versions of my ideas, and a William Rainey Harper Fellowship from the University of Chicago provided funding for an additional year of writing. Finally, the Faculty of Humanities and Social Sciences at Victoria University of Wellington, New Zealand, provided a grant for a trip to India for additional research materials. Without such generous support from a variety of institutions, this research and the book that has resulted from it would not have been possible.

Earlier versions of parts of this book were published as "The Autonomy of Tradition: Creating Space for Indian Medicine," in *Historicizing Tradition,* edited by Gregory Grieve and Steven Engler (2005); and as "Divorcing Ayurveda: Siddha Medicine and the Quest for Uniqueness," in *Modern and Global Ayurveda: Pluralism and Paradigms,* edited by Dagmar Wujastyk and Frederick M. Smith (2008).

Contents

Recipes for Immortality

1

Introduction

Advertisements for traditional siddha medicine in south India announce cures for a vast range of ailments. The SKM siddha medical clinic in Chennai treats everything from paralysis to hair loss to fertility problems.[1] An itinerant doctor based in Salem will cure "male problems" such as infertility, impotency, and even disturbing dreams.[2] One ashram cum clinic in Punjai Puliyampatti, in northwestern Tamil Nadu state, traces its medical recipes to an ancient yogi named Kollimalai Siddhar. It offers a memory power preparation of Indian pennywort and thirty-six other herbs, and claims to have developed and successfully tested a cure for AIDS, which it has exported to customers in New York, California, and Singapore.[3] Perhaps the most enticing product that the ashram offers is *racamaṇi*, a mercury amulet that makers prepare while reciting *mantras*. *Racamaṇi* is traditionally prescribed to cure many diseases and to counter sorcery, and it is a key ingredient in a pill that is held to enable celestial travel. This product, on offer for 250 rupees for a small amulet and 500 rupees for a large one, will make businessmen wealthy, families prosper, everyone in the household free of disease, and teenagers well-behaved and good at their studies.[4]

In India today, the sick can choose from a range of medical options, including Western biomedicine, homeopathy, Sanskritic ayurveda, Tamil siddha, Islamic unani, and Gandhian nature cure, among others. This variety might seem surprising, given the rapid globalization of the medicines, institutions, and explanatory apparatus of Western medicine. While penicillin cures many ailments, however, the complexities of human health and medical experience leave much to chance, to cultural interpretations of healing, and to the imagination. Traditional siddha doctors offer their clientele much more than the alleviation of physical distress: affiliation to a timeless and pure community, the fantasy of a Tamil utopia, and even the prospect of immortality. These doctors speak of a golden age of Tamil traditional medicine, drawing on broader revivalist formulations of a pure and ancient Tamil community. They characterize their medicines as uniquely suitable to the Tamil people, as rational and scientific, and as containing extraordinary potential to cure all ills. Narrating a history of the degeneration of Tamil civilization with the invasion of foreigners, first the Aryans from the north and then the British from the sea, they assert that the original potency of their medicine can be regained with the recovery of the purity of their tradition. They aspire above all to rediscover the lost formula for *muppu*, a medicine which they hold can heal all diseases and bestow immortality.

The high profile of traditional medicine in the public sphere in India, the proliferation of traditional clinics, and the support that these practices increasingly receive from local and national governments, testify to the vitality of traditional vocations in India today. There are currently seven colleges in Tamil Nadu, and one in neighboring Kerala, that offer BSMS degrees—Bachelor of Siddha Medicine and Surgery—which lead to registration in siddha medicine.[5] The Department of Ayurveda, Yoga and Naturopathy, Unani, Siddha and Homeopathy (AYUSH), part of the Ministry of Health and Family Welfare of the government of India, notes that in Tamil Nadu state there were 275 siddha hospitals, 435 siddha dispensaries, and 5,051 registered practitioners of siddha medicine in 2007, with 3,612 registered practitioners of ayurveda and 1,014 registered practitioners of unani in the state.[6] Nationwide in the same year there were 6,381 registered practitioners of siddha, 453,661 of ayurveda, and 46,558 of unani.[7] The number of unregistered practitioners with hereditary education is likely to be much higher than that of these officially recognized practitioners. These doctors continue to thrive in the modern world because they employ imaginative resources that speak to the sense of identity, hope, and duty of millions of people. In the pages that follow, I seek to illuminate the present success of traditional doctors by examining the ways that siddha practitioners in Tamil south India win the trust and patronage of patients. Contrary to popular perceptions and scholarly analyses that tradition and modernity coexist only uncomfortably, contemporary India has proved to be a hospitable place for people who earn their livelihoods through traditional knowledge.[8] Although traditional medical practitioners certainly face challenges today, they are keenly aware that medical patronage is won through appeals to a range of human concerns, emotions, and desires. They have at their disposal a variety of rhetorical and imaginative resources that they liberally and forcefully employ in championing their practices in a landscape marked by a plurality of medical choices. I argue here that the current popularity of traditional knowledge and practices in South Asia is due in large part to the effectiveness of traditional practitioners in justifying the contemporary relevance of their knowledge.

Vaidyas, traditional doctors in India, are not only resourceful in manipulating the modern world to their advantage but they are also active agents in shaping this world, and their influence increasingly extends beyond South Asia. The grounds of authority in any society are susceptible to constant revision, a process in which vaidyas are influential actors. In a medically pluralistic society such as contemporary India, medical systems must actively justify their effectiveness, and in the process they forge the criteria for medical authority in that society. This process often takes a polemical form, with promoters of one system attacking the specific medical practices and truth claims of others. The intensity of these debates is understandable, given that there is so much at stake in medical practice—it is literally a matter of life and death. Although the choice of the wrong religion might doom one to hell in the afterlife, the choice of the wrong medicine can make that afterlife come sooner than expected. Given the consistent popularity of traditional medicine in India, and the increasing diversity of medical options available throughout the world, it has become clear that there is no single medical authority that will render all alternatives irrelevant.

It is here that a study of the complex motivations of medical patronage and practice becomes important. In the pages that follow, I argue that the practices of doctors, and the decisions of patients, are forged out of a myriad concerns that are much more varied than cognitive evaluations of the efficacy of particular practices. In the context of competing medical systems, the politics of culture and identity are important factors in bids for medical authority. Siddha vaidyas invoke past and future utopias, conjoin the extraordinary and the scientific, appeal to patriotic sentiments, deliberately obfuscate their knowledge, and lament cataclysmic losses in their bid to confer value on their knowledge and to secure patronage for their practices. I will examine the discourses through which they promote their knowledge, paying more attention to the form of their arguments and to their rhetoric of authority than I will to the details of their practices. Although I acknowledge that patients take measurable physical amelioration into account when making medical decisions, I also assume a degree of autonomy between medical authority and the efficacy of particular healing practices. After all, not only are the criteria of healing themselves culturally variable but authority is also built on concerns that extend beyond judgments of efficacy, such as duty to tradition, for example, or adherence to captivating visions of personal and social identity.

In teasing out the nature of medical authority in contemporary India, the case of medical advertisements is instructive. Siddha vaidyas support their claims through appeals to the contemporary relevance of their tradition, juxtaposing symbols of the ancient and the modern. The new medical clinic in Chennai promotes the effectiveness of its medicine thus: "We prepare our medicines with substantial quality control, joining traditional medical methods, which have helped Tamil people live long, healthy lives, with new machines, under the supervision of degree holders in siddha medicine."[9] The practitioner from Salem refers to seven generations of continuous family practice, to 180 years of experience in a single family tradition, and to his new Web site.[10] The clinic in Punjai Puliyampatti boasts of its eight generations of continuous family practice, and of its "modern" and "scientific" research.[11] These traditional medical practitioners link together a rhetoric of science, community, autochthony, and the extraordinary potential of ancient knowledge, thus articulating a powerful vision of community that appeals not only to the rational demands of their clientele, or solely to their medical needs, but also to their common aspirations, desires, and hopes. These features they assign to their medicine, which I explore in the chapters that follow, highlight the underpinnings of traditional authority in the modern world.

Siddha Medicine as Traditional Medicine

The three generally, and officially, recognized traditional medical systems in India are Tamil siddha medicine, Sanskrit ayurveda, and Islamic unani. These are not the only medical options in South Asia; besides Western biomedicine, which is often called "allopathy" in India, patients seek alleviation through homeopathy, Gandhian nature cure, tantric practices, "country medicine," Reiki, goddess worship, and exorcism, to name a few.[12] Of indigenous South Asian medical practices, siddha, unani, and especially ayurveda enjoy a degree of hegemony with the independent Indian government because of their ascribed ancientness, their grounding in literary traditions, and their susceptibility to systematization. I focus on siddha medicine in the following pages, although other medical systems will often feature in this narrative, sometimes as allies but more often as foils against which siddha doctors define their knowledge and practices.

Although there are good studies of the spread of biomedicine in India with European imperialism and postcolonial globalization, there are few extended studies that address the response of indigenous practitioners to these processes.[13] Furthermore, as C. J. Fuller points out in his work on the Minakshi temple in Madurai, studies of modern India have too often focused on the writings of nationalist figures such as Gandhi or Nehru, largely ignoring the experiences of "ordinary flesh-and-blood people."[14] My study addresses these gaps by examining the efforts of siddha doctors, often marginalized in national and global contexts, to sustain their relevance in the modern world. I consulted a range of sources in the course of my research, conducted in 1997, 1998–99, and 2007, most in Tamil and some in English, including premodern medical texts, popular tracts that target broad Tamil audiences, government records, university textbooks and other didactic literature for siddha medical students and practitioners, newspapers, monthly magazines, conference proceedings, and commissioned histories. I conducted formal interviews with vaidyas and met with them in less formal contexts, and I spoke with textual scholars, patients, librarians, and anyone who had a view on traditional medicine. This included just about everyone I met in India.

Several practicing vaidyas were particularly helpful.[15] Kundrathur Ramamurthy, a registered Indian medical practitioner (R.I.M.P.), received a traditional training in siddha medicine, learning from his grandfather and from others. He runs a successful clinic in Kundrathur on the outskirts of Chennai, and is involved with shaping government policy on siddha medicine. He formulates nearly all his medicines in his laboratory adjacent to his clinic, and keeps a garden with dozens of varieties of herbs and plants. He has written two books, the first of which, *Mūlikai Pēcukiṟatu* (Speaking about medicinal plants), won an award from the Tamil Nadu government. It was first published in 1995 and remains popular among practitioners, and was in its third printing in 2004. Another vaidya, G. J. Parthasarathy, was also trained as a hereditary practitioner, and runs a clinic out of his home in Velachery, a suburb of Chennai. He has published a popular monthly called *Cittar Ulakam* (Siddhar world) since 2002, and he is active in promoting siddha medicine and in serving as a conduit for the exchange of medical knowledge. Finally, I was assisted by the well-established family of vaidyas that publishes the popular siddha medical monthly *Mūlikaimaṇi* (The wealth of medicinal plants). The magazine was founded by the late *mūlikai cakravartti* (king of medical plants) A. R. Kannappar of Vellore. His son, K. Venkatesan, has taken over the editorship of the publication and the management of the family's successful clinics in Chennai and Coimbatore, and has written a book called *Tamiḻ Ilakkiyattil Citta Maruttuvam* (Siddha medicine in Tamil literature), published in 1998. Dr. Venkatesan and his two daughters, K. V. Abirami and Ajita Porkoti, both siddha vaidyas, shared details of their family practice, their history, and their future goals. All these vaidyas generously offered their time, views, and publications, and I will often return to their spoken and written words in the pages that follow.

One written source has been especially influential in the modern formulation of siddha medicine and deserves special mention. This is T. V. Sambasivam Pillai's magisterial *Tamil-English Dictionary of Medicine, Chemistry, Botany, and Allied Sciences*, in five volumes, published in Madras by the the Research Institute of Siddhar's Science. This is a dictionary, as the title suggests, but it is much more, giving extensive commentary in both Tamil and English on many important words and concepts. It serves as a basic reference for medical terms, and the focus of the work is clearly on siddha medicine. A. R. Venkatachalapathy rightly compares Sambasivam Pillai's dictionary to the *Tamil Lexicon* that was produced at roughly the same time, and which is not much longer than Pillai's work, but which was composed with substantial government funding by a committee of scholars, whereas Pillai produced his dictionary solely through his own efforts and with his own funding.[16] He was born in 1880 in Thanjavur, and worked as a clerk and then a researcher for the Chennai police commission in the early decades of the twentieth century. He died in 1953. He first published sections of his dictionary in 1931, and the final volume was published posthumously in 1977. All five volumes were reprinted by the government of Tamil Nadu in 1990.[17] Besides being an excellent reference tool, Sambasivam Pillai's work reflects the south Indian Dravidian nationalism that was emerging in the 1920s and 1930s. The work is thus one of the earliest statements, and probably the most important, that places siddha medicine squarely in the realm of Dravidian and Tamil revivalism.

Contemporary siddha vaidyas trace the origins of their knowledge to a group of Tamil medical yogis called *siddhars*.[18] Premodern and recent mythologies describe the siddhars as ascetics who, through their yogic practice, attained supernatural powers. Writings attributed to the siddhars reject caste, emphasize a direct, internal relation with the divine, and ridicule brahmanic rituals. They cover a range of literary genres and subjects, which can be divided into two broad classes: philosophical poetry, on the one hand, and more applied disciplines, such as astrology, magic, yoga, and medicine, on the other. Here I will focus on the medical writings, and on the particular siddhars to whom these writings are attributed, although I will also occasionally refer to the siddhar poetry, as its antibrahmanism has informed contemporary views of siddha medicine.

From the early decades of the twentieth century to the present day, Tamil cultural revivalist writers have celebrated the siddhars as egalitarian and scientific, arguing for the modern credentials of Tamil tradition. Of the various subjects of siddha texts, it is medicine that has been taken up most fervently as a model for indigenous Tamil science. Vaidyas assert that the siddhars used their extraordinary knowledge to develop medicines that would preserve the body and prolong life, in this way formulating, in the words of Sambasivam Pillai, a "holy science" for the common person.[19] In their compassion for ordinary people, they transmitted this knowledge in the thousands of palm-leaf manuscripts that are today used as the canonical basis of siddha medicine. This is the legacy claimed by modern siddha practitioners, as they founded their vocation on equality, devotion to the Tamil people, and knowledge gained through extraordinary means.

The global spread of Western biomedicine continues to present the greatest challenge to people engaged in traditional medical vocations. Although today there are signs of change, biomedical doctors, buoyed by technologically sophisticated and well-funded institutions, and enjoying massive state support in India and elsewhere, have been the most vociferous critics of traditional medicine. The significance of this challenge is due in part to the physical efficacy of biomedical methods and medicines. As studies in the history of science and medicine have shown, however, the dominance of biomedicine is not simply the result of the slow but momentous diffusion of a potent science.[20] The history of the introduction of biomedicine in India and throughout the world is as much a history of imperialism as it is one of the spread of rationality. Even as colonial doctors consistently argued for their own superiority on the basis of rational considerations, their work was an integral part of the colonial project. As the historian David Arnold has convincingly demonstrated, British clinical medicine had a key role in colonizing India, attempting to "exclude its rivals and establish its monopolistic authority over the body."[21]

To a greater degree than in the pure sciences or mathematics, medical truth is difficult to adjudicate, given the complexity of bodies and the ambiguous nature of health. There has always been ample room to challenge the advance of biomedicine, which is perhaps part of the reason that biomedical critiques of traditional medical practices have been so passionate. In the matter of control over the bodies of Indians, indigenous medicine presented a much greater challenge to the British than did Indian literature, music, dance, yoga, and other traditional disciplines that could be relegated to the relatively innocuous realm of "arts," that is, those practices that did not impinge on British claims that they alone possessed the components of modern civilization. Medicine was a site of great contestation, as colonial powers claimed superiority in medical truth as a legitimating component of their imperial enterprises throughout the world.[22] The failures of any system of medicine are many, however, and it is in the gaps and uncertainties of Western medicine that traditional practitioners have argued for the relevance of their theories and practices.[23]

Additionally, since at least the early twentieth century, siddha vaidyas have had to respond to the homogenizing project of Indian nationalism. Unlike the British, who did not distinguish Indian medical practices, discounting them all as unscientific and degenerate, many Indian nationalists have sought to unify the diversity of indigenous practices into a single national system. As with other aspects of Indian nationalist culture, they base this medicine on Sanskrit texts, a bias that favors brahmanical learning and ayurvedic practices. In nationalist rhetoric, ayurveda is frequently considered to be the original medicine of India, and Tamil medical texts are often regarded as plagiarized versions of the Sanskrit.[24] In India and abroad, many ayurvedic practitioners continue to assert that ayurveda is the national medicine of India.[25] Siddha vaidyas, mostly non-brahmans who base their practices on Tamil texts, have been challenged in this way from within Indian society. Like all Indian vaidyas, they have had to respond to the critique of biomedical doctors who have a different history and tradition, and at the same time they have sought to distinguish their system from the history and practice of ayurveda, with which they share much.

These medical considerations are just particular instances of more general discourses of Indian culture vis-à-vis the British, and of Indian society vis-à-vis its fractured self.[26] In these debates, Tamil non-brahmans have fared particularly badly. Orientalist scholars writing on India tended to locate anything of value in Indian civilization in its Vedic, Aryan features, which they opposed to a Dravidian culture that they associated with non-brahman south India.[27] Indian nationalism utilized the categories and reflected the biases of this scholarship, envisioning an independent Indian state that would nurture a pure civilization that was Sanskritic in its features. With independence and the victory of the Indian National Congress in 1947, the locus of political power shifted to the north, fulfilling the fears of non-brahman leaders in south India. Political power in Tamil-speaking areas also shifted more squarely to brahmans at that time, as Tamil brahmans held the leadership of the Congress party in Tamil Nadu. This national bias toward Sanskrit culture continues to be expressed today at the national level, most influentially by the organizations of the Sangh Parivar and other groups of the Hindu right.

These broader political, social, and religious discourses have significantly shaped specific medical practices in India, and they have contributed models through which vaidyas assert their legitimacy. Given the importance of these larger discursive processes, I focus on more than medicine in the following pages. In doing so, I draw insights from medical anthropology and the history of science, which have made it clear that medical authority is won as much through appeals to culture and history as it is secured through the efficacy of medicines. Unfortunately, scholars of religion have not kept pace with these disciplines in examining healing phenomena. Although anthropologists have for decades considered medical practice to be embedded in specific cosmologies and symbols, historians of religion seem to have accepted the biomedical division between religion and science, and they have located medicine squarely in the latter. The discipline continues to fall prey to the misconception pointed out by Emiko Ohnuki-Tierney, when she criticizes the "tacit assumption . . . that although religion once played a major role in health care . . . the modernization process, especially scientific development, has separated medicine from magic and religion."[28] Medicine and religion share much, as both seek solutions to the ever-present problems of human suffering and mortality. Indeed, in promoting their knowledge, siddha vaidyas join discourses about medicine, science, religion, politics, and tradition, making this a germane topic for religious studies.

Although there has been a proliferation of scholarly literature in the past two decades that focuses on traditional medicine around the world, importantly attending to specific configurations of disease, the body, diagnostic procedures, and so on, there has been a surprising lack of attention given to the particular cultural and historical authority of the designation "traditional." As I began to examine the writings and practices of siddha vaidyas in south India, it became clear that the status of their practice as a particular, local tradition has been central in their bid for authority. In the past century, siddha vaidyas have self-consciously located their knowledge and practices in a revered, ancient past, and in a specific, idealized community. In this they share much with, and draw from, broader revivalist efforts to secure a place for Tamil tradition in the modern world. Vaidyas imagine their enterprise and shape their practices through the specific qualities by which revivalists define Tamil tradition: rationality, ancientness, egalitarianism, and timeless essence.

The centrality of medicine in formulations of Tamil tradition and vice versa should come as no surprise. Medicine is perhaps uniquely suited to justify a link between the bodies of a people and specific practices and knowledge. Just as bodies are the loci of individual identities, likewise a community's bodily practices and conceptions of illness and health are important components of collective representation. Medicine and tradition forge a comfortable alliance, because all medicine is perpetuated through tradition, and all traditions will position human bodies and health in larger frames of meaning. Among practitioners who describe themselves as traditional doctors or healers, this often implicit link is made explicit, usually as a result of radical social and cultural change that compels conscious reflection on traditions that were previously taken for granted.

When siddha vaidyas affirm that they practice traditional medicine, they assert an exclusive link between individual Tamil bodies and an imagined Tamil community. An international Tamil conference, held in Chennai in 1968, included an auxiliary seminar on siddha medicine. This conference was the second of a succession of international Tamil conferences that have been held periodically since the 1960s, and which have sought to promote Tamil culture with a significant revivalist orientation.[29] The published proceedings to the 1968 siddha seminar begins with a poetic eulogy to siddha medicine, written by A. Shanmuga Velan, a scholar of siddha medical texts at the Sarasvati Mahal library in Thanjavur.[30]

The country of the goddess Shakti is none other than our country;[31]
The language which bestowed the original medicine is none other than
our Tamil;
The Potigai Mountain which shines golden is the mountain of our
siddhar;[32]
There is no equal to this celebrated mountain;
The extremely rare and valuable *muppū kuru* medicine is ours and no
other's;

On this earth, what other medicine can match this, our *kaṟpa* medicine?[33]
The literature of the celebrated siddhars is none other than our literature;
And there is no other literature like this in the world.[34]

Shanmuga Velan joins the components of a Tamil tradition—language, geography, medicine, literature, and the siddhars—with the Tamil people in a relationship of possession. However, it is not clear who possesses what. The relationship between the Tamil people and their tradition is not a simple case of prior subjects possessing traditional knowledge, because this knowledge delineates and constitutes them in turn as Tamil people and as siddha vaidyas. Tamil tradition defines the essential nature of the community, which itself would be devoid of character if not for the tradition that describes it. While a tradition is continuously shaped by a people, it shapes them in turn.

According to siddha vaidyas and Tamil cultural revivalists more generally, the loss of any of these components of Tamil tradition would entail at least a partial loss of the Tamil community. In their bid to bring Tamils into their examination rooms, siddha vaidyas impress on potential clientele that, insofar as individuals identify themselves as part of a community, their actions have consequences beyond the individual. They disparage Tamil patronage of biomedical doctors as both a betrayal of self and an act of treachery toward the community. They also lament that this disloyalty undercuts their own livelihoods. Yet in their writings that I examine in subsequent chapters, vaidyas aspire to do more than assure the continuity of their practices, or even their vocations. They seek to establish a place in the modern world for themselves as important actors, for their knowledge as significant and relevant, and for their vision of Tamil tradition as one of the greatest the world has known. Their success in recent years makes their project worth examining.

The "Tradition" in Traditional Medicine

In its simplest formulation, tradition entails an orientation to the past. Any tradition joins content—the rituals, texts, heroic figures, and other substantial and ideal material (i.e., a canon)—with hermeneutics, interpretations of this ever-shifting canon that inform specific configurations of community. Actors formulate traditions to affirm a synchronic bond between contemporaries, and they extend that bond into the past into a diachronic community. Thus, traditional action involves reverence toward past events, actors, practices, and knowledge as holding a value that cannot, or at least has not, been superseded. Tradition, however, is not only about the past; it is also about the present in which the past is seen to retain its relevance, and it provides models for future action. When a siddha vaidya tells of a perfect medical tradition prior to Sanskritic influence, he criticizes a present in which Tamil knowledge is subordinated to Sanskrit knowledge in national and international contexts. He also implies an agenda for the future, which involves the purification of siddha knowledge of all its Sanskritic elements. In valuing the past, a traditional orientation will tend toward conservatism rather than innovation, but tradition is not as static as it is claimed to be.

This orientation to the past is held with greater or lesser degrees of consciousness. It is primarily the consciousness of action that distinguishes tradition as imitation from tradition as invention, to cite two dominant conceptions of tradition.[35] Tradition incorporates both of these extremes, insofar as both imitation and invention can be actions that entail the authority of the past in forging community. There are traditions that are unconscious, taken for granted, but that nevertheless are implicitly cognized, if not recognized. On the other end of the spectrum are rituals, forms of knowledge and practice, texts, and so on, that are deliberately articulated as traditional, and that serve as central, visible representations of community. They may or may not have been performed in the past, but they are employed to forge a link between present and past manifestations of an imagined, continuous community. Following Jean and John Comaroff's discussion of ideology, when tradition is engaged unconsciously, it is hegemonic, and when it is conscious, it is ideological. "Hegemony homogenizes, ideology articulates. Hegemony, at its most effective, is mute; by contrast, 'all the while, ideology babbles on.'"[36] That is, although sometimes tradition is implicit, taken for granted, naturalized, and habitual, it can also be explicit, articulated, and therefore open to contestation.

In looking at the writings of siddha vaidyas, I will examine articulations of tradition that are more conscious than unconscious, traditions that are debated, organized, formulated, and asserted. Actors deliberately and consciously represent something as traditional to perform the work of community building. Because explicit formulations of tradition actively construct human experience, they are more than cynical instruments (as implied by the language of "invention") with which one social group manipulates another. As Althusser holds for ideology, those who formulate the character and contents of a tradition are "caught by it, implicated by it, just when they are using it and believe themselves to be absolute masters of it."[37] Although traditions are themselves constructed and modeled, at the same time they provide models for a variety of practices and conceptions, and they govern the ways in which people discern meaning. They structure consciousness, history, and memories, providing representations through which actors come to understand their worlds. Therefore, siddha vaidyas do not act on their medical tradition as entirely autonomous agents, because they themselves are shaped by this tradition in important ways. This suggests a methodological approach that

I will follow throughout this study, which involves shifting back and forth between the past and the present, between the sources for the contemporary identity of siddha vaidyas and their projects to dictate the present and to shape the future.

Considerations of tradition must also take into account issues of authority. Specific practices and knowledge have frequently been criticized as "traditional" by those who seek to undermine their authority, usually by opposing them to the modern. At the same time, those whose practices have been identified as traditional have often run with this nomenclature, insisting that their traditions are modern, rational, and most important, essential components of their community. For these self-proclaiming traditional practitioners, what Marx called the "nightmare" of tradition provides a refuge into realms of human experience over which they can continue to exert control.[38] While for Marx tradition was the burden of the past that limited the possibilities for action, for those whose control over present circumstances is tenuous, whose agency in material worlds is limited vis-à-vis other societies, flights into the nonmaterial worlds of the past, or of religion, are efforts to master worlds of imagination in the midst of material and bodily subjection. Following Benedict Anderson, I hold imagination to be one of the primary arenas of human activity, not an illusion that gives consolation to those who lack material resources.[39] Indeed, tradition, reconfigured by contemporary agendas, is precisely that realm of human practices and forms of knowledge that communities consider to be their own.

Drawing from Slavoj Zizek, I will argue that among the interests that compel adherence to traditions are the ideological fantasy as well as the desire and enjoyment stimulated by this fantasy.[40] Those who actively shape traditions do not simply appeal to audiences to accept the truth of their message but also invite their audiences to participate in the narrative construction of a social self that provides the individual with comfort and enjoyment. The elaboration of a Tamil community and tradition is a call to non-brahman Tamils to imagine themselves as part of a utopian community, an ideal world in which the social body is absolutely unified. The price of participation is loyalty and adherence to the tradition and culture that constitute this community. Traditional leaders dictate that duty to tradition is necessary to maintain a harmonious conjunction of individual essence and social forms of knowledge and practice. Non-brahman Tamil leaders express the reward of adherence to tradition as the recovery of a utopian society, a reunion with the divine, a scientific revolution that will place the Tamil sciences at the apex of the world's systems of knowledge, and bodily health within the community culminating in, perhaps, longevity for all. Thus, narrative constructions of a pure and potent Tamil tradition offer a fantasy that itself is constitutive, providing the subject not only with the appearance of a unified identity but also, importantly, with enjoyment.

Tamil Notions of Tradition

The closest Tamil term that captures some of what I have described as tradition is *paramparai* (Sanskrit *paraṃparā*). The word is formed by conjoining *param* with *param*, where *param* means "other, another, remote." Paramparai, then, carries the sense of transmission between two people, from one to another. This transmission is not so much the dispersal of knowledge among contemporaries as it is the transmission of knowledge from one generation to the next. It designates a mode of education, the teaching that passes from a guru to a disciple. The term highlights the fact that knowledge will perish with its possessor if it is not transmitted to some other; this creates the need for a diachronic community of knowledge and the dedication to preserve the knowledge of preceding generations.

The South Asian conceptualization of paramparai as descent is one of lineage and not genealogy. As one traces descent through a genealogy, the number of ancestral figures increases twofold with each successive past generation, and so there is no single originary progenitor in a genealogical account of ancestry. The logic of the paramparai, on the other hand, is that of linear continuity, not dispersal through time, as its practitioners will trace their knowledge to a single origin in asserting a unified identity. Contemporary siddha vaidyas will often locate themselves within specific paramparais, citing proximate historical gurus as well as a founding siddhar for their lineages. For example, G. J. Parthasarathy considers himself to be in the lineage of his grandfather, who taught him medicine, but he also cites the siddhar Tirumular as the proto-guru of his knowledge. In placing himself in a lineage of teaching that began with Tirumular, Parthasarathy claims a direct connection to an original and true teaching that his particular lineage faithfully embodies. When two lineages claim the same progenitor, there may be contention between them over which one truly preserves the original teaching.

A derivative form of paramparai is *pāramapariyam*. As is the case with paramparai, the earliest South Asian occurrences of this word are in Sanskrit, pāraṃparyam. In Sanskrit, pāraṃparyam has the sense of "hereditary succession," "traditional instruction," or simply "tradition."[41] The Tamil pāramapariyam carries these same meanings, indicating anything that relates to lineage, and often can be translated simply as "tradition." It generally describes a particular body of knowledge or skill that is passed down through generations, such as *terukkūttu* street theater, siddha medicine, or any of the other "sixty-four arts" of the Tamils. Contemporary vaidyas often refer to "traditional experience" (*pāramapariyamāṉa aṉupavam*) or speak adverbially to describe something practiced in the manner of prior generations (*paramparaiyāka*). In both cases vaidyas use these terms today to indicate not only lineage but also the "old ways," and as such they oppose tradition to education and knowledge based on models introduced by the British. In this more recent usage, paramparai and pārampariyam carry a broader sense than lineage, referring more generally to the traditions of knowledge that define a Tamil community distinct from other ethnic or national communities. Indeed, the articulation of a single, unified Tamil medical tradition was unimaginable before the twentieth century, as the salient units of medical tradition, in the sense of communities within which knowledge and practices are shared, were hereditary lineages that traced their origins through a series of gurus to a founding siddhar, whether Agastiyar, Bhogar, or another of the dozens of siddhars whose authorship is ascribed to medical texts.

Siddha vaidyas generally have held that their medical knowledge originated with the siddhars, who were literally "perfected" beings. Members of a lineage therefore feel compelled to preserve this knowledge as carefully as possible. Contemporary vaidyas lament that the transmission of siddha knowledge and practice has been marred by foreign invasions, superstition, and the inevitable decay of palm leaf manuscripts. They hold that their knowledge is a pale reflection of the original, perfect teaching of the siddhars. Discursively, they often therefore discourage experimentation and innovation as detours from a primordial truth. In practice, however, vaidyas admit two modes of medical knowledge, *kaipākam* and *ceypākam*. Kaipākam designates practical knowledge of medical preparation, gathered through individual experience, whereas ceypākam is the process of preparation garnered through medical texts or according to theories laid out in these texts. Vaidyas often join these two ways of actualizing medical knowledge in formulating their medicines. For example, an herbal research institute has produced a medicine to cure AIDS through "joining our 45 years of herbal research with research on manuscripts written by Kollimalai Siddhar, in a way consistent with the modern scientific age."[42] Tension is apparent between the consideration of kaipākam as a proper approach to the innovative development of medical knowledge, on the one hand, and the desire to maintain claims to accurately, fully, and exclusively transmit an original teaching, on the other. This tension continues to be played out in contemporary debates over the future direction of siddha medicine, pitting those who wish to maintain the "purity" of siddha medical knowledge against those who wish to innovate in accordance with "the times."[43]

Tamils often speak of *Tamiḻuṇarvu*, Tamil-feeling, and *Tamiḻppaṟṟu*, Tamil-devotion. Tamil-feeling points to an emotional orientation, a centripetal movement toward a unified Tamil community. *Paṟṟu*, as Sumathi Ramaswamy has pointed out, carries the sense of adherence, devotion, attachment, and affection.[44] More literally, it means holding, grasping onto, or retention. In the context of tradition, then, Tamiḻppaṟṟu is a dedication to community, a particular sort of dedication that grasps or retains what has come before. Adherence to tradition is both a commitment and a duty to a community that existed in the past, exists in the present, and will continue to exist in the future, as long as its members do not abandon it. In other words, the character often attributed to tradition is *timeliness*, relevance in all times, and this attribute paradoxically becomes the grounds for a claim to the *timelessness* of tradition, its eternal essence. Adherence to tradition is an orientation toward an imagined timeless community, borne of the desire to submerge one's personal identity into a larger community that transcends that individual. The desire for tradition can therefore be seen as a desire for immortality. It is perhaps no coincidence that siddha vaidyas often assert that the recovery of their tradition in its original purity will enable them to formulate medicines that will cure all ills, from cancer to asthma to AIDS, and rejuvenate and preserve Tamil bodies for eternity.

The Sign of Science

As with many discourses on truth in the modern world, considerations of science come to the fore in south Indian debates over tradition and medicine. I will not use science here in an analytic sense, as siddha vaidyas incorporate science into their traditions in positively unscientific ways. Like Gyan Prakash, I consider science as a discursive sign in South Asian debates over the effectiveness of medical practices and the relevance of tradition. I will examine "science's cultural authority as the legitimating sign of rationality and progress."[45] The universality of science does not derive from its claim to the singular truth of its method, but rather from its multivalence as a sign of authority. Like other powerful signs, science is employed to claim authority in a variety of contexts, an authority that has as much to do with technology, politics, and imperial success as it does with a method of constructing knowledge. In other words, when Tamils invoke science as a central part of their tradition, they universalize it, not in its method but in its rhetorical link to power and authority.

Vaidyas generally qualify science by community, speaking of "Western science" and "Tamil science." They bifurcate science, marshaling its authority to legitimate Tamil tradition, and caricaturing its Western forms as grossly inadequate. They hold that Western science has disenchanted the world because it only considers the physicality of things, whereas Tamil science recognizes the divine in substances, in human individuals, and in the Tamil community. Vaidyas characterize Tamil science as ancient and thus as preceding Western science, and also as the culmination of Western science on account of its superior truth, which Western science will recognize in the future.

At the same time, siddha vaidyas often link Western and Tamil traditions by arguing that both share a rational, scientific account of natural processes. Many employ the language of science especially in rejecting the other "other" of Tamil revivalist discourse, the Aryan brahman (and his project of the Indian nation), whom they describe not only as ethnically and racially other but also as mentally other, his character being that of superstition, myth, and empty ritual. Nonbrahman Tamil authors narrate a history of science and religion among Tamils that begins with an original, rational Tamil society that was slowly corrupted with the growth of Hinduism and brahmanic religiosity. Siddha vaidyas thereby call upon racial and ethnic criteria in discerning this original scientific civilization, marking brahmanic cultural forms as superstitious and un-Tamil. Even as siddha vaidyas celebrate aspects of their tradition that are not scientific, claiming, for example, that a perfect and pure Tamil medicine can make a body free of illness, hard as a diamond, or invisible, they continue to emphasize the scientific nature of *Tamil paṇpāṭu*, or Tamil culture. Thus, defenders of Tamil tradition have appropriated notions of science that originated outside India, and they stereotype and manipulate scientific discourse in the service of their pointedly nonscientific agendas. While Western science has articulated critiques of Tamil traditions, these traditions have taken possession of science in a traditional space in which they can shape it as they please.

2

The Autonomy of Tradition

Creating Space for Traditional Medicine

The designation "traditional" has proved to be a double-edged sword for indigenous medical practitioners in India over the past century. Biomedical doctors have called Indian medical practices traditional to depict them as outdated and therefore irrelevant to modern civilization. Indian practitioners, however, have promoted the traditional character of their medicine, highlighting the sense of community and continuity entailed in tradition. It is under the mantle of tradition that Tamil vaidyas have asserted the sovereign character of their medicine and their culture, pointing to a unique essence that they discern in the products of an ancient civilization prior to foreign influence. In arguing that the purity of their tradition must be recaptured and preserved, siddha vaidyas take on the task of sealing the porous and ever-shifting boundaries of tradition. Thus, the formulation and promotion of traditional medicine in South Asia has been in part an apologetic activity, as indigenous practitioners have faced the challenges presented by an increasingly competitive medical market.

In nineteenth- and twentieth-century India, the status of tradition has been hotly contested; indeed, the dichotomy of universal science and local tradition is an historical one. Although much has been made of the way colonial authorities employed this dichotomy to relegate the knowledge of their imperial subjects to the past, less attention has been given to how notions of tradition have provided autonomous and impenetrable spaces over which Indians could exert control.[1] Partly as a response to the challenge of biomedicine, Indian indigenous practitioners have sought to establish their autonomy under the umbrella of Indian traditional medicine. In doing so, they determine the ground rules from which they make their claims, independent of the universalizing objectives of biomedicine or of any other tradition. Writing within their own sphere of influence, vaidyas have reconceived their practices, their traditions, and themselves in ways that unify an Indian community and establish the grounds for agency within that community. I will trace their strategic employment of the notion of tradition, suggesting not that vaidyas appropriated an imperial category and used it against the British, but that the dichotomy itself emerged from a cultural encounter that those on each side of the conflict used to their advantage. In interrogating contemporary assertions of unique and bounded traditional medical systems in their historical, colonial, and national contexts, I will offer an understanding of how one society has resisted cultural imperialism. This chapter, then, suggests in part an answer to a more general question: What motivates assertions of community boundaries?

Indian Medicine and Western Biomedicine

Before moving onto more local Tamil concerns in subsequent chapters, here I will outline the largest traditional compass within which siddha vaidyas have imagined their practices, their knowledge, and themselves, that is, as Indian in character. As we have seen, siddha vaidyas have emphasized the Tamil nature of their medicine in asserting the uniqueness of their healing tradition. However, these vaidyas have often joined with ayurvedic practitioners (also called vaidyas) and with unani doctors (*hakims*) in formulating a concerted response to Western biomedicine.[2] It is perhaps not surprising that the alliance of diverse indigenous medical practitioners in India emerged out of the confrontation with a common rival. In the past century, practitioners of all traditions of Indian medicine, like other specialists of non-Western medicine throughout the world, have seen the legitimacy of their knowledge challenged by biomedicine. Biomedical doctors have argued for a single, universal medical discipline, dismissing the possibility of an enduring medical landscape whose contours are constituted by disparate theories and practices. For the past two centuries in India, these doctors have assumed that the rationality of their own medicine is indisputable and therefore will, in accordance with a historical teleology of progress defined by the absorption of the traditional other, gradually effect the desiccation and ultimate demise of indigenous medicine.[3]

Debates over medical efficacy have been part of larger discussions of the future viability of non-Western cultural practices, especially those that impinge on disciplines that are classified as sciences. Since the early decades of the nineteenth century, one of the major issues facing indigenous medical practitioners in India has been whether their knowledge should be treated as unique and self-sufficient, or whether it should be supplemented by, or integrated into, biomedical learning.[4] Some indigenous medical practitioners have called for the synthesis of Western and indigenous knowledge into a single, universal medical system. The College of Integrated Medicine was founded in Madras in 1947 with this goal of integrating biomedical and indigenous medical knowledge.[5] Others have argued that, given the disparities of power inherent in colonial and postcolonial processes, traditional knowledge suffers neglect in the hands of the modern state and so is in peril of disintegration. These latter practitioners commonly delineate a realm of traditional activity with the defining feature of autonomy, in which they are free to formulate their own rules and insist on the relativity of truth vis-à-vis external critiques.[6] While these promoters of pure tradition often segregate themselves along linguistic lines—Tamil (siddha), Sanskrit (ayurveda), and Arabic and Urdu (unani)—they have been unified in their opposition to the universalizing goals of biomedicine. It was not without reason that they have felt the need to circumscribe and withdraw into an autonomous realm over which they might assume control. The global influence of biomedicine is due not only to its efficacy but also, just as importantly, to its connection with imperial force.

The British attempt to establish a medical school that incorporated both indigenous and British teachings is instructive in depicting colonial attitudes toward Indian medical practices. In 1822, the secretary of the Calcutta Medical Board proposed to establish a new school of medical education, in order to train Indians to serve the medical needs of the British.[7] A government order of June 21, 1822, established the Native Medical Institution in Calcutta, which would teach classes in Western and indigenous medicine in the vernacular languages.[8] This was the first time traditional Indian knowledge and techniques were taught in the classroom style of early nineteenth-century British education.[9] The purpose of the new school was to better train Indians to contribute to the medical needs of the East India Company, most commonly as assistants in military battalions.[10] These assistants, called "native doctors," served an eclectic range of tasks, some of which required basic knowledge of clinical medical techniques. The founding of the school had a further, covert purpose: those sitting on the Medical Board were confident that the conjoint presentation of allopathy and indigenous medicine would instill the realization in Indians of the "superiority of the new race."[11] Though convinced of the rationality of their medical practices, the British realized the necessity of an institutional apparatus to encourage its spread.

The status of indigenous medicine as a local tradition, not a universal science, was central in policy decisions of the British administration. The colonial administrators of the Native Medical Institution made no attempt to synthesize or integrate Indian and British theories and practices, but rather the curriculum consisted of the conjoint teaching of disparate systems. For the Western side of the course, physiology, anatomy, and pharmacology were taught in the first year, and the last two years consisted of instruction in clinical training in Calcutta hospitals. Students were taught ayurvedic texts and techniques at the Calcutta Sanskrit College, while the Calcutta Madrasa taught courses in unani.[12] At this early colonial moment, the British grouped indigenous medicine with literature and the arts, considering it to be a part of local tradition distinct from universal science. This is consistent with the changing English usage of the term "science," which in its earliest appearances in the fourteenth and fifteenth centuries was conjoined with notions of art. Only later in the seventeenth and eighteenth centuries did science come to represent disciplines of knowledge that were opposed to art.[13] The institutional divisions in the Native Medical Institution reflect this history, as the relegation of non-European medical traditions to a school of literature and the arts was a forceful statement that any future science of medicine would be carried out in the Western clinic, not on the basis of the ancient texts and hereditary practices of India.

It is no coincidence that the dissolution of the Native Medical Institution and the release of Thomas Macaulay's "Minute on Education" both occurred in 1835. Macaulay set the course of government patronage of Indian education for the next century. He dismissed vernacular scientific education, asserting the agreement of "all parties" that "the dialects commonly spoken among the natives of this part of India contain neither literary nor scientific information, and are, moreover, so poor and rude that, until they are enriched from some other quarter, it will not be easy to translate any valuable work into them." He admitted the poetic excellence of Sanskrit and Arabic, but asserted that "when we pass from works of imagination to works in which facts are recorded, and general principles investigated, the superiority of the Europeans becomes absolutely immeasurable." The classical languages may be appropriate for works of fiction, but their capabilities do not extend to the representation of facts, science, or truth.[14]

The school's dissolution is seen by many to have been a watershed in the victory of "Anglicists" over "Orientalists" in the debate over the proper relationship of Western and South Asian disciplines of knowledge.[15] However, as Zhaleh Khaleeli convincingly argues, the motivations for the founding of the Native Medical Institution were from the start utilitarian and imperial, and not borne out of a desire to promote native education or indigenous medicine.[16] James Mill had been one of the most influential critics of the scientific potential of Indian knowledge, arguing that "With respect to sciences it was worse than a waste of time to employ persons to teach and learn them in the state in which they were found in the Oriental books. Our great aim should be not to teach Hindu learning, but sound learning."[17] Subsequent to the closure of the Native Medical Institution, the Calcutta Medical College was founded to continue the education of native doctors, this time without the traditional component. Training would be carried out in English and would be exclusively dedicated to clinical medicine, as students would, in the words of a Home Department Public Branch document of March 7, 1835, "learn the principles and practice of medical science in strict accordance with the mode adopted in Europe."[18]

The Defense of Indigenous Theory and Language

Since Hobsbawm and Ranger's pioneering volume *The Invention of Tradition*, it has been clear that traditions have histories. What are less often examined are histories of the changing notions of tradition, and the authority entailed in specifying a particular practice as traditional. In nineteenth- and twentieth-century India, when British administrators classified indigenous medicine as traditional in order to relegate it to the arts, and also to the past, they did not anticipate the multivalence of the term, nor the resilience of the authority that it entailed. Indian vaidyas have fashioned tradition as a sovereign sphere within which they can exert control. The boundaries of tradition, they argue, provide a shield across which biomedical critiques lose their force. The British themselves acknowledged a degree of autonomy for traditional activity, as expressed in their noninterference policies in religious matters, which they regarded as concerns internal to Indian society, not public affairs.[19] Medicine, however, was a more active concern of colonial authorities, as the health of Indians affected the health of the British in India due to infectious diseases.[20] A debate over the efficacy of Indian medicines in the first quarter of the twentieth century highlights the ways in which the notion of tradition served the purposes of Indian and British biomedical doctors, colonial authorities, and traditional medical practitioners.

On November 26, 1915, A. S. Krishna Rao proposed a resolution in the Legislative Council of the Madras Presidency that the Madras government "direct a research and investigation of the Ayurvedic system of medicine, with a view to improve and encourage that system."[21] Rao proposed a study of ayurveda, to the exclusion of unani and Tamil texts and practices, consistent with an emerging Indian nationalism that formulated a national culture with Sanskritic knowledge and texts. The resolution was passed in 1917, though in a much revised form: "to direct a research and investigation of the pharmacological action of Indian drugs." The transformation of the resolution encapsulates several important historical presuppositions. The wording of the final resolution was dictated through the intervention of representatives of the colonial government and the biomedical establishment. A. G. Cardew, minister for medicine, objected to the proposal, simply saying that the government did not have the funds for such encouragement, requesting that the words "with a view to encourage and improve the systems [of indigenous medicine]" be deleted. T. M. Nayar then proposed that the words "ayurvedic system of medicine" be replaced with "the pharmacological action of Indian drugs."[22] Nayar's suggestion has two components. One is that "Ayurvedic" be replaced with "Indian," exhibiting either a sensitivity to non-brahman Tamil and unani practitioners and including their knowledge in the final proposal, or more likely dismissing the rich and diverse histories of indigenous medical practices, clumping them all together as "Indian" to facilitate a more comprehensive utilization of their possible medical and commercial benefits.

The more significant transformation was less subtle, entailing a shift from the initial goal of a broad study to encourage the development of ayurvedic medicine to an investigation of indigenous drugs in order to supplement and improve the biomedical system. Leading biomedical doctors and colonial authorities thereby expressed faith in the physical material of India but not in the knowledge produced and recorded in, as surgeon general G. G. Giffard put it, the "unintelligible" Sanskrit writings, a language of "priestly mysticism" that is unsuited for scientific truths. When M. C. Koman was appointed chairman of this committee and began to carry out the investigation, the nature of this inquiry was not lost on the local vernacular press. The *Andhrapatrika*, a Telegu paper, observed that "the appointment of Dr. Koman to make a research regarding these systems was not made with the object of improving them but for incorporating in the English pharmacopoeia the efficacious drugs which are used therein."[23] The *Andhra Medical Journal* also took on the issue in an article in November 1922 entitled "Is Ayurveda to Be Encouraged? Or the British Pharmacopea to Be Enlarged?"[24] The colonial plundering of native material wealth with a rejection of indigenous forms of knowledge was manifested in many realms, and medicine was no exception.

Koman submitted three reports to the government of the Madras Presidency from 1918 to 1920. In these reports, he considered a range of ingredients used for indigenous medicines and tested their effects on patients according to the standards of Western science. What I want to focus on here, however, is not the Koman Report itself, but the response to this report by the Dravida Vaidya Mandal and the Madras Ayurveda Society. The Dravida Vaidya Mandal represented primarily non-brahman vaidyas who based their practices on Tamil texts, and the Ayurveda Society represented brahman vaidyas who drew from Sanskrit works. Their *Reply to the Report on the Investigation into the Indigenous Drugs* was published in 1921. A response of this sort was necessary, these practitioners argued, because the "learned doctor, appointed by the Government, had thoroughly failed to understand the indigenous systems and had grievously erred on many vital points." Noting that Koman judged the effect of some indigenous medicines as "beneficial," the vaidyas continued that their protest "is not against what is declared as 'beneficial' etc., but against the mortal wound inflicted on the vital parts."[25] These "vital parts" are indigenous theories of health and the body, the areas of Indian medical knowledge that colonial health administrators did not consider worthy of consideration.

In his report, Koman asserts that "from what I have seen the science of Hindu medicine is still sunk in a state of empirical obscurity."[26] The vaidyas interpret this rightly: "To them [Koman, biomedical doctors, and colonial authorities] the use of drugs in Ayurveda is a matter of accidence [*sic*] which the learned doctor was kind enough to say as 'empirical.'"[27] Koman suggests that although there may be some useful medicines in the indigenous pharmacopoeia, these were chanced upon by practitioners, not systematically hypothesized through the application of theory. The vaidyas admonish Koman and the project in general for only being concerned with the properties of indigenous drugs while failing "to grasp the intricate principles of the indigenous systems."[28] For example, in his examination of the ayurvedic medicine for syphilis called Poornachandrodayam, Koman remarks that "the action of Poornachandrodayam is very slow and does not compare favourably with that of Salvarsan."[29] The vaidyas argue that Koman is influenced here by his biomedical background which values quick, temporary benefits over slower but permanent results. They counter that the report "carefully omits to mention that the treatment by Salvarsan does not thoroughly eradicate the disease from the body. Numerous cases of syphilis given up as hopeless by the allopathic physicians have been tried by the vaidyas with good and satisfactory results. The learned doctor has yet to learn why the action of Poornachandrodaya, though slow, is yet permanent while that of Salvarsan is transitory."[30] These vaidyas assert that the proper use of their medicines can only be understood in relation to indigenous theory, and that the biases of biomedical doctors prevent them from comprehending the efficacy of indigenous drugs. Medicines cannot be extracted from local traditions and integrated into a foreign system of knowledge without radically changing the nature of the medical applications. In broader terms, they claim the holistic nature of their tradition—Western medicine cannot benefit from indigenous medicines without first understanding indigenous theory. Though they might not put it in these terms, these vaidyas assert the relativity of knowledge within cultures, with the boundaries of tradition delineating spheres of effective medical understanding.

The authors of the *Reply* argue that one cannot understand the properties of Indian medicines outside of Indian traditions: what appears to be "slow" from the point of view of British medicine is considered "effective" from the Indian standpoint. Koman has dismissed the efficacy of Poornachandrodayam because he has failed to understand the traditional preparation of mercury, which causes a transformation that can only be understood through ayurvedic theory: "Ayurveda has recognized that there are seven important poisonous sheaths covering mercury which are highly injurious to the body and to remove them it has prescribed seven processes of purification as Sodhana, Jarana, Utthapana etc. By these processes mercury is made absolutely harmless. The British Pharmacopoea is quite a stranger to these methods."[31] When Koman asserts elsewhere that there is little for "us" to learn from vaidyas and hakims, his frame of reference is that of Western medicine. The vaidyas counter that Koman's lack of understanding of indigenous medical theories prevents him from successfully completing even the circumscribed task of testing the effectiveness of indigenous drugs.

The vaidyas trace Koman's misunderstanding to his use of translations and the fact that he "ridiculed" indigenous terminology that would have "greatly helped him to understand why one medicine acts either slowly or quickly or in a particular way in a disease."[32] They take Koman to task for his misunderstanding of the application of the preparation called *Vasaka* in Sanskrit. Although Koman tested Vasaka on patients with pulmonary tuberculosis, the vaidyas assert that it is specifically meant to remedy hemorrhage. To support their case, they quote a canonical ayurvedic text by Vagbhata: "*Vṛṣo jayatyasrapittaṃ sa hyasya paramauṣadham,*" or "Vrisha (Vasaka) conquers hemorrhage for it is an excellent specific for it."[33] They insert the Devanagari script into a polemic in English to mark the disjunction between different languages and so, by employing synecdoche, they suggest the disjunction between different worlds of understanding. This abrupt change of script implies that those without an understanding of South Asian scripts, languages, and texts cannot understand South Asian traditions well enough to offer an informed critique.

Whereas for Western doctors the impossibility of translation was an indication of the poverty of Indian languages and traditions, for these vaidyas the boundary of communication is a rampart against the attacks of an arrogant, uninformed foe. "So long as the properties of drugs are not known, to the practitioners of the Western system, in the terminology of Ayurveda also, so long will it have to be reckoned that all have not been 'already known' and that much is left which has to be known."[34] Indigenous medicine can only be understood, and therefore can only be critically scrutinized, by those with knowledge of South Asian languages and theories. This invocation of language boundaries parallels that utilized in other nationalist arenas. Partha Chatterjee argues that "bilingual intelligentsia came to think of its own language as belonging to that inner domain of cultural identity, from which the colonial intruder had to be kept out; language therefore became a zone over which the nation first had to declare its sovereignty and then had to transform in order to make it adequate for the modern world."[35] In countering biomedical attacks, Indian vaidyas invoke a relativity to language and theory, arguing that critique across traditions is impossible.

Alasdair MacIntyre has written extensively on the complexity of the issue of the translatability of culture. On one side of the debate are those who hold to the incommensurability of traditions, according to whom there is no independent standard that can be employed to adjudicate the claims of rival traditions, since there is no universal rationality that transcends historical contexts. The opposing position is that such incommensurability is an illusion, and that once one has the tools to translate both the arguments and standards of judgment of one tradition into the terms of another, common norms of evaluation can be ascertained.[36] Although MacIntyre's discussion is complex, he dismisses the possibility of an ethics and a rationality that can be universalized outside the contexts of particular traditions, arguing that "all reasoning takes place within the context of some traditional mode of thought."[37]

I relate these two positions not to engage in the philosophical debate on this issue, but because these two positions have been employed as rhetorical strategies by colonial authorities and by defenders of traditional medicine in South Asia over the past two centuries. That is to say, the translatability of culture is not only a philosophical or scholarly issue but a political one as well. In their critiques of indigenous medicine, biomedical doctors have argued for a single standard of rationality and a universal truth that they assert to be most fully exemplified in their own practices. Siddha practitioners invoke the principle of the incommensurability of traditions as a discursive strategy to counter the universalist challenge of those, both British and Indian, who have promoted biomedicine over the past two centuries. These vaidyas represent tradition as a sovereign realm which the critical gaze of an external, universalizing rationality cannot penetrate.

Orientalist Bodies

In addition to invoking the relative truth of tradition and the difficulties of translation to argue against a piecemeal appropriation of their knowledge, vaidyas make two sorts of spatial arguments about the uniqueness of Indian medicine. One of these spatial discourses speaks of internal and external aspects of the human body and of cosmic processes writ large, arguing that although Western biomedicine might hold its own in its understanding of the surface features of the body, Indian traditional medicine grasps the deeper, nonphysical elements of illness and healing. The second is a geographical argument that Indian medicine and Indian bodies are autochthonous, asserting that Indian medicine is compatible with Indian bodies and that Western medicine is alien to India and therefore ineffective for Indians.

Vaidyas claim a deep understanding of the interior, metaphysical aspects of the body. In doing so they reflect the conclusions of Orientalist scholarship, which hold that the expertise of the West is in its knowledge the physical world, and the strength of Oriental knowledge lies in its investigation of spiritual, mystical worlds. For some vaidyas, the coexistence of a materialistic Western science and traditional knowledge of the intangible person offers the possibility for the cooperation of medical systems, or even for their integration into a complete medicine. For example, in the proceedings of the decennial celebration of the Government College of Integrated Medicine, held in 1957, S. Nijalingappa, the chief minister of Mysore, wrote: "I think it is time that men of medical science should cast off prejudice or bias towards one system of medicine or the other and with an open mind learn from all systems and above all endeavour to know more of man—his heredity, his mental, spiritual and mystical potentialities—apart from what little of him is revealed by the application of the several branches of science such as physiology, pathology, psychology, etc."[38]

For other vaidyas, however, the disparity between Western and Indian medicine provides a space for traditional medicine apart from the universalizing, imperial aspirations of biomedicine. Whereas Europeans invoked Orientalist schemas to justify colonialism as a civilizing mission, vaidyas use them to define unique spaces for traditional knowledge.[39] They caricature the supposed mastery of physical processes achieved by Western sciences as superficial while claiming that Indian knowledge successfully accounts for both physical and nonphysical processes, and also that Indian practitioners correctly understand the relationship between these two spheres. Vaidyas have indeed long posited both physical and nonphysical matter and processes in the cosmos, both of which are relevant to illness and healing. Today, siddha vaidyas cite the siddhars as the first thinkers to have classified the world according to its inner and exterior components. They "had divided everything in the cosmos and the body into two classes: those physical objects that are composed of the five material elements and those subtle objects."[40] Likewise, drawing from yogic views of the body, scholars and practitioners of Indian medicine like T. V. Sambasivam Pillai distinguish a gross, physical body from an invisible, subtle body: "There are two kinds of structures in humans—one is the external structure of the body, and the other is the internal form. The former is conventionally known as the corporeal body and the other is called the subtle body. Therefore, if we know the structure of the internal body, then we will easily know, by means of the root substance, human diseases and their remedies."[41] Insight into this subtle side of healing processes requires the development of an intuition that comes through the spiritual insights of Indian traditions, not through mechanical apparatuses of the sort that the British so impressively possessed. "A physician or physiologist is concerned with the gross physical body. He is not aware of the subtle life force of the gross physical body which is not visible to his external sense organs. One who has developed his inner vision knows the subtle life force in him."[42]

Because this insight is garnered through South Asian religious practices, most notably disciplines of meditation, yoga, and asceticism, indigenous medical practitioners argue that knowledge of the inner workings of the body is an ancient and unique possession of Indian traditions. Siddha practitioner R. Kasturi wrote in 1970: "According to modern medicine, if one wants to see what is inside a body, one needs to dissect a corpse. Siddha practitioners, thousands of years ago, had clear knowledge about the body, and knew of all the body's internal organs with the mental eye.... Therefore, if one dissects and observes [a body] in this [modern] way, one cannot see the true structure. With the method of new medicine, it is not possible to discover the empty space in our bodies."[43] Biomedical doctors insist on the visibility (via two eyes) of knowledge and so they overlook the metaphysical composition of our bodies. They mistakenly approach the problems of health as solely physical, and so their remedies do not address the essence of diseases rooted in the subtle body. It is this "empty space" of the body that is only perceptible by means of traditional Indian methods, a bodily space that is likewise an epistemological space, an aspect of knowledge over which Indian tradition claims a monopoly of expertise.

This critique of biomedicine is at the same time a critique of the Western empirical scientific method, which demands a link between visibility and knowledge. "The ancient philosophers of Siddha School knew more about the powers that move the world and of communications of thought at a distance without the employment of any visible means which is thought current. Modern Western Medicine knows only the dead body of man and not the living image in him presented by Nature . . . and so, modern science knows more about the superficiality of things."[44] By claiming to understand both the physical processes that Western doctors address and intangible aspects of health and the body as well, traditional Indian practitioners carve out a discursive space that subsumes Western knowledge and so provides the grounds for a critique of Western medicine. At the same time, they claim that the spiritual essence of their traditional space lies apart from Western medical knowledge, invoking a distance that biomedical critique cannot traverse. Most important, they mark out a space below that of biomedicine, not in the sense of being inferior, but rather in the sense that traditional knowledge describes the root of things.

A second spatial argument that traditional practitioners employ in their bid for the medical patronage of Indian patients has been to assert autochthonous relations among the Indian climate, its flora, the diseases prevalent in India, and the bodily constitution of the Indian people. In their response to a questionnaire submitted as part of the 1923 Madras *Report of the Committee on the Indigenous Systems of Medicine*, a "Committee convened under the direction of the President of the Eastern Medical Association of Southern India, Madras," a guild of unani practitioners, invoking natural law rather than divine design, argued that local environments have all the material necessary to remedy diseases that prevail in a particular region. "It is one of the laws of nature that wherever we find a disease, in its very neighbourhood we do find cure for the same disease; that is to say, for the diseases prevailing in India, we need not go beyond India to procure medicines to efficiently cure the disease, for there is in India itself plenty of medicines to counteract the prevailing diseases."[45] Medical products of the land from which a people emerged are sufficient to cure the ailments of that people, an argument against the importation of foreign medicines.

This environmental correspondence is not limited to local medicines and local diseases, but extends to local people as well. These unani hakims assert: "The 'Ayurvedic' and 'Unani' systems of medicine are unquestionably and beyond a shadow of doubt more useful for this country than the so-called 'Allopathic' or the 'Western' principles of medical treatment, as they are operated on Indians by Indians through the media of Indian productions of herbs and drugs, on the efficacy of which climatic influences have not a little to partake of."[46] In his opening address of the 1935 "Exhibition of Indian Medicines," siddha vaidya A. J. Pandian declares that the founders of Indian medical knowledge, the "Saints, Rishis or Angels," developed "the subtle treatment that has been prescribed for the very many diseases of our land, particularly suited to the physical and mental constitution of our people."[47] These indigenous practitioners describe the conjunction of Indian bodies and Indian medicine as neither accidental nor conventional but rather historical and, even more important, essential, as the essences of each have a single origin and evolved in a symbiotic relationship.

This view of the suitability of Indian or Tamil bodies to the Indian/Tamil Nadu environment, and the effectiveness of local medicines in curing local disease, is common today among practicing vaidyas, and is often expressed through the "humoral" theory shared by siddha, ayurveda, and unani.[48] In siddha and ayurveda, there are three humors—wind, bile, and phlegm—called *tridoṣa* in ayurveda, and *tiridōca* or *muppiṇi* in siddha. In unani, there are four: blood, phlegm, yellow bile, and black bile.[49] In all these traditions, the humors are tied to health, as their imbalance or blockage can cause disease, and their relative strength can be manipulated through medicines, diet, and massage. Local environments influence the strength of the humors, and so climate, season, and land must be considered in diagnosis and treatment. G. J. Parthasarathy spoke to me in 2007 about the unsuitability of tea and coffee to the hot climate of south India.

> Here in Tamil Nadu . . . as soon as one wakes up, one should pour cool water on the head. If someone doesn't do that, they'll suffer from headaches for their entire life. Now, which headache is this? Is it a wind headache? Is it a bile headache? It is a phlegm headache? One needs to find this out. If one drinks tea 10–15 times a day, one will have headaches

> one's entire life. That's why I speak firmly about this. I am firm about it. Tea is fully bile. There is no need for tea in a hot country. It's only necessary in cold temperature places. In that way, after diagnosing the specific disease, next one needs to look at which season diseases come, and look practically at this. Patients go to an allopathic doctor, spend hundreds of thousands of rupees, and only after they can't do anything, they come quickly to us.

Parthasarathy links the consumption of too much bilious tea, in hot, bilious Tamil Nadu, to bile headaches. The inappropriateness of Tamils consuming tea, introduced by the British, is matched by the inability of allopathic medicine, with its lack of knowledge of process of the humors, to find an effective cure for the resulting headaches.

The linking of environment, disease, medicines, and bodies evokes the material, organic logic of autochthony. Vaidyas extend these organic links to apparently inorganic processes such as "culture" and "civilization." Thus, the Qaumi Report (on unani medicine), released on April 4, 1917, characterizes "indigenous medical practice whether Unani (Grecian) or Ayurvedic" as "an essential part of our civilization."[50] In a report released six years later, the siddha practitioner Ponnuswami Pillai writes from Kumbakonam,

> Just as each country naturally has a particular type of civilization, education, and religious practices, likewise medicine is appropriate for each country's natural environment, climate, and culture. India's own medical procedures, research and experience have been followed from the beginning of time by generations of great medical people. This medical system is structured such that it adheres to the culture of the people, it employs plants and metals that are found in the climates throughout the country, and it can be practiced without special expensive materials without compromising its perfection.[51]

This organic idiom calls for the exclusive and exhaustive conjunction of a particular people and a particular practice, both circumscribed within strict historical and geographic boundaries. This conjunction is most effective when these boundaries are hermetic, to keep foreign elements (whether bodies or ideas) out and prevent the escape of any traitors to tradition. The penetration of a foreign culture will upset this natural relationship, intervening between a pure culture and a pure people. In the nostalgic rhetoric of tradition, Indian medicine developed with the beginning of the Indian race and so its effectiveness on Indian individuals is undeniable and unsurpassable. Practitioners of Indian medicine envisage history as eternal nature, a timeless essence that nevertheless has historical effects.[52]

Indigenous doctors declare the importance of the local boundaries of Indian medicine, which here ironically coincide with the political boundaries drawn by the British, in order to create a geographic space for tradition. This traditional space is also an organic space, because practitioners distinguish Indian bodies from European bodies and propose an inalienable, material connection between disease, medicines, climate, and an autochthonous people. Western medicines, they say, do not have the proper organic material to effectively heal Indian bodies. Finally, this geographic and organic uniqueness is the basis for assertions of a unique cultural space, a site for indigenous medical theories and practices as a whole, as vaidyas celebrate the cultural products of their medical tradition as best suited to local people.

The Stagnation of Indigenous Medicine

Vaidyas carve out not only a unique space for their knowledge but also a temporality that is distinct from that assumed by biomedical doctors. We have seen one case in which indigenous practitioners defend the slow action of their drugs in response to Koman's critiques. They make this point often, for example with reference to a medicine called *Salmali* in Sanskrit or *Mullilavamaram* in Tamil. "This slow action of the indigenous drugs with permanent results is highly to be preferred to the quick action of the drugs of the British pharmacopea with fleeting results."[53] This claim that British medicine brings quick but only temporary relief, while the indigenous systems bring slower but permanent cures, is common throughout siddha and ayurvedic literature, and was often repeated by patients and doctors alike when I was conducting my research as a refrain on the superiority of traditional medicines. This attitude transposes the perceived endurance and longevity of traditional Indian knowledge onto its medicines and their effects, while denigrating the cures of an immature, fledgling biomedicine as transient and short-lived.

The values asserted in this temporal view can and were easily inverted. A cornerstone for British claims to possess a medicine more advanced than that of their colonial subjects was their conviction that European history advanced while Indian sciences had stagnated since classical times. To some degree, this view of stagnant Indian sciences was supported by both Tamil revivalists and Indian nationalists, who tended to regard history as a process of decay from an original perfection, a perfection that might be reestablished with the restoration of cultural and racial purity. This notion of history as degeneration in South Asia has precedent in the idea, first described in Sanskrit texts, that history proceeds as a succession of four epics (*yugas*), devolving from the first, utopian age to our present degenerate times, the Kali Yuga. History, however, does not just devolve but is circular, as the Kali Yuga ends in a great conflagration, followed by a time of regeneration, awakening again into the first, glorious, age. Similarly, formulations of Indian nationalism and Indian medicine, while narrating a history of decay, affirm the potential to reestablish the glory of Indian medicine in an independent state.[54]

Biomedical doctors seized upon Orientalist scholarship that told of the degeneration of Indian civilization from its ancient, Aryan roots, and asserted that indigenous practitioners had much to learn from British doctors.[55] In August 1918, A. G. Cardew, minister for medicine, objected to government plans to fund a school of indigenous medicine. Ayurveda, he argued, is only of "antiquarian interest" to the colonial government. "It is interesting as an old survival, just as the dodo was an interesting survival in the island of Mauritius when that bird was still alive. As an archaic system it is of interest. . . . But unfortunately it has stopped still at that stage and the enormous progress which science has made in the last century has been a closed book to it."[56] Like many colonial and biomedical authorities, Cardew considered Indian medicine to be of literary and historical, but not scientific, interest. Understanding medical difference through an evolutionary hierarchy of knowledge, he assumed a natural progression of history, a prognostic view according to which the eclipse of indigenous medicine by allopathy was inevitable. Like the dodo bird, which was not up to the demands of the new imperial world, indigenous medical knowledge lacks the strength to resist the force of truth, embodied in biomedical reason. Its time is past, and so it must, as all survivals from the past, "succumb before long."

In their *Reply to the Report on the Investigation into the Indigenous Drugs,* vaidyas respond to Cardew's views.

> Long ago Ayurveda developed a system of its own and reached a point beyond which it had become practically impossible to proceed. And that is why it is even now accused of having become stagnant long ago. Sir Alexander Cardew, late of the Madras Executive Council, bore testimony to this fact in a debate in one of the Legislative Council meetings. The practitioners of Ayurveda simply rely on those ancient theories and are even now doing their profession by administering the ancient medicines without even caring to introduce innovations. It is really therefore the western system of medicine that is still in the experimental stage or empirical. . . . Day after day we learn both from the medical papers and news papers that numerous experiments of various drugs and of vaccines invented by faddists who pose as scientific men, are being made on the lower and helpless animals and results pronounced with but dubious or trifling virtues only to be refuted and hooted down by other faddists.[57]

For these vaidyas, the unchanging character of Indian medicine is a sign of its perfection, not its inadequacy. They reject a teleology that equates invention with development, considering medical innovators to be erratic "faddists." For them, the knowledge of tradition is beyond history, contained in "immortal treatises" authored by a "noble galaxy" of "great souls" who were "illustrious, virile, and learned." In the view of these vaidyas, change is not a sign of progress toward a greater rationality but an indication of imperfection, as the notion that a practice that was once "'within the date' mysteriously becomes 'out of date'" is absurd.[58]

The authors of this response contrast innovation and the fickle ideas of individuals to the wisdom of countless generations. They quote "a well-known English authority on medicine," Dr. Clifford Albutt: "Prevalent opinions though not formal truths, contain truths and this the practical physician does not fail to perceive, nor does he forget that the observations of any person however profound, being the observations of an individual of brief life and limited faculties need some tampering by traditional lore by the embodied opinions of a vast number of observers over a long period of time."[59] The vitality of tradition is founded not on bold, impetuous innovations by individuals, but in its cautious measure, its sifting of all information by large numbers of people over vast stretches of history. In another Orientalist idiom, this one contrasting the individualism of the West to the community focus of Asia, indigenous practitioners oppose their careful and measured accumulation of knowledge afforded by a coherent community to the haphazard knowledge created by individualistic Western societies.[60]

The argument that there is no need to improve indigenous medicine serves to shield it from critique: a perfect medicine needs to import nothing, as medical value is measured by traditional purity. A. G. Natesa Shastri, a Madras vaidya, in an August 17, 1918, letter responding to Cardew's critiques, writes:

> The Hon'ble Sir Alexander [Cardew] says to the effect that Ayurveda is not a progressive science. Yes, because it has nothing to improve as it has propounded the theory of the three principles by which it has been able to generalize and bring into its fold the pathological developments of every disease ancient or modern so that it serves the purpose of the microscope for practical purposes. Similarly it has propounded the theory of panchakarma or the five methods of treatment which has enabled us to generalize the step by step procedure of treatment so that any and every disease ancient or modern may be successfully treated by it. It has understood these two principles so thoroughly that in spite of the twentieth century it cannot be destroyed. The real truth is that the "Ayurveda begins where western system ends."[61]

This last assertion, attributed to Mahamahopadhyaya Kaviraj Gananath Sen and cited probably more accurately elsewhere in the *Reply* as "Ayurveda begins where the Western system ends," draws a division between Indian and Western knowledge and asserts that the former supersedes the latter.[62] Inverting the view that biomedicine has progressed beyond traditional medicine, Sen argues for the timeless perfection of Indian medicine. His statement has been manifested in contemporary practice, as the points at which the failings of Western medicine are most explicit, with chronic ailments and incurable diseases such as asthma, diabetes, cancer, and AIDS, are precisely those areas in which vaidyas often claim expertise. In a very real way, then, the coexistence of traditional medicine with biomedicine in India today has led to the assertion of distinct specialities for each.

The notion of a traditional sifting and sorting of knowledge, discarding some and keeping the best, is in tension with the view of an original and perfect medicine founded by ancient, remarkable figures. Both siddha and ayurveda vaidyas trace their past perfection to the extraordinary insight of the founders of their knowledge, insight which modern people no longer possess. Equating innovation with fabrication, they assert that these first practitioners of their knowledge did not invent or author their medicine, but rather simply recorded truths that are inscribed in nature. That is, theirs are not human creations, but natural and divine: "The fundamentals on which the Ayurvedic system of medicine is based are so essentially true for all ages that they would have yielded to no changes. . . . The originators of the Ayurvedic system of medicine have not based their theories on any experiments. They were seers. . . . As their vision is far beyond the human reach and their knowledge all comprehensive, they could give a system which is far beyond approach."[63] Indeed, time itself testifies to the enduring truth of unchanging tradition. "Time which antiquates antiquity and hath an art to make dust of all things finds and shall find the Ayurveda unsurpassed and inexpugnable."[64] While the technique of an empirical science admits to current inaccuracies, the purportedly unchanging nature of traditional science is invoked as testimony to its perfection.[65] The orientation that vaidyas work to impress upon their audience, that of devotion to tradition, is this sort of orientation, a commitment to conserve knowledge in order to sustain the link to past community.

Although biomedical doctors admit that their current state of medical knowledge is imperfect, they argue that the value of their method lies in its constant innovation. From their point of view, any claim to possess an infallible lexicon of medical knowledge is absurd. However, innovation along the lines of biomedical development requires an expensive technological infrastructure on a scale that Indian medical systems cannot support. Arguments for the past and potential perfection of traditional medicine are in part motivated by the recognition of the technological and economic disparity between indigenous medicine and biomedicine. As both the colonial government and the independent Indian state give nearly all of their medical resources to biomedicine, traditional practitioners suggest that perfect knowledge is to be found in the teachings of the past, not in the discoveries of the future.

The Danger of Mixing Cultures

Perhaps the majority of Indians today use both biomedicine and indigenous medicine, either simultaneously to cover their bets, or else successively after failed attempts by one system to heal the illness.[66] Many indigenous practitioners integrate biomedicine into their healing repertoires, especially those who have studied in an indigenous medical college, as the curriculum would include some courses in the theories and applications of biomedicine. Charles Leslie notes that ayurvedic vaidyas in Bombay had incorporated "English medicines" into their practice as early as 1839.[67] This sort of concurrent practice of biomedicine and traditional medicine was institutionalized in 1947, the year of India's independence, in the College of Integrated Medicine in Madras.

It is notable, then, that rhetoric among many practitioners is often skeptical of the benefit or even the possibility of the coexistence, let alone the synthesis, of biomedical and traditional knowledge and practice. The Koman report was typical of colonial approaches to traditional drugs, that is, that they might serve to supplement the British pharmacopoeia. Indigenous practitioners feared that at the end of such a process of incorporation, the colonial government, satisfied that it had extracted everything of value in traditional knowledge, "will be able to declare clearly that since indigenous drugs and medicines are used in our Government Hospitals no special expenditure need be incurred in helping ayurvedic dispensaries and hospitals or the ayurveda itself in any other way." The result is that "soon will then ayurveda dwindle into oblivion."[68]

The danger is even worse than it might seem. It is not just that the benefits of ayurveda would barely endure in the context of biomedicine. The vaidyas propose a grim fantasy in which "Western chemists" analyze and lay bare the qualities of indigenous drugs "for their industrial enterprise." Discovering the value of these preparations, they will proceed to export Indian medicines in vast quantities, making them unavailable for use in India.[69] Their fear is not simply that tradition will be corrupted, transformed, or obliterated, but that it will be stolen and enjoyed by those who are other, depriving its rightful owners of their medical heritage.

Indian independence did not bring the enthusiastic acceptance of indigenous medicine that practitioners had anticipated. In line with the Indian Congress Party's emphasis on the scientific, technological, and industrial progress of the Indian nation, the first prime minister of India, Jawaharlal Nehru, set the agenda for the scientific scrutiny of indigenous disciplines. Speaking about the Government College of Integrated Medicine in Madras, he wrote: "The so-called conflict between Ayurvedic and modern medicine has to be studied and resolved. The only right approach has to be one of science, that is, of experiment, trial and error. In whatever type of medicine we may deal with, we cannot profit by its study unless we apply the methods of science. In this there should not be many conflicting methods but various aspects of one scientific approach."[70] This nationalist confidence in the potential of Western science derives in part from an awareness of the global diffusion of scientific knowledge. Thus, Srinivasalu Naidu, M.D. and former dean of the College of Integrated Medicine, argues that "India should evolve a system of medicine consistent with world opinion. India cannot be secluded in matters of medicine and cannot be content with what patriotism and emotion would stimulate people to adopt."[71] Indians with biomedical training ascribe patronage of a system of medicine that looks at ancient texts for perfect knowledge to patriotism, not to the pursuit of the objective, rational truth of science. Such patriotism, they argue, will lead to an isolated India, whereas the development of biomedicine will preserve for India a place among the great nations of the world. The high status of India on the world stage will be won at the expense of its native forms of medical practice, a price worth paying in the view of these educated, biomedical doctors.

For many indigenous practitioners, however, the integration of medical systems would be tantamount to admitting the inferiority of their own practices, and would initiate the demise of their vocations. Indeed, many defenders of cultural purity have asserted that the decay of traditional medicine began with the introduction of foreign culture into India. In his response to the questionnaire prepared as part of the 1923 Madras *Report of the Committee on the Indigenous Systems of Medicine,* Pandit V. Ponnuswami Pillai of Kumbakonam wrote about the "reasons for the decay of indigenous traditions": "As a result of the spread of foreign civilization in India from the West, and because of the recent lust [for that civilization] that has unfortunately taken hold of the Indian people, some perverse beliefs have taken root in their minds, changing many of their habits and customs. The people's belief in and appreciation of ancient principles and texts have decreased. These are the primary causes of the decay of our native (*cutēca*) medicine."[72] Far from benefiting Indian medicine, the mixing of healing traditions will lead to the deterioration of Indian medicine and its abandonment by the Indian people. The only way to stem this decay, in the logic of cultural purity, is to maintain its distance from ideas deemed to be foreign.

According to many siddha practitioners, the weakness of Tamil society in resisting this medical imperialism is due to the lack of unity among Tamils. Captivated by the materialistic promises of the West, many Tamils have abandoned the components of their tradition, creating dissension in the community.

> The Tamil people, who prospered since the time of creation, who justly and benevolently ruled many nations, who were the first to develop knowledge for medical texts, who knew events happening in many

> different places through their yogic practice (like radios), with the change of times, they forget their greatness, and with the changes of times they suffer without government support. A few among the Tamil people have learned English, deride their mother tongue, flaunt their ignorance of their mother tongue, and ridicule the Tamil people and Tamil doctors. The obstacles for native medicine have multiplied.[73]

For these promoters of Indian knowledge, traditional action is not the habitual imitation of one's forebears, but conscious allegiance to one's community and recognition of one's true identity. Imitative action consists not of blindly following one's own tradition, but of aping foreign culture. Siddha and ayurvedic vaidyas criticized Koman's report on indigenous medicines as flawed not only because Koman had misunderstood traditional theory but also because he had become a "slave to the western so-called scientific superstitions." The vaidyas connect the "degeneracy" of indigenous medicine to this "tendency to imitate the vanity of the West, that is now slowly devouring the indigenous vaidya," leading to the "maya [illusion] of bitter prejudice" and "prejudice against the ancient system."[74] Vaidyas see the patronage of Western medicine at the expense of indigenous medicine as part of a larger trend toward Westernization, which they warn is symptomatic of processes that will lead to the division of the Indian community and subsequently the destruction of all traditional practices. Thus in 1968, siddha vaidya C. Meykandar wrote, "We must realize that blindly following western ways will, in the course of time, result in the decline of siddha medicine and will result in grave danger to the country."[75]

Biomedical doctors and traditional practitioners are united in narrating a decay of traditional medicine, from its position as an "ancient system [that] possessed an imposing treasure of empirical knowledge and technical achievement" to the "decadent condition of the present day."[76] The language of decay was convenient for both colonial authorities and vaidyas. For biomedical doctors, degeneration was an excuse for intervention, as they could argue that Indians, when left to themselves, have stagnated and need external intervention to rejoin the modern world. Vaidyas, on the other hand, have located the source of decay in foreign intervention that culminated with British colonialism. What is required for medical revival, according to these vaidyas, is not a further influx of foreign culture and medical practice but rather a purification of Indian medicine of all its alien elements. The language of decay highlights the need to come to the defense of traditional medicine, and calls on patriotic Indians to support and "revive" their beleaguered tradition.

Arguing that foreign political and cultural imperialism led to the degeneration of Indian medicine, practitioners such as V. Perumal likewise link any hope for its revival in the unification of the community of tradition: "Modern medicine (allopathy), connected with Westerners, came just yesterday and showed its head. But siddha medicine, which emerged, grew, and lives with excellence in the Tamil land, today is in a state of decay. It is the duty of every siddha practitioner—indeed, of every Tamil person—to dispel this degraded state and to restore siddha medicine to its eminent position."[77] As if the effectiveness of siddha were not self-evident, siddha practitioners often assert the responsibility of all Tamils to patronize the siddha system, duty thereby bridging any gaps in confidence in siddha's healing potential. For those who hold the utopian ideal of a society following a pure tradition, duty to tradition is an essential precondition for the recovery of the greatness of Indian medicine. The boundaries of tradition, then, are asserted not only to keep foreign elements out but also to keep the members of the community in.

Conclusion

While the construal of one's knowledge as universal exerts an unambiguous authority, true for all people, the consideration of knowledge as traditional carries far more ambiguous implications for authority. To designate the knowledge of an articulated social other as traditional is often to ascribe to it the features of irrelevance, nostalgia, or even illusion. Yet those who characterize their own knowledge as traditional often do so to construct boundaries that separate their knowledge from that of rival traditions. This not only has the effect of reifying a relation of possession between a people and particular knowledges and practices but it also shields this knowledge from external critique. Their practices under attack as unscientific or forged, siddha vaidyas delineate a sphere of unique tradition within which they reject the scrutiny of outsiders.

This sovereignty of tradition shares much with the language that Emmanuel Levinas uses to describe the site of self-identification. It is a ground of possibility, an "'at home' which we inhabit."[78] The act of self-identification is forged not in isolation but begins with a relationship between an "I" and an external world that is radically other: "In a world which is from the first other the I is nonetheless autochthonous. . . . It finds in the world a site and a home. Dwelling is the very mode of *maintaining oneself*, not as the famous serpent grasping itself by biting onto its tail, but as the body that, on the earth exterior to it, holds *itself* up and *can*. The 'at home' is not a container but a site where *I can*. . . . The site, a medium, affords means. Everything is here, everything belongs to me."[79] Tradition is this sort of autochthonous ground, a site over which a social self can exercise control. It serves as a basis for constructions of selfhood, not a self that is prior to tradition, but a self which is forged in the very activity of formulating and promoting tradition. To paraphrase Levinas, this home, this residence and ground of the self, is not the end or goal of human activity but its condition, and so its commencement. That is, the space of tradition that Indian medical practitioners claim for themselves is not a domain of activity that is conferred on them by nature, or by divinity, but it is forged only through their active and consistent efforts.

From the early decades of the twentieth century, then, Indian medical practitioners have won expanded opportunities to participate in arenas of public debate that had been previously monopolized by British and like-minded Indians. Vaidyas secured this interest in official agendas through the assertive and conscious celebration of Indian traditional knowledge and practices. In this process, they began to regard their knowledge more consciously as part of a unique, coherent, and sovereign civilization, whose broad contours were drawn from both indigenous history and colonial political borders. Indian medical practitioners proposed new boundaries for their knowledge, utilizing the novel category of Indian medicine to reconceive the scope of their medicine and their clientele. The ways that they used colonial categories to delineate a sovereign traditional space suggests not that vaidyas were subject to the hegemony of these categories, but that they accepted these parameters precisely insofar as they recognized their potential for constructing authority.[80] These boundaries have come to define the contours of duty and of devotion to an Indian medical tradition, in order to counter the detrimental influences of biomedicine. Because these boundaries inaccurately reflect the nature of traditions, which are never pure, they are less descriptions of natural or social worlds than they are ideal constructions and hopeful aspirations, meant to establish models for social cohesion and exclusion within a circumscribed tradition and community.

3

The Miraculous Origins of Siddha Medicine

Oh poverty! Praise to you!
I am a siddha because of your grace.
I see the whole world,
but no one sees me.

—Sanskrit *subhāṣitam Devavāṇīpraveśikā*, quoted in Goldman and Sutherland, 99 (translation mine)

Although siddha vaidyas have at times considered themselves to be practitioners of Indian medicine, they have more commonly asserted that their knowledge is distinct from other traditional medical systems in India. In particular, they emphasize the Tamil character of their medicine, and they link elements of their knowledge and practice to local contexts. In this and the next two chapters, I will explore their assertions of an exclusive Tamil medicine, with particular attention to the relationship between siddha and its two major competitors, ayurveda and biomedicine. Their assertions of a pure Tamil tradition has necessitated reworking a tradition that in the past often celebrated its links to Sanskrit culture, as well as incorporating notions of science that figure prominently in the contemporary rhetoric of siddha medicine. I will begin with a detailed examination of the eponymous founders of siddha medicine, the siddhars.

During my research in Tamil Nadu, siddha vaidyas and nonvaidyas alike regaled me with stories of the extraordinary feats and the elusive character of yogis who they call siddhars. The siddhars, many said, live forever, yet they are never seen because they avoid the haunts of ordinary people, using their abilities to fly or to become invisible in order to remain hidden from society. They can, as the epigraph above suggests, see the entire world, even if the world cannot see them. In many ways, this equally describes the position of siddha vaidyas and other traditional healers throughout the world today.[1] While the invisible, all-seeing siddhar is an omnipotent being, however, siddha vaidyas lament their lack of recognition in Tamil Nadu, in India, and in the world. In local and national medical landscapes, both Western biomedicine and ayurveda enjoy advantages in infrastructure and in central government support. In less regulated spheres of Tamil-speaking communities, on the other hand, the popularity of the siddhars appears to be on the rise. In my perusal of Tamil bookshops, the number of books on the siddhars increased dramatically from 1998 to 2007. Others have noticed a surge in interest in the siddhars. Layne Little notes the growing importance of the siddhar Bhogar "in the minds and imagination of the pilgrims" to the famous Murugan temple at Palani.[2] In his *Cittarkaḷ Collum Tirāviṭa Āṉmīkam* (The Dravidian spirituality of the siddhars), Kalai Arasu notes that recently a "market" has emerged for the siddhars.[3] S. P. Ramachandran, editor of a large number of siddha medical manuscripts, in his *Cittarkaḷ Varalāṟu* (History of the siddhars), similarly notes growing interest in the siddhars.[4] "Shivamayam," a popular Tamil serial on the siddhars, aired on Sun TV beginning July 10, 2004.[5]

This unofficial popularity of the siddhars is consistent with the radical, unorthodox qualities ascribed to them in their rich Tamil mythologies. Tamil literature on the siddhars, and those writings attributed to them, portray them as performers of miracles and as critics of religious and social orthodoxies, in particular of brahmanic hegemony. In narrating the fantastic powers of the siddhars, my interlocutors took obvious pleasure in challenging my skepticism, and imbedded in their often entertaining narrations of the miraculous was a critique of what I represented to them: the modern, the West, science, and materialism. Here I consider their accounts, and those advanced by siddha vaidyas and Tamil revivalists, as performative acts through which these speakers seek to move their audience in specific ways. In particular, they ascribe extraordinary foundations to siddha medicine not only to describe an objective reality, or just to entertain, but also to justify their claims for the unlimited potential of their medical knowledge and practices, and to garner prestige for their specific healing practices and for Tamil tradition more generally. When vaidyas narrate the exceptional mastery of the siddhars over the natural world, they strive to reconfigure Tamil, Indian, and global social worlds. Insofar as they attribute to the siddhars particular identities and presumed loyalties, their articulation of miraculous abilities speaks to social relations, to aspirations of community harmony, and to social discord.

The Rhetorical Power of the Miraculous

At the Second World Tamil Conference, held in Chennai in 1968, P. Muttukkaruppa Pillai gave a typical account of the abilities of the siddhars: "Through their unwavering effort, the siddhars obtained the power to manipulate their bodies and internal organs at will, a great power which ordinary people are not able to achieve. They fastened onto the inner animating force, stimulated the root fire, and with the help of great medicines, consuming the immutable mental nectar, they conquered the natural world, with its gray hair, wrinkles, old age, disease and death. The siddhars obtained indestructible bodies, achieved liberation, and lived forever as those who know truth."[6] Vaidyas continue to make miraculous claims about the origins of their knowledge. Even though the spread of biomedical institutions, discourses of science, and technology has not rendered statements about the miraculous absurd, it has significantly shaped the character of recent statements of the extraordinary potential of siddha medicine and the powers of the siddhars. Even further, in many instances, siddha vaidyas pronounce their medicine as miraculous not in spite of the requirements of a rational science, but indeed because of the attempts of biomedical and scientific discourse to dictate the limits of what is possible and what is rational. In this chapter, I will argue that siddha vaidyas lay claim to the extraordinary in order to assert a potential that lies beyond the limitations of biomedicine.

I will analyze the statements of vaidyas primarily as performative acts, not as principally expressions of belief, nor as emerging out of a specific, restrictive cultural milieu, though I accept that both belief and cultural conditioning are aspects of their statements. When I was first told that siddhars inhabit the hills of western Tamil Nadu, that they fly through the air, and that they live for thousands of years, I asked myself whether these raconteurs "really believed" what they were telling me. By focusing on belief, I assumed that their statements were primarily descriptive, meant to give an account of an objective reality. I was not wrong in taking belief to be an important consideration, as their statements made a claim to truth. Siddha vaidyas, in their bid for cognitive legitimacy, or at least plausibility, place the siddhars beyond scrutiny, in the ancient past or on distant mountaintops. In this way they locate the extraordinary just on the other side of experience, and therefore beyond what might be falsified, a strategy to make these statements appear credible.

What this focus on belief ignores, however, is that the work that vaidyas intend their statements to accomplish is much more than the work of description. Byron Good has pointed to the problems in considering "belief" to be the primary motivation for medical behavior.[7] When used in medical contexts, belief generally indicates a cognitive act, a considered judgment that something is true according to some relevant criteria of authority. Siddha vaidyas certainly take this sort of belief into account when they describe the character of their knowledge. There are serious limitations, however, in making belief the sole, or even the primary, link between people and their traditions. Belief, after all, cannot be separated in clear ways from motivation and interest. That is, we often believe things because it is in our interest to do so. When siddha practitioners assert that the founders of their medicine had extraordinary power, they never do so solely because they believe it but also because such assertions accomplish particular sorts of work. Donald Lopez distinguishes between believing something and believing *in* something.[8] To believe something is a cognitive, reflective act which asserts a particular relationship between a subject and an external object. To believe *in* something is a creative act, in that the statement of belief itself creates its object. An affirmation that "I believe in you" confers value and confidence on the person addressed. It is this latter sense of belief that more accurately describes the relationship between siddha vaidyas and their extraordinary statements, in that these elegies themselves in part create the object of which they speak. Their formulations of the origin, history, and nature of their knowledge are perhaps most accurately statements of self-belief, formulations that are meant to confer self-respect on a medical tradition that has been so roundly criticized by biomedical science. These articulations are acts of self-creation because they specify the *value* of the self, that is, they argue for the glory of the siddha medical tradition, and they also define the *nature* of the self, that is, they delineate the character of their system and who can participate in their community of knowledge. Insofar as they emphasize the Tamil character of the siddhars, and thus of the miraculous, such statements celebrate the glory of Tamil civilization and community. When siddha vaidyas exclaim about the extraordinary origins of their system, then, they do so to garner prestige for their knowledge. They recount these stories not only because they believe that they are true but also because they know that they are useful.

Recent scholarship has tended to examine accounts of the extraordinary within emic webs of cultural and semiotic meaning. That is, rather than discounting such statements as superstitious, or as expressions of mistaken logic, as did Victorian anthropologists such as Edward B. Tylor, it has become commonplace to analyze supernatural claims within their historical and especially their cultural contexts. This orientation has also become the primary mode through which historians of medicine and medical anthropologists study the knowledge and practices of traditional doctors. Byron Good, for example, sees medical practices as meaningful within what he calls the "semiotic networks" of culture, language resembling Geertz's definition of culture as "webs of significance."[9] These networks provide members of a society with ways to reflect on, and to actively construct, meaning of experiences. As such, they are primary to any cultural study of health and healing, because they are as constitutive of the experiences of Western biomedical doctors as they are of those of Swazi herbalists, for example.

I accept much of this approach, and will argue here that the narratives that siddha vaidyas tell must be considered in the context of broader Tamil revivalist social, religious, and political discourses. One thing this contextual model fails to highlight, however, is the porous, cosmopolitan nature of cultures and traditions. Siddha vaidyas engage in medical discourses that cannot be typified as purely Tamil nor understood in the context of a single culture that is distinct from Western culture, or Sanskritic culture, even if they themselves describe their knowledge as pure, as unique, and as essentially Tamil.[10] If we accept that the boundaries of traditions are fluid, we must treat their statements about traditional medical knowledge as both intradiscursive and interdiscursive. That is, although we need to understand the writings of Tamil vaidyas within their particular history, we should not contextualize their thought too narrowly in seeking to render it intelligible. This is because these vaidyas have a keen sense of contexts outside of the specific discourses within which they are writing, discourses about science, religion, natural law, and political power. They seek to speak across contexts, self-consciously and strategically articulating their tradition within a plurality of traditions. They narrate the miraculous abilities of the siddhars in order to garner status for their medical knowledge and practices in a globalizing world, in order to rectify the invisibility that limits their influence and their development. While theirs are local discourses, siddha vaidyas indeed "see the world," even if the world does not see them.

Recent Tamil narrations of the miraculous powers of the siddhars emerge not in the comfortable center of a coherent and homogenous Tamil culture, but at the edges of cultural encounters and contestation. They address colonial critiques of Tamil medicine and society as primitive and ineffectual. In addition to religion, medicine played an important role in the legitimation of colonial intervention, and science and technology were often brought to bear on the British encounter with Indians, both in the material and military advantages they enjoyed, and also as signs of a superior civilization.[11] I will not here detail the nature of European critiques of non-European technical and medical accomplishments, but rather propose that three features of recent depictions of the siddhars—namely, their Tamil character, their extraordinary powers, and their scientific sophistication—in part respond to these critiques. Like others in the modern world, Tamil vaidyas and cultural apologists are aware that science and technology are essential to the domination not just of nature but also of human societies. Although they are falling behind in the material competition with Western medicine, their imaginative and ideological formulations of the miracles of Tamil science have been powerful tools in their bid for patrons and authority.

The view that Tamil narratives of the siddhars and their medicine are rhetorical, that they are strategic responses to shifting historical circumstances at the same time that they conform to and shape symbolic meanings, takes us beyond synchronic accounts of meaning suggested by a Geertzian approach.[12] Kenneth Burke has called for the analysis of magic as a form of rhetorical language, characterized by persuasion and sharing with rhetoric the capacity and intention to move people.[13] Although here I focus on the narration of the miraculous rather than on the performance of magic, the rhetorical component of these narrations is readily apparent. When siddha vaidyas speak of the extraordinary abilities of the founders of their knowledge, they do so not so much to make themselves feel secure in an uncertain *natural* world, as Malinowski would have argued, but to invite an audience into accepting visions of tradition that celebrate a Tamil community in a competitive social, economic, and political world. Their narratives are rhetorical acts through which they seek to persuade Tamils, Indians, and increasingly those outside India to accept siddha medical knowledge and practices as relevant to the modern world. This approach thus compels attention to shifting political situations, patronage networks, and criteria of authority that contribute to the modern production of siddha medicine. In this chapter, then, I will look at shifts in accounts of the miraculous origins of siddha medical knowledge from precolonial to contemporary times. I will then trace the evolution of narrative accounts of Tirumular, whose mythological and textual history is among the oldest and richest of the Tamil siddhars. I will end with recent statements by siddha vaidyas about the extraordinary powers of the siddhars, with a particular focus on the way they employ the language of science.

The Literature of the Siddhars

Siddha vaidyas today depict the siddhars as the founders of Tamil traditions of medicine, astrology, and chemistry. They base their formulations of siddha medicine on the thousands of palm-leaf manuscripts that hereditary vaidyas have used for centuries, and which now more often than not are housed in libraries and archives throughout Tamil Nadu state. Each of these premodern texts is attributed to one of the siddhars, and represents a particular lineage of knowledge that begins with the deities Shiva and Shakti. Although diverse in content, these texts share common conceptions of the human body and its relationship to the environment, and they all detail recipes, rituals, astrological criteria, and devotional practices through which physical processes can be manipulated in extraordinary ways. Vaidyas assert that the siddhars, in their compassion for ordinary people, transmitted this knowledge in palm-leaf manuscripts, "singing" them in texts which vaidyas consider to be original redactions of their knowledge.

In using *siddhar* rather than the Tamil *cittar* or the Sanskrit *siddha*, I follow the convention of most scholarly, popular, and medical literature about Tamil traditions in English. An etymological analysis of *siddhar* immediately highlights the long history of Tamil/Sanskrit interaction in South Asia, and also the contradictory nature of revivalist assertions of the pure Tamil credentials of the siddhars. The Tamil *cittar* is a transformation of the Sanskrit *siddha*, while the English rendering *siddhar* transcribes the Sanskrit *siddha* and adds the Tamil personal suffix *ar*. Thus *siddhar* appears only in English, and by incorporating Sanskrit, Tamil, and English features, it is a linguistic hybrid that neatly encapsulates the cultural hybridity of the broad usage of the word. *Siddha* is derived from the Sanskrit verbal root *sidh*, meaning to accomplish or succeed, so a siddha is one who is accomplished or successful.[14] In Sanskrit and Tamil mythological and didactic literature, the term generally designates an adept in yogic practice, a being perfected through the performance of austerities, one who has achieved mastery over the natural world and is possessed of extraordinary powers known as *siddhis*. While Tamil revivalists argue for the pure Tamil origins of the siddhars, the word *siddhar* itself highlights diverse cultural links to these figures.

The siddhars of Tamil mythological and medical traditions share much in their attributes and abilities with the eighty-four mahasiddhas of Tibetan and Sri Lankan Buddhist traditions, with siddhas of the Nath traditions of north India, and with those of Sanskrit epic and Puranic narratives.[15] At the same time, most of these siddhars of Tamil fame are unique characters, with names and myths that do not occur outside of Tamil literature, Agastya being the significant exception. R. Venkatraman usefully classifies the Tamil siddhars into four types, which roughly correspond to chronological progression as well as subject matter.[16] These are the *sanmārgasiddhars*, the *ñāṉasiddhars*, the *kāyasiddhars*, and other Tamil ascetics who did not call themselves siddhars but to whom are attributed extraordinary abilities. The first group, the sanmārgasiddhars (caṉmārkkam—path of truth), includes just two individuals, Tirumular as author of *Tirumantiram*, and a certain Bhogar who is mentioned in that text. The two most important types for our analytic purposes are the ñāṉasiddhars, or the siddhars of *ñāṉa*, profound knowledge, and the kāyasiddhars, or siddhars of the *kāya* or body.[17] The ñāṉasiddhars are the attributive authors of philosophical and polemical poetry, whereas the kāyasiddhars are the purported authors of a huge number of texts on medicine, alchemy, ritual, astrology, and yoga. Many of the writings of the ñāṉasiddhars are collected in the *Periyañāṉakkōvai* (The great collection of profound knowledge), which is widely available today in bookshops and street stalls throughout Tamil Nadu as the popular *Cittarpāṭalkaḷ* (Verses of the siddhars).[18] These poems are philosophical and unorthodox, promoting a direct, personal relationship with divinity, usually Shiva, and criticizing caste and brahmanic ritual monopoly.

Kāyasiddhars are those siddhars who have gained the power called *kāyasiddhi*, the ability to control the body, to master the world through the body, and to keep the body eternally youthful.[19] This power is often secured by consuming magical medicines. The writings of the kāyasiddhars are texts on Tamil traditions of knowledge such as alchemy, medicine, astrology, yoga, and tantric ritual. Whereas the siddhars of the philosophical works claim to possess supernatural powers and eternal youth, the texts of the kāyasiddhars detail ways in which ordinary people can obtain these powers, through yoga, mantras, or mineral compounds. These practical writings are often obscure, written in parts in *paripāṣai*, highly technical and idiosyncratic language, and they have been passed down in family lineages of doctors, astrologers, and other hereditary vocations for centuries. These works are Shaivite, like the writings of the ñāṉasiddhars, but they promote the worship of the goddess Shakti somewhat more than Shiva and appear to have been influenced by Shakta tantrism. They assume tantric views of the human body, with *chakras* or energy points in the body and a *kundalini* or serpent which, when stimulated through meditation or ritual, winds its way through these chakras. Medical texts are the most numerous of all the writings attributed to the siddhars. Many of these give medicinal formulae for everyday ailments such as eye problems, or women's diseases, while others outline the ingredients for occult medicines like muppu, which their authors claim will cure all diseases, bestow extraordinary powers, and restore and preserve youth.

The texts of the kāyasiddhars have been preserved for centuries on palm-leaf manuscripts, and while some of these have been printed, many remain unpublished. G. John Samuel puts the number of extant Tamil palm-leaf manuscripts in India and abroad at about 100,000.[20] C. Arangarajan estimates that there are 50,000 Tamil manuscripts in Tamil Nadu state, of which about half are medical manuscripts.[21] Although some siddhars, such as Agastya and Tirumular, are the attributive authors of both the philosophical and practical sorts of texts, most are either ñāṉasiddhars or kāyasiddhars. For example, Bhogar is one of the most famous medical siddhars and so can be classified as a kāyasiddhar, while the writings of Pattinattar are only of the philosophical sort. The premodern texts attributed to the siddhars often speak of ninety million siddhars.[22] Current convention holds that there are eighteen siddhars, but there is no standard authoritative list, nor do the various lists distinguish different types of siddhars. The *Periyañāṉakkōvai* lists thirty-five siddhars, and a survey of the medical manuscripts at the Government Oriental Manuscript Library in Madras lists medical texts attributed to sixteen different siddhars, many of whom do not appear among the thirty-five ñāṉasiddhars found in the *Periyañāṉakkōvai*.[23] The *Usman Committee Report on Indigenous Medicine* of 1923 lists fifty-four siddhars. In the *Encyclopaedia of Tamil Literature*, P. Raja and M. Mathialagan count fifty-eight siddhars, a number tallied from a comparison of several lists of siddhars, not distinguishing between different types of siddhars. T. N. Ganapathy has compiled a list of twenty-five lists of siddhars.[24] Although the differences between the two genres of siddhar writings are important, all the texts attributed to siddhars are written in an informal, colloquial style, and their authors invariably claim to possess extraordinary powers, including that of immortality.

The dates of the medical texts are difficult to determine, given their lack of historical references. Few extant manuscripts are older than 250 years, and most date from the nineteenth century.[25] Scholars of these texts usually do not even attempt to date them. For example, V. R. Madhavan, one of the foremost authorities on Tamil medical texts attributed to the siddhars, in his edition of *Agastya's 1500 Medical Verses*, cites precise dates given in the colophons of the extant manuscripts that he consulted, one from 1786, the other from 1844. He concludes that this text was in wide use 200 years ago, but does not venture a guess as to its approximate date of origin. "Because of its obvious widespread utility, the text must have been preserved for ages (*kālaṅkālamāka*) in manuscript form so that it was available in many places and as many manuscripts."[26] The desire to depict siddha medicine as a timeless tradition, and the role played by many manuscript scholars in the promotion of siddha medicine and Tamil tradition, has discouraged more precise dating of these texts.

There are some clues, however, that allow tentative speculations on their date of redaction. The extant manuscripts contain errors typical of those made when recopying a text, so they are probably copies or compilations of earlier texts. One indication of the date of authorship is their language, which is relatively modern and colloquial. R. Venkatraman dates most of the texts attributed to the siddhar Agastya to around the fifteenth century, noting that in no literature prior to that time is Agastya linked to medicine.[27] P. M. Ajmalkhan dates the medical and alchemical writings of another siddhar, Yacob, to the fifteenth century on the basis of the style of writing and notes that no other evidence exists to determine more accurately the date of his writing.[28] Kanchana Natarajan argues for a terminus post quem of the twelfth century for Yacob's work *Vaittiyam* (Medicine), based on a reference to the twelfth-century Sufi mystic Mukiyadeen Abdul Kadir Jailani. Natarajan dates Yacob's writing to between the fifteenth and seventeenth centuries on the basis of its literary style.[29] In describing his conversations with scholars of siddha medicine, Hartmut Scharfe reports a similar date, that is, the oldest medical texts are no older than the sixteenth century.[30] Although many of the medical texts were probably composed around this time, some of the philosophical texts attributed to the ñāṉasiddhars are older. The earliest and most well-known text attributed to a siddhar is the *Tirumantiram* of Tirumular, which was probably composed toward the end of the first millenium.[31] Sanskrit and Tamil mythologies of the siddhars are even older. The figure of Agastya in Sanskrit literature appears in the *Ṛg Veda* (c. 1200–900 B.C.E.) and in the *Mahābhārata* and the *Rāmāyaṇa*.[32] He first appears in Tamil literature in the *Maṇimēkalai*, which dates to about 500 C.E.[33] I will follow Venkatraman in dating the oldest Tamil medical texts attributed to the siddhars to approximately the fifteenth century.

Narrating the Origins of Siddha Medicine

The juxtaposition of early formulations of the origins of medical knowledge with recent accounts highlights some important historical shifts in Tamil medical considerations of the miraculous from precolonial to recent times. The earliest available accounts of the origins of siddha medicine are found in texts long preserved on palm-leaf manuscripts, many of which are available today in cheap, printed editions. Agastya, the most prolific of the medical siddhars, describes the foundations of his teaching on the rejuvenative medicine muppu in his *100 Verses on the Regenerative Compound Muppu*.[34]

> Daily I did puja to the feet of Shakti, and I placed myself at the feet of Shiva, adorned with the crescent moon, before I proclaimed the method to prepare muppu.[35]
>
> I sang many great texts, oh noble one. I gathered the appropriate parts on *kaṟpam* that were in those myriad texts, and I put them in this one without technical language (*paripāṣai*) for the survival of the people of the world. . . .[36]
>
> Holding the feet of Shakti in my mind, I saw the method to prepare muppu which is the means to immortality. While on the densely forested Potigai Mountain, many great siddhars came, ate kaṟpam, and asked me about this unique herb used to calcinate all types of minerals. I taught them, summarizing the chemical process. . . .
>
> I taught the method for preparing muppu. . . . No one else in the four directions knows this method. I will sing this openly to you. If you understand this correctly, you too will become a rishi-siddhar!
>
> I will tell you now about the wondrous muppu which is used to make *centūram* and *paṟpa*.[37] Notice that I have condensed this knowledge in one hundred verses. Manonmani [Shakti] taught it to me, and I taught it in this text exactly like she did, without errors, for the benefit of the people of the Earth.[38]

The author of this text ascribed to Agastya traces the origin of siddha medical knowledge to the divine couple Shakti and Shiva, who taught Agastya through a vision as he was worshiping them. Agastya in turn taught other siddhars and then committed the medical formulae to writing for "the benefit of the people of the Earth." By tracing their lineage back to Agastya, Shakti, and Shiva, those vaidyas who employ this text can claim divine authority for their medical knowledge and practices, an authority not susceptible to the fallibility of ordinary people. Contrary to the contemporary characterization of siddha medicine as the special dispensation of the Tamil people, there is no reflexivity in this text about the fact that it is written in Tamil, and there is no designation of the earthly benefactors of this knowledge as Tamils.

Contemporary siddha medical practitioners tell at least two kinds of stories to account for the origins of their knowledge. One type resembles the premodern accounts, depicting the siddhars as mediators between divine and human realms, while other narratives describe the siddhars as ancient scientists. S. Chidambarathanu Pillai gives a typical account of the first type: "For the relief of the suffering of souls, the eternal, highest Shiva took form and taught many arts to the likes of Umadevi [Shakti], Kumaravel [Murugan], Tirumular, and Agastya. Siddha medicine, which contains all of the arts, came to the Tamil land, which is the Dravidian country, through the siddhars. With the assistance of this great art, people conquered wrinkles, gray hair, death and disease, living long lives of great bliss."[39] Like the premodern narratives, many contemporary accounts locate the origin of siddha medicine in the realm of divinity. They trace its descent to the sphere of human knowledge through a hierarchy of divinity beginning with Shiva, and including Murugan, whose worship is limited to south India and who, with Shiva, is the primary deity linked to the Tamil revivalist community. Although vaidyas today continue to hold that the siddhars were the conduits of medical knowledge from divine realms, the earthly destination of this knowledge is not "the Earth" in general as it was in Agastya's text, but the "Tamil land" (*Tamiḻakam*). In these contemporary narratives, the siddhars mediate divine knowledge and the human realm in the same way that they do in earlier accounts, but they also link medical knowledge and an ethnicized Tamil community. The premodern Tamil medical texts simply speak of the knowledge of muppu, kaṟpam, centūram, and paṟpam medicines. Chidambarathanu Pillai joins all these methods under the rubric of siddha medicine, assigning to this knowledge a systematic designation that the older texts do not suggest. In order to speak of a siddha medical system, he traces the descent of medical knowledge to more than one siddhar, thus linking the texts and practices of previously separate lineages into a single body of knowledge. Although the premodern texts describe this knowledge in connection with specific siddhars who would correspond to particular lineages of vaidyas, Pillai considers siddha medicine to be the preserve of a unified linguistic, ethnic, and racial Tamil community.

According to Chidambarathanu Pillai's account, Shiva, in his compassion for humans and empathy for their suffering, teaches them the arts, which besides medicine include music, dancing, astrology, yoga, and magic. In extolling siddha medicine as the most comprehensive of the arts, Pillai contributes to contemporary constructions of Tamil tradition, in which Tamil community is actively imagined and expressed through classical and folk performative traditions, literary societies, and applied disciplines of knowledge such as astrology and medicine. Of these arts, which Tamil tradition holds to number sixty-four, Pillai asserts that siddha medicine has pride of place because it contains all the others and is the best suited for the purpose of all the arts, the mitigation of suffering. This suffering is not primarily that of the body (*uṭal*), but that of the *āṉmā* (Sanskrit *ātman*), the part of the individual that is distinguished from the body and the mind, the seat of the human person. This is the *uyir*, the animating force of life that Western science does not perceive.[40] This linking of medical formulae with spiritual aims is not one that the premodern text makes, nor does it count siddha medical practice as one of the arts. The aims of the knowledge transmitted in the older text are physical, as the survival of the body is not an opportunity for higher spiritual practice but a goal in itself.[41]

In addition to accounts of the divine origins of siddha medicine, contemporary siddha practitioners tell a second, very different sort of narrative, one that is absent in the premodern texts. In their bid to establish siddha medicine as a rational alternative to Western medicine, vaidyas sometimes characterize their knowledge not as a gift from the gods but as a medical science developed by the siddhars through their research of human bodies and the natural world. According to this narrative, it was the ancient Tamils, exemplified by the siddhars, who in their compassion for ordinary people developed and bestowed siddha medicine on the Tamil land and later on the world.

> Many centuries ago, Tamil Nadu was one of the greatest countries in the world in all ways. At that time siddha medicine flourished. . . . Tamils were the first in the world to discover cures for human disease. When disease entered the body, there were great medical people who would examine the sick person and his body, determine the precise nature of the disease, and prepare and administer the medicine appropriate for the cure. Because those great medical people lived as sages (*muṉivarkaḷ*) who have completely renounced the world, and because they were geniuses who knew the past, present, and future, they were called siddhars.[42]

Consistent with revivalist assertions that ancient Tamil society was the font of all civilization, assertions that I will explore more fully in the next chapter, siddha vaidyas claim that their tradition is the original medical system of the world. They characterize the medical siddhars as geniuses, scientists who discerned the principles of the body and developed effective medicines to counter illness. As vaidyas today emphasize the Tamil nature of siddha medical knowledge, so too they depict the siddhars according to the qualities they ascribe to Tamil community, as scientific sophistication is one of the key features in their argument that Tamil tradition remains relevant in the modern world.

While vaidyas attribute scientific achievement to the siddhars, they often link this technical mastery to spiritual attainment. In his massive and meandering *History of Siddha Medicine*, sanctioned by the Siddha Science Development Committee and published by the Tamil Nadu government for use in the education of students of siddha medicine, N. Kandaswamy Pillai speculates that in the course of their spiritual quests, "the ancient Siddhars were constrained to make a research in the field of medicine also. . . . In this process the Siddhars came by a knowledge of medical science which surpassed the then known knowledge of all the learned doctors in the field. As the Siddhars knew all about the body and the functions of its various parts, it was easy for them to compound medicine to remedy any type of ailment. The Siddhars' knowledge of the human anatomy was perfect. Their single-minded concentration was unique. So, when they set out to perform any work, it was achieved with a perfection. Thus did the Siddhars who aimed at turning into Doctors of the soul, incidentally turn into doctors of the Body also."[43] Siddha vaidyas today frame the origins of their medical knowledge as a coalescence of spiritual and material goals, where the immortality sought by the siddhars is simply the physical component of their religious aims. They speak in the idioms of science when describing the deliberate researches of the siddhars, even as they imbue these processes with the aura of the extraordinary by asserting the miraculous medical outcomes of these investigations. The physical effectiveness of the siddhars' knowledge is only the external "sheath" of a much deeper transformation, as their ultimate goal is not the mastery of natural processes but the transcendence of nature. It is in articulating this goal of liberation that vaidyas distinguish their knowledge from a Western medicine that, they say, aptly describes the physical world but overlooks the inner essence of things.

The Identity of the Siddhars

The Hindu ascetic, yogi, or sadhu is perhaps the figure presented most often in pictorial or descriptive accounts of Indian religious life. For many non-Hindus, these renouncers exemplify the sensationalist extremes of an exotic religion. For many Hindus, they embody the limits of human possibilities, whether in their control over their minds, desires, and bodies, or more compellingly in their purported mastery of the physical world and the ability to manipulate it in extraordinary ways. For millennia, South Asian mythology and bodily disciplines have pointed to the extraordinary powers, or *siddhis*, that an adept can develop through yoga and ascetic practice. The *Yoga Sutras*, attributed to Patañjali and dating probably to about the third century C.E., speaks at length of the siddhis, which it holds can be gained through yogic concentration, mantras, ascetic practice, or even magical herbs. These siddhis include the ability to make the body extremely light, big, or small, subduing others to one's will, control of desire, and acquiring whatever one wishes.[44] There is a rich Sanskrit mythology of siddhas that dates to the *Rāmāyaṇa* and *Mahābhārata*, and siddhas are important figures in Jain and Buddhist imaginings.

Several factors conspire to give South Asian asceticism the sheen of the eternal. Traditions of yoga and renunciation strive to achieve enduring truths by transcending mundane, historical, and social worlds. Texts of a variety of South Asian traditions prescribe disciplines or outline philosophies through which adherents might leave behind the particularities of history in order to grasp a never-changing self, whether the *ātman* of the Upaniṣads or the *puruṣa* of Saṃkhya and Yoga. Yoga texts teach of the possibility of escaping death, and South Asian myths in various languages commonly recount stories of immortal yogis. Premodern and contemporary Tamil mythologies describe the siddhars as a group of ascetics who, through their yogic practice, attained supernatural powers and immortality. Scholarly accounts of South Asian asceticism have contributed to this rhetoric of the eternal, often tracing renunciation from archeology (a horned god on an Indus Valley seal) to the Vedas (the "long-haired one") through to the present (focusing on dramatic religious spectacles such as the Kumbha Mela), giving the impression that yogis have been an ever-present, unchanging feature of South Asian life. Thus Mircea Eliade considers yoga to be an indigenous practice with origins prior to the historical record, while yogis are survivals from pre-Aryan India, the true autochthons of the subcontinent.[45] Siddha vaidyas concur, often considering the siddhars to be the last surviving denizens of ancient Tamil Nadu.[46]

This view that South Asian asceticism is immune to history is itself a particular, historical story. I will here examine instances in which tales of yogis are radically historical, marked in obviously modern terms.[47] In addition to those enduring characteristics that have been attributed to yogis in South Asia for millennia, vaidyas today describe the siddhars with the ideals celebrated by twentieth-century Tamil revivalism: rationality, science, egalitarianism, and possessing intuition into the natural laws that govern the cosmos. According to their accounts, the siddhars are scientists, defenders of the common person, opposed to caste and superstition, and the original proponents of human equality. They interpolate the siddhars into the lineage (*paramparai*) of the Tamil people, celebrating them as the authors of Tamil civilization. What is new in these recent depictions, then, is not the siddhars' mastery of nature but the nature of their mastery, and the character of the natural and social worlds that they are seen to control.

According to siddha scholars and vaidyas, the siddhars were, or still are, real people. Some assert that because one of their powers is time travel, they cannot be dated.[48] Others hold that the siddhars are immortal, and that they continue to live far from society in the mountains and jungles of Tamil Nadu.[49] Another writes: "Even today there can be siddhars, but we do not gain any positive knowledge about them because of our negligible knowledge and confusion."[50] T. V. Sambasivam Pillai holds that they are generally invisible, and in any case they prefer "solitude in the jungles and on the mountain tops."[51] Others assert that there are indeed siddhars today who can be seen in our midst. A. Shanmuga Velan writes of Balayogi, a modern-day yogi of Mummidivaram who claimed to have gone without food for sixteen years.[52] Srirangam Siddhar has published several books about his own experiences as a siddhar. One includes an advertisement for his teaching of "Vasi Yoga," which brings "relief from Asthma, obesity, lunacy and other incurable diseases."[53] He also wrote a book outlining a practice of just thirty minutes a day, through which one can become a siddhar.[54] Layne Little has recently written on the new popularity of a siddhar lineage that traces its line back to Bhogar through Yogananda, the author of the 1946 *Autobiography of a Yogi*, and through Yogananda's guru Babaji, who was invoked in a recent Tamil film, *Baba*, starring Tamil superstar Rajnikanth.[55]

Most, however, locate the medical activity of the siddhars in a utopian Tamil past. T. V. Sambasivam Pillai posits that the siddhars developed their knowledge sometime between 10,000 and 4400 B.C.E., or in any case before the introduction of ayurveda into south India. Such narratives locate the founding of siddha medical knowledge in a past before the earliest historical records, the "once upon a time" of nostalgic Tamil origins. "Siddhar's period was one of intense intellectual activity in all the arts and sciences. In the realm of medicine, it was indeed a golden age. New ideas took root and flourished."[56] Consistently with assertions that the siddhars desired bodily longevity for spiritual ends only, vaidyas often claim that after the siddhars attained their spiritual goals they chose to abandon their bodies. In his book on the alchemy of the siddhars, M. C. Subramaniam ridicules those who hold that the siddhars, having mastered themselves and the world, would remain in their bodies: "After achieving an ideal state, a state in which there is nothing left to achieve, would there be any greater foolishness than wandering the world, burdened by a useless body? The siddhars, having reached a state of seamless union with god, regard the body to be insignificant and discard it. This is why none of them today walk in our midst."[57] In other words, the siddhars achieved bodily immortality but they chose not to take it. They retained their absolute mastery of nature, indeed realized it most fully, in voluntarily giving up their bodies.

This is to say that the siddhars, the only people who have perfect knowledge of the siddha medical tradition, are no longer active participants in the perpetuation of this tradition. In 1968, the Tamil government sponsored the Second World Tamil Conference, a forum to celebrate and promote Tamil traditions. The conference was a major undertaking of the newly elected DMK (Dravidian Advancement Party), a pro-Tamil party that has done much to support Tamil language and literature since the middle of the twentieth century. At an auxiliary conference on siddha medicine, S. K. S. Kalimuttu Pillai asserted that only the siddhars have mastered medical knowledge, and they have stayed away from the conference because they have no need for it. All those present have not mastered the siddhars' art.[58] According to Kalimuttu Pillai and other vaidyas, the perfection of siddha medicine resides with the siddhars, who themselves reside in the nooks and crannies of Tamil Nadu and of history itself, in times and places inaccessible to the present. Tamil vaidyas locate the extraordinary in a place beyond scrutiny, constructing an imaginative world of possibilities that cannot be falsified by the criteria of a mundane science or a subsuming nationalism.

Those who attended that conference, and all who promote siddha medicine, are working to bring this shadowy siddha medical knowledge into the light of public recognition. To borrow a term from Hugh Urban, contemporary vaidyas seek to "exotericize" an esoteric tradition, to shift the locus of the most effective medical knowledge from private to public space, from jungles and mountain caves to libraries and conference centers.[59] Thus the Tamil Nadu government has attempted to collect palm-leaf manuscripts from hereditary practitioners to house in archives for public use. But although the siddhars' absence is cited as the reason that siddha medicine has not retained its former perfection, their inaccessibility is itself a condition for the credibility of the glorious claims for siddha medical knowledge.

Tamil revivalists also make them autochthonous, claiming their emergence from the soil of Tamil Nadu along with all other pure, non-brahman Tamils. Although there are Sanskrit traditions of siddha alchemy and yoga that have thrived in the north, Tamil revivalists locate the origins of all siddhar traditions on Tamil land:

> Our great Tamil siddhars bestowed the first medicine to the world for the redemption of the world many thousands of years ago. Our country is extolled as the country of the siddhars. Thiruvavadudurai is the city of ninety million siddhars. Palani Mountain is considered to be the

> mountain home of siddhars. The Katcamalai siddha temple is associated with Kalangi siddhar. Historical details of the siddhars, who have obtained the eight supernatural powers, are contained in our ancient Tamil literature. Siddha medicine, the original medicine (*ātimaruntu*), has been studied in Tamil Nadu from ancient times. Such great medical methods shine as the unique artistic wealth of Tamil Nadu.[60]

For A. Shanmuga Velan, the landscape and literature of Tamil Nadu is suffused with the presence of the siddhars. He posits that the components of Tamil tradition—a people, a medicine, a culture, and a language—form an organic unity because each emerged from Tamil soil. In his preface to A. R. Charangapani's *Citta Neṟi* (Path of the siddhars), C. Meyyappan, former professor at Annamalai University, celebrates the siddhars' "wealth of knowledge that conquered time. . . . The Tamil land is a land on which a treasury of knowledge lived, and still lives. This soil contains a richness of knowledge. Siddhars have appeared throughout history, planting the deep roots of the siddhar path in this land."[61] V. S. Parvati posits a genetic link between the siddhars and contemporary Tamils, as the eighteen siddhars are "our ancestors."[62] She holds that the siddhars are not only founders of medical knowledge and science writ large but that they are also the progenitors of the Tamil community, this paternal role a strange one for celibate yogis.

The "siddhars are the sages of the Tamil soil. . . . They should always be praised as the leaders of the Tamil race (*iṉam*)."[63] To contemporary vaidyas, the siddhars are the first and the greatest of all Tamils, the exemplary models of what it is to be Tamil. In tracing their knowledge to the siddhars, siddha practitioners claim the appropriateness of this knowledge to Tamils. If the *Tamil* nature of siddha medical knowledge seems overemphasized, it is only because the connection between the Tamil people and their knowledge has been called into question, both by Indian nationalists who promote ayurveda as the essence of Indian medicine and by biomedical doctors who assert the universality of their knowledge and thus its appropriateness, indeed its truth, for all people.

A History of Tirumular

I will explore the shifting association of the siddhars with an ethnic Tamil community by tracing the chronological progression of mythologies about, and literature attributed to, Tirumular. Tirumular is interesting for a number of reasons. He is one of the most well-known siddhars, and with Agastya is the siddhar who is connected to the greatest diversity of literary contexts. Tamil mythologies celebrate Tirumular as the author of the celebrated *Tirumantiram*, the oldest Tamil text attributed to a siddhar, and thus many consider him to be the first Tamil siddhar. Tirumular is the only one of the siddhars to be counted among the sixty-three saints (*nāyaṉmār*) of orthodox Shaivism, and as such he is depicted as a devotee of Shiva in the twelfth-century *Periya Purāṇam*. There are a number of Tamil medical texts attributed to Tirumular, and thus he is a popular siddhar among vaidyas today.

Tirumantiram

The dating of the *Tirumantiram* is not clear. The *Periya Purāṇam* (3590) claims that Tirumular wrote the "Tamil 3000," and describes that text as a *tirumantira mālai*, a garland of holy verses, giving us a terminus ante quem for the text of the mid-twelfth century. Cuntarar's *Tirutoṇṭattokai*, which David Shulman dates to the first half of the ninth century, is the first text to name Tirumular as one of the sixty-three nāyaṉmār. However, this text does not help us to date the text, as it does not mention Tirumular as the author of the *Tirumantiram* or any other text, simply stating "I am the servant . . . of our lord, Tirumulan."[64] The *Tiruttoṇṭar Tiruvantāti*, attributed to Nambiyandar Nambi, is of more use. It speaks specifically about "Mulan," describing him as entering the body of a cow herder, as a devotee of Shiva, and as he who, "using the speech of the established Vedas, praised Shiva with perfected Tamil."[65] This is an accurate description of the *Tirumantiram*, which often extols the Vedas and describes its teaching as Vedic in character. The dating of the *Tiruttoṇṭar Tiruvantāti* is not clear, however. The *Periya Purāṇam* states that it draws from the work of Nambiyandar Nambi, which is probably the *Tiruttoṇṭar Tiruvantāti*, giving us, again, a terminus ante quem of the mid-twelfth century, and probably a date somewhat earlier. Zvelebil assigns a date of late tenth or early eleventh century to Nambiyandar Nambi. More recently, Anne Monius places him in the tenth century. S. Vaiyapuripillai dates the *Tirumantiram* to the first quarter of the eighth century. Dominic Goodall points out that certain features of the *Tirumantiram* are shared only with later Sanskrit Shaiva Siddhanta texts, presenting a convincing argument for a date later in the range we are considering.[66]

The *Tirumantiram* incorporates features of the texts of both the ñāṉasiddhars and the kāyasiddhars. As Venkatraman points out, however, the text prescribes ritual practices that the ñāṉasiddhars would later reject, which leads him to classify the Tirumular of the *Tirumantiram* as a *sanmārgasiddhar*, rather than a ñāṉasiddhar or a kāyasiddhar.[67] The text is included in the canon of orthodox Tamil Shaivism, the *Tirumuṟai*, as its tenth book.[68] Written in the voice of its ascribed author, the *Tirumantiram* offers few biographical details of Tirumular, but it does include some elements of narratives that would feature in later Shaiva tradition. In the four editions that I consulted, two agreed in their numbering of verses, and as I will point out shortly, some verses were tellingly omitted from certain editions.[69] Here I will follow the numbering of the Shaiva Siddhanta edition, as this seems to have been the most widely disseminated edition for a number of decades.

The text depicts Tirumular as one of eight disciples of Nandi who received the title "master" (*nātar*) (129). Presumably this period of study was spent on Mount Kailasa, Shiva's abode in the Himalayas in the north. He spent much of his time in devotional meditation. "Daily thinking of the feet of Shiva, who wears the twilight moon, I propounded the Āgamas. . . . Reaching gracious Nandi's feet, after seeing Shiva's matchless dance in the flawless hall, I lived an unequalled seventy million eons (*yukam*)" (135–136). The "matchless dance" refers to Shiva's dance in the hall at Chidambaram, in his form as Natarajan, indicating that Tirumular also lived some of his eons among ordinary people. The Āgamas are Sanskrit liturgical texts of orthodox south Indian Shaivism, which took shape as a genre in roughly the same period as the composition of the *Tirumantiram*.[70]

This association with Nandi, residence on Kailasa and in more mundane environs, and longevity, are biographical details that are consistent with those of later, more coherent narratives. Other skeletal elements of later narratives appear in the *Tirumantiram*, such as his association with Mulan.

> I received the title of "master" by Nandi's grace.
> I found Mulan only through Nandi's grace.
> Without Nandi's grace, what can be accomplished?
> With Nandi showing the way, I remained on the earth. (130)

This "finding" of Mulan is narrated in later texts as an entering into the dead body of a cow herder named Mulan near Avadudurai, a town in the Tamil Kaveri delta. In the *Tirumantiram*, Tirumular "dwells at the feet of the beautiful goddess of the cool land (*tuṟai*) of Shiva's Avadu" (139). He stayed there in Avadu, not far from Chidambaram, "chanting the names of Shiva in the shade of Shiva's *pōti*," where pōti is either wisdom, or a bodhi tree (140). "I was in this body for countless millions of years, I was in the place beyond day and night, I was at the blessed feet of god, I was below the two feet of my Nandi" (142). He entered the "city of Nandi," apparently here a reference to Avadu, where he remained for ninety million eons (143). He "came by way of Kailasa" (155). "This body" seems to be that of Mulan, who would compose the *Tirumantiram*: "Mulan was born long ago in the enduring, virtuous path of the seven holy orders. On the edge of the monastery, he rendered the beautiful words of the Āgamas in 3,000 verses, divided into nine treatises."[71] "Mulan composed the *3000* in Tamil for the wisdom of the world."[72] The biographical details given in the text are scattered, however, and they could be ordered into any number of coherent narratives, so one must not give in to the temptation to organize them into the narrative that is given in later texts.

Much of the text is didactic, instructing the persevering reader on the nature of Shiva, the causes of entanglement in the world, and the techniques and benefits of yogic practice and devotion to Shiva. Tirumular claims extraordinary powers throughout the text, a result of his devotion and yogic practice.

> In order to rid myself of flaws, I searched out the feet of the one whom the celestial beings adore;
> I saw the space of brilliance and purity.
> Nothing is difficult for me now;
> He gave me the great gift of the eight siddhis, and cut off my future births. (621)

The eight siddhis, the extraordinary powers possessed by all siddhars, are gifts from Shiva, achieved through deep devotion. Tirumular makes it clear that that the siddhis are not gained through "artistic learning, genius, or subtle wisdom" (626). The siddhis he lists resemble those of Sanskrit traditions of yoga, such as the ability to become tiny, to become large, to prevail everywhere, and, especially salient to later narratives of Tirumular, to enter into the bodies of others (648).

For Tirumular, and also for the later medical tradition, the most important extraordinary power is the ability to preserve the body and extend life. The reason to preserve the body is that, "with the destruction of the body, life departs, and one is destroyed. One will not achieve the eternal, true wisdom" (704). Tirumular recounts that he "used to regard the body as base," but that he began to protect the body after he realized that "god put a temple inside it" (705). The techniques he gives are primarily yogic. For example, he outlines practices of breath control through which one can live for a thousand years submerged in water, or buried in the earth, without the deterioration of the body (702). The retention of semen and other ascetic practices likewise preserve youth, as does the recitation of mantras (715, 719). There is almost no instruction in medical preparations, with the exception of the drinking of "potent drinking water that resides in the body," which commentators universally take to refer to urine (825). If one drinks this liquid, the body will become golden (826). This water may be mixed with pepper (*miḷaku*), Indian gooseberry (*nelli*), turmeric (*mañcaḷ*), and neem (*vēmpu*). When this concoction is consumed, the body will become supple and the hair on the head dark (829). Here, the text names some of the central ingredients used today in siddha medicine, and specifically calls this formulation "medicine" (*maruntu*). Like the naming practices of later medical texts attributed to the siddhars, the *Tirumantiram* gives various names for this formulation: heroic medicine, medicine of the celestials, *nāri* medicine, primordial medicine, and radiant medicine (830). Another verse puts tumors and throat ailments alongside thunder and snakes as things that will not afflict those who adhere to duty (*tarumam*), while those who do not do their duty will be susceptible to cough, anemia, asthma, and fever (120). The text asserts that Shiva is medicine (284, 947); that all medicine is simply his two feet (1578); and that Nandi's grace is like medicine that makes a madman lucid (2037). However, the *Tirumantiram* is not a medical text in the sense that the later texts of the kāyasiddhars are: it does not detail medical formulae, analyze types of diseases, outline methods of diagnosis, and so on. It can even be read as an explicitly antimedical text, at one point stating that aside from urine, no other medicine is necessary (827).

The *Tirumantiram* is not particularly interested in medicine, then, nor does it highlight Tirumular as a siddhar. The text defines siddhars as those who "see clearly that space enters and pervades space, that love contains love, and that light dissolves into light. Siddhars have realized that this here is Shiva's world. They embody sound and the limits of sound" (168–169). "They are siddhars who, in addition to attaining the eight [siddhis], reach the highest heaven. They dwell in the heavenly world, and in them is established the sought-after vision of god. They transcend the eight directions" (651). The text views the siddhis as great accomplishments, but ultimately subordinated to the power of the divine. These extraordinary powers can be gained through yogic practice: "Along with the eight siddhis, all wisdom is illuminated through the eightfold yoga" (670). However, although the yogi might achieve the siddhis through his own effort, "the eight siddhis become attainments only through the grace of [the goddess] Tripura Shakti" (670). Human effort is successful only with divine assistance.

Although Tirumular certainly claims to have attained what siddhars have attained, he does not use this designation when speaking of himself or of his accomplishments. Often he refers to siddhars in lists of types of beings. "Gods (*tēvar*), demons (*curar*), siddhars (*cittar*), semidivine beings (*vittiyātarar*), the three and the original thirty-three [Vedic gods], ascetics, the seven rishis, pious people, and beings moving and unmoving, all these dance when my god dances" (2685).[73] The text even lists the siddhars, along with immortal celestial beings, as those who "think of Shiva constantly, but don't really know him" (2975). If this is more of a statement of the greatness of Shiva than it is of the limitations of siddhars and celestial beings in particular, verse 271 is less ambiguous. "Even the siddhars don't deeply comprehend the divine light, but to those devotees (*aṭiyār*) who worship with devotion, he appears before them and grants liberation." Thus, while the *Tirumantiram* considers the attainment of the siddhis and of siddhar status a high state of accomplishment, it is not given particular eminence. Just as often, the text uses *yōgis*, *civayōgis*, *ñāṉis* (those with profound knowledge), and other terms to refer to those who have achieved the highest states of yogic practice and devotion.

One of the fascinating features of the *Tirumantiram* is its reflection on language. It regards Tamil highly, both as an effective means to communicate the greatness of Shiva and as having value unto itself. Tirumular reflects, "God gave to me a good birth, so I could sing about him with skill in Tamil" (147). The "triple Tamil"—Tamil traditions of music, literature, and drama—is valued as a goal to be realized, set alongside Shiva in his form as bestower of salvation, philosophical truth, and the Vedas (149). "Shiva is salvation, wisdom, and the sound of the triple Tamil. For those who worship him always, the spotless one is always in them, just as milk is contained in butter" (2076). The Tamil region is celebrated as a place of knowledge. "They roam the world spreading wisdom that is abundant in the five Tamil regions (*maṇṭalam*). A heart melting in devotion, and knowledge of my lord, are the basic characteristics of the five Tamil regions" (1619). Two verses, notably absent from the Shaiva Siddhanta edition but present in the other editions that I consulted, speak of Shiva communicating in both Sanskrit and Tamil. "He shows compassion to her [Shakti], speaking in both Sanskrit (*āriyam*) and Tamil" (65).[74] Shiva "reveals [truth] in both Tamil words and Sanskrit words [*vaṭacol*, literally, northern words]" (66).[75] The omission from the Shaiva Siddhanta edition is consistent with the project of non-brahman Shaiva orthodoxy in the twentieth century to purge the Tamil language and literature of Sanskrit words and influence.[76] Here it is important to note that although the text extols Tamil, it does not reject Sanskrit as an effective vehicle for communicating the glories of the divine, nor does it demonstrate a geographical preference for devotional practice, instead employing tantric imagery to locate the divine within the body.

Periya Purāṇam

The next contribution to the literary history of Tirumular, and the earliest rendering of the expanded story of his exploits, is found in the *Periya Purāṇam*.[77] Attributed to Cekkilar, a minister of the Chola court, the *Periya Purāṇam* is one of the canonical texts of Tamil Shaivism, and dates to the middle of the twelfth century. It recounts events in the lives of the sixty-three nāyaṉmār, Shaiva devotees who lived between approximately the sixth and ninth centuries C.E. The account of Tirumular, the "Tirumūlatēva Nāyaṉār Purāṇam" (Story of the devotee Tirumular), begins:

> On Kailasa Mountain, home to the one who wears the crescent moon as a wreath, there was a yogi of the four Vedas. He received the grace of Nandi, who guards the eternal temple there and teaches the path of Shiva to the celestial gods like Indra, Vishnu, and Brahma. (3564)
>
> That yogi, who had achieved the ability to become extremely small (*aṇimā*) and the other siddhis, lived on Shiva's holy Kailasa Mountain.

> He set out to spend a few days with his friend Gurumuni [Agastya] on Potigai Mountain, the mountain of excellent Tamil. (3565)[78]

He traveled south and eventually came to Avadudurai, in the heartland of the Tamil-speaking Kaveri Delta. There he worshiped Shiva in his form as Pasupati, lord of animals (3572). As he moved on from the town,

> he saw a herd of cattle on the land by the bank of the Kaveri River, bellowing in grief. (3573)
>
> In the town of Sattanur, inhabited by brahmans, there was a shepherd named Mulan. Born into a family of herders, he was engaged in the family vocation of tending cattle. He was out with the herd when his karma ran out, and the cruel strong poison consumed his life. He fell to the ground, dying. (3574)
>
> That herd of cows gathered around the body and bellowed with grief, turning in circles, sniffing the air. The yogi of great austerities, as an act of god's grace, decided to remove the suffering of the cattle. (3575)
>
> Reflecting that "the distress of the cattle won't disappear unless he comes to life and rises up," that austere sage, in his mercy, decided to insert his life (*uyir*) into the shepherd's body. He safely stored his own body, and by controlling his breath, he entered into that body. (3576)
>
> After entering that body he rose, now as "Tirumular." (3577)[79]

The yogi, now Tirumular, finished the work of grazing the cattle and returned home. He encountered his wife, who was distressed by his strange appearance and refusal to touch her. He renounced her, and the villagers unsuccessfully tried to appease her by telling her that Mular has become focused on "Shiva-yoga" (3583).

The yogi meant for this transformation to be temporary, but on returning to the place where he deposited his body, it had disappeared. "Deliberating on these events, he realized clearly what had happened. Shiva hid the body out of grace, so that Tirumular would propagate in Tamil to the world the meaning of the Āgamas, bestowed by the one who wears the cool moon in his matted hair [Shiva]. With complete insight, he realized, 'This is Shiva'" (3585–3586).[80] Tirumular returned to Avadudurai and sat focused on Shiva. He lived there for 3,000 years, each year composing a single verse.

> To remove the poison of being born in bodies of flesh, and so that people of the earth will attain liberation, he lived happily on this earth for three

> thousand years. Each year he adorned the *Tamil 3000* with a single verse, composing a garland of holy verses (*tirumantira mālai*) with the four flowers that begin with wisdom.[81] This garland of truth considers the one who wears the boar's tusk, the supreme god, as "the only one."[82] By the benevolence of the one whose head is adorned with the moon, he reached Mount Kailasa, never to be separated again from the feet of Shiva. (3589–90)[83]

The story ends where it began, on the slopes of Mount Kailasa in the north.

Like the episodes of other nāyaṉmār of the *Periya Purāṇam*, the story of Tirumular is a vehicle to portray the strength of his devotion and to extol the greatness of Shiva, not to showcase Tirumular's extraordinary powers or knowledge. Although the text does attribute to Tirumular the attainment of the siddhis, it refers to him as a yogi, not a siddhar. The characterization of Tirumular as rendering in Tamil the truths of the Sanskrit Āgamas is consistent with the *Tirumantiram*, as is Tirumular's residence in both the northern and southern regions. The *Periya Purāṇam*, however, presents a coherent narrative that clearly depicts the ascetic as a non-Tamil speaker, only gaining facility in Tamil through his occupation of the body of the herdsman. His possession of this body for an extended period of time is something thrust upon him by Shiva, and although he lives happily on the earth for three thousand years, by Shiva's grace he eventually leaves the Tamil land and resides at the feet of Shiva on Mount Kailasa. The text's account of the life of Tirumular clearly idealizes Kailasa to the north as the home of Shiva, not the southern Tamil land.

Contemporary Narratives

The site of Tirumular's residence in the *Periya Purāṇam*, Avadudurai, is now home to one of the most influential Shaiva monasteries in south India, Thiruvavadudurai Adinam. On the grounds of the monastery and its adjacent temple is an image of Tirumular, marking the place where, another narrative tradition holds, he sat in meditation for 3,000 years, emerging once every year to compose a verse of the *Tirumantiram*. The Thiruvavadudurai monastery publishes literature on the *Tirumantiram* meant for a popular audience, such as *Tirumantira Muṉṉurai* (Introduction to *Tirumantiram*), and *Tirumantiram Vaittiyappakuti* (The medical portion of the *Tirumantiram*), a compilation of verses from the *Tirumantiram* having some reference to the body and health.[84] The monastery dates from the sixteenth century, long after Tirumular is said to have lived.[85] Kathleen Iva Koppedrayer has noted that the monastery does not include Tirumular in its lineage.[86] Even so, the preface of the *Introduction to Tirumantiram* suggests a connection by stressing the history of siddhars in Thiruvavadudurai, noting that the town itself is sometimes called "the city of 90 million siddhars."[87] The preface highlights the claim that the heads of the monastery are in "the Kailasa lineage, in Nandi's order," further cementing the link to Tirumular.

These works by the monastery for the most part downplay Tirumular as a siddhar, drawing rather from the *Periya Purāṇam* narrative in considering him one of the sixty-three *nāyaṉmār*. Desikar recounts in English the story of Tirumular, expanding on narrative elements of the *Periya Purāṇam* such as Tirumular's residence at Thiruvavadudurai, "where he sat under a Bodhi tree and passed into a state of deep contemplation. Once a year he woke up, and each time he composed a stanza containing the cream of his spiritual experiences during the year."[88] Desikar's interpretation of the narrative is fascinating. First, he stresses that Tirumular took on the body of a shepherd in order to demonstrate to the world that "any person be he of high or low birth, can see to attain Shivananda (Shiva's bliss)," reading an egalitarian message into the narrative that is consistent with modern portrayals of the siddhars as opponents of caste.[89] Second, he posits that Tirumular traveled from Mt. Kailasa to the South on account of his "strong condemnation of the pretensions of impostors masquerading as saints and seers. . . . The true import of the Vedas and Agamas was allowed to be lost in the jungle of rituals and dogmas. Tamil nadu [sic] the cradle of Saiva Siddhanta, had become the breeding ground of false prophets who used religion and philosophy for securing personal advantanges."[90] The antiritualism that Desikar refers to is a standard message of many of the ñāṉasiddhars, though this is not stressed in the *Tirumantiram*. Desikar also introduces an idea not found in the *Periya Purāṇam*, that Tirumular's journey to the south is a *return*, namely, of "the true import of the Vedas and Agamas," of "the principles of Saiva Siddhanta," to the "land of [their] birth."[91] This acrobatic interpretation effectively takes this knowledge that the *Tirumantiram* and the *Periya Purāṇam* depict as traveling from north to south, or from the heavens to the earth, or from Sanskrit to Tamil, and gives it Tamil origins and thus Tamil credentials.

Desikar's narrative is, however, ambivalent about the ethnicity of Tirumular himself. Other authors go further, ascribing Tamil character not only to the agamic knowledge transmitted in the *Tirumantiram* but also to Tirumular himself. Some simply ignore his exploits on Kailasa. N. Manikkavasagam, the editor of a popular compilation of the verses of the ñāṉasiddhars, *Cittar Pāṭalkaḷ* (Verses of the siddhars), gives a short biographical introduction to Tirumular's verses. He mentions the yogi's entry into the body of the shepherd Mulan, but makes no reference to his residence in the Himalayas.[92] He consistently emphasizes the Tamil character of the siddhars and their verses, calling the literature of the siddhars "honey pots of refined Tamil." Tamil is the "chief throne of philosophical wisdom," and the Tamil land is the "famed shield of knowledge in the South."[93] Reference to Tirumular's ascetic practice and revelations on Mt. Kailasa would undermine the Tamil credentials of the siddhars, so Manikkavasagam omits this part of the story.

Others introduce new narrative elements that make Tirumular a Tamil by birth. In an edition of the *Periya Purāṇam*, following the section on the life of Tirumular, A. Chidambaranar gives a contemporary, expanded life history of Tirumular.

> In the *Periya Purāṇam*, Cekkilar has discussed at length the latter part of the history of Tirumular Nayanar, but he has included few details about the earlier portion. . . . Tirumular was named "Sundarar" by his mother and father.[94] He was from southern Tamil Nadu. In his youth, he joined the Tamil academy of the sage Agastya on Mt. Potigai. He learned the texts of the world, and excelling as a student, he became friends with Agastya, the head of the academy. Afterward, after learning philosophical texts under Agastya's tutelage, he joined the school which was functioning at North Kailasa. There he learned the eternal Vedic Āgamas from Nandi, fully in Tamil, along with Janaka . . . [he lists six other students]. After completing the examination, he received the title of "master" from Nandi, and remained in Kailasa performing austerities.[95]

Chidambaranar (1883–1954) was active in the Shaiva Siddhanta movement and in efforts to recover details of prehistorical Tamil lands.[96] According to Chidambaranar's revisionist history, Tirumular's residence on Kailasa was temporary, and he eventually returned to the south, rejoining the events as they are narrated in the *Periya Purāṇam*. Instead of his life in Avadudurai being a transitory period (3,000 years!) between more enduring periods on Kailasa, Chidambaranar inverts this history. He also makes Tamil the language of instruction on Kailasa, a departure from *Tirumantiram*'s statement that Shiva taught in both Tamil and Sanskrit, which itself would have been a radical departure from the Sanskrit Āgamas.

Recent dating by Tamil revivalist authors puts Tirumular somewhere between scholarly accounts (which range from about the fifth century C.E. to the twelfth century C.E.), and calculations based on the *Tirumantiram*, in which Tirumular claims to live for seventy million yugas or eons, by which he means not a specific number of years but simply a very, very long time (136). T. V. Sambasivam Pillai dates him to the first century B.C.E.[97] In an introductory essay to the Shaiva Siddhanta edition of the *Tirumantiram*, A. Chidambaranar concludes that he lived at the time of the events of the *Rāmāyaṇa*, about 6000 B.C.E., and holds that he lived for 5,900 years.[98] In his *History of the Siddhars*, S. P. Ramachandran follows Chidambaranar in naming the yogi Sundarar, and puts Sundarar's time in Mulan's body as occurring between 200 and 150 B.C.E.[99] He does not speculate on the date of Sundarar.

Others are less specific, simply dating Tirumular and the other siddhars "many thousands of years B.C."[100]

Contemporary narrations of Tirumular emphasize not only his Tamil character but also his medical expertise, focusing on the scant medical material found in the *Tirumantiram*, invoking the later medical literature attributed to Tirumular, and adding narrative details to his hagiography. Siddha vaidyas consider Tirumular, along with Agastya and Bhogar, to be one of the foremost medical siddhars and thus one of the main founders of siddha medical knowledge. In her *History of Medicine in South India*, R. Naranjana Devi cites A. Shanmuga Velan in asserting that Tirumular founded a school for siddhars, and that he ran a medical education center for siddhars.[101] A. Shanmuga Velan calls him the "father" (*tantai*) of siddha medicine, stressing his role in training other siddhars. "Tirumular is the reason for the spread of the siddhar path."[102] Other influential authors of siddha medicine emphasize Tirumular as the original siddhar preceptor of Tamil medicine. K. N. Kuppusami Mudaliyar, H.P.I.M. (Higher Proficiency in Indian/Indigenous/Integrated Medicine), was formerly a professor at the Government College of Indian Medicine, Madras. He wrote an introduction to siddha medicine, *Citta Maruttuvam* (Siddha medicine), for use in courses on siddha medicine at colleges throughout the state. The book was first published in 1954, and a second edition was published in 1987 by the Tamil Nadu government's Siddha Medicine Publications Commission. I purchased the book in 1999 from the Department of Indian Medicine and Homoeopathy, part of a health, research, and education complex in Chennai. The complex includes a hospital with clinical facilities, a research department, a Tamil Nadu government siddha medical college, a library, and a publications division. Kuppusami Mudaliyar's book, which I will consider in more detail later, cites verses from the *Tirumantiram* as "evidence" that places Tirumular in a lineage of medical knowledge that began with Shiva. "Shiva taught Nandi, Nandi Tirumular, and Tirumular the other siddhars."[103] He considers another popular account of the siddha medical lineage, that of Shiva to Parvati to Murugan to Agastya, but rejects this, arguing that Agastya is not one of the group of Tamil siddhars, and that he was not the author of siddha medicine. Many siddha vaidyas display similar ambivalence toward Agastya, as his northern origins are not as easily ignored as Tirumular's.

Siddha vaidyas practicing today continue to identify their knowledge with Tirumular. G. J. Parthasarathy runs a successful siddha medical center in Velachery, a suburb of Chennai, and publishes a popular monthly medical journal called *Cittar Ulakam* (Siddhar world). He named his medical center the Tirumular Radha Siddha Medical Clinic and Information Center. Although Parthasarathy considers the flesh-and-blood vaidyas who have taught him siddha medicine to be his gurus, and cites his grandfather as his primary guru, he regards Tirumular as akin to a guru. "Tirumular is for all the doctors in Tamil Nadu. Agastyar, Tirumular, Bhogar, people embrace one of these and practice medicine. For medical practice they are like gurus." He considers Tirumular to be the siddhar who most closely embodies the ideals of siddha medicine, especially its purported egalitarian character, since Tirumular authored the *Tirumantiram* in the body of a common cowherd. Parthasarathy is himself from the *iṭaiyar* community, a caste of cattle and goat herders. As Tirumular embodies the ideals of siddha medicine, the *Tirumantiram* teaches a philosophy appropriate to Tamil Nadu. Parthasarathy spoke to me of the conjunction between Tirumular, the *Tirumantiram*, and life in the Tamil land. "*Tirumantiram*. A man, as long as he is of Tamil Nadu, how should he live? . . . Who am I? Why was I born? What sort of work should I do? To understand these things, you need to read Tirumular's *Tirumantiram*." He cites verses from the *Tirumantiram* in his monthly publication as well as in the conversations I have had with him. In the February 2003 edition of *Cittar Ulakam*, Parthasarathy recounts the history of Tirumular, using the variant of the sage's birth as a Tamil named Sundarar, who first learned "worldly literature" on Potigai Mountain with Agastya before traveling to the north to study "wisdom literature" and the Āgamas with Nandi.[104] Thus he consistently stresses the Tamil credentials of Tirumular.

There are several premodern medical texts attributed to Tirumular, and many contemporary vaidyas interpret the *Tirumantiram*'s verses on the body, health, and longevity as early instances of siddha medical knowledge.[105] K. Venkatesan, a registered practitioner of siddha medicine and editor of what is perhaps the most well-known siddha medical publication, the monthly *Mūlikaimaṇi*, completed a PhD on siddha medicine in the Tamil department of Madras University. In his dissertation, published in 1998 as *Tamiḻ Ilakkiyattil Citta Maruttuvam* (Siddha medicine in Tamil literature), Venkatesan presents a comprehensive collection of medical details contained in Tamil literature from sangam times. The *Tirumantiram* figures prominently. "The excellence of the Shaiva Āgamas, the explanation of the path of yoga, the makeup of the body, the functioning of the body, mantras, chakras, and medicine, all these are discussed at length with subtlety and in esoteric fashion. . . . Details of the art of medicine evident in the *Tirumantiram* are especially valuable."[106] An eminent scholar of siddha medical texts, V. R. Madhavan, writes: "it is only in *Thirumandiram* that the fundamentals of the Siddha system of medicine have been described. Just as the basic concept for modern medicine is physics, chemistry and biology, Thirumoolar tells us the essential factors of the Siddha system of medicine."[107] Most vaidyas, and people writing about siddha medicine in the last half-century, accept that a single siddhar named Tirumular authored the *Tirumantiram* and the various medical texts attributed to him, such as the *Tirumantiram 8000*, a medical and alchemical text written in the style of other premodern Tamil medical texts.[108] A. Shanmuga Velan calls the *Tirumantiram 8000* the "medical *Tirumantiram*," and considers this "priceless" text to be the original siddha medical text.[109] S. P. Ramachandran, in his introduction to another medical text attributed to Tirumular, *Tirumūlar Vaittiyam 1000* (Tirumular's 1000 verses on medicine), asserts that this medical text shares the same author as that of *Tirumantiram*, because of the beauty of the Tamil used in each. "Tirumular's *Tirumantiram* is a feast without equal for those who desire to see the Tamil language as a Tamil girl, sweetly prattling and playing, as a girl in her tender youth, as a dancing woman adorned with jewels. . . ." "No one other than Tirumular could have written the verses in *Tirumūlar Vaittiyam 1000*," because of the fineness of its verses and the proper ordering of its words.[110] He assigns to Tirumular "the first place among siddhars," and interprets his assertions of long life in the *Tirumantiram*, and his 3,000 years in Tirumular's body, as his practice of *cākāk kalai*, the art of deathlessness, one of the primary aspirations of siddha medicine. "Every Tamil son can rejoice with justification, reflecting that the siddhars lived, indeed, they are still living, having perfected the art of deathlessness, which is only in this good world called Tamil."[111] The final verse of the text, however, identifies the text as ayurvedic, highlighting the diverse literary history of Tirumular and the disjunctions between modern and past traditions.[112]

Siddhars and the Mastery of the World

The narratives of Tirumular are typical of those of other siddhars. Siddha vaidyas today often assign an indigenous, Tamil character to the siddhars' extraordinary powers. They speak of these powers in particularly modern ways, employing the terminology of science and stressing that the siddhars attain their powers chiefly through their own efforts rather than through divine grace. I argue that in identifying the attributive founders of their medicine with the extraordinary and the indigenous, vaidyas seek to infuse their knowledge with miraculous potential and with the authority of tradition. In typifying this knowledge as both extraordinary and scientific, they make a claim to its modern relevance, and yet also critique the limits of Western science. They draw on more than a millennium of Tamil literary testament to the powers of ascetic practice and devotion in launching a critique of the imperial agenda of Western medicine and science, arguing that siddha medicine satisfies the criteria for credibility of a rational science while not being limited by those criteria.

Premodern and contemporary literature on the siddhars, as well as the writings attributed to the siddhars, depict their relationship to the world as one of mastery and domination. The texts of the ñāṉasiddhars speak about the siddhars' mastery of their bodies and of the world around them. These stories of supernatural powers are repeated in later Tamil literature, as well as in the recent, burgeoning "pulp nonfiction" on the siddhars.[113] The siddhars control their appetites and sexual desires through asceticism and their bodies and minds through yoga and meditation. On successfully mastering themselves, they gain powers through which they can control the physical world in extraordinary ways. Insofar as they link mastery of desire, of their bodies, of health, and of the physical world, the siddhars are apt figures to place at the beginnings of siddha medical knowledge. For contemporary vaidyas, the siddhars' somatic mastery is the basis for their medical authority. In conquering death, the siddhars achieved the absolute limit of mastery that is the aspiration of all medicine and that signals a perfection of medicine.

S. P. Ramachandran, editor of numerous siddha medical texts, distinguishes siddhars from devotees (*paktarkaḷ*), even such great devotees as the Shaiva nāyaṉmār. "There is a major difference between siddhars and devotees. Devotees are immersed in devotion through god's grace. They forget the realities of the world and devote their lives to divine service. The siddhars, on the other hand, master the path of the noble life. They live embracing the practice and performance of medicine, alchemy, yoga, and wisdom." Their contribution of a variety of forms of knowledge to the world is possible because of their ability to perform miraculous feats through their own power. According to Ramachandran, miracles happen to devotees through god's grace, uninvited and unexpected. "But the siddhars, when they desire that something happen in such and such a way, they make it happen, demonstrating the power of their knowledge and the strength of their asceticism."[114]

Siddha vaidyas generally describe the siddhars' mastery of nature as resulting from their deep insight into the natural laws that govern the cosmos, a characterization that asserts the scientific credentials of a medicine that claims to have the power to bestow immortality. They portray the siddhars as scientists whose rigid investigation, indeed, whose *research*, results in their control over nature. T. V. Sambasivam Pillai writes that the siddhars

> had investigated and studied fully the cause and effect of diseases and all kinds of drugs, mineral and poisons; and thereby came to realize what is beneficial and what was not, to their existence in life. They can even, if they choose, retain their bodies for ages or disintegrate them at their will; and can also dematerialize or rematerialize their bodies as they like. Their knowledge of the inherent nature and the therapeutic and magnetic effects of different drugs, combined with the practice of regulating their breathing in vasi yogam [yoga of the breath], is supposed to give them longevity and superhuman powers quite beyond our comprehension.[115]

Beyond our limited comprehension, certainly, but not beyond comprehension per se. The extraordinary powers of the siddhars are not transgressions of natural laws, but rather are made possible by their exhaustive knowledge of nature and its principles.

Vaidyas often speak of the siddhars' skills of intuition in physiological terms. A. Shanmuga Velan wrote a popular book on siddha *kalpa* or longevity medicine, and on the siddhars' ability to remain youthful for long periods of time. A registered medical practitioner (Indian medicine), he was the founder and president of the Tirumular Siddha Medical Academy in Madras in 1959. He writes, "The seat of the inner eye is in between the two eyebrows. The siddhars who conquered death and attained perfection in life had developed the inner eye or wisdom eye which revealed to them the great truth about the inner mechanism of human life, valuable medicinal properties of herbs as well as the invisible objects and secrets of the heavenly bodies."[116] According to Shanmuga Velan, the siddhars do not transcend the dictates of natural law, but they differ from modern scientists in their realization that natural law is not limited to physical processes. Their perception extends beyond the five physical senses, as they have developed an "inner eye" that reveals "great truth." It is this sort of instrument, not possessed by modern scientists, through which the "inner mechanism of human life," "invisible objects," valuable medicines, and even the distant stars are known. The deficiencies of science are exposed in the superior faculties available to the siddhars, faculties that enable knowledge of the universe beyond the imagination of scientists.

Vaidyas consistently emphasize the rational nature of siddha medicine and of Tamil tradition more generally. Yet this rationality incorporates the depth of tradition and a sixth sense, a "mental eye" or a "wisdom eye" that intuits processes beyond the mere physical.[117] As T. V. Sambasivam Pillai puts it, what is required for medicine is a "holy science," by which he means a science that has "true knowledge and understanding of natural laws." These natural laws require intuitive modes of perception to be discerned. "The mysteries of curing and healing [are] hidden from the eyes, but open to the spiritual perception of the Wise." Ancient siddha medicine is this very perfection of science. According to Sambasivam Pillai, the siddhars "were the greatest scientists both material and spiritual," and the "Siddhars' Science" is "the fountain head of all knowledge and sciences."[118]

The characterization of the siddhars as investigating the natural world, doing their research in a considered way, and gaining knowledge through careful measurement, stands out as more specifically modern when we compare these twentieth-century writings with premodern medical texts. In these texts, and similarly in the *Tirumantiram*, the siddhars are great devotees who gain their powers and their medical knowledge not through personal insight into the nature of things but through their devotion to Shiva and Shakti. Thus Bhogar, one of the most popular of the medical siddhars, writes of a devotee of Shakti: "Because he did *puja* and recited the mantra 'Om,' worshiping Shakti's feet, he achieved extraordinary power (*citti*, Sanskrit *siddhi*). . . . He made a pill for bodily immortality (*kāyaccittam*)."[119] Similarly, the text I quoted earlier states that Agastya gained knowledge of muppu through devotion. "Holding the feet of Shakti in my mind, I saw the method to prepare muppu which is the means to immortality."[120] The premodern texts do not hold that the siddhars discerned medical formulae through careful explorations of the natural world, but that they received this knowledge as a reward for their extraordinary devotion.

Furthermore, according to these older texts, the siddhars' extraordinary medicines were often the *cause* of their great powers, not the fruit of their insight into the natural world. In a text on "subtle muppu" (*cūṭca muppu*), Agastya speaks of a medicine called *vañciṉi*, prepared by combining mercury, a salt called *ām*, and copper sulfate. On eating this, one can run all the way past the peak of the mythical Mount Meru and will even see the siddhars, and will there have the opportunity to serve them![121] As Agastya points out in another of his texts on muppu, "If you understand this [formula for muppu] correctly, you too will become a rishi-siddhar!"[122] Another siddhar, Kailasa Sattamuni, holds that simply eating a plant called *ceruppaṭai* will put one in a deep meditative state of *camāti* (Sanskrit *samādhi*), the highest goal of yoga.[123] Rather than Tamil intuition or research penetrating the secrets of the physical cosmos, premodern medical texts posit that material nature itself, in the form of a mere creeper, stimulates the highest possibilities of human achievement.

In depicting the siddhars as Tamil scientists, and in overlooking the devotional, ritualistic elements of premodern medical texts, siddha vaidyas today demonstrate a keen awareness that their medical authority depends on an adequate response to their two major challengers, biomedicine and ayurveda. T. V. Sambasivam Pillai explicitly addresses this competition in contrasting ayurveda, which he views as a superstitious component of brahmanic Hinduism, with the works of the siddhars, who were "the greatest scientists in ancient times. Their works in Tamil are supposed to be more valuable than many that have been written in Sanskrit; and they are said to be works less shackled by the mythological doctrines of the original ayurveda."[124] The celebration of the siddhars as scientists not only meets the competition of biomedicine, then, but also responds to the challenge posed by ayurvedic practitioners. Siddha vaidyas typify ayurveda, in its connection with Sanskrit, as inseparable from brahmanic Hinduism, which in revivalist non-brahman polemic is an upper-caste scheme to dominate lower castes.[125] As such, they assert that no properly scientific medicine can emerge from Sanskrit culture—only rational Tamil traditions, formulated according to the vision of Tamil revivalism, can produce effective medicine. Indeed, it is the particularly Tamil science of the siddhars that makes their extraordinary accomplishments possible.

> The said animated mercurial pills according to Siddhar's process would, if retained in the throat, not only enable one to travel in the aerial regions, but also neutralise the action of fire, dematerialise the body, lead one to the path of wisdom, throws [*sic*] the Astral light and serve for various other purposes. No books so far, either in Sanskrit or in any other language except in Tamil Siddha works could be found treating on such a subject; and no nation in the whole world except Tamilians, was aware of this wonderful art. This in itself is a sufficient proof that the highest attainments of the Siddhars in spiritual science are marvelous and awe inspiring.[126]

More interesting than simply claiming that the siddhars have mastered worlds, siddha vaidyas suggest specific techniques through which the siddhars have conquered these worlds, and they give these worlds particular characteristics that they say biomedicine and ayurveda overlook. Yet vaidyas do not recount the discipline and rational insight exhibited by the siddhars merely to legitimate their knowledge—they also revere the siddhars as models of behavior. They ask contemporary Tamils to exercise mastery of their desires by avoiding the superficial pleasures and treatments offered by foreign medical systems, and to satisfy their duty to tradition by becoming patrons of siddha medicine. In their superior control of nature, the siddhars have laid the groundwork for the hope of all siddha vaidyas, that their knowledge will eventually master current national and global medical markets.

The global aspirations for this rhetoric of indigenousness are expressed by recent writers who exalt the siddhars on the world stage, not only as masters of nature or just as the progenitors of Tamil society but also as founders of the civilizations of the world. Vaidyas depict the siddhars as the world's first scientists, drawing on revivalist narratives of Tamil civilization as the impetus for all civilization and science. N. Kandaswamy Pillai asserts that the siddhars were the original authors of all the world's civilizations. "The racial memory of Tamilians and some section of the Egyptians speaks of a very ancient period in the human history in which civilised people from the submerged Tamil continent came to Egypt led by Siddhas, and laid the foundations of a civilization which is the mother of all modern civilizations."[127] According to Kandaswamy Pillai, world civilization has devolved from its Tamil original, and so all scientific traditions are degenerate versions of the foundations established by the siddhars. However, some traditions are less degenerate than others, and it is Tamil tradition that most fully embodies the foundational knowledge of the siddhars. "Though the Siddhas and their cult are spread over the whole world and the glimpses of their existence were seen in all ages, Tamilians used to claim closer relationship with them because of the land of their origin and continuous existence of their cults in Tamil land."[128] In his work on siddha alchemy, M. C. Subramaniam argues that although all science began with the siddhars, only the Tamil sciences have maintained their links to these origins: "All of today's research methods in chemistry came into being on the basis of the chemistry research conducted by the siddhars. It is an established historical truth that the siddhars' research methods in chemistry spread to the Western countries by way of the Turks, Arabs, Greeks and Romans. Therefore, it is completely appropriate to consider the siddhars to be the pioneers of chemical science."[129] In championing Tamil knowledge as the root and essence of all modern science, Subramaniam makes a case for its prestige in an environment in which biomedical doctors and modern scientists discount Tamil siddha traditions of alchemy and medicine as false or superstitious. He argues that the siddhars are not just the founders of Tamil science but are the founders of science per se. This narrative is of Tamil origins and also of the origins of science, thereby making all science, even Western science, properly Tamil. It is a totalizing discourse both spatially and temporally, identifying science as essentially Tamil, everywhere and at all times. This includes the future development of science: because Tamil tradition has maintained the closest connection to the source of all science, it must be the basis of any attempt to recover this original perfection.

This rhetoric of origins emerges out of a globally competitive medical world, and this competition is central to some of the ways that vaidyas describe the siddhars. They routinely juxtapose accounts of the extraordinary powers of the siddhars with the technical accomplishments, or lack thereof, of other societies.

> The *cittu* is called the atom, the smallest yet complete particle. Modern scientists have been immersed in unceasing research to know better these small particles. But from the conception of time, our great siddhars have succeeded in this as a result of their extensive research. In this research, they split atoms and combined atoms using the fine instruments of the grinding stone, rolling pin, and so on, and they attained greatness resulting from this research. They would roam for millions of years, emerge from their state of meditative bliss (*camāti*) and take on an indestructible body, and would give darshan.[130]

The siddhars, Muttukkaruppa Pillai argues, did all that modern scientific researchers do, yet they did it thousands of years ago. They did it with less, making all the same discoveries with primitive technologies. They also did more than modern science can do, living for millions of years in deathless bodies. In the context of a narrative of Tamil tradition, Muttukkaruppa Pillai celebrates the accomplishments of the siddhars not only to claim the glory of the siddhars' knowledge for Tamils but also to argue for its universal applicability and global relevance.

Muttukkaruppa Pillai describes the method of the siddhars as "research" (*āyvu*), the same word which denotes modern scholarly and scientific methods. So while he argues that Tamil science should set the universal criteria for truth, he employs the language of Western science in describing and validating Tamil science, implicitly acknowledging that all forms of knowledge that intersect with the Western sciences must in some way justify themselves in terms of these sciences. What results is an explanation of extraordinary accomplishments using quasi-scientific language, an explanation that aims to enhance the value of the extraordinary, not to make it more ordinary. Science is a sign of modern authority, of truth, and of power. Like any sign, it can take on different meanings for those who invoke it. Muttukkaruppa Pillai here claims its authority while rejecting the rigidity of its method and its omission of the metaphysical. In emphasizing the spectacular achievements of this "siddhar science," he seeks to elevate it to a position above Western science, since the siddhars have already achieved all that Western scientists might achieve, and much more.

What sort of research did the siddhars do? Although it is in part research that used instruments and testing, its distinguishing tools are extrasensory. T. V. Sambasivam Pillai describes the ancient siddhars as men of "very high culture and intellect," and their methods "are of a high degree of perfection and many of which cannot be solved by even Modern Scientists, because they truly had an encyclopoedic mind guided by intuition."[131] Kundrathur Ramamurthy, speaking to me about the origins of siddha medicine, described the siddhars' intuition as aural.

> The eighteen siddhars were in the mountains, on Potigai Mountain. . . . The plants would speak to them as they would walk along. "I'm useful for this, or for that" they would say. They didn't have any books or notes at that time. They just had staffs in their hands. They wrote on palm leaves. How did the songs come to us? They told their students, they sang to them and told them again and again. They knew [things] immediately on seeing them. That's divine knowledge (*ñāṉam*). The siddhars were *ñāṉis*, those with divine knowledge. Ñāṉis have divine knowledge, while scientists have scientific knowledge (*viññāṉam*). For any process, scientific knowledge analyzes how the process works, and describes this for others. Divine knowledge can't be measured, scientific knowledge can. . . . How's that? There's a plant. You can see its name, its use, analyze it, and know. But the siddhars, without analysis, spoke about the plant's use.

Kundrathur Ramamurthy distinguishes the knowledge of the siddhars from scientific knowledge, but he does not posit an essential difference between their conclusions. For him, the difference lies in the way knowledge is gained, and he also suggests that their great powers of intuition allow them to see more deeply into the nature of things.

This view has been prevalent in siddha medicine since the beginning of its modern formulation. T. V. Sambasivam Pillai writes, "They arrived at conclusions . . . from introspective reflection and mental vision rather than by the toilsome and tedious researches of the laboratory from the imaginary knowledge rather than intuitional one. So the only conclusion to be arrived at lastly, is the spiritualism which is the real, and in that reality, they saw further and deeper beyond the ordinary comprehension, and achieved more than it would have been possible for the West."[132] The accomplishments of Tamil science are achieved through the power of the Tamil intellect, while those of Western science are won through mechanical apparati. Sambasivam Pillai contrasts "the spiritualism which is the real" with the "tedious" material researches of Western scientists that bring "imaginary knowledge," thereby inverting colonial critiques that the Tamil sciences are based more on fancies of the imagination than on evidence. His stereotypes of the West are typical of a reverse Orientalism according to which the essence of all things Western is materialistic, superficial, and mechanical, knowing "only the dead body of man and not the living image in him presented by Nature."[133] The siddhars are not only the historical founders of science but also the exemplary models of what it means to be scientific. Faced with the clear technical advantage of biomedical institutions, vaidyas posit that the most powerful forms of mastery are gained through natural mental ability and tradition, and not with technical superiority and innovation. They thereby leave open the possibility that the Tamil sciences might assume their prior and rightful position at the apex of the world's sciences.

> We know how to make this *iracamaṇi* pill from Tirumular's 8000-verse text, and we know that at the beginning of time, the siddhars circled many worlds. While today Westerners think of going to celestial bodies in their rockets with scientific methods, our siddhars went to the moon and other worlds thousands of years before with the help of the *kavaṉa* pill. When will the day come when Tirumular's 8000-verse text, which contains all these details, will be published? That will be a great day for our medical world. Long live the siddhars, geniuses who have seen worlds beyond the reach of scientists! Long live the arts of the siddhars![134]

The siddhars mastered not only nature and the world but time itself. The systems of knowledge they developed were not only the first sciences but remain the highest aspirations for future sciences. In achieving immortality, the siddhars achieved timelessness, in that to be immortal is to have already survived forever, that is, to stand outside of history. This is also the claim and hope of siddha vaidyas for their medical tradition, and of Tamil revivalists for Tamil tradition as a whole. Tradition is, in T. V. Sambasivam Pillai's words, a "real science" because it "holds good at all times—the past, the present and the future. The facts well-ascertained in our ancient books of some thousands of years ago have never been disputed or in any way criticized and so cannot lose their ground being nothing short of truths, and nothing but absolute and universal truths."[135] The characterization of the siddhars and Tamil tradition as timeless and immortal is less a description of history than it is a hopeful vision for a lineage of Tamil knowledge whose future, given the forceful challenge of biomedical technology and Indian nationalism, appears uncertain.

Conclusion

In eulogistic writings of the founders of their medical knowledge and practices, siddha vaidyas consistently link the siddhars' Tamil character with their mastery of nature, society, and the world. Tamil authors are aware that civilizations are judged on the basis of their technological and scientific accomplishments. They also know that the development of technological superiority, aside from its ideological value, has played a major role in the mechanics of imperialism and remains an advantage in competitive global economic markets. In *Dialectic of Enlightenment*, Max Horkheimer and Theodor Adorno speak of the enlightenment project to demystify and subsequently to master nature. For them, Francis Bacon best embodies the goals of the enlightenment, primary among which is the "happy match between the mind of man and the nature of things."[136] But Bacon's optimism was premature, Horkheimer and Adorno add:

> The concordance between the mind of man and the nature of things that he had in mind is patriarchal: the human mind, which overcomes superstition, is to hold sway over a disenchanted nature. Knowledge, which is power, knows no obstacles: neither in the enslavement of men nor in compliance with the world's rulers. . . . Kings, no less directly than businessmen, control technology; it is as democratic as the economic system with which it is bound up. . . . What men want to learn from nature is how to use it in order wholly to dominate it and other men.[137]

This has been borne out with European imperialism, with the globalization of technology, and, in medicine, with the explosive development of biomedicine and its challenge to indigenous medical practices. In competing for medical resources, siddha practitioners are acutely aware of the challenges posed by both ayurveda and especially biomedicine, and by the scientific, institutional, and political authorities and structures that support the claims of their adversaries. Also cognizant that technological mastery translates to social control, they claim a legacy of mastery of nature far superior to that displayed by the contemporary technologies of their competitors, and locate Tamil technical achievements in the past, in the future, and in the extraordinary powers of the elusive siddhars. Their discourses on the siddhars construct realms of narrative imagination over which they can exert control, providing accounts of Tamil medical superiority that draw patients into their clinics and hospitals. Their narratives of the siddhars are therefore rhetorical devices meant to identify their medicine with an idealized community; to extol the greatness of that community, and so to celebrate the self; and to assert a hierarchy of communities, insofar as they recount extraordinary power in the context of competing knowledge systems. In more general terms, their rhetoric seeks to win a position of respect for Tamil language, culture, and individuals equal to that of other societies.

4

The Invasion of Utopia

The Corruption of Siddha Medicine by Ayurveda

One of the most captivating features of many Tamil revivalist histories is their vision of utopia. Siddha vaidyas join other authors of Tamil tradition in imagining a prehistoric island called Lemuria in the Indian Ocean, home to the first Tamils and to the first human civilization.[1] They describe this ancient society as harmonious, prosperous, and peaceful, enjoying a medical system that could cure any ailment and that even offered the possibility of bodily immortality. According to these narratives, Tamils lived happily on Lemuria until foreign invasions initiated the deterioration of their medical traditions and hence the decline of their health. Drawing on Orientalist histories of Aryan incursions into India from the north, siddha vaidyas tell of a brahman invasion of their ancient civilization, which led not only to the political subjection of indigenous Tamils but also to the corruption of their pure traditions. They lament that these intruders introduced ayurveda into Tamil society, diminishing the truth of their knowledge and the potency of their medicines.

The last chapter examined the ways in which siddha vaidyas relate to perhaps their greatest medical challenger, biomedicine, but for them the specter of ayurveda becoming the national traditional medicine and the representative of Indian medicine globally looms large. Contrary to those affirmations of Indian medical solidarity that I detailed in chapter two, many traditional practitioners have redrawn and magnified the lines of division that distinguish indigenous knowledge, promoting their specific practices over other Indian medical traditions. The borders they have established closely parallel the political divisions that developed with Indian nationalism. Hindu/Muslim tensions are reflected in ayurveda/unani formulations, while an emergent Tamil revivalism has characterized siddha medicine as absolutely distinct from ayurveda. Siddha vaidyas, fearing that their practice would be eclipsed by biomedicine, or absorbed by ayurveda in the name of a united India, have participated in broader revivalist imaginings of a unique Tamil tradition. In the following two chapters, I build on the body of excellent scholarly work on Tamil nationalism and revivalism.[2] This work has not, however, addressed the contribution that siddha medicine has made to articulations of Tamil identity. The project to bring siddha in line with Tamil revivalism has decisively shaped siddha medicine over the last three-quarters of a century. Siddha medicine has, in turn, provided Tamil revivalism with something unique: the prospect of an ancient Tamil science that could serve as an important component in the formulation of an advanced, self-sufficient civilization.

Like other utopian narratives, these visions of ancient Tamil civilization contrast sharply with present realities, thereby providing a critique of the present and an agenda for the future. Paul Ricoeur highlights the critical distance afforded by utopia formulations, which emerges out of the gap between the imagined ideal and the perceived present. "Does not the fantasy of an alternative society and its exteriorization 'nowhere' work as one of the most formidable contestations of what is?"[3] By narrating a history in which Aryan brahmans from the north destroyed their perfect medicine, vaidyas contribute to a politics of Tamil identity that culminated in a call for Tamil political sovereignty from the Indian state in 1939. My goal in this chapter is to highlight the resonances between these political, medical, and utopian discourses, and to address the historical processes through which non-brahman Tamil leaders began to work for an independent Tamil political and cultural sphere. I will also inquire into the particular power of utopian narratives in projects of identity construction, with a specific focus on the role others are called upon to play in narratives of self.

Agastya, a Sanskrit Tamil Sage

Whereas the future of siddha medicine is threatened by the ascendancy of biomedicine, the challenge to its unique identity vis-à-vis other Indian medical practices reaches into both the future and the past. In asserting a distinct historical trajectory for their knowledge, siddha practitioners overwrite a past in which the lines between two discrete medical systems called ayurveda and siddha were not clearly, and rarely even faintly, drawn. Scholars, practitioners, and patients today too often assume the durability of these lines that have come to distinguish South

Asian medical systems. The histories through which siddha practitioners seek to build authority are as much about establishing the contours of Tamil self as they are about promoting the effectiveness of their medical practices. Their narratives of original unity assert that the natural order of Tamil society has been shattered by history, but they also suggest that this order can be recaptured through revivalist projects. The utopian promise of these narratives therefore lies as much in the future as in the past, its imaginative culmination being the perfect harmony of Tamil bodies, medicine, and tradition. By examining some of the motivations and strategies by which siddha vaidyas have articulated a distinct medical system, I will suggest a genealogy in Foucault's sense. "The search for descent is not the erecting of foundations: on the contrary, it disturbs what was previously considered immobile; it fragments what was thought unified; it shows the heterogeneity of what was imagined consistent with itself."[4]

As we saw in the last chapter, mythologies of the siddhars raise the specter of the intimate connections between Tamil and Sanskrit that non-brahman Tamil leaders and siddha vaidyas ignore or dismiss. The mythological history of the siddhar Agastya exemplifies this cultural hybridity, and so a brief look at the shifting literary representations of this popular siddhar will illuminate some general contours of linguistic and identity politics in recent medical and social debate. Of all the Tamil siddhars, it is Agastya whose Tamil credentials are most often questioned, as he is the only Tamil siddhar to feature in Sanskrit literature, where he is depicted as an Aryan, brahman sage. As a Tamil siddhar, more Tamil medical texts are attributed to him than to any other siddhar, approximately one-third of all extant manuscripts.[5] Many vaidyas therefore consider him to be the founder of the siddha medical system and the primary mediator of siddha medical knowledge to the Tamil people.[6] Tamil literary traditions celebrate Agastya as the "father of Tamil," the author of its first grammar and, perhaps, of the language itself.[7] This tradition can be traced to the commentary of Nakkirar on an eighth-century work of rhetoric, the *Iṟaiyaṉār Akapporuḷ*, which cites Agastya as the author of a Tamil grammar called *Akattiyam*. The *Iṟaiyaṉār Akapporuḷ* speaks of three successive Tamil literary academies (*caṅkam*, often "sangam"), all patronized by the Pandya kings. The first of these lasted 4,440 years, and was held in "Madurai which the sea claimed." The text cites Agastya (Akattiyaṉār) as the first participant of the first sangam, along with Shiva, Murugan, Kubera, and others. Agastya also took part in the second sangam, which lasted 3,700 years, according to the text.[8] There is no historical evidence for either of the first two sangams, but literature attributed to the third sangam is extant and forms the corpus of what is often called "sangam literature."

Agastya first appears in the *Ṛg Veda*, but fuller accounts of his activities appeared later in Sanskrit epic and puranic literature and also in a number of Tamil Purāṇas. According to both Tamil and Sanskrit mythologies, Agastya is a northerner who only reluctantly traveled south in order to balance the world's burden of significant beings, which had shifted north with a gathering of great beings for Shiva and Parvati's wedding in the Himalayas. The *Tirumantiram* speaks of Agastya as the "ascetic sage of the northern region," who was asked to balance the earth when it was leaning to one side.[9] The *Kañcippurāṇam* tells us that Agastya, after being summoned by Shiva to go to Potigai Mountain in the south, "was extremely upset, and protested vehemently," but finally submitted after Shiva promised to reveal himself to Agastya there.[10] Historians such as K. A. Nilakanta Sastri see Agastya myths as having a historical basis in the movement of Aryans to the south.[11] Agastya's knowledge of both Sanskrit and Tamil is what wins for him status as the greatest of sages, as Tamil is the culmination of the Vedic path, its newest addition. David Shulman accurately sums up the premodern Tamil literary history of Agastya: "Agastya is thus a symbol of Tamil learning, not as independent from or opposed to Sanskrit, but rather in harmony and conjunction with it."[12]

Agastya's connection to Sanskrit and the northern regions has led many vaidyas to deny him a role in the founding of siddha medicine. In his textbook for siddha medical students, K. N. Kuppusami Mudaliyar rejects one of the commonly held lineages of siddha medical knowledge, from Shiva to Parvati, Murugan, Agastya, Pulattiar, and then to the other siddhars, in favor of the lineage of Shiva, Nandi, Tirumular, and then the other siddhars. "It is not true that Agastya authored siddha medicine, because he cannot be accepted as one of the siddhars."[13] Agastya's legacy as a brahman and a northerner has led others to depict him as a foreigner who corrupted a previously perfect medical system. T. V. Sambasivam Pillai writes,

> In about 750 B.C., the Aryans began penetrating [the south] around the Vindya Mountains . . . and their entry is preserved in the tradition regarding Agastya's coming to the south. It would appear that the Aryan migration to South India refers to this period. The Dandhaka forest marked the Aryan frontier, and the Aryan immigrants came into the Tamil land under the lead of Agastya.
>
> This Agastya carried ayurveda to South India and founded a new school of medicine after his name. . . . It is only after the coming of Agastya, that the Siddha System and the school received a death blow, as he was responsible for introducing the Aryan culture into the Tamil country. The siddhars period of culture ceased to exist from this date. . . . It is presumed that the Arya Agastya is responsible for innumerable changes in the Siddhar's Science in his attempt to secure an equal footing to ayurveda.[14]

Here, Agastya is not the original redactor of the Tamil language but the leader of the Aryan invasion of the south, the brahman who corrupts the Tamil language, arts, and medicine by infecting them with Sanskritic elements. Sambasivam Pillai disparages the medical texts attributed to Agastya, saying that he mixed siddha and ayurveda in an attempt to degrade the superior Tamil medical system. The clear distinction here between two systems of medical practice is certainly an anachronism, as premodern Tamil medical texts do not consider their medical formulae to be part of a unified system. Sambasivam Pillai goes on to excise the Aryan Agastya from the group of eighteen siddhars by positing that there were two medical siddhars called Agastya. Besides the brahman Agastya was an Agastya of pure Tamil birth, who was one of the original eighteen siddhars and founders of the Tamil sciences, including pre-Aryan siddha medicine. This Tamil Agastya was of the Vellalar caste, the very caste of Sambasivam Pillai himself and the community that has been the primary force in the Tamil revivalist movement.[15]

Tamil revivalist historian A. Chidambaranar, whose narrative of Tirumular we have already discussed, distinguishes a variety of Agastyas in Tamil literature history, and gives short biographies of thirty-seven of these. He writes that Agastya is an "eminent Tamil name" that was first used in the Tamil country, before being taken up by Aryans, Sumatrans, Burmese, Sri Lankans, and Europeans. He delineates the early regions of Tamil civilization according to a geological landscape that precedes the rising of the Himalayas. "The Himalaya Mountains appeared 20 million years ago. Before that, there was a great sea between the Vindhya Mountains and Tibet. Tamil Nadu spread from the Vindhya Mountains to the South Pole. This is the place of origin of the Tamil race." He dates the origin of the Tamil people to this early time.[16] In describing the relation between the Tamil people and this land, Chidambaranar uses the term *uṟpatti*, to originate from, to spring or emanate from, a word that is used to describe the origin of rivers or the production of crops. Tamil revivalist rhetoric and siddha practitioners commonly employ such natural or even agricultural metaphors in linking the Tamil land, people, and medicine.

According to Chidambaranar, after the Himalayas appeared, Tamils established their civilization in the northern reaches of South Asia, and the Tamil Chola and Pandya kingdoms intermittently ruled those areas. However, in 16,500 B.C.E. a group of Africans came to rule the southern portion of the Tamil land. They ruled for five hundred years, a time in which Tamil Nadu was "plunged into calamity." The Tamil kings, not able to defeat the Africans who had built great forts made of gold, silver, and iron, went to Mount Kailasa and complained to Shiva. This was at the time Shiva was engrossed in preparations to marry Uma, the daughter of the Himalayan king, so he was not able to go himself. Instead he called "Agastya, who was his equal, and sent him south with great armies to help the Tamil people." Chidambaranar describes this Agastya as the first Agastya, hailing from a family of "Oḷināṭṭu Vēḷāḷars." That is, he is from a land-owning Vellalar Tamil community from Oḷināṭu, one of the twelve provincial regions contiguous with the central

Tamil land. Agastya has Shiva teach him Tamil grammar, and he leaves Kailasa as an "expert in the triple Tamil." He continues south and defeats the African armies at the Vindhya Mountains before rooting them out of the Tamil land. He then establishes a Tamil academy on Potigai Mountain in order to enrich the Tamil language, and there authors a Tamil grammar called *Akattiyam* and teaches a coterie of students.[17] Chidambaranar distinguishes this first Agastya from a later, tenth-century "siddha Agastya," a Tamil who was one of the eighteen siddhars and an eminent doctor.[18]

Chidambaranar's narrative is interesting in its elision of any features of Sanskrit, while at the same time it incorporates many episodes included in Sanskrit mythologies of Agastya. Although Agastya is a Tamil, he is from the provinces of the Tamil land, not the central region, the Centamiḻnāṭu or land of refined Tamil. Thus he needs to be taught Tamil grammar before establishing himself in a career of teaching in the south. Chidambaranar's interpolations that frame his Agastya narrative, such as the geographical and geological shifts, the specificity of the dates, and the presence of African kings, cast a new, revivalist light on much older narratives. He seeks credibility for his narrative by giving it the veneer of science and history, integrating features of geology (the rising of the Himalayas) with remarkably specific dates. Unlike the narratives of the miraculous discussed in the last chapter, Chidambaranar does not highlight extraordinary events, instead presenting Agastya, and even Shiva, as great warriors, benevolent leaders, and wise scholars. By expanding the Tamil region to cover much of the Southern Hemisphere, Chidambaranar is able to argue that Agastya is called the "sage of the South" (*teṉmuṉi*) not because he is a northern Aryan who went to far-flung regions in the south, but because he is a Tamil who established his residence and school in the southern heartland.

Tamil Medicine and Ayurveda

We must read these narrative shifts in the ethnicity of Agastya and in the geography of the subcontinent in the context of significant changes of Tamil identity and community from the beginning of the twentieth century. Political and literary changes have also significantly influenced, and have been influenced by, medical debates in south India. The connection between ayurveda and siddha has been a major preoccupation for siddha vaidyas, government officials, and scholars since the early decades of the twentieth century. Opinion runs the gamut from asserting that they are absolutely different to basically the same, and inherent in both positions is the assumption that these are coherent medical systems. The historical precedence of one over the other, with subsequent plagiarism, is often part of the histories they tell. The question of the historical relation and development of medicine in India has tended to be more a political issue than a medical one.

Siddha and ayurvedic practitioners for the most part share the concepts that structure their medical techniques.[19] Both use the notion of the three "faults" or *tōcam* (Sanskrit *doṣa*) in characterizing ailments and formulating remedies. The Tamil terms for these three, *vāta* (wind), *pitta* (bile), and *kapa* (phlegm), transpose Sanskrit words. Hartmut Scharfe has traced the semantic shifts in the term *doṣa* in ayurvedic literature, and concludes that the later usage of the term in Sanskrit literature corresponds to its understanding in siddha medicine. He consequently argues, convincingly, that the concept went from Sanskrit to Tamil, not vice-versa.[20] Both siddha and ayurvedic vaidyas use pulse reading as a method of diagnosis, but this plays a more central role in siddha medicine. Both siddha and ayurveda theorize 72,000 *nāṭi* or "veins" running through the body, and use the same terms for the primary three nāṭi.[21] Much of the technical terminology in siddha medicine is of Sanskrit origin. The forms of medical preparations have Sanskrit equivalents that are also ayurvedic medicines, such as *lēkiyam* (electuary; Sanskrit *lehyam*); *tailam* (oil; Sanskrit *tailam*); and *paspam* (ash, calcinated powder; Sanskrit *bhasma*).

Both use plant and, to a lesser degree, animal ingredients in their medical preparations. Inorganic substances, most notoriously mercury, seem to play a more central role in siddha than in ayurveda, and this is certainly one of the features that siddha vaidyas today cite as a distinctive feature of their medicine. This use of minerals and metals, and the importance of tantric views of the body and yogic practice, indicate the influence of tantra and alchemy on siddha medicine. None of this, however, is entirely absent from ayurvedic texts or practices.[22] The inorganic preparations described in premodern siddha medical texts share much with the Sanskritic traditions of *rasaśāstra* (alchemical teaching) or *rasacikitsā* (alchemical treatments).[23] David White, in his study of north Indian siddha writings, distinguishes therapeutic and alchemical writings, noting that whereas the former seek to alleviate suffering, the latter promise to transform the successful alchemist into an immortal siddha. Therapy, the province of ayurvedic practitioners, primarily uses herbal preparations, while alchemy has been mostly carried out by yogis and alchemists who work with mineral substances.[24] The siddha medical writings of south India are somewhat different, as therapy and alchemy are more closely integrated, and the pursuit of extraordinary medicines made with mineral and metal ingredients is a common goal among siddha vaidyas.

Although siddha vaidyas today consider themselves to be part of a distinct medical system, many do not view their practices as radically different from ayurvedic practices. When I asked Kundrathur Ramamurthy what the differences are between siddha and ayurveda, he said "siddha, ayurveda, and unani are all the same. Small, minor differences." He went on to describe some of these differences, first of which is the use of baspams and cendurams. Baspams are medicines of powder or ash produced through calcination, and cendurams are any chemical or metallic compound (usually mercury) used as medicine. G. J. Parthasarathy responded in precisely the same manner, asserting that "There's not that much difference. But there are differences," and citing the use of baspams and cendurams as the first difference.

Due to the considerable overlap in indigenous medical practice in south India, in the early decades of the twentieth century many Tamil vaidyas did not clearly define their practices as either siddha or ayurveda. In 1921, the government of Madras appointed a committee to look at "the question of the recognition and encouragement of the Indigenous Systems of Medicine in vogue in this Presidency."[25] The work of the committee, headed by Mohammed Usman, led to the publication in 1923 of the *Report of the Committee on Indigenous Systems of Medicine* and, two years later, to the founding of the Indian Medical School in Madras. As part of the 1923 report, a questionnaire was distributed to practitioners of indigenous medicines, and 183 replies were received in several Indian languages and in English. The responses of many practitioners to the question of "which system do you practice" suggest that the lines dividing medicine into distinct siddha and ayurvedic systems were in the process of formation at that time. While most vaidyas who traced their practices to either Sanskrit or Arabic texts clearly identified themselves as ayurvedic or unani practitioners, there was much ambiguity among those who employed a Tamil literary canon. Veluswami Pillai, a vaidya responding in Tamil, declared that he practices "Tamil Ayurveda," which Shiva taught to Devi, who taught Nandi, who taught the devas (gods), the munis (sages), and the siddhars (yogis), expressing one of the founding narratives claimed by contemporary siddha practitioners.[26] Another Tamil practitioner, Shanmukanandaswami, wrote: "I will speak about siddha medicine, Tamil medicine, or Tamil Ayurveda medicine, which has been practiced in Tamil Nadu from ancient times." Subramaniya Pillai claimed a lineage that has been practicing "Ayurveda Siddha Vaidya" for generations. In a joint submission, Murugesa Mudaliyar and Shanmukasundara Mudaliyar identified their practice as the "Siddha system . . . the age-long Ayurvedic system obtaining in Southern India."[27] They then went on to cite Tamil texts and a legacy of divine transmission of medical knowledge that siddha vaidyas today consider to be central components of their tradition. The key distinction highlighted by these practitioners was not between medical techniques, theories, or preparations, but between the languages of the texts that serve as authoritative corpuses of medical knowledge. In calling their practices "*Tamil* Ayurveda" or "*Tamil* medicine," they emphasized that they followed a medical tradition that drew upon Tamil texts rather than Sanskrit texts. Yet in calling their practices "Tamil *Ayurveda*," they also assumed an overlap between the medical practices and theories contained in these Tamil texts and those of Sanskrit sources.

In the same report, Ponnuswami Pillai of Kumbakonam spoke of the diversity of Indian traditional medical practices as having a single origin, only distinguished today by language differences.

> The three fields of medical knowledge, generally called "ayurveda," meaning the path to bodily health, were bestowed by the eighteen great siddhars for the benefit of the human world. Though there are no differences in their general principles, and only small differences in their methods of treatment, they are called by the names ayurveda, unani, and siddha (Tamil) medicine, as they are written in the three important languages of our country, Sanskrit, Hindustani, and Tamil. I will speak of siddha medicine, preeminent in the South and born in the Tamil country.[28]

Ponnuswami Pillai was correct to describe the basic principles of these systems as similar, and also to specify language as one of the most significant markers of difference among traditional medical histories and practices. However, he was wrong in attributing the origins of all Indian medicine to the eighteen siddhars, as this tradition of siddha authorship is unique to Tamil texts. In the course of my research in Tamil Nadu in 1998–99, practitioners always clearly affirmed their medical affiliation as siddha, ayurveda, or unani, and they generally asserted these as discrete systems of practice. I never heard anyone cite the siddhars as the authors of ayurveda or unani. In 1923, although practitioners acknowledged that they drew on different textual traditions—Sanskrit, Tamil, or Urdu—in formulating their contemporary practices, they were not insistent that these traditions reflected distinct medical practices.

Against these fuzzy lines that distinguished indigenous medical practices in India, Tamil non-brahman vaidyas began to assert a radical distance from ayurvedic practitioners, who were, and are today, primarily brahmans. They did this by narrating a history and character of their knowledge and practices. Paralleling, drawing from, and contributing to a political discourse of Tamil separatism that was gaining momentum in the early decades of the twentieth century, these vaidyas told a story of an original, perfect medical system that was corrupted by Aryan influence. They tried to "untangle" this history of Tamil and Sanskrit interaction by locating the origins of pure Tamil medical knowledge on the primordial continent of Lemuria.[29] Siddha vaidyas today continue to tell similar narratives, though now they are more certain that their practices compose a distinct system of medicine.

How do we account for this shift of identification, this crystallization of the murky division between siddha and ayurveda? To address this question, I will consider the broader discursive arenas in which siddha vaidyas have participated from the early decades of the twentieth century up to the present day. In doing so,

I suggest that the "traditional" aspect of traditional medicine is a site in which practitioners link medical techniques to broader, self-reflexive discussions of identity and community. When siddha practitioners employ a rhetoric of tradition to legitimate their practices in the modern world, they do so with an awareness that tradition continues to provide powerful resources for the construction of authority. Thus I will consider their promotion of siddha medicine as part of broader projects of non-brahman Tamils to define their identity, their history, and their community.

The Utopian Origins of Tamil Civilization

Since the early decades of the twentieth century, authors of Tamil identity have searched for the roots of their tradition behind history. In his quest to discern the essential character of the Tamil people, P. T. Srinivas Iyengar, reader of Indian history at the University of Madras, in the first of a series of lectures given in 1929, describes his methodology as cutting through the accidents of history to the origins of identity: "If the culture of a people is indigenous to the soil on which they live, if it appears to have grown *in situ* before they came in contact with other people, it must be solely due to the influence of their physical surroundings. A culture that has grown as the reaction of a people to their milieu is due to geographical and not historical causes, like the influence of foreign people who have come in touch with them by conquest or trade or other forms of peaceful intercourse."[30] According to Srinivas Iyengar, the vagaries and transactions of history obscure the real identity and traditions of a people. Cultural and racial purity, that is, the true self, is not found in history but rather in a primordial, autochthonous connection between people and the soil on which they grow.[31] Tamils do not merely live on the soil, or even off the soil, but they are, most important, *of* the soil, in which we can find, almost literally, their roots. Because they are born of the soil, their character develops in relation to this soil and takes on its qualities. Srinivas Iyengar opposes autochthony to history, locating the era of Tamil racial and cultural purity just prior to the onset of history. In seeking the essence of the Tamil people apart from historical events, Tamil authors and siddha vaidyas are compelled, to some degree, to ignore the evidence of history, though as we will see, they also bring historical data to bear on their visions of Tamil self. Moreover, by positing an unchanging Tamil self that is immune to history, revivalist writers overwrite the messiness of history with its humiliations and failures, celebrating the exemplary character of Tamils in historical narratives that suggest the opposite: Tamils are courageous in defeat, generous in folly, and justified in wreaking havoc.

It is not accidental that Tamil cultural revivalists have located pure Tamil society on an island. Geographically and imaginatively, islands offer the most protection from outside influences, where the possibility of a society insulated from foreign corruption seems most plausible. David Harvey calls utopia "an artificially created island which functions as an isolated, coherently organized, and largely closed-space economy (though closely monitored relations with the outside world are posited)." The perfect isolation of an island is not just spatial but also temporal, affording distance from the vicissitudes of history. As Harvey notes, in utopian thought "time's arrow, 'the great principle of history,' is excluded in favor of perpetuating a happy stationary state."[32] Siddha vaidyas conceive their roots in a place apart from time and space, in which the first siddha doctors selflessly and effectively served a prosperous and peaceful society. Most important, perhaps, they hold that Lemuria was utopian because of its perfect racial and cultural homogeneity, enjoying unanimous compliance to a single tradition as the natural order of things.

In accounting for Tamil origins, revivalist authors have drawn on Tamil literature, archeology, geological speculation, Orientalist histories, and their own imaginations. The ancient continent of Lemuria in the Indian Ocean was first hypothesized by European geologists and biologists in the second half of the nineteenth century. In 1864, the British zoologist Philip Sclater first theorized a continuous land mass linking India, Madagascar, and continental Africa. Because his hypothesis emerged from his attempts to explain the existence of lemurs in Madagascar, Africa, and India, he named this continent "Lemuria."[33] In 1870, the German Darwinian biologist Ernst Heinrich Haekel further speculated that this submerged continent was the original home of the human species.[34] The first in India to pick up on the Lemurian theory appears to have been neither scientists nor Tamil revivalists, but rather the leaders of the Theosophical Society in Madras. In 1877, one of the founders of theosophy, the occultist Helena P. Blavatsky, cited Lemuria as home to the third of the "Root Races" of humans, inhabited by apelike, egg-laying hermaphrodite Lemurians. Annie Besant, who led the Theosophical Society well into the twentieth century, continued to fill in details of this lost continent.[35] By the late 1890s, Tamil writers began to use the theory of Lemuria to describe a lost continent that was the ancestral home of the Tamil race.[36]

Tamil scholars link the Lemurian theory to Tamil literature that depicts an ancient Tamil land, beginning in the north at the Vindhya or Venkata mountains and extending to the south far beyond the tip of contemporary India. In a 1937 paper, Navalar Somasundara Bharathiar wrote:

> The ancient Tamil classics now proved to be over two thousand years old, expressly identify the home of the Tamils to be a region bordered by the Venkata Hills in the north, and extending southward very much further into the Indian Ocean than Cape Comarin [the present southern

> tip of India] and the Island of Ceylon, forming one contiguous country where the Tamil people were the Indigene. In fact one of the poems in Kalithogai [extant literature of the third sangam] expressly speaks of a deluge causing the subsidence of a large slice of land in the south of Tamilaham, and driving the survivors from their submerged lands to colonise in the northern territories of their great Tamil continent. The consciousness of the Tamil people as evidenced by their literature from the earliest times has always been that they were the aboriginal natives of this southern continent.[37]

By the mid-1930s, the Tamil name "Kumari Kandam" began to find favor as a designation for this ancient continent. First cited in Kacciyappa Shivacharya's fifteenth-century *Kantapurāṇam*, Kumari Kandam was one of nine divisions of Bharatavarsha, a place free of barbarians and enjoying a population of brahmans.[38] Tamil revivalists, counter to this literary depiction, speak of Kumari Kandam as a non-brahman utopia. According to their accounts, this ancient island stretched roughly from Africa in the west to Australia in the east, and from the middle portions of India in the north to thousands of miles south past the present southern tip of India. Although individual accounts differ, typical is N. Mahalingam's assertion that Tamil culture first flourished on Kumari Kandam in approximately 30,000–25,000 B.C.E.[39] With the end of the last ice age and the subsequent rising of the seas, much of this land mass was submerged and its inhabitants were forced to scatter to Africa and Australia, though some remained in the last remaining Tamil land, present-day Tamil Nadu.[40]

According to these revivalist narratives, Tamil prehistoric society was characterized by social harmony, benevolent governance, and natural prosperity. As the first civilized society, Kumari Kandam was ruled by kind and just leaders, enjoying technological and artistic achievements that scholars and Indian nationalists have tended to link to early Vedic, Aryan societies. Tamil revivalists invert these prejudices by stressing the absence of Aryans in this Tamil utopia: "The Augustan or Golden Age of Tamil was undoubtedly that of the First [literary] Academy, when there was no foreign influence of any sort, when even the racial name 'Aryan' was not derived or coined, when the literary production was in full bloom, when the people were at the zenith of prosperity under a benign government, when the social division was based on occupation, and when the whole Tamilagam [Tamil land] was virtually an El Dorado."[41] Although Tamil literature and contemporary revivalists cite three literary academies that advanced Tamil literature and the arts, the earliest extant writings are an early grammar, *Tolkāppiyam*, and a number of anthologies of poems attributed to the third academy. These writings date from approximately the first to the third centuries C.E., yet even these contain Sanskrit vocabulary.[42] There is no Tamil literature, then, that indicates a Tamil civilization free of Sanskrit influence. So, in order to locate pure Tamil culture and identity, before the presumed invasion of the Aryans, Tamil revivalist leaders historicize beyond history, speaking in authoritative, hopeful tones about the nature of Tamil beginnings.

The siddhars are also drawn into this narrative, and with them siddha medicine. As he does with Agastya, A. Chidambaranar employs the notion of a large, prehistoric Tamil continent to bring Mount Kailasa into the Tamil realm and thus also the entire scope of Tirumular's wide-ranging exploits. He dates Tirumular to 6000 B.C.E., about ten thousand years after the first Agastya. According to Chidambaranar, this was the time of the *Rāmāyaṇa*, a time in which Sanskrit and Tamil were interacting.[43] Tamil was still the predominant language of the subcontinent, however, spoken from the northern mountains to Kumari in south. Indeed, Chidambaranar draws on an intriguing verse of the *Tirumantiram* to argue that the influence of Tamil extended throughout the world. "They roam the world spreading wisdom that is abundant in the five Tamil regions (*maṇṭalam*). A heart melting in devotion, and knowledge of my lord, are the basic characteristics of the five Tamil regions" (1619). Chidambaranar interprets *Tamiḻ maṇṭalam aintum* not as five regions of Tamil-speaking people in the south of the subcontinent, but as a reference to five continents, Asia, Europe, Africa, America, and Australia. Although the subject "they" of the verse is unspecified, Chidambaranar takes it to be "groups of Tamil Nadu siddhars" wandering those five continents, spreading their knowledge. This was also a time in which Tamil gave rise to eighteen languages, which include Sinhalese, Chinese, Javanese, Burmese, Bengali, Kannada, and Nepalese, among others.[44] These details about the siddhars are consistent with some of Chidambaranar's other writings, which include poems to *Tamiḻttāy* (mother Tamil). He is perhaps best known for his specious "discovery" of a text of the first sangam, *Ceṅkōṉraraiccelavu*, a text celebrating the exploits of a Tamil king named Sengon.[45] Chidambaranar held that this text told of "the oldest civilization of the Tamilians" on the "submerged land called continent of *Lamoria* [sic]." This land, a "thousand miles south of present Ceylon . . . was called Tamilagam by the Tamilians. Many pandits and scientists hold the opinion that the human species first evolved in the Great Indo-African Continent. . . . This large continent is of great importance for being the probable cradle of the human race."[46]

Siddha vaidyas contribute to these accounts, locating the origins of their medicine in a variety of foundation narratives. Although there are some differences in their formulations, they consistently cite the ancientness, ethnic purity, and extraordinary capabilities of the beginnings of their medicine, and they insist on an enduring link between the Tamil people, land, and siddha medicine. When I spoke to Kundrathur Ramamurthy about the early history of siddha medicine, he located the origins of his knowledge on Lemuria. "It started on Lemuria. Then Lemuria and Lanka were one. It started in Lemuria and spread to northern lands, then to China and then to Arabian countries. This is how it happened. That's the correct history." P. Muttukkaruppa Pillai, head of the Madurai Siddha Medicine Association, also speaks of the siddhars founding and teaching siddha medicine on Lemuria. There they "established a siddha committee at that time under Agastya's leadership . . . and they shone with divine qualities."[47]

V. Narayanaswami, a licensed practitioner of Indian medicine and a retired lecturer in the Government College of Integrated Medicine in Madras, wrote his *Introduction to the Siddha System of Medicine* at the request of K. Anbazhagam, the Tamil Nadu minister of public health at the time of the book's publication in 1975. In his forward to the book, Anbazhagan recounts that "till recently it was the practice of the Government of India to refer in their records to Siddha as 'Ayurveda including Siddha' as though both the systems were the same and that the Siddha system was only a minor variant." Objecting to this, he had asked Narayanaswami to write a book "highlighting the special features of the Siddha system."[48] Narayanaswami, a practiced ayurvedic specialist with knowledge of both systems, begins his book with a history of siddha medicine. "The recorded history of the Tamils is millions of years old. . . . A civilized society must naturally have had a system of medicine which catered to the health needs of its people. This was the Siddha system." He attributes authorship of this ancient system to eighteen siddhars, who he describes as historical rather than mythological figures. Although he insists that he does not want to enter into the debate on the primacy of siddha or ayurveda, he ascribes greater antiquity to siddha medicine. "It is well established that before the Aryans occupied the Sind region and the Gangetic plain, there existed in the south, on the banks of the rivers Cauvery, Vaigai, and Tamiraparani, a civilization which was highly organized. This civilization had a system of medicine to deal with the problems of sanitation and treatment of diseases. This is the Siddha system." Although siddha and ayurveda later came into contact and "enriched each other . . . from the beginning the Siddha system has maintained its identity."[49]

N. Subramaniam, a licensed Indian medical practitioner and graduate of the Government Indian Medical School of Madras, wrote a short booklet on the development of siddha medicine, published in 1940. He begins by thanking his *kāraṇakuru*, his selfless spiritual guru, none other than A. Chidambaranar, who encouraged his entry into medicine. He begins his account in language reminiscent of that of his teacher. "Experts do not doubt the ancientness and greatness of the Tamil people. . . . Tamils were cultured people 12,000 years ago."[50] Subramaniam locates the beginnings of siddha medicine at that early date, which coincides with the beginning of the first Tamil sangam. These ancient Tamils enjoyed mental and bodily health, respecting nature and living hygienically.[51] Subramaniam emphasizes that these ancient Tamils lived in ways appropriate to the Tamil soil, employing the language of autochthony common to formulations of siddha medicine. He follows Chidambaranar in giving precedence to Agastya, who received medical knowledge from the god Murugan, which he then taught to other Tamil siddhars, as well as to the Chinese. Agastya and other siddhars attained youth and health for themselves, and they selflessly cared for others.[52] N. Kandaswamy Pillai draws on the Lemuria narrative for his history, locating the origins of Tamil civilization and siddha medicine on "a vast continent several millions of years ago. The present Tamil Nadu is only a tiny corner of the extensive continent which once covered the large expanse of the Indian Ocean and beyond. The fragmentation and submersion of that vast landmass, though a fact of millions of years old, still lingers in the racial memory of Tamilians."[53] Dr. Circapai writes from Kanchipuram that siddha is the oldest medicine in the world, and that it never borrowed from any other system. "Before Aryans, Mongolians, and other foreign peoples entered into medical research, the Tamil peoples' siddha medicine had attained full fruition, like other arts such as astronomy. This eminent art is unique to the Tamil land."[54] Siddha vaidyas consistently highlight the ethnic purity of Tamil cultural traditions as a response to histories that locate the achievements of Indian civilization in Sanskritic culture.

The Lemurian narrative is not the only myth of origins that vaidyas invoke. In 1983, the Siddha Medical Textual Research Center gave first prize in an essay contest to Lakshmi Renganathan. Her essay begins, "Tamil medicine, known as 'siddha medicine,' appeared on this earth on the third day as the waters dried and the land spread. When humans and other species were established on the earth, Shiva taught Uma the art of medicine in order to remove disease, increase health, and extend lives. Because this medical method was transmitted by the grace of the mother goddess to the siddhars, and from the siddhars to the people, it is called 'siddha medicine.'"[55] Renganathan frames the origins of the Tamil people with the Genesis account of the six days of creation, and in turn she reads this account as a story of Hindu creation, not by Yahweh but by Shiva and Uma, appropriating the authority of Christianity for a narrative of Tamil origins. Although she has authored a unique account of Tamil beginnings, her narrative is consistent with other accounts in its assertion of the co-origination of humanity, the Tamil people, and siddha medicine.

S. K. S. Kalimuttu Pillai, a registered practitioner of Indian medicine, locates siddha origins in puranic cosmic history.

> Siddha medicine, or Tamil medicine, has been in practice since the appearance of the Earth, from ancient times. It is the medical method which was enjoyed by the wise, ancient people; these are the medical

> techniques which provided them the means to live without disease. . . . My textual research of siddha books, my research conclusions, the experience that was gained through this research, and my personal opinion based on this research, indicate that except for the emptiness of the deluge at the end of the eon, at all other times there must have existed people, gods, siddhars, wise people, the cosmos and its creatures. . . . We know through research that people, the country in which they live, those things which are natural to them, the Tamil language, Tamil medicine, that is, siddha medicine, all must have existed throughout the world."[56]

By eon, Kalimuttu Pillai refers to the puranic notion of the yugas, temporal cycles of cosmic creation and destruction that end in a great deluge. He argues that because the world's first language was Tamil, Tamil medicine, which he equates with siddha medicine, was the first medical system in the world. "Just as other languages operate taking Tamil as their basis, other medical systems and medical fields take siddha medicine as their basis."[57] Pillai imagines a time in which all language was Tamil, all civilization was Tamil, and all medicine was siddha medicine. That is, he conceives Tamil beginnings in a time of no otherness. The time of which Pillai speaks, even though the Lemurian narratives claim particular dates for Tamil utopia, is more a "once upon a time" than it is a part of history. It is a time in which anything is possible because, being beyond history, it is imagined.

The Invasion of Utopia

According to the historical narratives siddha vaidyas and Tamil revivalists tell, this blissful seclusion was not to last. The demise of Lemuria came with the end of the most recent ice age and the rising of the seas. The majority of the pristine Tamil land was submerged, and Tamils were forced to migrate elsewhere. Finding themselves in many places in the midst of barbarians, they had to begin their courageous struggle with history. According to many accounts, Tamils settled in Africa, Australia, and Asia, civilizing barbaric people as they migrated, and intermarrying to create new races, languages, and civilizations. Tamils, according to this narrative, are the source of all civilized culture in the world, including that of European peoples. The final haven for Tamil purity was within the borders that define present-day Tamil Nadu. Most hold that this area was the only part of Lemuria to survive the deluge, the last remnant of the great primordial Tamil land.[58] In Tamil Nadu, unlike Africa or Australia, there were no indigenous others to corrupt the blood of the Tamils, so Tamil civilization was able to retain the glory of Kumari Kandam for a few millennia. But their peace was not to last—the Aryans were coming.

Vaidyas today lament the loss of Tamil purity and political autonomy, which many see as culminating in recent times with the incorporation of Tamil-speaking areas into an independent India that is dominated by people, regions, and languages in the north. G. J. Parthasarathy complained to me about the marginal place of siddha medicine in India today.

> No one has given to siddha the importance given to ayurveda. Not in India. They support ayurveda fully in north India. It is very important in Kerala, and the Kerala government supports it. Siddha is just for Tamil Nadu. Why is Tamil the primary Dravidian language? Lineages like ours that came as the base of Mohenjo Daro, Harrapa, that they call Dravidian, these have a unique culture, are unique among civilizations. The central government has not given sufficient support to siddha medicine. This is a travesty. They need to do more. Siddha is not inferior in any way to other medical systems. When that's done, many benefits can be provided to the people.

Siddha vaidyas and other authors of Tamil tradition posit an Aryan invasion of the Tamil land that was to prove catastrophic to Tamil civilization. If it was first the sea, and then the Aryans, that buried Tamil culture and language, it was European archeologists who dug up artifacts that vaidyas cite as evidence of early Aryan incursions. Excavations of sites at Harappa in 1922 and Mohenjodaro in 1923, in the Indus Valley in present-day Pakistan, provided evidence that a thriving, sophisticated urban society predated the presence of Aryans in north India. Determining the identity of the Indus Valley people and deciphering their script are among the great uncompleted projects in archeology. Scientific uncertainty has its advantages for those whose purposes are other than descriptive, and Tamil forces of identity construction advance their own claims to the identity of these people. Paul Joseph Thottam, in his introduction to siddha medicine, traces the beginnings of siddha knowledge to the Indus Valley civilization, which he dates to about 6000 B.C.E. He argues that this civilization was Tamil by linking current siddha medical practice to archeological evidence unearthed by John Hubert Marshall, one of the early leaders of this excavation. Thottam attributes to the Harappan people the "worship of the neem and peepal trees," both of which are used today in formulating siddha medicines. He also cites the "widespread use of different kinds of salts" in the Indus Valley civilization. Thottam reasons that because the use of salts is less common in ayurveda than in siddha, especially the use of complex salts, this civilization must have been Tamil, not Aryan, and siddha medicine "originated in the Harappan civilization."[59] In linking of the details of current practice, the premodern siddha textual tradition, and ancient archeological evidence, Thottam assumes a continuity of tradition and an unchanging essence of siddha medicine.

In his work linking the Indus Valley civilization to Kumari Kandam, Nathan reports that Marshall compared archeological finds with cultural descriptions found in early Sanskrit Vedic literature.[60] Finding no evidence of horses or sacrificial halls, two key elements of Vedic culture, Marshall concluded that this civilization was not Aryan.[61] The absence of sacrificial halls is significant to archeologists and Tamils alike: many Tamils claim that Vedic ritual, indeed, all religious ritual was absent on Kumari Kandam, and that brahmanic rituals were introduced with Aryan incursions in order corrupt the minds of Tamils. For Nathan, the absence of sacrificial halls is evidence of an ancient scientific society that he links to Kumari Kandam. According to Nathan, Marshall not only asserted that the Indus civilization was not Aryan but also confirmed that "for centuries the Aryans went to other countries and destroyed the great civilizations of others. Only later were they to slowly develop their own civilization."[62] He concludes that the Aryans do not create civilizations, but destroy them.

In Tamil revivalist writings, Aryans not only have no connection to the Tamil land but they also have been wandering for so long that they no longer have any connection to any land. Nathan describes them as "wanderers" or "nomads," using the Tamil term *nāṭōṭikaḷ*.[63] *Nāṭōṭikaḷ* is variously translated as "vagabond; wanderer; tramp." The Tamil definition given in a recent dictionary is even more telling, indicating a way of life, or the nature of a people: "*nāṭōṭikaḷ*: one who lives his life never residing in a single place but survives moving from place to place." The examples of its usage clarify this further: "the census does not take into account *nāṭōṭikaḷ*." "A *nāṭōṭi* race."[64] Insofar as the purity of a people and the stability of their identity depend on their relation to their ancestral land, the Aryans are an empty people, without substance because they are without a land. In E. Valentine Daniel's excellent ethnography of a Tamil village, brahmans of Kalappuur are likewise considered to be a "transient caste that lacks attachment to a particular place or a particular soil."[65] Non-brahman Tamil leaders concur, characterizing brahmans as wanderers and so as people of unstable and unclear identity, a shifty, deceitful people. Brahmans belong nowhere, and so they destroy autochthonous harmony wherever they go, bringing darkness to civilized societies.

The contrast with Aryans is central to the ways that Tamil revivalists and siddha vaidyas characterize the Tamil people and Tamil tradition. "The Tamilian was a born optimist, full of humour and buoyancy, joyously clinging to the rosy side of life, prone to be happy in family life and inclined always to revel in a righteous yet merry life on earth. The Aryan grew to be a sullen cynic, sour to pleasures of every kind, hating all existence as a misery to be avoided, preaching asceticism therefore as the only panacea for all ills of life and vehemently given to otherworldism."[66] Somasundara Bharatiar uses the verb "born" to describe the relation between the

Tamil subject and the Tamil character, and emphasizes the natural and enduring quality of this character, not learned but inherent. Thus, the Tamil lives happily, connected to the earth. The Aryan, on the other hand, is not born with enduring qualities, but "grows" to be cynical and pessimistic. Character for the Aryan is not a natural essence but is developed through history, and it is therefore composed of contingent, unstable qualities. It is not surprising, then, that the attitude of the Aryan to the earth, which in this discourse symbolizes natural essence and stability, is one of alienation. The otherworldism that Bharatiar speaks of here refers to Hinduism, which Tamil revivalists have vehemently attacked as an ideological tool that brahmans have employed to subjugate non-brahmans.

Rama Dharmaniti distinguishes four essential qualities (*kuṇaṅkaḷ*) of the Tamil people of Kumari Kandam: rational thought (*pakuttaṟivu*), working hard, struggling courageously, and sharing in eating.[67] He carefully chooses these qualities to contrast with Aryan characteristics. For example, sharing food differs sharply with the caste prohibitions that he links to brahmanic oppression. Brahmans also lack rational thought and a good work ethic, as they adhere to superstitious mythologies and parasitically enjoy the fruits of Tamil labor. Dharmaniti considers these *kuṇams*, qualities, to be intrinsic to the Tamil people, a part of their natural essence that underlies their history. "The reason that Tamils follow these four qualities is because good (*naṉmai*) and bad (*tīmai*) are inscribed into the natural structure of the world, which rotates and changes from day to night. Therefore, the beings that appear in this world are divided into two types, good animals and people, and bad animals and people."[68] In the predeluvian world, these moral divisions corresponded to terrestrial boundaries. "According to the laws of nature, there were two types of people: Tamils who lived in Kumari Kandam, and people who lived outside of Kumari Kandam." Only the Tamils enjoyed the components of civilization, while others lived as animals.[69] Perhaps the most important of these *kuṇams*, courage, is necessary in this post-Lemurian world, where Tamils have had to encounter barbaric, and often violent, peoples. According to Dharmaniti, they have been only partly successful in resisting these foreign influences. Yet while Tamils have been corrupted by Aryan religion, their original *kuṇams* have only been temporarily obscured, and so the potential to live as the original Tamil people remains. Indeed, the author asserts that despite this foreign corruption, "despite the fact that most Tamils have lost their way and changed, I continue to live as proof that even today there are Kumari Kandam Tamils."[70]

These utopian narratives are discourses of desire, inviting non-brahman Tamils to participate in a fantasy of the glory of their tradition. Yet as soon as they offer the pleasure of a utopian fantasy, they narrate the *loss* of utopia, their incongruity with contemporary society providing the basis for a critique of the present. It is precisely at this juncture between contemporary realities and these utopian imaginings—at the point in which those participating in a fantasy of pleasure realize that their pleasure exists *only in fantasy*—that the other, the Aryan brahman, is placed, a menacing figure that initiated the descent of the Tamil self into history. Again, this raises the issue of the central place that the Aryan other occupies in these identity narratives. How did the Aryan come to inhabit this intermediate, contemptible place in these stories of the Tamil people? Like all historical writing, these projections into primordial, prehistoric pasts, unknowable futures, unfindable locations, or other misty locales, are more about the here and now than they are about the there and then.[71] The "here and now" of these narratives is twentieth-century south India, and the reasons for this demonization of brahmans are not difficult to find.

Aryan and Dravidian Medicine

The division of south Indian society into ethnically distinct and coherent non-brahman and brahman communities ignores a vast amount of historical and literary evidence that suggests complex interrelations between a multiplicity of caste communities, and highly stratified relationships among non-brahman caste groups. The association of brahmans exclusively with Sanskrit is also misleading, as Tamil brahmans speak Tamil as their mother tongue, and they have made significant contributions to the composition and study of Tamil literature and to its promotion as one of the world's great literatures.[72] Sheldon Pollock has pointed to the problems of such exclusive linking of Sanskrit and brahmans, observing that by the beginning of the second millennium, "Sanskrit had long ceased to be a brahmanical preserve, just as brahmans had long taken to expressing themselves literarily in languages other than Sanskrit."[73] There is no literary evidence of a Tamil society without brahmans, nor is there evidence of a Tamil culture free of Sanskritic elements that are generally associated with brahmans.[74]

On the other hand, the caste composition of south India has particular features that have made this radical social dichotomization a credible and effective narrative. There is an extremely small population of intermediate caste groupings, that is, kṣatriyas (royalty and military) and vaiśyas (merchants).[75] The majority of the population has been classified as shudra and dalit, with brahmans a small minority of about three percent.[76] Without intermediate castes, there has been great potential for the isolation of brahmans, yet certain factors limited such isolation in precolonial and early colonial times. Among the shudra castes, the landowning Vellalars, who had ritual and economic ties with brahmans, distinguished themselves from other shudra castes by maintaining certain brahmanic standards of ritual purity.[77] As long as these groups prospered economically, and as long as they maintained a relationship with brahmans, brahman castes did not enjoy a clear political or economic dominance.[78] Many of the major figures of Tamil revivalism and siddha medicine are from these Vellalar castes.[79]

Robert Caldwell, a Scottish missionary and student of Tamil, wrote one of the most important linguistic works of nineteenth-century India, *A Comparative Grammar of the Dravidian or South-Indian Family of Languages*, published in 1856. His book, still often cited by Tamil scholars and revivalist writers, argued that India is linguistically and ethnically divided into an Aryan north and a Dravidian south.[80] His scholarship challenged a prior generation of Orientalists and Sanskrit pandits, who had asserted that all Indian languages and culture descended from Sanskrit. Caldwell's work builds on that of earlier scholars, especially Francis Whyte Ellis, to argue that south Indian languages formed a distinct family of languages that has an origin and history distinct from that of the north Indian languages. Caldwell tells a narrative in which the Aryans came to the south, introduced caste distinctions, and designated the indigenous people as "shudras" or worse.[81] Caldwell's work was to significantly influence later generations of Tamil scholars, politicians, and the creators of new narratives of Tamil identity. These non-brahman leaders followed Caldwell in asserting that Tamils are the native inhabitants of the Tamil soil, of an entirely different origin than the Aryans of the north and their brahman representatives in the south, and that caste was imposed by Aryans on Dravidians. For nearly a century, these assumptions have constituted the dichotomies of Tamil non-brahman identity politics.

Although my primary concern is to examine the recent historical causes of the alienation of brahmans in Tamil identity narratives, it is fitting to note that the opposition of Aryan and Tamil, or of Sanskrit and Tamil, is not entirely modern. One of the earliest works of Tamil literature, the *Tolkāppiyam*, composed in the early centuries of the Common Era, defines the use of *vaṭacol*, Sanskrit words, in Tamil.[82] The association of Sanskrit with the northern direction and Tamil with the southern also finds place in the *Tēvāram*, a compilation of devotional Shaiva poetry that dates from the sixth century. In a verse by the devotee Appar, Shiva is celebrated, among other things, as the site in whom "Sanskrit of the North and southern Tamil" meet.[83] In the epic *Cilappatikāram*, composed circa fifth century C.E., the Tamil king Senguttuvan's conquest of the "Arya kings" of the north is depicted as a clash of communities distinguished by language and geography.[84] Nevertheless, the division was never so clearly drawn along historical, racial, and caste lines as it was by nineteenth-century missionaries and Orientalists, who speculated that groups of Aryan invaders migrated into India from the north and conquered the indigenous people.[85]

Several factors provoked the animosity of a newly imagined community of non-brahmans toward brahmans in south India in the early decades of the twentieth century. The advent of colonial administration and education in the creation of the Madras state created many opportunities that favored literate applicants, and brahmans overwhelmingly filled these positions. For instance, in 1912, 55 percent of government positions were filled by brahmans, compared to 22 percent by non-brahman Hindus. These percentages are significant when one considers that brahmans composed only 3 percent of the population, as opposed to 86 percent for non-brahman Hindus. Brahmans also enjoyed a disproportionate share of educational opportunities, making up 71 percent of the graduates from Madras University from 1901 to 1911, as compared to 18 percent non-brahman Hindus.[86] The elite shudra castes found themselves at a significant disadvantage in competition with brahmans for education and government positions. These non-brahman elites also lost a certain amount of social prestige with increasing urbanization. In the anonymity of cities, there was a tendency to classify all shudras together as low caste, even those who had enjoyed privileged ritual, economic, and social status in the village as landlords.[87]

Aside from these social, economic, and scholarly developments, changes in the political realm were also important in mobilizing non-brahmans. Here again the Theosophists played a role, with Annie Besant founding the Home Rule League in Madras in 1916. Its purpose was to work closely with Mahatma Gandhi's Indian National Congress as a southern-based lobbying force for independence from the British and for the establishment of an Indian state. Besant was also president of the Theosophical Society, an organization whose leaders extolled the virtues of Aryan civilization and Sanskrit literature. In Madras and its outlying districts, the Theosophists founded Sanskrit schools and established societies for the promotion of Vedic morals, and Besant was herself viewed as "the outstanding revivalist of Smarta [orthodox Shaiva] Hinduism in South India."[88] Besant worked closely with brahman politicians in Madras on her Theosophical projects, ties that she would exploit in her Home Rule efforts. Non-brahmans feared that brahman leaders would replace colonial rulers, leading to brahmanic political domination that would further the social and economic advantages enjoyed by brahmans.

These tensions were expressed in medical discourse as well, as the brahmanic, Sanskritic bias of this emerging Indian national culture extended to medicine. Indian nationalists and ayurvedic practitioners celebrated an encompassing ayurvedic system as the appropriate medicine of an independent India. "Ayurveda is the National system of medicine. . . . There can be no doubt whatever that it is a veritable science, superior to the Western system in its curative value in relation to certain diseases, and indubitably well-adapted to Indian bodies and to Indian constitutions."[89] In line with Gandhi's formulations of an Indian nation that placed classical Hindu sources at the center of a unified Indian culture, nationalists most often promoted a corpus of Sanskrit medical texts as the basis of an original medical system of a unified Indian people. They emphasized the natural differences between Indian and British bodily constitutions as primary criteria of medical and social differentiation in order to mask the linguistic, ethnic, and cultural disparity within India, a move they hoped would unify the diversity of South Asian societies and histories in opposition to colonial domination.[90]

Sanskrit sources, therefore, would set the agenda for the future of all Indian traditional medicine, and medical texts in other Indian languages were often viewed as flawed translations of Sanskrit originals. In his response to a survey that was included in the 1923 *Report of the Committee on the Indigenous Systems of Medicine*, M. R. Pandit Narayana Ayyangar, an ayurveda practitioner, wrote, "the classification . . . in the Ayurveda, Unani or Siddha is not quite correct; strictly speaking, both Ayurveda and Siddha are comprised in what may conveniently be described as the Sanskrit system of medicine dealt with in the ancient Sanskrit books."[91] The authors of the *Report* presented a similar opinion, identifying siddha as a branch of ayurveda and thus proposing to examine only ayurveda.

> All our general observations and recommendations are meant to be equally applicable to all schools of Indian medicine . . . having regard to the views of our experts as to the common foundations of all these three schools [ayurveda, siddha, unani], we have thought it best to consider them all as one triune whole, rather than as so many isolated and independent entities; for we have it on the high authority of Janab Hakim Ajmal Khan of Delhi that Arabian medicine was founded on Ayurveda; and it is well-known that the Siddha and the Ayurveda have very many things in common.[92]

Those who contributed to the creation of this report, that is, local political and medical leaders, assume ayurveda to be the root of all Indian medicine, and so they consider traditional practices together, but not equally. The threat to Tamil practitioners was not simply that their practice would be subsumed by Western medicine but also that they would be viewed as practicing a secondary, inferior form of ayurveda, a vernacular approximation of the Sanskritic national medicine. Just as Tamil separatist leaders lobbied for an autonomous Tamil state, vaidyas who employed a Tamil literary corpus and who traced their medical lineages to the siddhars began to argue for an autonomous medical space predicated on their formulations of a unique siddha medical tradition.[93]

With the emergence of influential Tamil non-brahman political parties in the 1920s, Tamil vaidyas increasingly identified themselves along caste and racial lines. In response to the question "What, in your opinion, are the causes of decay of the indigenous systems of medicine," a Tamil vaidya named Shanmukanandaswami wrote: "Because medical texts in Tamil and medical texts in Sanskrit are both generally called 'ayurveda.' Because even though brahmans are a minority, many of them are educated and they have most government jobs. They support only their own texts and their own language, without allowing Tamil and Tamil medicine to flourish. Tamil doctors have experience but no education. Our Aryan brothers in South India deceptively practice Tamil medicine but call themselves ayurveda practitioners. Tamil medicine is not supported by local chiefs, wealthy people, or merchants, who are confused by the brahmans' deception."[94] Shanmukanandaswami did not speak of indigenous medicine as a homogenous whole as the primary authors of the report suggested, but rather he distinguished Tamil and Sanskrit medical knowledge and practices, lamenting that confusion between the two has been to the detriment of the former. He characterized the historical interaction of Tamil and Sanskrit medical texts and practices in south India as the Aryan appropriation of Tamil knowledge, a process that he held must be reversed if Tamil medicine is again going to realize its pure utopian origins, its true nature, and its effectiveness.

Since that time, non-brahman Tamil vaidyas have drawn on revivalist identity narratives, and they have increasingly staked out a traditional space separate from ayurveda. One way they have done this is to date siddha to a period before ayurveda. In a report to the dean of the Government College of Indian Medicine, Madras, concerning the establishing of a chair in the history of medicine at the college, P. M. Venugopal, a lecturer in the Department of History of Medicine (Indigenous) at the college, seeks to invert the views of many "North Indian authors," who have a "preconceived notion that the Tamil medical works contain little or nothing that was original . . . that Siddha system is part and parcel of Ayurveda or that it is mere copy or translation into Tamil form."[95] He dates the origin of siddha medicine by splitting the difference between the dates of the first sangam reported in the *Iṟaiyaṉār Akapporuḷ* and the geological evidence presented by "the Western author Tennets," who dates the "first deluge" to 2800 B.C.E. He concludes that siddha medicine dates "at least from 5000 to 4000 B.C., from the earliest inhabitants of the Southern Hemisphere," while the beginnings of ayurveda were 2,000 years later, in approximately 3000 B.C.E.[96]

R. Kasturi, a Tamil scholar and member of the Coimbatore District Agastya Siddha Medical Association, argues that siddha medicine is the only indigenous medicine of Tamil Nadu: "Ayurveda, unani, allopathy, and homeopathy, though practiced in our land at present, are medical systems that entered our land [from elsewhere]. The Aryans came to our land, and over a thousand years later, they created the ayurvedic system, written in Sanskrit. Then the Muslims conquered our land and after establishing their rule, they introduced the unani system, written in Arabic and Urdu. After that the Europeans came and took control, bringing with them allopathic medicine, written in English and in other European languages."[97] Tamil scholars write of blatant Aryan and Muslim plagiarism of Tamil medicine, a plundering of the intellectual and practical wealth of Tamils. In his review of Tamil literature, M. S. Purnalingam Pillai narrates a history in which the practice of Aryan ayurvedic medicine began in 500 C.E., long after the origin of siddha medicine. According to Purnalingam Pillai, early authors of ayurvedic texts wrote their treatises based on "borrowed knowledge" after learning medical techniques from treatises written by the siddhars, claiming this knowledge as their own: "Now that the Aryans have in course of time enriched their medical science in the way pointed out above [plagiarism from Tamil science], they have come forward to assert the Ayul Vaithiam as their own and to look upon their ancient Tamil masters with contempt. The followers of the Siddha School have begun to expose the Aryan indebtedness and prove its comparative modernness to the vexation of the ungrateful."[98] Purnalingam Pillai calls ancient Tamil medicine *Ayul Vaithiam*, where ayul is a term used in both Sanskrit and Tamil meaning "life" or "life span," and *vaithiam*, again used in both languages, means medicine. In Sanskrit, *ayus* combines with *veda*, knowledge, to form the term *ayurveda*, or "knowledge of life." By calling siddha medicine the original and true "medicine of life," Purnalingam Pillai appropriates the very term *ayurveda* and makes it Tamil.

T. V. Sambasivam Pillai describes Sanskrit medical texts as "literary forgeries [of Tamil texts] mingled with the ideas of Ayurveda in Sanskrit translation." He goes on to characterize Muslims as "avowed borrowers of science," noting the opinion of a "Prof. Wilson" that "the Arabs followed the Siddha works on medicine more closely rather than of the early Greeks."[99] More than fifty years later, V. R. Madhavan, a scholar of Tamil manuscripts, blames the confusion between ayurveda and siddha for "causing heavy damages to the independent development of Siddha." The narrative he tells is one of Aryan invasion and pillaging of the "greatness of Tamil culture in all its branches" in order to "enrich their culture by the assimilation of the highly civilized culture of the Tamilians." In spite of the harm this plagiarism has caused siddha, however, Madhavan credits ayurveda for its "great service to the medical world in collecting, preserving, arranging and incorporating in a marvellous method all the facts then available about the Siddha medicine." The origins of siddha medicine that have been obscured by history can be recovered, then, by looking at the best parts of ayurveda. Indeed, because of its contemporaneity with "Egyptian, Mesopotomian, Chinese and Grecian medicines," Madhavan reasons that literary research into the origins of siddha medicine, to be "scientific and useful, should commence with a comparative study of the medicines of those ancient civilizations, which will illuminate many of the dark corners of our system."[100] Reversing the view that siddha medicine developed out of ayurveda, siddha vaidyas emphasize the primacy of their knowledge, following a logic of tradition according to which older is better because it is closer to the origin of things.

Like all narratives of community, these Tamil narratives are not yet finished, and suggest endings that are nevertheless left open. Although the original utopia has been destroyed by history with the intervention of the other, the future holds the potential to reestablish the perfect Tamil society. Paul Ricoeur, highlighting the "escapist" aspect of utopia, contends that "no connecting point exists between the 'here' of social reality and the 'elsewhere' of utopia. This disjunction allows the utopia to avoid any obligation to come to grips with the real difficulties of a given society."[101] Ricoeur's characterization of utopia, however, fails to take into account the very real social projects within which utopian visions are articulated. Even if the primary site of any utopia is in the imagination, the imagination itself is a key site of social experience.

Utopia and the Narrative Role of the Other

While Indian nationalists exploited the lack of rigid distinctions in traditional medical practices in early-twentieth-century South Asia in order to articulate and shape a homogenous medical system Sanskritic in character, practitioners who looked to Tamil texts for medical authority felt threatened by this very same contiguity of practices. In line with political developments, non-brahman Tamil vaidyas began to consider their knowledge and practices as a coherent and unique medical system. Drawing on broader revivalist narratives of Lemurian culture, they founded a distinct siddha medical system on the very histories that told of its degeneration. Their stories of a fall from grace, a descent from utopian origins, are just as much accounts of beginnings as they are tales of destruction. In their narratives of the history of their knowledge, siddha vaidyas not only speculate on a past about which they know little but also provide the reasons for the challenges of the present that they know all too well. They blame the introduction of foreign medicine into the Tamil land as the principal cause for the deterioration of siddha medicine from its lofty beginnings. To return to one of the questions that frames this chapter: what is the relationship between self, other, and utopia in identity narratives?

Emmanuel Levinas describes the site of the self as enabling "the utopia in which the 'I' recollects itself in dwelling at home with itself."[102] Indeed, Tamil utopian society is precisely that in which the other does not exist, in which the purity of Tamil society is unspoiled. The role of the other, then, is as the destroyer of utopia. Because the state of isolated self is perfect, the downfall of utopia *must* be due to the influence of some other. The Aryan resides at the interstice of the utopian past and the dystopian present, between the impossible nowhere and the painfully real here and now. It is this position that makes the other a demon, the one responsible for the nonrealization of the utopian fantasy. It is only with the destruction of the other that the utopia will be realized. This narrative, then, is not merely a flight of fancy, or fiction for the sake of artistic enjoyment, but is also a call to action, a call to purify Tamil society. For Tamil society has only been corrupted, some hold, at the level of the *putti*: it is just the intellect that has been made impure, while the seat of their identity, their unchangeable *kuṇam*, is only submerged and therefore can be recovered. Although the deluge of Lemuria is irreversible, the flood of migrant Aryans can be turned back. The survival of the Tamil tradition, one is led to believe, depends on it.

It appears, then, that the coexistence of Aryans and of pure Tamil civilization is impossible in contemporary Tamil Nadu. However, although these narratives conceive of Tamil utopia as characterized by the absence of brahmans, these same histories inextricably link Tamils, Aryans, and utopia in their narrative structure. The Aryan is an unceasing threat to Tamil utopia, and his enduring presence lurks throughout these narratives. Furthermore, this revivalist rhetoric of utopia occurs most often in relation to the historical conflict between brahmans and non-brahmans, and between siddha and ayurveda. The recurrent emphasis of Aryans in Tamil utopian imaginings compels closer examination. I will pursue a line of inquiry here in which the Aryan is as responsible for the possibility of utopia as he is for its alleged downfall. That is, I will argue that without the Aryan other, the Tamil utopia is not even imaginable.

Slavoj Zizek's characterization of unrealizable fantasies and the prohibitions we construct between subject and fantasy provides the model for my discussion. Zizek, drawing from Jacques Lacan, distinguishes the Oedipus narrative from the "underlying purely formal structure of symbolic prohibition," a move that opens the Oedipus structure up to more general applicability.[103] The Oedipus complex requires that one assume a fundamental obstacle or prohibition (the father), that prevents the subject (the son), from realizing an object of desire (the mother). This prohibition is necessary for the ordered functioning of society. However, there is a certain irony here, which is that if the object of desire were in fact achieved, its character as fantasy would be destroyed. Real consummation, falling far short of the imagined ideal, would be replaced by another fantasy, another object of desire. The ultimate object of desire, the realization of fantasy as fantasy, is therefore unattainable. Zizek proposes that prohibitions in fantasy not only symbolically represent impediments to our ultimate aims but also sustain the feasibility and potency of fantasy. "Far from acting as the 'repressive agency preventing us gaining access to the ultimate object of desire,' the function of the paternal figure is thus quite the opposite, to relieve us from the debilitating deadlock of desire, to 'maintain hope.'"[104] In spite of the fact that, or more accurately, precisely because the desired object is beyond reach, one imposes on oneself the prohibition in order to entertain the possibility that one need only overcome this prohibition to achieve the object of desire. It is because of the prohibition that the elusive goal appears to be within our grasp. Such prohibitions therefore give credence to fantasy because they supply the reasons for its nonrealization.

For those whose lives are invested in Tamil traditions, the Aryan provides this sort of imaginative and symbolic prohibition in their narratives of self. They depict Aryans as demonic others, the destroyers of Tamil utopia and the conspirators against its reestablishment in the modern world. This Tamil utopia, like other utopias and like the fantasies that Zizek describes, is not realizable outside of the imagination.[105] Although the word "utopia" plays on the ambiguity between the Greek "eu-topia" (good place) and "ou-topia" (no place),[106] the place of utopia is in the imagination as fantasy. Lemuria, then, does not exist at the bottom of the Indian Ocean, but in the narrative imaginings of Tamils. The Aryan lends credibility to this narrative, standing as a symbolic, superfluous prohibition that creates the illusion that the impossible can be obtained if only he can be expelled from the Tamil soil. The Aryan invasion is not only responsible for the downfall of Tamil utopia but is also a necessary element of the narrative that enables Tamils to "maintain hope."[107]

By portraying foreign medical systems as threats to the survival of siddha medicine, vaidyas call on Tamils to heroically defend their beleaguered tradition. At the same time, it is their characterization of siddha medical knowledge as conquered and thus impure that makes its past perfection appear credible and, just as important, retrievable. Medical others, whether ayurvedic vaidyas or biomedical doctors, serve as both the reason for the present failure to realize the full potential of siddha medical efficacy and the enablers of hope that this potency merely lies dormant at present. These narratives of Tamil identity thus perform a spectacular acrobatic, where many who literally reside at the designated cultural center are displaced as outsiders, and real Tamil identity is located in the past, in the future, on a submerged continent, and in the innermost core of every non-brahman Tamil. Although not all Tamils who participate in these formulations of Tamil tradition advocate a real, physical expulsion of brahmans from Tamil Nadu, it is one of the formal tendencies of such narratives to self-destruct, to generate hopes that are expressed politically in attempts to remove the very element that makes them possible.

5

Reviving the Utopian Character of Siddha Medicine

At the same time that they narrate histories of Tamil tradition, siddha vaidyas and Tamil revivalists ascribe particular characteristics to this tradition. Responding to critiques that Tamil traditions are superstitious, and aware of the authority of science in the contemporary world, Tamil non-brahman leaders have placed science and rationality at the center of Tamil traditions, a strategy common to traditional medical practitioners, leading teachers of yoga, and others engaged in traditional practices across India today. In a March 8, 2000, editorial in *The Hindu*, Chennai's popular English daily newspaper, a commentator speaks of the scientific basis of Indian traditions.

> One among the very important reasons which had prompted our ancestors to construct towers (Gopuram) in temples was to preserve valid vital documents relating to the area round. These deeds were kept on the top tiers of the structure. Even if there were unprecedented floods, this tradition ensured that these documents would not get affected. Whenever needed, they were taken out of these "safe vaults." Many of our customs, being adopted even now, though mechanically or blindly or as empty formalities, were developed on scientific basis. Benefit will accrue if their significance is understood and the genius of our forbears could be appreciated. . . . All our customs and traditions thus reveal the positive nature of the thinking of our ancestors.[1]

Defenders of tradition read science back into ancient Indian history to legitimate the components of tradition. The author of this editorial asserts that modernity has no monopoly on scientific knowledge, as it was the ancient thinkers of India who built temple gopurams as safe repositories for valuable texts. According to his view and consistent with narratives that place the apex of Tamil civilization in the ancient past, history has been a descent into ignorance. Modern Indians have forgotten the rational genius of their ancestors, and today mechanically and blindly follow the scientific practices instituted in ancient times. Defenders of Indian traditions tend to view history through such a teleology of degeneration, contrasting ancient creative genius with modern, blind mechanization of ritual practice. Contrary to the teleological view that human history progresses toward greater rationality, in this narrative it is modernity, not ancient tradition, that lacks rationality.

At stake in these divergent teleologies is the relevance of the traditional in the contemporary world. Those who promote traditional medicine as a realm of effective and credible cultural practices, theories, and narratives, have liberally appropriated science as a discursive sign, and to a lesser degree they have employed empirical scientific methods in their medical research and practice. For example, in the town of Thanjavur in 1997, I met with a siddha doctor who wore a stethoscope when she saw patients. She did not use this as a diagnostic tool but rather as a sign of scientific authority, saying that the patients trusted her more when she wore it. She also directed me to a laboratory in which siddha medical researchers were testing the properties of siddha medicines by using rats, machinery, and other tools employed in biomedical research. Government siddha medical institutions, such as the College of Indian Medicine and Homeopathy in Anna Nagar, Chennai, engage in research with controlled subject groups, careful observation of results, and other methods drawn from empirical science.[2] Numerous articles are published in scientific journals that test the pharmaceutical properties of a variety of plants used in siddha medicines. For example, an article by R. S. Ranga and colleagues on *rasagenthi lehyam* (RL) sought to determine "whether RL could be recommended as a CAM [complementary and alternative medicine] for prostate cancer." One of the authors of the study produced RL based on its formulation by IMPCOPS, Indian Medical Practitioners Co-operative Pharmacy and Stores. This formula employs thirty-eight botanicals and eight inorganic compounds in a base of hen's egg and palm sugar. Extracts of the medicine were then tested for anticancer activity, the authors finding that "n-hexane, ethyl acetate and chloroform extracts of RL significantly inhibited the growth of PC-3 cell." They conclude that "the present study was a preliminary scientific validation of the anticancer properties of RL. We propose to conduct further studies to find the relevance of this Siddha therapeutic modality in the modern context . . . and to establish RL or a variant of it . . . as an effective alternative medicine for prostate cancer."[3]

For the most part, this scientific research on traditional medicine is not carried out to discover new medicines or to produce new knowledge, but rather to put existing practices on a scientific footing. The advancement of siddha medical knowledge, most Tamils agree, will entail the recuperation and legitimation of past insights rather than the discovery of anything new. Vaidyas hold that this is entirely consistent with scientific reasoning, because they locate the highest achievements of science in the primordial past. They argue that contemporary siddha medical practices appear dubious today because their scientific basis has been forgotten, and also because their truth is so deep that it is beyond modern understanding. Vaidyas thereby promote their medicine by citing the sanctity, the genius, and the rationality of traditional practice, an assertion that, paradoxically, relies on the legitimating force of a particular discourse of science which, in its specific features, was absent from this tradition. The scientific proclamations that announce the end of superstitious tradition have their echo in which science is made, discursively and effectively, an element of tradition.

The rationalization of the siddha medical tradition has been incomplete, however, not because its practitioners cannot dispense with the superstitions of their tradition, but because the juxtaposition of the ancient, the familiar, the extraordinary, and claims to rationality is particularly powerful. In an article in *Mūlikaimaṇi*, K. V. Abirami links siddha medical practice to temple traditions through the religious and medicinal benefits of temple trees. Many of the trees commonly found on temple grounds, such as the pipal (*aracu*), neem (*vēmpu*), bael (*vilvam*), and jaumoon (*nāval*) are auspicious to view (*darshan*) when coming to the temple and also have medicinal qualities when their leaves are chewed and swallowed, and so they cure diseases of the body and also give "inner peace."[4] The Shri Amirtagateshvarar temple in Tirukkataiyur has two temple plants, a bael tree and a jasmine (*mullai*) with big flowers called *jātimalli*. To have *darshan* of these plants at the temple, to behold them with reverence, is an auspicious act. They also have medicinal properties. "Daily, if one takes ten bael leaves, chants *om namacivāya* [praise to Shiva] five times, chews them and swallows them with a little buttermilk or warm water, afflictions of the body and mental anguish will be brought under control." Similarly, jātimalli gives "vigor to the circulatory system and peace to a disturbed mind. . . . The divine history of temple trees shows that in siddha medicine, the worshop of god and medical treatment are joined together."[5]

By characterizing their medicine in particular, and Tamil tradition more broadly, as rational, spiritual, ancient, and effective in harnessing the power of nature, the proponents of siddha medicine assert that their knowledge supersedes the possibilities of science. They hold that the value of their medicine derives not only from its inherent effectiveness, or just from its adherence to the principles of nature, but also because it is part of a tradition. They consistently stress that their knowledge was developed within a community, and they link its potency to the prestige of that community, holding that the effectiveness of their medicine testifies to the sophistication of their society. While one might not call a present-day archivist a genius for constructing an elevated room that keeps documents off the floor of a leaky, monsoon-besieged building, the presence of such reasoning in the past, developed and presented within a form of architecture that has come to represent a culture and a people, as well as the endurance of this practice over the centuries, are the grounds on which the term "genius" here appears appropriate to both author and reader. Rationality is only one way in which Indians and siddha vaidyas have asserted the value of their cultural practices, while ancientness and the location of these practices within the realm of tradition are additional forms through which siddha vaidyas argue for the effectiveness of their practice and its worthiness to be sustained.

Models of Tamil Tradition

There is no typical content for tradition, and no criteria of rationality by which a particular practice can be determined to be traditional or modern. Thus the qualities assigned to a tradition, its canonical texts, its practices, and any of the other elements that compose a tradition are often highly contested. Traditions have histories and are marked by constant innovation, even if the rhetoric of tradition employs the language of the unchanging, the eternal, and continuity with the ancient. In describing traditional medicine in India as stagnant, the British accepted (and distorted) this rhetoric, as do, in more nuanced ways, modernization theorists who portray tradition as in decline, its decay due to its inability to innovate in line with the modern world. The historical study of tradition is susceptible to the same dangers that Bruce Lincoln notes for religious studies. Whereas religious actors speak of "things eternal and transcendent," history "speaks of things temporal and terrestrial. . . . History of religions is thus a discourse that resists and reverses the orientation of that discourse with which it concerns itself."[6] Likewise, we must read history into the rhetoric of hoary tradition of siddha medicine. In their assertions of the unchanging, scientific nature of their medicine, siddha vaidyas deftly imply that their ancient tradition has always been modern, yet in doing so they characterize their practices in novel ways.

As I argue throughout this book, the successes of those engaged in traditional livelihoods over the past century attest that the modern world is amenable to traditional activity. To account for these successes, we must recognize that those invested in traditional practices engage in significant and ongoing projects to maintain the vitality and relevance of their practices in the modern world. Throughout the twentieth century to the present day, a central aim of Tamil leaders has been to fix the forms of tradition proper to Tamil society in ways that they deem consistent with modern sensibilities. Disputes around this issue have resulted in numerous and shifting alliances and fissures among politicians and others who seek to define Tamil identity. From the atheism of one of the leading cultural nationalists, E. V. Ramasami, popularly called E.V.R., and his contemporary political heirs, to the reform agenda of Maraimalai Adigal and the Shaiva Siddhanta movement, to the Congress Party's agenda to unify India under thinly veiled Hindu symbols, several influential groups have worked to demarcate the essence of Tamil society. Religion, or the lack thereof, has been a central concern in these debates. The most radical formulations of Dravidian cultural politics, expressed most forcefully by Ramasami from the 1920s through to the 1970s, have claimed that the character of the Tamil people is wholly rational and that their ancient stance on religion was that of atheism.[7] The Shaiva Siddhantins have argued for a rational, egalitarian Tamil Hinduism that teaches a direct, unmediated relationship between the devotee and the divine. Both of these groups claim to articulate the content of a non-brahman Tamil tradition, and both have formulated Tamil identities that shape the ways siddha vaidyas speak about their medical knowledge and practices. I will focus here on qualities that vaidyas ascribe to their medicine—egalitarianism, rationality, linguistic excellence, accessibility, and concordance with nature—paying particular attention to the ways in which these qualities relate to broader discussions of Tamil tradition, community, and identity.

The Egalitarianism of Siddha Medicine

Vaidyas most often begin with the siddhars when they characterize their medicine as egalitarian. Mythologies of the siddhars describe their caste affiliations as varied, from brahmans to Vellalars to shepherds to hunters.[8] Vaidyas extol the siddhars not only in their control of their bodies, their minds, and the natural world but also in their mastery over social relationships within Tamil society. In their manipulation of nature, the siddhars represent awesome power, and in their disregard for social norms, especially the dictates of caste, they are invoked as models of particular social values. Tamil revivalist writers include them in the genealogy of a pure Tamil race because of the writings of the ñāṉasiddhars, which at times are stridently anti-caste, anti-brahman, and anti-Vedic. Kamil Zvelebil describes the writings of the ñāṉasiddhars as "a protest, sometimes expressed in very strong terms, against the formalities of life and religion; rough handling of priests and brahmins in general; denial of the religious practices and beliefs of brahmanism, and not only that: an opposition against the generally pan-Indian social doctrine and religious practice; protest against the abuses of temple-rule; emphasis on the purity of character."[9] Contemporary non-brahman Tamil leaders have singled out for abuse those components of Hinduism that support brahmanic privilege, such as priestly rituals and prescriptions of caste duties. They have found support for their criticisms in the writings of the siddhars, who were "rationalists and rejected all types of rituals and ceremonies."[10] Vaidyas and other Tamil revivalists depict the siddhars as representing the lower castes of Tamil society, usually in the idiom of "the common people" (*potumakkaḷ*).

The writing style of the ñāṉasiddhars, while sometimes poetic, is more often colloquial, as is the style of the medical texts attributed to the kāyasiddhars. Ironically for figures who reside beyond the limits of society, the siddhars' poems are considered by some to be the most accessible of premodern Tamil literature, speaking not to the literary elite but to the common person. According to Purnalingam Pillai, a historian of Tamil literature, the writings of the siddhars "are the most popular works in Tamil and there is no pure Tamilian, educated or uneducated, who has not committed to memory at least a few stanzas from one or other of them. . . . They were the haters of the Aryan social fabric, religious rites, and the Vedic authority."[11] Consistently with revivalist formulations of a Sanskrit-free Tamil tradition, non-brahman Tamil leaders celebrate the siddhars in their intimate connection with colloquial Tamil and with "pure Tamilians." Mu. Varadarajan, in his *History of Tamil Literature*, writes that the language of the siddhars was "easily understood by the people. . . . Even today the siddhars' verses are sung by street singers."[12] The siddhars are Tamils who identify with non-brahman castes, the very communities that Tamil revivalists are trying to win to their vision of Tamil society.

Vaidyas and Tamil revivalists often invoke the insight with which the siddhars penetrate and manipulate both physical nature and social configurations as the basis for a critique of caste, Sanskritic culture, and brahmanic ritual dominance. Tamilpriyan writes, "The siddhars were noble people, born to serve humanity. They were great men who lived for others, not for themselves. Even though they won immeasurable powers, they didn't use this rare power even a single time for their own good. They happily used their rare power only for the benefit of the common person (*potumakkaḷ*)."[13] Among the rules and regulations of the South Indian Siddha Vaidya Association in 1952 were the injunction to publicize siddha medicine so that "the common person can live without disease," and the decree that all its members must work with the conviction that "all Tamils born in Tamil Nadu are a single race, without differences of caste and religion."[14] Paul Joseph Thottam recounts a story from a text attributed to Bhogar, *Pōgar 7000*, that links extraordinary abilities to compassion for ordinary people. Konkanar, a powerful yogi, was intrigued by the extraordinary powers of two acquaintances. When he inquired into their powers, one of these acquaintances, a butcher, explained. "We have no extraordinary powers. We say what we feel, and we feel for others as much as we feel for ourselves. We carry out our duties to the best of our abilities. There is nothing more to it than that." These householders gained great power through their empathy for ordinary people, not through rigorous ascetic practice. On hearing this, Konkanar "went about healing and helping people," beginning his career as a well-known medical siddhar.[15]

G. J. Parthasarathy named his clinic after Tirumular to highlight the egalitarian nature of his work and siddha medicine in general. For him, it is Tirumular more than other siddhars who embodies the quality of inclusiveness, presumably because of the sage's occupation of the body of a shepherd. "Tirumular is for all the doctors in Tamil Nadu. . . . Many people who I know take on Bhogar and Agastyar. Those who take on Tirumular are rare in Tamil Nadu. I'm one of those. If you want to understand why . . . he wanted all people to know all the practices which he learned, which he knew, all the medicines he used, his wisdom and his knowledge. But if you ask what other siddhars said, only the good people should know. They thought their knowledge should not go to bad people." Indeed, this depiction of the medical siddhars as keeping their knowledge secret is faithful to the way that the premodern medical texts portray the siddhars, but as we will see in chapter six, Tirumular is no different from the other siddhars in this regard.

Most vaidyas take the ñāṉasiddhars to exemplify an egalitarianism that all medical siddhars share, and they speak of their own practices as being specifically for the common person. In his short editorial comments at the beginning of several issues of his *Cittar Ulakam*, Parthasarathy states that "my service is transforming siddha medicine into a movement of the people."[16] He repeated this to me as we spoke. "I don't run this magazine for intellectuals. [It's for] ordinary middle-class, low-class people." His editorials address the concerns of his target audience. In one he defends quotas for tribal peoples, which will be necessary to maintain "until there is social equality . . . until caste is destroyed."[17] In another he urges the party holding power in Tamil Nadu, the DMK, "who desire the best for our people," to give pensions to hereditary vaidyas who do not have them, and to increase the pensions of those who do. He suggests that the government provide siddha medicines to the poor. "If the Tamil Nadu government gives bank loans to farmers to grow medicinal plants, and then purchases those plants, they can provide free medicines to our people."[18] For Parthasarathy, Tirumular is the model for his public service, because he "desired that everyone has medical knowledge. For doing my public work, he is a great help to me. I have taken him on as a guru."

Like many other siddha vaidyas, Parthasarathy considers the "common people" who need help to be those in the villages. He criticizes siddha doctors who earn siddha medical degrees for their neglect of ordinary Tamils. "None of the doctors who have studied here go to the villages and do fieldwork. They are just in the city.

Now, even though they adhere to siddha medicine, they have an allopathy mentality, and treat according to allopathy methods. That shouldn't be." His criticism of vaidyas with degrees invokes a significant division among practitioners, between those educated in government colleges and hereditary vaidyas. Parthasarathy and many other hereditary vaidyas consider themselves to embody the egalitarian spirit of siddha, while criticizing vaidyas with degrees as ignoring the Tamil masses and with being corrupted by Western methods, which have been often taught alongside siddha medicine in colleges and universities. While many vaidyas blame social inequality in Tamil society on caste and brahmanic influence, Parthasarathy sees it as a legacy of British rule, and medical neglect as the corrupting influence of Western medicine: "When the British government was here, they only used allopathy for themselves and a few wealthy [Indians]. Those in high society used it. Other, common, poor people . . . for them, this hereditary siddha medicine, herbal medicine, these protected them. This is true. This was a period in history in which these siddhars had basically a lot of respect and affection for people. I have a lot of affection for people. I'm very concerned with what I'm going to do for people. For that reason I've come to this [medical] field. I didn't come to make money." As we spoke, Parthasarathy repeatedly mentioned his service to people in villages, which includes running workshops and providing cheap or free medical attention. He also spends time in villages to prepare medicines that he has collected in forests and on mountains, the ideal land for medical herbs. Taking Tirumular as a model, he seeks not only to promote siddha medicine qua medicine, but also to transform it into a vehicle of liberation for the disenfranchised of Tamil Nadu.

The Rationality of Siddha Medicine

In his editorial preface to the July 2006 edition of *Cittar Ulakam*, Parthasarathy argues for the continuation of reservations and quotas for the "ancient inhabitants" (*paḻaṅkuṭiyiṉar*), or tribal peoples, of India. He considers such reservations to be integral to the "principles of social justice" followed by India's southern states, and credits quotas with producing many great doctors and engineers. He attributes these social principles, which are consistent with his own efforts, to "Tantai Periyar," or "Father Periyar," perhaps the most influential non-brahman Tamil leader of the twentieth century.[19] E. V. Ramasami or E.V.R., known later in life as "Periyar" (Great One), has been one of the primary authors of modern Tamil identity. He stressed the basic equality of all Tamils, was fiercely opposed to brahmanic hegemony, and depicted the Tamil people as essentially rational. His characterization of Tamil society has had a significant influence on discussions of the siddhars and siddha medicine.

Ramasami was born in 1879 into the Naiker caste, a land-owning shudra caste that follows rigid standards of purity with respect to non-landowning communities. In 1904 he became a renouncer, wandering through pilgrimage sites in north India, where he repeatedly witnessed, and was a victim of, caste discrimination. Disillusioned with the caste inequalities of Hinduism, he subsequently gave up the religious life and joined the Congress Party in 1919 to fight social inequality in Indian society.[20] In 1925, he left Congress after witnessing eating facilities in a Congress school that segregated non-brahmans from brahmans. In the same year, he started the Tamil Self-Respect Movement, declaring that "hereafter my work is to dissolve the Congress."[21]

Ramasami's leading position in the Self-Respect Movement established him as one of the most influential cultural critics of brahmanic domination. His primary target was Hinduism, which he saw as a brahman "scheme" (*cūḻcci*) to "make Aryans superior, to put other people in the dark so that they could be ruled for the benefit of the Aryan."[22] He viewed Hinduism as a cornerstone of caste inequality. Hinduism "is founded by a small group for their own power interest and built on the ignorance, illiteracy and exploiting of the people." In his own writings, Ramasami extolled "man and his wisdom rather than talk of God and his power." In a 1947 speech, he asserted that atheism and rationalism are a "scientific alternative to religion. Man's reason alone can further true progress." He advocated scientific education as the means to spread rational principles through which Tamils would free themselves from repression.[23]

Ramasami drew from, and contributed to, Tamil narratives of a rational, ancient Tamil society, arguing that religion in any form is foreign to Tamil culture. He held that although modern Tamils might think of themselves as Hindus, the genuine character of Tamils is that of rationality, and their ancient position on religion was atheism. "That is why I say that Tamils have no gods at all. The gods that they pray [to] are all the gods and deities of Aryans . . . genuinely Tamils have not accepted the four vedas as their scriptures." While many Tamils think of themselves as Hindus, their "gods and goddesses were imported from foreign soil." He wrote, "there had been no god, no temple, no holy place and no holy tank for the Tamils of ancient days. What are existing to be [sic] for the sake of the Tamils have been fabricated and institutionalized by Brahmins for the sake of their livelihood. They have done so, to maintain their religious hegemony and to keep us in perpetual subordination, besides fooling all of us."[24] To reestablish a rational Tamil society, Ramasami argued, it is not enough to expel Aryans from Tamil soil, but Tamil culture itself must be purified of the Hindu beliefs and practices that they introduced.

Ramasami inscribed notions of truth and deception into social identity, making rationality an inherent possession of particular communities and traditions.

However, his attitude toward Tamil traditions was ambivalent at best, as he felt that present traditions were so deeply corrupted by Hinduism that they were irremediable. His criteria for what would constitute an ideal Tamil tradition were based rigidly on Western views of science, and he was unable to salvage much that had survived to the present age. "Ours is an obstinate society. Even after more than three-fourths of the people of the world have progressed, our society is still in a backward and barbaric stage, adamantly following customs of yore, because they have been adopted for a long time by its forebears."[25] He relentlessly compared the progress of other nations to his own country, where "men believe only in rituals and ceremonies, in God, in religion and such other rubbish."[26] He was dismissive of any form of custom or ritual, and at times was impatient with nostalgic formulations of non-brahman tradition. He urged Tamils: "Don't think about past glory, see today's degradation."[27] He was often frustrated that the reality of contemporary Tamil society was far different from his vision, and he often lashed out at Tamils for being naive and blinded by superstition. Recognizing that a majority of Tamil speakers are in fact deeply affected by Hindu symbols and identify with Hindu ideals, he lamented, "I do not know for how many centuries our people have to wait for attaining reason and maturity. I have to believe that Tamil Nadu will have no salvation unless she is razed to her foundation by a catastrophic deluge or storm, a flood or an earthquake, and then renewed."[28]

Ramasami's critique of Hinduism and brahmanic traditions, his refusal to glorify Tamil history, and his conviction that present Tamil culture was irreparably tainted by Aryan superstitions led him to commend a model for Tamil society that was based on the industrialized countries of Europe. Much like the British, Ramasami saw value only in those cultural traditions, such as music or drama, that were not in direct contradiction to science. However, his critique of religion led him to disregard all practices that were counter to science and its institutions. Indigenous medical practices were among his targets: "Much earlier than the advent of allopathy and when belief in god, prayer, magic, mantra were in vogue, the average age of an individual was only 15 and after the debut of allopathy, it increased to about 60 or 70. . . . Are these [facts] not due to a scientific approach and deep knowledge? Only those who are blind and ignorant of these progress [sic] do believe in god."[29] Ramasami accepted the universal truth claims of allopathy and disparaged the current state of indigenous medicine. Although I was not able to find any writings of his on siddha medicine, his conviction that ancient Tamils were rational and scientific would appear to leave some room to entertain the recovery of an ancient Tamil medicine. This is indeed what a prominent member of the Self-Respect Movement, Sami Chidambaranar, proposed.[30] Chidambaranar advocated the development of the Tamil sciences, and therefore actively promoted the siddhars as embodying the goals of Tamil revivalism, and siddha medicine as a native science with great potential.

Sami Chidambaranar (1900–61) wrote a number of books on Tamil literature and culture, including an influential biography of Ramasami.[31] He was one of thirteen "Tamil National Authors" to have his books "nationalised" in 1997.[32] He applied Ramasami's egalitarian and rationalist principles to the siddhars and siddha medicine in *The True Science of the Siddhars*.[33] Siddha medicine is, according to Chidambaranar, the Tamil art of most benefit to all people. "The siddhars, wise men who lived in this very land in ancient times, developed the art of medicine, so that the common person (*potumakkaḷ*) would live without disease, so they would live a long time with strong bodies. . . . [Medicine] is the one art which helps all people regardless of differences of caste, religion, language, and race. All, from the poor to the wealthy, experience the benefits of this art."[34] Although Chidambaranar shares Ramasami's concern for the ordinary person, he expresses this concern in a more inclusive vision, with little of the strident anti-brahmanism that made Ramasami such a controversial figure. He blames modern society and Western ways, not brahmans, for current neglect of siddha medicine, and says that he has written this book to help revive the siddhars' medicine and philosophy. The benefit of this revival will be unity and affection among people. "The siddhars' philosophy is that there is only one human society, only one human race. Creating divisions between people is counter to truth and to nature. If the siddhars' philosophy spreads, can anyone deny that this will benefit the country and the people?"[35]

Chidambaranar interprets much of the data of siddha medicine through a rationalist lens, but does not discard many features of Tamil tradition, as Ramasami was wont to do. Chidambaranar affirms that the extant siddha medical texts are only four to five hundred years old. At the same time, he maintains the antiquity of siddha medicine by claiming that these texts were late redactions of medical techniques that are thousands of years old.[36] He also accepts that the siddhars had the eight yogic powers or siddhis, but denies that these transgress rationality or the laws of nature, so their performance of wondrous acts should not be considered miraculous. "No doubt, those who have obtained great knowledge perform rare acts that common people cannot do. It's true that ordinary people praise such difficult acts as miracles."[37] In similar ways, he rationalizes their use of astrology and their recitation of mantras. He gives the Sanskrit *mantra*, or *mantiram* in Tamil, a Tamil etymology, formed by combining *man* (mind) and *tiram* (firmness), to give "steadiness of mind." The recitation of mantras makes the mind firm, and those who recite mantras gain confidence through their belief in their effects. They become fearless. This fearlessness is essential for those who, like the siddhars, "wandering through mountains and forests for medicinal plants and metals, face many dangers. Mantras help them escape from poisonous creatures and vicious animals. Those people will shout out mantras with confidence and strength of mind, and those dangerous animals will run away."[38]

The relative importance of alchemical materials and processes is one of the features that many vaidyas say sets siddha medicine apart from other medical systems. Chidambaranar cites this use of metals as the primary distinction between siddha and ayurveda, and he sees the transformation of metals as one of the major contributions of the siddhars to scientific knowledge. He defines the Tamil *vātam*, most often translated as alchemy, as the investigation into transformations of the physical world. Research that employs artificial means to study these natural changes is vātam. This method of inquiry results in the discovery of truths, and it is the basis of medical knowledge. Chidambaranar quotes Tamil aphorisms that suggest the emergence of medicine from the basic goal of early alchemy, the transformation of base metals into gold. " 'Alchemical medicine'; 'engaging in alchemy, the vaidya was born'; 'when alchemy doesn't work, medicine emerges.' . . . Many people, engaging in alchemy out of a desire for gold, became great vaidyas."[39] Through their research into the character of metals and other materials, the siddhars came to know the medicinal qualities of various substances that they began to use for curing disease. Of primary importance was mercury, which was employed for the most intractable diseases. Chidambaranar characterizes the siddhars' vātam as chemistry (*racāyaṉam*), not alchemy, emphasizing that it is a mode of scientific research that leads to true knowledge of the qualities of nature. He ridicules those who continue to spend resources in attempts to formulate gold from other metals, arguing that each metal has a different nature.[40]

As the selfishness of those who seek riches through vātam signals their scientific ignorance, it is the selflessness of the siddhars' research that distinguishes their efforts from that of Western scientists. Chidambaranar emphasizes that "the siddhars' medicine and philosophy are equal to today's scientific methods," yet he distinguishes the siddhars' scientific discoveries from those of modern science on the basis of their relative benefits to humanity.[41] That is, the siddhars developed medicine for the good of the common person, and this knowledge continues to serve all levels of society today. Although "today's scientists" make discoveries that advance society, they also "discovered terrible destructive power, capable of wiping out humanity and civilization and turning the earth into ash. This is the power of grenades and bombs. The world today trembles with such discoveries of today's scientists." The effects of these discoveries are fear and distrust, which he holds plague the modern world. The uniqueness of the siddhars' science, according to Chidambaranar, was not in their rational discoveries, which are mirrored by those of Western science, but in their refusal to harness the destructive powers of nature. These "ancient scientists of the Tamil land laboured only for the life of humanity . . . and for the happiness of human society."[42]

More recently, Kalai Arasu has written a rationalist account of the siddhars that is perhaps more true to Ramasami's principles. In his *Dravidian Spirituality of the Siddhars*, Kalai Arasu is vitriolic in his anti-brahmanism, which he sees as the most enduring legacy of the siddhars. He dates the history of the siddhars to the time of the āḻvār and nāyaṉmār of the late centuries of the first millennium, when "Aryan customs violently took hold in the Tamil land." The ālvār and nāyaṉmār bhakti saints destroyed a prior, Jain society and spread superstition, irrationality, caste distinctions, and Aryan dominance throughout the Tamil land. "In the name of devotion to god, the uniqueness of the Tamil language and of the Tamil people was destroyed completely." Along with the ñāṉasiddhars, the medical siddhars emerged at this time, spreading a Tamil medicine in the common language of the people, a medicine that employed potent plants available in Tamil Nadu.[43] Kalai Arasu holds that the siddhars were the first Tamils to resist the domination of brahmans, creating a legacy of non-brahman resistance that was continued in the twentieth century by Ramasami. "This earlier opposition to the Vedas and to brahmans continues in our time, evolving into E.V.R.'s Dravidian Movement and rationalist movement." Ramasami rose to establish non-brahman rule against the "brahman leaders who took the Congress Party by force."[44] Kalai Arasu thus considers Ramasami's Self-Respect Movement, and its attempt to establish a rational, scientific tradition, as a recent manifestation of the legacy of the siddhars.

Kalai Arasu, consistently with Ramasami's rationalism, rejects the more incredible aspects of the siddhars' narratives. He considers the recent proliferation of popular literature on the miraculous powers of the siddhars to detract from the real value of the siddhars' writings, the wisdom and social egalitarianism that they stressed. Narratives of their fabulous powers are "baseless myths, downright lies. They are composed . . . to depict the siddhars as having circus knowledge, ignoring that they were noble, wise people." Kalai Arasu recounts a number of stories of the siddhars, like that of Karuvur Devar, who fashioned the main image of the great Thanjavur temple of Rajaraja Chola by chewing betel leaf and spitting out the twelve-foot Shiva linga that is the focus of worship in the temple to this day. Kalai Arasu discounts such stories as "cosmic lies, fairy tales" propagated by brahmans to detract from the true message of the siddhars, their opposition to brahmanic hegemony. Thus, while he can accept siddha medicine as rational and scientific, and as non-brahman and Tamil, he discounts its more extraordinary claims, such as the siddhars' discovery of rejuvenative medicine, and their formulation of a medicine for immortality.[45]

Siddha Medicine and the Deep Rationality of Shaivism

In contrast to Ramasami's atheism and rejection of Tamil traditions, most vaidyas are far more accepting of the religious elements of their tradition and emphasize the Shaiva character of their medicine, citing the fact that the siddhars' medical and philosophical texts express devotion to Shiva. Historically, the writings of the siddhars have posed a challenge to temple-based Shaivism. Despite their professed devotion to Shiva, the anti-authoritarian character of the writings of the ñāṉasiddhars has resulted in an ambivalent, often confrontational relationship with Shaiva Siddhanta orthodoxy.[46] Prior to the twentieth century, south Indian Shaiva institutions placed brahmanical rituals and temple worship at the center of their prescribed practices. The philosophical writings of the ñāṉasiddhars, on the other hand, often targeted these brahmanic rituals for ridicule. Typical of these siddhar poets, Sivavakkiyar, whom Zvelebil dates to the tenth century C.E., rejects the same religious forms that Tamil revivalists would later attack as foreign elements in the Tamil community.[47]

> What are temples, tell me! And what are sacred tanks?
> O you poor slaves who worship in temples and tanks!
> Temples are in the mind. Tanks are in the mind.
> There is no Becoming, there is no Unbecoming, none, none whatever![48]
>
> Why, you fool, do you utter mantras, murmuring them, whispering,
> going around the fixed stone as if it were god, putting garlands of flowers around it?
> Will the fixed stone speak—as if the Lord were within?
> Will the cooking vessel, or the wooden ladle, know the taste of the curry?[49]

Over half a millennium later, in the *Ñāṉaveṭṭiyāṉ*, a work of the sixteenth century, the siddhar Valluvar writes, "While we worship the *atmalinga* [soul] within us, these Brahmins worship a *linga* [phallus] made of stone."[50] Valluvar posits a clear social divide between brahmans and "us," a distinction based on their different approaches to religious practice, a distinction that was later emphasized in the project of Tamil revivalism to unite a non-brahman ethnic community. It is unclear who the "we" cited above is, but it most likely refers to Valluvar's own Sāmbhavan caste, a caste that buries carcasses and cremates corpses, which he celebrates throughout the text at the expense of upper castes.[51]

This tension is often expressed today through comparisions between the siddhars and the nāyaṉmār. As we have seen, Tirumular is considered both a siddhar and one of the nāyaṉmār, his story is recounted in Cekkilar's *Periya Purāṇam*, and the *Tirumantiram* is the sole text attributed to a siddhar that has been included in the *Tirumuṟai*. However, some authors who promote siddha medicine and the views of the ñāṉasiddhars reject any association between the siddhars and the nāyaṉmār. Kalai Arasu gives an account in which the nāyaṉmār sought to impose brahmanical ritualism on the non-brahman Tamil people, and the siddhars rose to fight against those efforts. S. P. Ramachandran is careful to distinguish the siddhars from the nāyaṉmār and sees the siddhars as possessing more power to transform human society than the nāyaṉmār, though he does not resist Tirumular's inclusion among the orthodox saints.[52] Likewise, A. V. Subramania Iyer, in discussing Tirumular, distinguishes devotees from siddhars, noting that "while all Bhaktas have not been Siddhars all Siddhars have been Bhaktas."[53] Shakti P. Subramaniyan likewise distinguishes devotees and siddhars, describing the Vaishnava ālvār and the nāyaṉmār as adhering to organized religion (*camayam*), while the siddhars adhere to spirituality (*āṉmīkam*). While devotees perform external rituals, the siddhars consider the interior as a temple.[54] R. Venkatraman distinguishes two Tirumulars, the first being a nāyaṉmār and the second a siddhar.

Despite these tensions, most vaidyas today take the siddhars and siddha medicine to be comfortably Shaiva, if not Hindu. Siddha vaidyas rarely describe their medicine as "Hindu," a designation that is largely reserved for ayurveda. Hindu nationalists and ayurvedic practitioners often consider ayurveda to be *the* Hindu system of medicine, reflecting earlier Orientalist studies that depicted ayurveda as the medicine of the Hindus.[55] Ayurveda, particularly its early textual forms, is certainly susceptible to analysis in its connection to classical religious considerations, as Francis Zimmerman has brilliantly done.[56] However, Jean Langford has pointed out that the nationalist construction of ayurveda reaches back to a distant, pre-Muslim past to locate a pure, Hindu medicine, "erasing centuries of exchange between vaidyas and hakīms."[57] This characterization of ayurveda as Hindu invites the accusations that non-brahman Tamil revivalists make of other elements of Hinduism: it is superstitious, elitist, and foreign to Tamil tradition.

The professed Shaivism of siddha knowledge, on the other hand, does not compromise the revivalist credentials of the siddhars or siddha medicine, as vaidyas link their medicine to twentieth-century Shaiva Siddhanta and its strong anti-brahmanism and rationalism. The siddhars have found more favor in this modern, revivalist Shaivism than they have in the past. Kamil Zvelebil was right when he noted back in the early 1970s that "It is only very recently that the Siddha doctrine is, so to say, being 'rehabilitated' . . . as the expression of 'pure' Tamil indigenous thought, as *the* Tamil medicine, *the* Tamil philosophy and so on."[58] This is due in large part to the modern convergence, under the mantle of Tamil revivalism, of depictions of the siddhars and contemporary Shaiva Siddhanta. In their consideration of the Shaiva nature of the siddhars and their medicine, vaidyas follow Maraimalai Adigal, probably the most prominent proponent of Shaiva Siddhanta in the twentieth century, who vehemently attacked caste yet took a moderate stance on Hinduism, advocating its reform rather than its destruction.[59] Tamil Shaiva Siddhanta is a Shaivite philosophical and devotional tradition centered on the *Tirumuṟai* corpus, the Shaiva Āgamas, and subsequent philosophical literature. Shaiva Siddhantins today consider Shiva be the prototypical Tamil god, often citing an Indus Valley seal depicting a figure in a meditative posture as material proof both that this civilization was a Tamil civilization, and that the worship of Shiva among Tamils dates to thousands of years before the common era.

The relationship between the Shaiva Siddhantins and members of Ramasami's Self-Respect Movement was extremely ambivalent. On the one hand, they were unified in their opposition to the Congress and in their attacks on brahmans and Sanskrit. However, E.V.R.'s strident atheism limited close ideological links between the two groups. The *Dravidian*, the official periodical of the Self-Respect Movement, attacked Maraimalai Adigal as the bedfellow of Hindu brahmans. "Theism, faith in God, Hinduism (both Saivism and Vaishnavism) all belong to the Aryan brahmins. Maraimalai Adikal who supports these is a slave of the Aryans. Only those who support atheism are genuine Tamils."[60] Yet others, usually Shaiva Siddhantins, made attempts at reconciliation. Thus Ilavalaganar, a student of Maraimalai Adigal, wrote,

> Saivism is not one iota different from the primary aim of the Self-Respect Movement. The Self-Respect Movement arose to dispel the illusion of Brahminism from the Tamil people and infuse self-respect into them. Saivism also does the same. The Self-Respect Movement detests the Aryan Brahmins. Saivism too doesn't like the Aryan Brahmins one bit. . . . The Self-Respect Movement wishes to uplift the depressed classes. That is also the basic idea of Saivism. . . . The Self-Respect Movement is against caste differences among the Tamil people. Saivism too emphasizes the same point. . . . When there are so many common points, why should Saivism and Saivite apostles be deprecated and condemned?[61]

The two groups did cooperate in certain anti-brahman activities, especially in their defense of Tamil when Congress attempted to introduce the mandatory study of Hindi in all schools in the Madras presidency in 1938.[62] Shaiva Siddhanta writings that celebrated the greatness of Tamil civilization preceded the founding of the Self-Respect Movement, and Maraimalai Adigal claimed that E.V.R.'s movement was based on Adigal's own views and principles.[63] Even so, it is important to note that the two groups drew from one another in their formulations of Tamil identity, and both asserted that intelligence and rationality were defining qualities of the Tamil people.

Maraimalai Adigal (1876–1950) was born R. S. Vedachalam and later changed his name to the Tamil equivalent, Maṟaimalai Aṭikaḷ.[64] In his English preface to *Tamiḻar Matam* (Religion of the Tamils), Adigal emphasizes the racial and cultural differences that divide Indian society. He employs the distinction between Aryan and Dravidian and claims the autochthony of Tamils by bringing together archeological findings with Tamil literature.

> If Sir John Marshall had had a first hand knowledge of the Tholkappiam and some other ancient classics of Tamil, he would have easily shown in corroboration of what he stated as regards the pre-Aryan antiquity of one of the Dravidian languages, that Tamil alone, and not any other as he vaguely affirmed, must have been the language spoken and cultivated by the pre-Aryan inhabitants of the Indus valley. . . . We are now in a position strong and unshakable to correlate with the above archaeological evidence, the proofs afforded by the ancient and genuine literary works of the Tamil language.[65]

For Adigal, in addition to archeological evidence, Tamil literary works, "ancient and genuine," can also serve as "proofs" for historical arguments. Adigal equates the authority of Tamil literature with that of science, arguing that it was Sir John Marshall's ignorance of Tamil literature that prevented him from discovering the true, Tamil identity of the Indus Valley people. Whereas Ramasami discounted most Tamil literature as irrational, Adigal advocates a method of historical inquiry that combines literary and scientific evidence. He argues that Tamil literature and culture are no less true than the truths of science, and indeed, insofar as they are more ancient than science, they supersede the authority of even the most incontrovertible claims of science.

Siddha medical leaders and vaidyas make similar arguments about the historical and scientific veracity of the evidence of tradition, joining the Shaivism of the siddhars to archeological remains. They often refer to perhaps the most famous of the Indus Valley seals, which portrays an apparently ithyphallic man, seated with his knees splayed to each side and feet meeting at his groin. Paul Joseph Thottam sees the figure as evidence of early siddha medicine, taking the posture to be *siddhasana*, a yogic posture "named after the siddhars."[66] In his textbook for first-year students of siddha medicine at the College of Indian Medicine, K. C. Uttamarayan similarly enumerates a chain of connections that link siddha medicine, Shaivism, and the Indus Valley civilization. "Many siddhars appeared in Tamil Nadu, developed a medical system, and wrote medical texts. Therefore, the medicine of the Tamils is called siddha medicine. The religion of the siddhars is Shaivism. The Tamil mode of worship is worship of the linga. This is apparent because of the many lingas that can be seen in a variety of places, beginning with Mohenjo Daro."[67] T. V. Sambasivam Pillai links linga worship specifically to ancient Tamils and to the siddhars, who "metamorphosed" their bodies into lingas after attaining their goal of union with Shiva. Linga worship is "practiced by the civilised and not by the barbarous." It is found throughout Asia, Africa, America and Europe, and phallic symbols are apparent on Egyptian pyramids. While Sambasivam Pillai does not mention the Indus Valley seal here, he does refer to the "labours of Anthropologists and Archeologists" in uncovering evidence of early linga worship. He also asserts that it was the siddhars who first spread this linga worship throughout the world, as they "used to go abroad in those days in order to initiate people into the tenets of the Hindu creed."[68] Adigal identifies pieces uncovered in the Indus Valley as Shivalingas and as anthropomorphic representations of Shiva and Uma, concluding that Shaiva worship was common across India five or six thousand years ago.[69]

P. Ramanatha Pillai, the commentator of the Shaiva Siddhanta edition of the *Tirumantiram*, takes verse 1619, "they roam the world spreading wisdom that is abundant in the five Tamil regions," as evidence that the siddhars spread their knowledge throughout the world. He expands on this verse, envisioning that in Tirumular's time, 6000–100 B.C.E., Tamils were living throughout the world, and the siddhars wandered throughout the world spreading Tamil doctrines, such as the Tamil language, the Shaiva religion, and the worship of the Shivalinga. He asserts that epigraphical evidence across the globe, and the dispersal of Shivalingas throughout the world, support this.[70] P. M. Venugopal, lecturer in the Department of History of Medicine (Indigenous) at the Government College of Indian Medicine, Madras, wrote a report on the history of siddha medicine for the Madras state government on the history of siddha medicine using a significant number of books purchased from the South India Shaiva Siddhanta Society.[71] At the end of his report, he concludes that not only were Shaivism and siddha medicine closely intertwined in their origins, but also that in "the Tamil Sangam Age the Physicians of Siddha System of Medicine were the founders of Saiva Siddhantha Philosophy and they were also the ardent followers of Lord Siva. In as much as the Lord Siva was a super-human or a hero warrior, he was considered the first propounder of medicine and Tamil Literature."[72]

This linking of the siddhars, medicine, and Shiva has premodern precedents, as we have seen, both in the medical texts that claim Shiva as the original redactor of medical knowledge, and in the siddhars' philosophical texts that take Shiva as the source of all things. What is new in more recent medical and revivalist considerations is their emphasis on the rational character of Shaivism. There is also a greater stress on the Tamil character of Shaivism and especially of siddha medicine than in earlier texts, though this is a matter of degree. Literary references to Shiva's connection with the Tamil language are not new, but they are absent from the medical texts attributed to the siddhars, which do not identify their medical formulae as specifically Tamil. Thus, while medical knowledge in premodern texts carried the authority of divinity (Shiva and Shakti) and semidivinity (the siddhars), contemporary narratives retain these and add another, the authority of Tamil revivalism. Here I will focus on the rational Shaivism advocated by Adigal and by siddha vaidyas, and in the next section I will look at the place of Tamil in these revivalist and medical visions.

It is Maraimalai Adigal who has been most influential in conceiving a rationalist Shaivism that vaidyas employ in describing their medical knowledge. Adigal followed the Lemuria narrative in describing a history in which a pure Tamil race inhabited ancient India before Aryans, Muslims, and others invaded from the north and mixed with Tamils, forming new mongrel races. These mongrel races are those presently found in north and central India, while "the [Tamil] stock in the south has remained pure and intact." Adigal contrasts Tamil intelligence, and the truth which Tamils seek, to the character of the Aryans, whose lack of a homeland, whose "fluidic condition, on account of their long nomadic life bred in them a disinclination for honest work and led them to live upon plunder and cattle-lifting."[73] Present day Tamilians are no longer attuned to rational arguments,

> having, for the last four or five centuries, come under the influence of the Aryan priesthood, [Tamils] have lost their independent and rational way of thinking and have become slaves to the Aryan laws, customs and manners . . . . Their observances of rites, of religious practices and social customs are formal and inflexible, for they care little to understand the significance of what they so strictly but unwittingly observe. This slavishness, this petrified conservatism has so thickened the gloom of their ignorance as to render them thoroughly impervious to the ray of light coming from the critical and historical spirit of the modern culture.[74]

Adigal complains that contemporary Tamils are unaware of the true significance of the rituals they support. He distinguishes those religious practices that are ancient and Tamil from those introduced later by Aryans. Whereas the former were established for rational, spiritual reasons, the latter were perpetuated by brahmans to enslave Tamils. He cites Vedic texts which prescribe animal sacrifices, calling these "Aryan rituals" that are "revolting and barbaric to the Tamilian mind."[75] Here Adigal's antiritual views coincide with those of Ramasami, who, in one of his famous revisionary *Rāmāyaṇas*, writes: "If one asks why Ravana hated devars, rishis and munis, there is no reason other than because, in the name of sacrifice, they tormented and killed living beings. . . . He denounced brahmans only after seeing them performing sacrifices and drinking the intoxicating somarasam."[76] Adigal focuses his critique on temple pujas, marriage ceremonies, death rites, and other rituals through which brahman priests gain their livelihood, objecting to their use of Sanskrit on Tamil land, and also to their monopolization of these rituals. Unlike E.V.R., Adigal was not opposed to the performance of ritual per se, and he engaged non-brahman ritual specialists on various occasions.[77] By selectively, rather than thoroughly, incorporating rationalist considerations into his new vision of Shaivism and of Tamil society, Adigal was able to draw significantly on the materials and authority of tradition.

The view voiced by many vaidyas that the siddhars initiated a rationalization of South Asian religion is unsustainable. The writings of the ñāṉasiddhars substitute for one hidden quantity, the material efficacy of ritual and symbolic constructions, others such as the potential to gain knowledge through extraordinary means.[78] Medical texts attributed to the siddhars do not criticize rituals often linked to brahmanic temple practices, such as puja or archana. For example, Uromarishi, in his *Muppu Sutra 30* (Text on muppu in thirty verses) warns the vaidya not to forget to do puja in conjunction with formulating medicine.[79] Although many vaidyas today reject this employment of ritual in formulating medicine, they continue to emphasize that the siddhars, and by extension their medicine, have a direct relationship to divinity. A pamphlet entitled "The Principles of Siddha Medicine" traces the "treasure" of the siddhars' knowledge to their internal realization of divinity.

> With the sixth sense, siddhars have been successful in their attempts to attain the power which animates the world. . . Through their learning and experience, the siddhars have mastered great knowledge. So that ordinary people can obtain the permanent bliss that they achieved, they described in songs the way to acquire that power. All their verses are the invaluable treasure of the holy Tamil land (*tamiḻttirunāṭu*). The special characteristic of siddhars is that they have attained the divine state of permanent bliss. Realizing this divine state within themselves, the siddhars transcend institutional religion (*camayam*) and ritual.[80]

This transcendence is made possible by the dismissal of the physical technologies of worship, by the location of divinity within each individual self, and by the assertion that the method to acquire "great bliss" and the "power that moves the world" does not require "institutional religion" that involves the mediation of brahmans but is contained in the verses of the siddhars. Unlike much temple ritual performed in Sanskrit, the siddhars' verses are in Tamil, the colloquial language of rickshaw drivers, street vendors, and other ordinary people who compose the primary audience of this rhetoric. Vaidyas usually criticize only those technologies that have been controlled by brahmans: rituals, temples, and Sanskrit texts and mythologies. At the same time that they reject external religious activity, they celebrate internal processes that are less directly subject to control by others. This move from external to internal is in part an attempt to assert control over religious and medical worlds dominated by brahmans and by biomedical doctors. For Tamil revivalists, the siddhars' "sixth sense" that I earlier discussed as a means of scientific knowledge here describes a direct, internal, intuitive relationship between Tamils and divinity. It is a sense that sees into the extraordinary, not mundane, nature of things, a sense that penetrates to the true state of nature and also to the true, egalitarian nature of society.

Maraimali Adigal expressed confidence in the potential of modern historical and scientific disciplines to liberate Tamils from the oppressive and superstitious character of Hinduism. These tools for liberation also provide tools to achieve knowledge of the cosmos, but they are not sufficient in and of themselves. The most potent path to truth, Adigal held, is to apply this "critical and historical spirit" to ancient Tamil texts, which "depict nature and human nature as they truly appear."[81] "The ancient Tamil works describe things as found in real life.... Because of a critical and deep study of the ancient Tamil classics and the tenets of the Saiva Siddhanta by the Tamils, the evil Aryan influences on Tamil and the Tamils have begun to fade away. The great researches conducted by Western scholars in Tamil and the study of English have greatly helped in exploding the myth of Aryan superiority and wiping out the evil traces of Aryan way of life among the Tamils."[82] The subject of science is not just the physical world but also Tamil tradition, a view that vaidyas have taken on wholeheartedly in their studies of Tamil literature, medicine, and the writings of the siddhars. Like Adigal, they hold that the conjunction of modern science and research into the components of Tamil tradition will not only reveal great truths to the world but will also initiate a reconciliation of Tamils with their true character.

Whereas for Ramasami the measure of civilization was solely determined by its conformity with Western science, Adigal includes religious sensibility in his articulation of a rational Tamil tradition. According to Adigal, ancient Tamil society enjoyed absolute religious conformity, and so sectarian dissension was nonexistent. There was only one school of religious thought, that propounded by Adigal's Shaiva Siddhanta, and there was little conscious reflection on religious belief, because the truth of Shiva as the only god was clear to everyone. Ancient Tamils, simply, absolutely, and unanimously, "were paying their worship to the one Almighty." Religious dissension was only later introduced by brahmans. "Before this intrusion of the northern people, all the cultured and civilized Tamils were as a body strict monotheists paying their worship only to Siva as the almighty God of the universe and therefore had no occasion to bring in any religious or philosophic discussion among them."[83] Adigal characterizes Tamil religious inquiry as a scientific spiritualism in which people "think for themselves and examine their beliefs in the light of reason."[84] While lesser civilizations come up with religions of fancy, illusion, or deception, the genius of Tamil culture, he asserts, has been to develop a religion of truth ascertained through reason. The "ancient Tamilians" had "intuitive perception of the existence of God in light and fire aided, of course, by an acute discriminative understanding." He wrote, "strongly convinced therefore of the existence of such an infinite being, the acute intelligence and the highly developed instincts of the ancient Tamils anxiously set out to search for the principle in which it could reside in a way perceptible to the outer and inner vision of man."[85] While temporarily deluded by the false Aryan religion, Tamils can restore their relationship to truth and reestablish their utopian society by returning to ancient Tamil religion. "All Tamils must abandon worshiping the multitudinous gods and goddesses and deified heroes and return to the monotheistic belief of their ancestors and worship only the one almighty God Siva."[86] For Adigal monotheism is the most rational form of religion, entirely in agreement with scientific sensibilities.

Adigal held that one of the primary qualities of the Tamil people that distinguish them from all others is their superior intellingence. "There might be seen at a glance a perceptible general characteristic running through them which marks off the Tamils from all other people who have come into India at different periods of time and settled. Many an acute student of ethnic studies has noted in the eyes and features of the Tamils a certain brightness and alertness due to a suffusion of superior intelligence which is naturally denied to others."[87] Vaidyas invoke the rational superiority and natural intelligence of the Tamils in claiming the effectiveness of their knowledge. In his article for the "Siddha Medicine Seminar Special Souvenir," presented at the Second World Tamil Conference in 1968, Dr. Circapai writes, "Characteristically, Tamils are lively researchers. They are eminent thinkers. Their hypotheses, abilities, and knowledge are amazing. One can even call them the brain of the world."[88] Most vaidyas consider the siddhars themselves to best embody this Tamil propensity for rational activity. If the siddhars are paragons of Tamil character, they vary from contemporary Tamils only in degree, dramatically expressing the genius that all Tamils possess.

K. N. Kuppusami Mudaliyar holds that this genius was most fully realized in ancient Tamil society, when the only god worshiped was the only true god, Shiva, and the only medicine practiced was siddha medicine. In his introduction to siddha medicine, a textbook for students at siddha medical colleges, Mudaliyar closely links Shaivism with siddha medicine. He begins with a verse from the *Tirumantiram*.

> What is a living being (*cīvaṉ*)? What is Shiva? There is no difference
> between these.
> The living being does not know Shiva.
> When the living being knows Shiva,
> It then becomes Shiva.[89] (1979)

This verse plays on the similarity between *cīvaṉ*, which is life, soul, living being, and *civaṉ*, the god Shiva. Mudaliyar cites this verse to emphasize that indeed, the science of life, siddha medicine, and the science of god, Shaiva Siddhanta, are no different, and that both must be understood together. He further attributes this idea to the ancient Tamil people. "Tamil Nadu, which takes life to be Shiva himself, arose in the beginning of time. It's the tenet of geographers that this country was the first to appear on the earth."[90]

Kuppusami Mudaliyar begins his narrative by expressing the debt of the Tamil people to Western researchers who, through archeological and geological research, have uncovered the ancient history of the Tamil people. It begins on Lemuria, which was eventually broken up by earthquakes and volcanoes, and parts submerged by the sea. Only the central Tamil lands remained stable in this catastrophic geological time. The Tamils developed a sophisticated and peaceful civilization, and worshiped the linga and god. They founded the Shaiva Siddhanta philosophy, and wrote many Shaiva philosophical texts during the first sangam 12,000 years ago. They were blessed with rational thought. Mudaliyar writes at length about the principles of Shaiva Siddhanta, and then turns to medicine. The physical goal of medicine, the maintenance of healthy bodies, is not an end in itself but more importantly extends the length of time that one can experience knowledge of god. He gives a lineage of the descent of siddha medicine, from Shiva to Nandi to Tirumular to other siddhars and finally to the people of the world.[91] In the remainder of his lengthy introduction, Kuppusami Mudaliyar connects Shaiva philosophy to the details of siddha medicine through what he sees as a basic Tamil adage, the equation of divinity and the life of the body. He cites a common tripartite division of Hindu divinity, with Brahma as creator, Vishnu as protector, and Shiva as destroyer. He relates this by homology to the life that animates the mind and the body. Even though this life is unitary, it has three roles, which it manifests as the three humors of siddha medicine that flow through the body, with wind as creation, bile as protection, and phlegm as destruction. "There is a god for the world, and a life for the body." He links the siddhars' alchemy with Shaivism, asserting that the siddhars considered mercury to be the stuff of Shiva. Among the many names for mercury in medical texts attributed to the siddhars are words that refer to Shiva's semen, such as *civapītam* and *civavintu*. He emphasizes alchemy as the special expertise of southern India, where there is no higher medicine than mercury. He goes on to assert that the siddhars traveled through Egypt, Greece, and Arabia, teaching people about alchemy. He consistently brings medical details back to Shaiva language and tenets, such as the six important centers of the body, the chakras, each of which has a different form of Shiva and Uma. The fourth, the *aṉākatam* chakra, located twelve finger breadths above the third chakra, on the left side of the middle chest, in the place of the trachea, has Rudra and Parvati as deities, while the sixth, the *ākkiṉai* chakra, between the eyebrows, has Sadashiva and Manonmani as deities.[92]

For Kuppusami Mudaliyar, the Shaiva Āgama texts written by the early Tamils outline the "Shiva science," the path for reaching the "Shiva state." The means of knowledge set out in these texts can also be used to ascertain "the subtleties of medicine." "Southerners saw god expressed as light everywhere, not just here and there." They dwelled in bliss, their desires satisfied, flourishing in god's grace. "Taking all things as Shiva-Shakti, they knew the workings of the universe thousands of years before today's scientists, and they used this knowledge for the benefit of our countrymen. . . . In that way, siddha medicine was joined with Shaivism, in order to extend the life span as necessary to attain a place beyond birth." He chides today's Tamils for neglecting to research the subtle details and medicines of siddha medicine, citing their lack of courage and their disinterest, and concludes with a passionate plea that the government and the Tamil people show more zeal in this research.[93]

The particular genius of Tamil Shaiva science is this penetration of the essence of things beyond mere physicality. G. Subramania Pillai, a Shaiva Siddhanta scholar, describes the method of the Tamil philosopher, the Siddhantin, as going deeper into things than the level of *mulaprakriti*, root physicality: "The Siddhanta has excelled all other systems of philosophy in its wonderful progress in the scientific diagnosis of nature. While the other systems pursued the analysis of the Maya or matter down to the substratum of Mulaprakriti only, the Siddhantin plunged deeper and detected that even behind it there could be found a dozen more tatvas or reals of a far more refined type than Mulaprakriti."[94] Such insight into the invisibility of things is not mysterious but in absolute correspondence with nature. "One important feature of Siddhanta is that it gives more value for Reason, than for anything else. . . . It has not said anything which is relegated to the realms of the mysterious."[95] It is this common perception of the *depth* of Tamil tradition, its ancientness and its primacy, as well as its claim to rationality, that make these assertions of the superiority of siddha medicine over an immature Western science persuasive to a Tamil audience. Insofar as these assertions appear plausible, they are also pleasurable, and so this is a discourse not only of truth, not only of authority, but also of desire.

The deep rationality that siddha vaidyas claim is modeled more on Maraimalai Adigal's formulation of Tamil identity than on that of Ramasami. Although Ramasami thought Tamils might only progress after a "catastrophic deluge" destroys the community and their traditions and enables them to start anew, siddha vaidyas have not been anxious to abandon their livelihoods and begin a study of biomedicine. The deluge they invoke is not one that will lead them back to rationality, but the floods that destroyed their rationality in the first place, that is, the rising seas that submerged Lemuria and the subsequent waves of foreign invasions. They seek to recover their medicine as they imagine it in its predeluvian origins, before the flow of history clouded the scientific essence of their knowledge. Although the tools of modern science and the methods of historiography might verify the rationality of their medicine, they hold that siddha medicine, when fully recuperated, will supersede Western science.

Tamil Language, Siddha Medicine, and the Root of Things

For Maraimalai Adigal, other Tamil revivalist authors, and siddha vaidyas, the genius of the Tamil people and their success in early scientific endeavors was reflected in, and partly due to, the nature of the Tamil language. They argue that as the original language, Tamil was formed in accordance with nature, and therefore is the ideal language for communicating scientific truths. Rama Dharmaniti, in his work on the Kumari Kandam civilization, attributes the loss of rationality of the Tamil people to the loss of their respect for, and knowledge of, pure Tamil language. The Aryans blinded the rational nature of the Tamils with their "magic and illusions," tainted their original purity, and made them indifferent to their language.[96]

> With the change of the times, foreigners entered the Tamil country, attained a high social place, made the Tamils slaves, dug a hole and buried the Tamil language and Tamil civilization. The majority of Tamils, seeing the magic and illusions demonstrated by the foreigners, were mentally corrupted (*putti keṭṭa tamiḻarkaḷ*), and bit by bit they lost the four good qualities and became arrogant like animals. No longer knowing the incomparable greatness of Tamil, Tamils, like beggars grasping onto spit, took an interest in the poison [foreign] language. They regarded Tamil as insignificant, and forgot it, rejected it, despised it.[97]

Dharmaniti holds that it will be the recovery of the Tamil love of their language, and the subsequent restoration of their rationality, that will reunify the Tamil race, reveal to them the greatness of their traditions, and set them on the path to a new, ideal Tamil society.

For siddha vaidyas, this restoration involves the purification of siddha medicine of its foreign elements. K. N. Kuppusami Mudaliyar recounts that as he was collecting books and information for writing his introduction to siddha medicine, every Tamil book he came across had many Sanskrit words. The names of diseases were in Sanskrit, for example, and so the common people would not be able to understand the meaning of these books. He questions the appropriateness of considering the medicine of these books "ancient Tamil medicine," and asks "how is this of use to any Tamil person?" For this reason, Mudaliyar wrote his book rendering the names of all medical words in Tamil, so that all Tamils can understand them. "My goal is that many others will try to compose books with pure Tamil words, without mixing Sanskrit." He criticizes those Tamils who "use many Sanskrit words in their books, in order to show their facility in the northern language. This is disastrous and cause for offence. Those who write books in pure Tamil demonstrate their courage and their patriotism. The excellence of siddha medicine, the relationship between siddha medicine and Shaiva science, and the pride in Tamil Nadu, all of these shine through in this preface."[98] Mudaliyar skillfully avoids using Sanskrit words, except for a few that are indispensable, such as Caiva Cittāntam (Sanskrit: Śaiva Siddhānta), or Ākamam (Sanskrit: Āgama), for example. He gives Tamil derivations for some words with Sanskrit origins, such as medicines called *kāya kaṟpam*, from the Sanskrit *kāya*, body, and *kalpam*, a cosmic length of time, millions of years. In ayurveda, as in siddha, *kāya kalpam* refers to rejuvenative medicines. Mudaliyar derives *kāya* from the Tamil *kāy*, unripe fruit, and takes *kaṟpam* as *kal-pōl*, stonelike. "The word *kāya kaṟpam* is two words, *kāya* + *kaṟpam*. *Kāyam* refers to the mind and body which do not age, remaining young like unripe fruit; *kaṟpam* is the way to make the body [hard] like a stone."[99]

The purification of the Tamil language, and the coining of Tamil words for technical and scientific communication, has been part of the project of Tamil revivalism since the early decades of the twentieth century. Maraimalai Adigal founded the Pure Tamil (*taṉit Tamiḻ*) movement in 1915 to purify Tamil of Sanskrit influence, which was a project to restore it to its ancient glory and full scientific potential.[100] This consisted of expunging words that Tamil shares with Sanskrit, and it also involved the formulation of new, "pure" Tamil words that describe scientific knowledge and technological developments. This was a project that Ramasami's Self-Respect Movement and the Shaiva Siddhantins shared. Sami Chidambaranar advocated that the scope of literature in Tamil, until then dominated by works on religion, be extended to include "modern sciences": biology, economics, chemistry, and so on, a prescription repeated by many others. A. Ponnambalam, a Tamil pundit and Self-Respect member, tried to introduce reform on the legislative level, proposing that Tamil literature be purged of the devotional Tamil puranas, and that temple festival funds be diverted to Tamil schools with a rationalist agenda.[101] With government support and under the leadership of Adigal, the Madras Presidency Tamil Association founded the Committee for Scientific and Technical Terminology, which published a glossary of ten thousand Tamil technical terms.[102] Adigal saw this project in part as the development of a lingua franca for the world, arguing that "unless a common language comes to be spoken and written and cultivated, real unity among people cannot be imagined to come forth." The "new tongues" such as English are of "artificial and external beauties" and are "no match for the ancient Tamil tongue of rare worth and rarer works." Sanskrit, though ancient, is a language of superstition and deception, and Hindi is both superficial in its recent development and spurious due to its descent from Sanskrit.[103] The responsibility for the global spread of Tamil falls to Tamil youth, who have a duty "to give deep thought to the innate worth of Tamil the ancient tongue and do the needful to make its treasures known through the length and breadth of the world of many tongues."[104] As the original language of humanity, the language of nature and the language of human harmony, Tamil is best suited to this globalizing task, but first it must be restored to its original state.[105]

These formulations of pure Tamil tradition are not simply hopeful and appealing visions, but they also impel action, demanding that Tamils work with tradition. The development of Tamil as a language of science and technology has continued to this day. M. Karunanidhi, who has intermittently been chief minister of Tamil Nadu since 1969, has a political lineage that goes back to E. V. Ramasami, and is head of the DMK, the party that descended from Ramasami's DK party. As chief minister in the late 1990s, Karunanidhi was instrumental in providing government support for a conference, TamilNet99, that sought to facilitate the computer (*kaṇippoṟi*, *kaṇiṉi*) utility of Tamil by standardizing a Tamil keyboard and digital coding for the Tamil script. More recently, in order to stop the increasing use of English in Tamil film titles, he has pushed through legislation that give exemption status from an entertainment tax to Tamil films that use only Tamil words in their titles.[106]

The emphasis on the exclusive use of Tamil words emerges in part out of an argument that Tamil is a natural language, not a conventional one. This leads many to attribute certain mystical qualities to the language. An article published in the siddha medical monthly *Mūlikaimaṇi* stresses the transformative effects Tamil has over the natural world. "Only the Tamil language, which appeared many thousands of years ago, has sounds that directly influence the workings of the five elements and the nine planets, and letters that are written representations of those sounds." The five elements, or *pañcapūtaṅkaḷ*, are earth, water, fire, air, and space. Vaidyas generally cite this notion as one of the foundational doctrines of siddha and use it to explain a range of medical practices. The nine "planets" (*navakkirakam*) are planets and other astrological bodies: the sun, the moon, Mars, Mercury, Jupiter, Venus, Saturn, and the mythological *rāku* and *kētu* which are associated with eclipses. Their positions are the basis of astrological considerations, and they are said to have effects on personal destinies and health. The unnamed author of this article asserts that Tamil has the power to manipulate these basic processes of our universe, stressing the importance of giving people Tamil names in order to avoid calamity.[107]

At the incipience of Tamil revivalism and at the time of the founding of the Pure Tamil Movement, P. V. Manickam Naicker wrote a book that sought to prove Tamil's divine origins, concordance with nature, and power to influence the physical world. He describes the "Mystical School" of the origins of Tamil as holding that "the Tamil language was given by God Siva to Agasthia, who, in turn, prescribed it to the South Indians, and that its use was to reach God." Manickam Naicker distinguishes this view from that of the "Rational School," which "would not accept anything without a reason." His purpose in his book is to "discover the *rationale* of the Mystic."[108] He does this by describing an uncanny relationship between the language and nature, first correlating Tamil letters to the five elements, hoping to demonstrate that in discovering the "rationale" of the mystic, "the word mystic loses its mystery and begins to signify that it only engenders more subtle laws of nature than the ordinary ones and consequently more generic in their application." He gives a theological reading of various aspects of Tamil according to Shaiva Siddhanta categories, implying that Tamil was formed by a "master hand." He cites the pervasive "system and order" of the language as proof of its divine origins.[109] He finally rejects the rationalist view that Tamil and its products are artificial, that is, "the products of man," by pointing to similarities between the shapes of the "products of nature or God, if you choose to call so," and the shape of the "anchor" of the most important sound, the mantra *ōm*, which he holds to be wholly Tamil. He presents pictures of cross-sections of the human brain, kidney, spinal cord, and other parts of the human body, all having the shape of the Tamil *ō*, as do the embryos of a number of animals. The numbers of folds in the necks of the embryos, five, is the same as the number of syllables in the Shaiva mantra, *nama civvāya*, or "praise to Shiva."[110]

Maraimalai Adigal too argues that Tamil corresponds to the reality it describes in a physically appropriate, consubstantial way, and makes a strong argument for the Tamil provenance of *ōm*.

> At a time when people were not producing sound, sound was naturally being produced. The first sound was *ōm*. Listen to the ocean, and you will hear *ōm*. Or, try blowing on a conch, and see what sound is audible. . . . Even if one focuses internally, this sound *ōm* is clearly perceptible. From the time when there were no people, there has been a sound in nature, and it has been, naturally, this sound *ōm*. . . . This sound *ōm* is the great possession of Tamil. . . . And Tamil is great because of this sound *ōm*. It was the Tamil people and no other who first discovered the sound *ōm*.[111]

According to Adigal, phonic Tamil is mimetic, developed in imitation of nature, and in this way differs from subsequent languages that are arbitrary and conventional.

He extends this presumed connection between language and nature to considerations of health, recounting a story that attests to the contrary effects of Sanskrit and Tamil.

> In my youth, I would recite the [Sanskrit] Vedas. After reciting, blood would flow from my mouth. I went to many doctors to discover what the reason was for the bleeding. The doctors gave many different answers. For every doctor there was a different answer. I didn't understand it at all. When I'd recite Sanskrit shlokas in the morning, I would become depressed. As soon as I would wake up and recite them, my body would become very weak. After a half an hour, I would recite Tamil songs. Then my sadness would disappear, and I would be happy. One doctor told me to stop reciting the Upanishads and Vedas for fifteen days. I stopped reciting the Upanishads and the Vedas and only sang Tamil. Then the blood stopped! From that time, I decided that Sanskrit is the "blood language." I did some research into the reasons for this difference. Tamil is the language of the great ascetics. Tamil words are constructed in such a way that the strength of our bodies will not dissipate.[112]

Maraimalai Adigal holds that because Tamil is a natural language, it is not antagonistic to the body, and he pathologizes other languages and, by extension, other traditions. He does not speak metaphorically when he proclaims that "Mother Tamil (*Tamiḻttāy*) protects us. Mother Tamil is not seduced by others. Tamil ceaselessly protects us!"[113] He means this literally, that the physical well-being of the Tamils depends on the continuation of their relationship with Tamil. In addition to being the language of science and of social unity, Tamil is also the language of health, a view that is also expressed by siddha vaidyas when they promote the Tamil character of their practices.

In his introduction to a compilation of verses of the ñāṉasiddhars, N. Manikkavasagam rhapsodizes about the sweet Tamil of the siddhars' writings. Their deep meaning reveals the "profound heart of poetry," and their literary excellence allows the reader to enjoy the "thoughts of ancient Tamil" and to relish the "benefits of the sweetness of ordinary Tamil." He compares the siddhars to honey bees, who go out and collect the sweet wisdom of the world for our benefit. Their verses are "honey pots of refined Tamil. It is the nature of honey not only to cure disease but also to bestow ageless youth. It doesn't spoil, and anything made with it will not go bad. The siddhar's verses are just like that. They give the reader joy, benefit, and the sweetness of austere knowledge."[114] S. K. S. Kalimuttu Pillai, a registered practitioner of Indian medicine, asserts that the rational character of siddha medicine derives from the mimetic perfection of the Tamil language. Echoing Adigal's depiction of Tamil as the only natural language, Kalimuttu Pillai claims that Tamil coincides precisely with the natural world and therefore is the best language for science. He continues,

> It is known through research that what is natural to people—the Tamil language and siddha medicine which is Tamil medicine—must have been prevalent throughout the ancient world. The evidence for this is that Tamil is the language which resounds with nature. The best of all animals is the cow. . . . Calves of cows which are abundant in Tamil Nadu today, and calves of cows of foreign countries, think of their mothers and cry only *ammā*! They don't cry "mother" in English which is the language of foreign countries, nor do they cry *mātā* in Hindi, the north Indian language which is now stirring up language controversy. Therefore, that Tamil is the mother tongue that resounds with nature is not just something I say but a fact that everyone can agree with. . . . Because Tamil was the only language that corresponded to original nature at the time of the world's creation, all the people of the world must have taken it as their mother tongue. After that, with changes due to the grip (*vacam*) of time, other languages must have emerged, taking the sounds of eminent Tamil as their basis. I say this with authority based on the conclusions of my research.[115]

The natural language of people is Tamil, and the natural medicine of people is siddha, Kalimuttu Pillai argues, because both emerge from "original nature" (*mutal mutal iyaṟkai*). In this narrative of degeneration from pure origins, Tamil tradition and siddha medicine are universal not only because they are the font of all human civilization but also because they correspond absolutely to nature. V. R. Madhavan holds that the language itself has healing qualities. "Tamil means Amiltam (Ambrosia) and as one takes amiltam it will bring bliss to oneself. Amiltam or Nectar is also a restorative and reviving medicine towards diseases. Logically the language itself is a medicine."[116]

This celebration of the Tamil language led Maraimalai Adigal to exalt Tamil literature and those forms of knowledge that he characterized as traditional. Proponents of siddha medicine have responded to Adigal's call to employ Tamil literature in the revival of tradition, citing early Tamil literature to testify to the antiquity and scientific credentials of siddha medicine. K. Venkatesan, in his *Tamiḻ Ilakkiyattil Citta Maruttuvam* (Siddha medicine in Tamil literature), interprets medical references throughout Tamil literature as details of an emerging yet already coherent siddha medical system, a move that equally posits that all Tamil literary texts compose a unified literary corpus that embodies a single diachronic Tamil community. For example, he cites verse 941 of the *Tirukkuṟaḷ*: "Authors enumerate three constituents: wind, etc. If these are excessive or deficient, disease will occur." "Wind, etc." is apparently a reference to the three humors, which both ayurveda and siddha medicine hold to cause disease when in excess or deficiency. The humors first appear in classical ayurvedic texts that predate siddha medical texts by at least a millennium, but Venkatesan takes this reference as early evidence of siddha medicine.[117] "Wind, etc. in this verse refers to the three constituents of life, wind, bile, and phlegm, which are referred to in siddha medicine. 'Authors' refers to the textual scholars of siddha medicine at that time."[118]

The *Tirukkuṟaḷ* occupies a certain pride of place in the interpolation of siddha medicine into the Tamil revivalist canon, even though it dedicates only one chapter out of 133 to medicine, and even this chapter gives as much space to the perils of overeating as it does to the details of health.[119] Attributed to Tiruvalluvar, the *Tirukkuṟaḷ* is a collection of 1,330 aphorisms written around 450–550 C.E.[120] It has characteristics that make it well suited for projects to formulate a nonreligious Tamil tradition: it contains almost no references to divine beings, being primarily concerned with ethical rather than devotional conduct. The text even appealed to Ramasami, for whom it "is impelled by ideas that are in accordance with practical knowledge, and in tune with Nature and Science. . . . The author of the Kural did not accept God, Heaven and Hell. You could find only virtue, wealth and love in the Kural."[121] There is a rich oral narrative tradition that takes Tiruvalluvar to be of mixed brahman-paraiyar birth, and depicts him spending time on Potigai Mountain studying with Agastya.[122] V. R. Madhavan sees the essence of siddha medicine contained in the text, which "addresses itself without regard to caste, people or beliefs, to the whole community of mankind. It formulates sovereign morality based on reason. . . . The important and fundamental principles of the Siddha system of medicine are embedded in the Tirukkural."[123] N. Manikkavasagam, editor of a collection of verses of the ñāṉasiddhars, includes Tiruvalluvar as one of the ñāṉasiddhars, but distinguishes the siddhar Tiruvalluvar from the author of the Tirukkuṟaḷ.[124] Most vaidyas, however, like R. Kasturi, conflate the author of all texts attributed to Tiruvalluvar and consider him to be a great medical siddhar.[125] In his book on Tiruvalluvar, "Siddhar" P. Murukaiyan discusses the ethical teachings of the *Tirukkuṟaḷ* alongside medical formulations drawn from medical texts attributed to the kāyasiddhar Tiruvalluvar, as "Tiruvalluvar was also a siddhar engaged in medical research."[126] S. Chidambarathanu Pillai gives a summary of the *Tirukkuṟaḷ* chapter on medicine, and calls Tiruvalluvar a "genius of great experience in siddha medicine."[127]

In an article that argues for the healthy character of Tamil culture, K. Venkatesan notes that the titles of three texts of the literary collection *Patiṉeṇkiḻkkaṇakku*, the *Eighteen Shorter Works*, are also the names of medicinal formulae. These eighteen works, which include the *Tirukkuṟaḷ*, were probably composed in the second half of the first millennium.[128] Venkatesan examines works in the collection which have been written "with medical names and medical structures." These works are like other works in "emphasizing moral positions that remove mental disease, but they also, in their didactic structure and titles, take on the names of three types of medicine, *tirikaṭukam*, *ciṟupañcamūlam*, and *ēlāti*, medicines that destroy diseases of the body."[129] Venkatesan holds these works to be both didactic and medical, curing the "internal" ailments of readers. For example, *tirikaṭukam* is a medical combination of dried ginger, black pepper, and long pepper. Just as the combination of these three "transforms physical disease and brings joy," likewise the three moral teachings of the text "destroy ignorance, an internal disease, and give delight." Venkatesan cites these texts as early evidence of the use of siddha medicine. "*Tirikaṭukam*, appearing 1,800 years ago, is still used today in siddha medicine as a complementary medicine. This text demonstrates the antiquity of this medicine and its power to transcend time." Conflating the moral with the medical, and the literary with current medical practice, Venkatesan formulates a versatile tradition that spans thousands of years. He extends the healthy character he ascribes to Tamil literature to all aspects of Tamil tradition, its customary practices, its culture, and its food, in each of which "good health shines."[130]

As Yogi Shuddhananda Bharati exclaims in his foreword to Maraimalai Adigal's polemic against Hindi, if we consider Tamil's "fertility to produce new works in tune with the time spirit, taking into consideration its vitality to measure the heights of Scientific technology, we can very well maintain the invincible capacity of Tamil to develop into a universal language."[131] Most siddha vaidyas would agree with this assessment, emphasizing the universal potential of their medicine. Venkatesan considers siddha medicine, as it is formulated in the *Tirukkuṟaḷ*, to be based on a "universal medical theory," its doctrine leading the way "for doctors everywhere in the world." He cites *Tirukkuṟaḷ* 948: "One should inquire into the nature of the disease, its cause, and the way to cure it, and then do what is appropriate." He holds that the spirit of this *kuṟaḷ* expresses the ideal of all doctors, an ideal that would be an appropriate motto for any "global association of doctors" that might be formed.[132] Vaidyas would happily extend Adigal's description of Tamil to siddha medicine: "Tamil will never be destroyed. Those who seek to destroy Tamil will themselves be destroyed. Tamil was born and developed rooted in nature. No one can destroy nature. Therefore, no one can destroy Tamil."[133]

Recovering a Natural Medicine for the World

Vaidyas speak of the local character of their medicine to emphasize its enduring presence in Tamil tradition and in the Tamil land, despite non-Tamil cultural influence and political rule. In promoting siddha, they play on a consistent tension between the local character of their medicine and its universal aspirations. They resolve this tension through appeals to history and nature, invoking the Lemurian narrative in asserting that siddha medicine is the original medical science of humanity, and depicting their medicine as essentially natural. They use "nature" (*iyaṟkai*) in conjunction with siddha medicine in at least two ways. The first describes siddha as adhering to nature, where nature carries the sense of the "nature of things," with which siddha medicine, like the Tamil language, is in perfect accordance. The second speaks of siddha as "natural medicine," employing natural products that are local and available, not requiring the complex processes of fabrication of biomedicines. As I have already discussed the former, here I will focus on depiction of siddha medicine as a natural medicine.

Kundrathur Ramamurthy spoke at length to me about the natural character of siddha medical products. He advocates the use of medicines formulated from plants rather than metals or minerals. He was first drawn to siddha medicine by the use of local plants to cure illnesses, when he was in the ninth standard at school in the early 1950s. He told me of his introduction to siddha medicine by his neighbor, a vaidya.

> He made all medicines and cured diseases. They were simple remedies. I was amazed. . . . When he was making medicines he had me help him. I was amazed—it was very useful. He had me pulverize greens and plants. The two of us did research on plants. Plant flowers. Small plants captivate me very much. Gloriosa superba, a small plant, you can take it and mix it with gingelly oil. It will cure migraine headaches. It cured someone who had migraines for 10–15 years. I was very amazed. I was completely captivated. After that I did teacher training. They put me in many different schools. In all the places where I was placed, I asked local tribal people about plants. They don't give away their knowledge easily. However, because of the respect I got from being a teacher, they told me. I learned very much. In the teachers' associations . . . I spoke of the uses of all the plants. Finally that itself became my full-time work. Many people began to seek me out, and I began to prepare and give medicines. I who was a teacher became a vaidya.

Kundrathur Ramamurthy was captivated by the local nature of siddha medicine and its accessibility to everyone. He sees the world around him as filled with ingredients for medicines: "One can prepare medicines from all ingredients used in our siddha. Soil, rocks, leaves, sprouts, nine metals, nine minerals, everything is medicine. Even hair is medicine. . . . After eating eggs, even the egg shell is medicine. There is calcium. Crab is medicine. Even water in the crab's shell is medicine. That is a special medicine. Anything can be medicine." Unlike many vaidyas, who emphasize alchemy as the distinguishing feature of siddha medicine, Kundrathur Ramamurthy does not use metals and minerals in his medicine, as this undermines the simplicity that should define medicine, and it also results in medicines that are beyond the budgets of ordinary people.

> Preparing medicine with metal and mercury is difficult. One needs a lot of practice. It's costly. A patient is bitten [by a snake]. One needs to give costly medicine. For the patient this is difficult. Only those with means can afford to take it. This is a problem. If one doesn't prepare medicine well, side effects will occur. The kidney and liver will be ruined. That's why I decided to use only plant medicines. From the time I was young I have only had belief in plant medicines. Preparation is easy. And the medicines are good. They are effective immediately. Cheap and best. Medicine should be available for everyone. And everyone should be able to afford it. I don't believe that only those with money, buying gold powder and eating it, should be healthy.

Among Kundrathur Ramamurthy's publications are two books that are practical guides to the use of local ingredients for health. One, *Uṭal Nalam Uṅkaḷ Kaikaḷil* (Bodily health is in your hands), gives local ingredients and their medicinal properties.[134] His first book, *Mūlikai Pēcukiṟatu* (Speaking about medicinal plants) won an award from the Tamil Nadu government. He begins with a plea to Tamils to use herbal medicine, "our country's medicine." "Grass, bulbous roots, plant, and creepers, these grow with us, around us and for us. They are appropriate to our country's climate and our bodily physiques. We should know their usefulness in curing disease. This herbal medicine has no side effects, is simple, and can give extended benefits."[135] He narrates a history in which herbal medicine was the medicine of Lemuria, which the siddhars later codified in their texts. For Ramamurthy, this medicine is not ordinary medicine but has fantastic potential. The medicine itself has obtained the siddhis, the yogic powers of the siddhars. Yet it is available to everyone. After its formulation by the siddhars, its early employment and reputation spread "in the hands of women of every household. Plants which grow around our homes are just like people who live around us, who play a role in our well-being and misfortune. Our mothers took these plants and used them to satisfy our daily needs, and also to cure simple physical ailments."[136] Ramamurthy goes on to detail the construction of planters one can build at home, the plants one can grow in these, and the medical uses and health benefits of these plants.

Biomedicine and its formulations seem increasingly incomprehensible and artificial to many Tamils, who complain of its expense and "side effects."[137] An article by K. Venkatesan warns of the dangers of allopathic medicines, which he holds responsible for "side effects" throughout the world, including ulcers, heart palpitations, joint pain, and sometimes even sudden death. He compares these to "natural, herbal medicines that are of high standard, without side effects, and inexpensive," and that are effective in treating cancer, ulcers, asthma, and heart disease.[138] He holds that herbal medicine does not accept the explanations of modern science, and a few medical plants give "amazing" relief. Tamil "ancestors" discovered the uses of many medical plants through practical experience, and the "truths" of that experience is of "many times the power of the basics of science." Venkatesan describes himself as having learned, and been astonished by, "2,000 years of history of herbal medicines," and as having been engaged in "service" to herbal medicine for the last forty years. He sums up his estimation of this natural medicine and its eternal usefulness with an aphorism: "Yesterday, today, and always, herbal medicine nourishes life."[139]

Given the distrust of the products of biomedicine and their expense, the possibility of a medical approach that uses local ingredients has much appeal. Tamil bookstores today offer a variety of books that describe ways that nonspecialists can take their health into their own hands. One finds, for example, *Cittar Kaṇṭa Mūlikai Maruttuvam* (The herbal medicine of the siddhars). Its author, P. C. Manian, wrote a daily column in a regional newspaper from 1980 to 1982 called "Easy Home Medicines of the Siddhars." The present book offers a number of essays on home remedies, so that its readers "can cure their diseases themselves with simple cures, without spending money on doctors. These effective remedies have been followed for ages in the custom of the siddhars. These medicines have no side effects for the body and present no risks, and the medical ingredients described in these essays are easily available."[140] Singaravelu Vaittiyar is the author of *Ārōkkiyam Tarum Cittarkaḷiṉ Kīraikaḷ, Mūlikaikaḷ* (The siddhars' greens and medicinal plants that bestow health). He describes the health benefits of thirty-seven green leafy vegetables, of thirty-six leaves of plants, and of the leaves of twenty-four types of vines. For Vaittiyar, this knowledge of herbal medicine is ancient, hearkening back to a time when "country medicine" (*nāṭṭu vaittiyam*) cured diseases naturally, with "tubers, roots, leaves, etc." This was at the beginning of human history, when "many diseases of unknown name began to spread and increase." The siddhars discovered the uses of many leafy plants, and "took their awls and wrote on palm leaves, with great poetic skill, the specific effects of particular leaves, and which are to be avoided."[141] With his book, Vaittiyar follows in the path of the siddhars, spreading this simple, natural knowledge for the benefit of the people.

The Chengalpattu Siddha Medical Association published a short piece on the vine called *piraṇṭai* or *vacciravalli* (*vitis quadrangularis*), which grows in southern and eastern Africa, Arabia, and India. It is "one of the medical plants that can be commonly seen in all forested and mountainous areas in Tamil Nadu."[142] The association goes on to describe different types of this vine, and the different qualities of the plant's stem, leaves, flowers, and so on. This is a "wondrous medical plant that cures diseases from the mouth to the anus (mouth, esophagus, stomach, small intestine, large intestine, and anus). The women of our country, through the course of their experience, make *piranṭai* relish. This relish cures indigestion and stimulates hunger." The juice of the plant is also used as an unguent for broken bones to reduce swelling and pain. It can also be processed into a salt, and in calcinated form it can cure asthma, fatigue, diabetes, and other ailments.[143]

The juxtaposition of local ingredients, medical knowledge, and Tamil culture is perhaps best exemplified in the notion that Tamil food itself is medicine. Kundrathur Ramamurthy speaks of Tamil cuisine as the most rudimentary medicine. "This siddha medicine began as home remedy. Rasam, tamarind, salt, pepper, siddha began by using things like this that are around the home." In an introductory note to *Cittarkaḷ Kaṇṭa Uṇavu Maruttuvam* (The food-medicine of the siddhars) by Nelvay Sanguppulavar, N. C. Teyvasigamani writes that Sanguppulavar wrote this book with the goal that "you will get rid of disease and achieve health with food items that you use daily. We implore Tamils to buy this, read it, and obtain its benefits." Sanguppulavar gives a range of Tamil foods and their beneficial qualities, but warns about some non-Tamil foods like apples, which are "grown abundantly in Kashmir," which have a "severe character" and which "create phlegm and increase lust."[144] A publication of the Directorate of Indian Medicine and Homoeopathy asserts that for Indian systems of medicine, "medicine is not a separate entity. It is part and parcel of our daily diet and our hygienic principles start from our daily ablutions, community ceremonies, etc. So Indian Medicine starts from our Kitchen." The pamphlet goes on to give daily food ingredients used for medicinal purposes, and rationalizes "community ceremonies" as having their origins in procedures of hygiene and health.[145]

Vaidyas often highlight the natural character of siddha medicine to distinguish it from Western civilization and biomedicine. Thus S. Chidambarathanu Pillai, founder of the Siddha Medical Literature Research Centre, attributes today's physical ailments to the modern world in which humans indulge their materialist tendencies: "The simple life is excellent for the health of the body and the tranquillity of the mind. People who submit to the modern life have no piece of mind, and suffer from diseases like high blood pressure and cancer. As civilization advances, the body becomes emaciated and the opportunity for liberation of the soul decrease. . . . The siddhars maligned this approach to life and saw success in the simple life. They purified the body with natural living, and took a keen interest in spirituality."[146] For Chidambarathanu Pillai, it is the disenfranchised of this modern world who are most suited to learn siddha medicine, in particular women and the world's poor. His Siddha Medical Literature Research Centre teaches siddha medicine "in a systematic way to people throughout the world who lack opportunities and conveniences, to each woman who shines as the virtuous lantern of the family, so that 'granny medicine' (*pāṭṭi vaittiyam*) and women's medicine, forgotten by the mothers of the Tamil land, will thrive again."[147]

Chidambarathanu Pillai links siddha medicine as natural medicine with siddha medicine as in accordance with the nature of things. That is, because siddha medicine grew in nature and is accessed through nature that surrounds us, the siddhars enumerate abstract principles in accordance with nature. "The siddhars' prescriptions and medicines are sweet nectar that have grown in nature. . . . Siddha medicine was created in harmony with nature. The siddhars erected this medicine on the basis of the three doshas, wind, bile, and phlegm. . . . They categorized the physical matter of the world according to the five elements, and enumerated their qualities. . . . They classified diseases and assembled remedies for those."[148] G. J. Parthasarathy also spoke of the doctrine of the five elements as highlighting that siddha knowledge is attuned to the workings of nature. "The basic science in this world, that is, the theory of the five elements—space, earth, water, fire, and air—siddha medicine works on these subtle principles."

Parthasarathy's mention above of the five elements was only part of his answer to my question, "What is the unique value of siddha medicine?" His response began by stressing the antiquity of Tamil and of siddha medicine, both of which appeared at the "beginning stages" of the world. Siddha adheres to "the basic principles of things," as evidenced by their development of scientific theories like the five elements. It contains a diversity of medicines, including those that can be formulated without machinery by people of any means. Parthasarathy highlights the accessibility of siddha medicine and its use of local resources with a hypothetical scenario.

> I'm a siddha vaidya. [Suppose that] suddenly a world war comes, they set off an atomic bomb and attack all places. You come to a medical shop, looking for medicine. There's no medicine to buy. What will an allopathic doctor do? No matter where you take me, in that place I'll make medicines. Whatever is available there, I'll take it and make medicine. From the soil, I'll use the worms that are in the soil, whatever insects are there, I'll take them and make medicine. I can make medicine from any plant there. That which can make any medicine, from any environment on any land, that is siddha. . . . It all comes from nature. It's completely natural.

It is this ability to improvise with local resources that sets siddha medicine apart from other medical systems. This is, for Parthasarathy and other vaidyas, the basis of medicine, the state of medicine at its origins before the sophisticated artifices of modern civilization, a time when human society existed in harmony with nature, indeed, before there were divisions between human society and nature.

If civilization suddenly were to revert back to this primordial state, through the destructiveness of Western science, which Sami Chidambaranar warned us of decades before, and which today has its quintessential embodiment in the atomic bomb, it will be siddha medicine which will set humanity back on the road to health. The artificial advances of biomedicine are precarious, while siddha medicine, the natural and basic medicine, is as eternal as the immortality it sometimes promises.

A Global Medicine for the Modern World

Vaidyas conceive the qualities they ascribe to siddha medicine—egalitarianism, science, rational spiritualism, adherence to nature, and natural character—as forming a logical and coherent whole. All are qualities that Tamil revivalism ascribes to the beginnings of the world, and that it holds to be the defining principles of a prosperous and virtuous civilization.[149] And all these qualities describe the Tamil people, which, like siddha medicine, emerged at the origins of the world, a time when siddha medicine was at its most effective because it most closely reflected the essence of the Tamil people. Vaidyas invoke this autochthonous concordance of qualities between nature, medicine, and the Tamil people not only to assert a contiguous, organic relationship between Tamils and siddha medicine but also to assert a *right* over this medicine, and a duty of Tamil people to patronize it. Addressing a medical landscape in which Tamils have a variety of options, R. Kasturi argues, "Siddha medicine is ours. Just as the Tamil language, the culture of the Tamil people, and the Tamil land (*tamil̲akam*) are ours, in the same way the techniques of siddha medicine are ours. The art of siddha medicine is an enduring treasure which was discovered and passed on by our ancestors. Its excellence suits the Tamil race. Siddha medicine is the method of our country."[150] Kasturi uses an essentialist argument to claim that siddha medicine is particularly suited to the culture, language, and racial constitution of the Tamil people. He considers it to be a cultural possession, distinguished from other medical systems currently practiced in Tamil Nadu because of its status as the original medical system of the land and people. The Lemurian narrative and the qualitative conjunction of the Tamil people and siddha medicine thereby provides vaidyas with a powerful justification to assert an exclusive right to practice in Tamil Nadu and on Tamil bodies.

The relativistic logic of these assertions of the appropriateness of a medicine to a people would appear to compel vaidyas to recognize all medical systems as equal, and to acknowledge that there can be no universal medicine. If siddha medicine is the most effective medicine for Tamil bodies, the same should be the case for ayurveda on Aryan, brahman bodies, and biomedicine for Europeans. However, Tamil vaidyas often juxtapose their claims to relative uniqueness with aspirations for medical imperialism. While utilizing the buffer of relativity offered by the autonomy of tradition, they assert that the very cultural and historical specificity of their practice affirms that its universal potential is greater than that of other medical systems.

In its most basic formulation, the essences that non-brahman Tamil leaders assign to various salient communities in south India have been as follows: Tamils are rational, Aryans deceitful, the British materialistic, and Muslims carnivorous. Vaidyas read these characteristics into medical practice. R. Kasturi speaks of the relative effectiveness of various medical systems in their treatment of damaged organs. Biomedical doctors do transplants, or use artificial organs, corresponding to the propensity of the West to discard prior traditions in favor of new innovations. These British doctors focus only on material realities, believing that if the damaged material is replaced by new material, health will be restored. Kasturi also aligns ayurveda with the illusion and superstition that Tamil revivalism ascribes to the Aryan character. The ayurvedic doctor applies medicine that misleadingly appears to effect a cure, that only affect the "outer appearance of organs" while the organs remain damaged. "According to ayurveda, the reasons for the occurrence of disease are god's will, fate, the anger of the gods, or sins committed in past lives." Unani practitioners give medicine made from animal organs, reflecting a common stereotype of Muslims as carnivores due to their consumption of beef. "Therefore, these other medical systems do not give the final, true causes of disease. The causes given in siddha medicine are in accordance with reason." Unlike these other medical systems, siddha medicine effects permanent relief because it values durability and continuity, salvaging old things, whether traditions or organs, rather than discarding them. "Once a patient is cured according to the Siddha medical system, that disease will never return. Siddha medicine cuts disease at its root."[151]

This perception that siddha medicine is the only medicine to address the basic cause of disease is common among vaidyas. G. J. Parthasarathy spoke to me about this. "If you ask what the basic difference is between this [siddha] medicine and other medicines, we challenge, can others cure disease permanently like our medicine can? We can cure a disease permanently. Should one take temporary medicines for one's entire life? It's the firm doctrine in siddha that one should not." Siddha medicine cuts disease at its root is because it is the root of all medicines. L. Krishnamurthy, in language similar to Kasturi's, asserts that siddha medicine has certain features that make it both unique and highly effective. Of the medicines currently practiced in the world, "English medicine (allopathy) and German medicine (homeopathy) are the most influential and are used by common people. But do these medicines cut at the root all diseases that appear in the body? Do they destroy suffering and give happiness? If one ponders this, it is clear that they do not." Because allopathy and homeopathy have not been successful at curing diabetes, tuberculosis, and other chronic illnesses, Krishnamurthy asks: "have those medical systems understood basic, essential medical details, such as the natural classifications of the structure of the human body, the details of that structure, and the natural bases of those classifications? Without a doubt we can see they have not." He adds ayurveda and unani to his list of medical systems that do not clearly understand "the nature of disease, the reasons for the onset of disease, the medicines that can remove disease, the supplements that make medicine effective, and the time to give medicines. . . . Is there not a single medical system that can cure all diseases fully?"[152]

Krishnamurthy answers his question in the affirmative: that medical system coming "from our Tamil Nadu," the medical system that is the "mother" (*tāy*) of ayurveda and unani, that is, "siddha medicine," or "Tamil medicine." He claims that siddha medicine is at least 5,000 years old, and that siddha vaidyas have intuition into the human condition that practitioners of other systems lack. Tamil medical practices attend to more than the physical body of the patient, taking into the account the heart (*uḷḷam*) and soul (*uyir*). Thus siddha vaidyas can cure all ailments. Today's Western experts do not know how to stop disease because they do not attend to the heart and soul.[153] *Uḷḷam* literally means that which is internal, and more specifically refers to both heart and mind. *Uyir* is most simply "life," but in its more active sense it is that which animates things, the "life breath" of living beings. Because Western doctors do not consider *uḷḷam* and *uyir* to be important, they are inadequate in their understanding of nature. Western science sees the world as dead matter, and so it is itself lifeless, all brain and no heart.

The characteristics siddha vaidyas ascribe to their medicine are suited for a global medicine of the modern world. Contrary to the nationalist promotion of ayurveda as the medical system of India, and to the conviction of biomedical doctors that their medicine is the global medicine of the present and the future, siddha vaidyas argue for the universality of siddha medicine. In 1984, V. R. Madhavan wrote that the "Siddhars were Dravidian in their origin and they were the greatest intellectuals of ancient time. The science of medicine expounded by them, namely, 'Siddha system of medicine,' comprehends the entire system of Indian Medicine."[154] More than sixty years earlier, Virudal Sivagnanayogigal, writing from rural Koilpatti in 1923, juxtaposed the uniqueness of siddha medicine with claims to its universality: "According to Tamil medical texts, there are 112 mineral substances, 9 metals, 25 types of salt, 64 types of mineral poisons . . . and thousands of other medicines. These are not suited for the Sanskrit, Unani, or English medical systems, only for Tamil medicine. Therefore, there is no need for Tamil doctors to learn Western medicines. But if Western doctors learn and use siddha medicines, the differences between the two will disappear, I think."[155] Sivagnanayogigal prescribes the absorption of all medicines currently practiced in India into siddha, with siddha serving as the root of these because it is the root of all the world's medical practices. The cultural specificity of Tamil tradition has served both as an autonomous realm over which vaidyas assert control, and at the same time it has become the basis of their global aspirations.

Besides the local/global dichotomy, a further tension siddha vaidyas address is that between their narratives of medical decay and their assertions of the contemporary relevance of their medicine. They do this by positing an ideal, interior traditional space in which pure Tamil medicine bides its time, waiting for revival. Just as the true identity of the Tamil people has been obscured by history yet remains at the core of each Tamil person, the knowledge of siddha medicine is only submerged, not destroyed. B. Anandaraman, a registered Indian medical practitioner, writes, "The eminent siddha medical art has continued for ages in the Tamil land, passed from guru to student in the proper manner. Even though the conclusions set out in medical texts have been clouded by history, by the cruelty of foreign governments, by ignorance, and by poverty, the life breath of siddha medicine lives on even today among the Tamil people. Thus it is clear that siddha medicine has divine features and stable theories."[156] Tamil medicine, like the pure Tamil society of Lemuria, can be purified and revived. Like the utopian homeland of Lemuria, the enduring character of siddha medicine has been inundated by history yet remains unchanged. This submerged essence of tradition is both behind history and beyond history, its ancientness, its present relevance, and its future potential testifying to its timeless.

With their articulation of the essential qualities of siddha medicine, and their conviction that these qualities are timeless, vaidyas provide specific blueprints for the recovery of the extraordinary potential of their medicine. They propose that Tamils return to conformity of character and absolute allegiance to Tamil traditions that gave the Tamil land its ancient utopian character. The recovery of medical utopia therefore requires the participation of all Tamils, beginning with local and national governments. Although it was foreign invasion that set back Tamil medicine, most vaidyas hold that it is current governments, infatuated with Western medicine or favoring ayurveda, who betray it at present. G. J. Parthasarathy spoke in harsh terms about the Indian government: "The central government has not given sufficient support to siddha medicine. This is a travesty. They need to do more. Siddha is not inferior in any way to other medical systems. When support is given, many benefits can be extended to the people. All people throughout the world can use it. Many good medicines can be given to all people. In America allopathic medicines can be relegated to the margins, to the degree that Americans take siddha medicines." This recovery of identity will not only benefit Tamils, then, as the extraordinary effectiveness of this original medicine can be enjoyed by all of the world's people. Yet again, its benefits entail responsibility and are only manifested through participation, and so the global aspirations can only be realized when all the world's people support siddha medical practices. G. Srinivasamurthi, one of the forces behind the founding of the Government School of Indian Medicine in Madras in 1925 and its first principal, gives voice to the hopes of many siddha practitioners.

> The recent excavations in the North West India had shown that learning and culture had, in very ancient times, gone from South India to many parts of the world, and a day will soon come when through translations from the original difficult Tamil, people all over the world could understand the wonderful Siddha literature which is still mostly a closed book. Then the value of the Baspams and Chendoorams and other preparations would come to be realized. In my vision of the future, I have the picture of students from all over the civilised world coming here, to South India, to learn what only this land could teach.[157]

Such a universalization of Tamil knowledge does not make this knowledge less Tamil in character. Vaidyas conceive the spread of siddha medical knowledge as part of a process of making the world and its people Tamil. When I would tell people about my research, they would often say I must have been Tamil in a prior birth. My interest in siddha medicine marked me as Tamil. Siddha medical knowledge is not only thoroughly ethnic, then, but obtaining it is a process of ethicizing the possessor of knowledge: siddha medical knowledge transforms its keepers into Tamils.

Conclusion

Defenders of Tamil culture argue that their tradition embodies the ancient, the rational, the natural, and, most important, the self. The congruence between the content of siddha medicine, as it has been formulated in the past century, and non-brahman articulations of Tamil community has developed through the historical interweaving of diverse discourses. Siddha vaidyas have actively aligned the content of their tradition with broader notions of Tamil identity so that the conjunction of their medicine with prevalent conceptualizations of Tamil identity appears natural. When siddha healers situate their practice within a narrative of Tamil identity, they contribute to that narrative, and that narrative in turn frames and shapes the nature of their practice. By this active mirroring of traditional knowledge and community identity, they suggest an essential and eternal link between the Tamil community and particular medical practices. This is, however, a historical process—traditional actors consistently transform the constituents and qualities of their tradition, as they do community identities.[158] These formulations of tradition are myths in the sense offered by Roland Barthes, transforming history into nature and the particular into the eternal.[159]

One can, however, overstate the degree to which traditions can be invented. Ramasami, after all, failed in his ambition to create an entirely new tradition that Tamils would accept as their own. At the same time that a historical argument compels us to recognize the innovations and transformations of tradition, it also requires that we acknowledge the continuities of tradition through generations. The formulation of the content of tradition is a reciprocal process, in which actors assign particular qualities to their tradition, but also, insofar as that tradition transcends the individual in history and community, these actors are themselves shaped by tradition. One of the reasons that siddha vaidyas have been successful in promoting their practices is that they have highlighted their continuity with prior Tamil community, and at the same time they have argued that this past community was entirely modern. As indicated in contemporary siddha medical advertisements, vaidyas insist on the longevity of their knowledge and practices, typifying these in ways that have resonated with Tamil notions of health and healing that have been prevalent in south India for centuries. They simultaneously contemporize these long-standing practices, describing the features of their medicine in ways that are consistent with signs of authority in the modern world.

It would be easy to conclude that these formulations of tradition are ideologies in the Marxist sense, that is, sophisticated discourses that mask underlying material interests. The most obvious of these interests would be the economic and social fortunes of the elite non-brahman castes, who have been leaders in both the non-brahman movement and in the practice and promotion of siddha medicine. Although these articulations of Tamil character are certainly in part motivated by material concerns, they are not just the means to material ends, but they are also ends in themselves. That is, celebrations of tradition are themselves interests, providing a social vision that people enjoy narrating, constructing, enacting, and if necessary, defending. The success of siddha vaidyas depends on the appeal of their formulations of tradition and identity to broader Tamil and increasingly global audiences. Their celebrations of tradition thereby speak to the desires of their patrons, eulogizing the Tamil community and individuals within that community. Ramasami recognized the importance of this celebration of self when he named his campaign the "Self-Respect Movement," aiming to encourage the self-respect of each Tamil individual and the Tamil community as a whole.

While articulations of tradition provide legitimating narratives for particular groups to pursue material interests, and, as I have argued, they are interests in themselves, these visions of tradition also shape the very material interests that many would argue are the underlying motivation of ideology. The imaginative formulations of siddha medicine dictate, to some degree, the goals that siddha vaidyas seek to accomplish. These are fantasies in the sense indicated by Zizek, who holds that fantasy "does not simply realize a desire in a hallucinatory way: rather, its function is similar to that of Kantian 'transcendental schematism': a fantasy constitutes our desire, provides its coordinates; that is, it literally 'teaches us how to desire.' . . . Fantasy does not mean that when I desire a strawberry cake and cannot get it in reality, I fantasize about eating it; the problem is, rather: *how do I know that I desire a strawberry cake in the first place? This* is what fantasy tells me."[160] Narratives of community not only function in a manner analogous to fantasy but they also contain elements of fantasy that shape desire. In narrating their visions of Tamil social and medical utopias, siddha vaidyas invite individual Tamils to participate in a social fantasy, a fantasy that itself constructs desire and, quite often, compels action. Their visions have a didactic component, meant to teach Tamils who they are, how they should imagine their social situation, and how they might rectify social and historical injustices suffered by the Tamil people. They provide maps through which Tamils experience society and the world, and they encourage social change, foster social stability, and create enmity between communities. Siddha vaidyas reject the notion that the only authority is a science of medicine or a national Sanskritic tradition that others possess, and instead assert that their tradition encompasses Western science, Indian civilization, and more. Siddha medicine is not only scientific but just as important, it is *theirs,* and it testifies to the glory of the Tamil community. As Dr. Circapai holds, "If siddha medicine flourishes, the Tamil land can be proud. The Tamil people will live sweetly."[161]

6

Secrecy, Hereditary Education, and the Immortality of Siddha Medicine

In promoting their medicine, siddha practitioners evoke the extraordinary healing potential of their knowledge. Many claim to have discovered cures for cancer and AIDS, and some even suggest that their formulas might bestow bodily immortality.[1] Given the blatant gap between these ambitious claims and the lack of evidence for them, what makes these assertions of extraordinary healing potential appear possible, or even reasonable? What features of siddha medical knowledge do vaidyas employ to lend credibility to claims that their medicine might indeed cure all ailments? As I have argued earlier, one of the ways that vaidyas have imbued their knowledge with the aura of the extraordinary has been by assigning it a perfect essence in a time and place beyond historical data. In so doing, they have colored their medicine with certain romantic attributes such as timelessness, perfect correspondence to nature, and profound effectiveness. Another way that siddha practitioners have positioned their knowledge beyond the ordinary is by describing their knowledge as obscured, either actively concealed by vaidyas protecting their unique techniques, or transmitted in coded language by the siddhars who wished to maintain their preeminence over ordinary people.

The Authority of Obscurity

By circumscribing their knowledge within a unique and bounded realm of tradition, siddha vaidyas seek to shield their medicine from the scrutiny of others. Perhaps in no way is the withdrawal from the penetrating, critical gaze of others more explicitly effected than in the obfuscation of siddha medical knowledge. Such obfuscation entails both active dissimulation, usually in the name of loyalty to the hereditary lineage, and also the unanimous acknowledgment of siddha practitioners that their knowledge is so esoteric that even they do not know all of its secrets. They highlight the obscurity of their knowledge in part to differentiate a community of knowers from others who are ignorant of their secrets. Because secrecy assumes a bounded social group within which a secret is held in common, a secret is the exclusive possession of an individual or group. Georg Simmel points to the power of secrecy in encouraging social differentiation: "The strongly emphasized exclusion of all outsiders makes for a correspondingly strong feeling of possession. For many individuals, property does not fully gain its significance with mere ownership, but only with the consciousness that others must do without it. The basis for this, evidently, is the impressionability of our feelings through *differences*."[2] This notion that specific forms of knowledge can be possessed by a particular group is one of the premises of tradition. When vaidyas withhold the medical formulae of their hereditary lineage from those outside that lineage, they draw a line between the lineage and the rest of the world, which includes, first and foremost, their medical competitors, both other siddha practitioners and doctors of other medical systems. The secrets of the paramparai, the lineage, therefore highlight the competition between medical practitioners in south India.

Simmel goes on to observe that because what is of value is jealously guarded, the converse also appears to be true, that is, that what is exclusively possessed must therefore be valuable.[3] This is certainly the case for siddha medical knowledge, which vaidyas celebrate as the unique possession of the Tamil people, and to which they further attribute extraordinary efficacy. Insofar as the possession of secret knowledge excludes others, it is a marker of social differentiation, and at the same time it unites an internal, coherent community. It also serves as a basis for hierarchy, as insiders claim a prestige that they deny to those outside their group.[4] It is important to note that the value of such exclusive knowledge is determined not only by the community that holds it. If outsiders are indifferent to, or deride, a group's knowledge, then this knowledge will have little value outside the group, which may affect its value within the particular community. In an increasingly global medical market, the value of particular medicines derives in part from their demand beyond the boundaries of regional communities.[5] Siddha vaidyas have worked to expand their community of knowledge to encompass the entire Tamil non-brahman community, and they seek to further extend its influence globally, lamenting that their medicine has not achieved worldwide recognition. Part of their goal, then, is to proclaim their obscure knowledge to the world, revealing some of the tensions inherent in the promotion of siddha medical knowledge as both an exclusive possession of the Tamil community and universal in its healing potential. They engage in what Hugh Urban calls the "advertising" of secrecy, the "dialectic of lure and withdrawal," in order to entice outsiders to desire the knowledge that is unavailable to them.[6]

Simmel remarks that "inner property of the most heterogeneous kinds, thus, attains a characteristic value accent through the form of secrecy, in which the contentual significance of what is concealed recedes, often enough, before the simple fact that others know nothing about it."[7] Here I follow Simmel, and Hugh Urban in his treatment of secrecy in the Kartābhajā sect of Bengali tantrism, in focusing not on the specific content of obscured knowledge but rather on "the forms and the strategies through which secret information is concealed, revealed and exchanged."[8] Such a focus reflects the discourses that vaidyas employ in their ambitious pursuit of regional, national, and global authority. When they argue for their relevance in the modern world, vaidyas emphasize the grand narratives of their medicine, its essential characteristics, and other attributes that transcend the details of medical practice. Furthermore, as we will see, they relate a history of secrecy that has been so successful that even they have forgotten the most secret and valuable medical formulae, thereby positioning a portion of their knowledge not only beyond the critical gaze of others but even beyond their own present understanding. What is known, they lament, is only a dim shadow of the glory that siddha medicine once enjoyed and that might be reestablished in the future, a view that often leads them to pay less regard to the tangible content of current medical practice.

The Hereditary Transmission of Medical Knowledge

Prior to the nineteenth century, medical knowledge in India was generally transmitted in paramparais. From the time that Indian medicine began to be taught in the Native Medical Institution in 1826, numerous schools, colleges, and universities of traditional medicine have been founded in various configurations throughout India.[9] Although this mode of education currently carries the most authority in the eyes of the Indian government, and although public medical institutions will only employ registered medical practitioners, many people continue to pursue medical education in hereditary contexts and engage in private practice. There have been many attempts to regulate these hereditary practitioners by setting up certificate courses and examinations, and by requiring official registration, but thousands of vaidyas continue to practice without state authorization.[10]

For centuries in south India, medical knowledge and practices have been shared within paramparais that trace their origins to a founding siddhar such as Agastiyar, Bhogar, or any of the other medical siddhars. Vaidyas consider the knowledge of each paramparai to have been "seen" by the siddhar whom they consider the first guru of the lineage, either through intuitive vision granted by Shakti or another deity, or through their own researches into the properties of nature.[11] The siddhars "merged with Virgin Nature to fathom her depths and span her expanse. At long last when they emerged with new light on their quests, people adored them as Siddhas—the accomplished ones. Their crystallized thoughts transcended time and spoke across centuries during which scores of disciples endeavored to unravel their mystic and cryptic utterances."[12] The authority of individual vaidyas is in part derived from the prestige of their paramparai, which is itself founded on that of the siddhars. Insofar as the individual paramparai has defined the boundaries within which medical knowledge is transmitted, this knowledge is generally considered to be uniquely possessed and exclusively employed by those within the paramparai. Thus, the medical landscape of Tamil medicine has always been characterized by a variety of practices and medical options.

Across this diversity of medical practices and formulae, however, the basic forms of medical knowledge overlap considerably across lineages. As Gananath Obeyesekere argues, medicine is "part of the public domain and, however esoteric the medical theory, physician, patient, and community are linked together in an intersubjective network defining the nature of the symptoms as well as types of medicine and their relative efficacy."[13] Medicine and healing are implicated in culture, and so there is much correspondence in the general features of traditional south Asian medical practice. Tamil premodern medical texts, attributed to different siddhars and representing the knowledge of different paramparais, detail similar methods of diagnosis (such as pulse reading, examination of feces, urine, and mucus) and similar views of the body (such as having 72,000 *nāṭi* ["veins"], three humors, etc.). This overlap in the forms of medical practice indicates that even though lineages have touted the uniqueness of their knowledge, the boundaries between them have been porous enough to allow the exchange of ideas.

Although the form of Tamil medical knowledge is shared widely, the *details* of medical formulae vary significantly from practitioner to practitioner. Thus the contemporary view that there has always been a coherent system of siddha medicine composed of cooperating paramparais is an anachronism. The exclusive teaching of knowledge of particular medicines was sustained and controlled by direct transmission from a guru to a student.

> The siddha system of medicine in the beginning was taught by "Guru-Sishya" method only. Here, it is important to note that, the Siddha system of education in ancient Tamilnadu was not imparted or organized on the scale of mass education like schools and colleges, but the ideal of education is, to treat it as a secret and sacred process, for the reason that the process of individual growth (inner) can only be achieved

by a close and constant touch between the teacher and the disciple in their personal relationship from which the whole world was excluded.[14]

The boundaries that defined what was "inner" were not only those of the individual student but they also circumscribed the intimate connection between the guru and student. This intimacy has been a key component in the hereditary transmission of siddha medical knowledge. Although there are many written manuscripts in which medical knowledge was transmitted, the direct, physical (oral, aural, and tangible) relationship between guru and student gave greater control over the dispersal of knowledge. Ideally, knowledge would only be offered to a student after initiation (*tīṭcai*), ensuring that this knowledge stayed within the lineage. The concealing of siddha medical knowledge was always, and is still often, a strategy to highlight the unique medical techniques of independent paramparais in a competitive medical arena. As I will demonstrate in the next chapter, secrecy is therefore often in tension with attempts to forge a broader siddha medical system and community.

Palm-leaf manuscripts have served as aids in the transmission of medical formulae in south India for centuries. Today vaidyas consider these manuscripts to be symbols of an ancient past, presenting concrete evidence that siddha medicines have a mystical, obscure origin. The vaidya who can read them demonstrates his literacy, though the sort of literacy thus demonstrated has changed, from literacy per se (the ability to read), which set him apart from his illiterate clientele in the past, to literacy of ancient tradition, which sets him apart from his modern, often educated, contemporaries. Take, for example, K. R. Krishnan's description of a typical siddha practitioner of the late eighteenth century. "The doctor boasted of secret knowledge from a palm-leaf-book heirloom and quoted verses ostensibly from it, to impress his client, before he proceeded to make the remedy for a stipulated fee."[15] The ability to read a palm-leaf manuscript, the medium of ancient knowledge, continues to captivate observers. G. John Samuel, the founder and head of the Institute of Asian Studies, a large research institute situated just outside of Chennai that edits and publishes texts preserved on manuscripts, recounts his youthful observations of an astrologer. "I was amazed, watching him reading palm leaf manuscripts, searching them and then speaking to those who had come for their horoscopes."[16]

The recording of medical knowledge in manuscripts was an enterprise fraught with the danger of leaking information to those outside of the paramparai. Thus vaidyas point out that their texts were written in technical language, *paripāṣai*, which can only be deciphered by those students who have been taught its meaning by a guru.

There is no denying the fact that the fundamental principle underlying the process of calcination of the metals and the minerals successfully

> eliminating their evil effects but not losing at the same time their beneficial ones is a great secret; but the difficulty is that one has to learn the secret of manufacturing the Siddhic medicines from a learned and experienced Guru, since the correct scientific terminology of the different kinds of formulae relating to kalpa drugs was given in the ancient Siddha texts are not only fully comprehensive and expressive but also shrouded in symbolic words.[17]

Velan voices an opinion common among many hereditary vaidyas, that siddha medical knowledge has inherent qualities that can only be taught by a guru, and that textual education is incapable of teaching the secrets that are transmitted in traditional modes.

A look at some premodern Tamil medical texts sheds light on some of the meanings of secrecy in precolonial times. Here, the lines of secrecy were drawn in at least two different ways. One was drawn between types of beings, on one side the ordinary people of the world and on the other the extraordinary siddhars, the knowers, who concealed their knowledge from common people. Another line is that between hereditary medical lineages, which kept their knowledge secret from one another. The text *Akastiya Muṉivar Aruḷiya Kaṟpa Muppu Kuru Nūl 100* (Agastya's 100 verses on the regenerative compound muppu) narrates a typical story of Agastya's initial redaction of medical knowledge in textual form, a redaction that other siddhars strongly resisted.

> I say this in clear language to all of the wise people of the world. This text is without equal among such texts. I collected information from many texts and recorded it in this one. If this text is not available to scholars, I previously gave a text called "205 verses," which is the first text in healing and is the same as this one. . . . Knowing this, the siddhars, who were in a mountain cave, took this text and hid it in that cave.
>
> I called the siddhars who had hid it and I retrieved the text, telling them it is for the good people of the world. If those who know this clear text on muppu don't reveal it to people who revile the guru, then they will become knowledgeable with the grace of the undivided Shiva-Shakti. I have given the complete formula of the restorative medicine (*kaṟpam*) which gives yogic powers (*citti*).[18]

The author of this text portrays the siddhars as a whole as selfishly protecting the knowledge that separates them from ordinary people. It is the acquisition of the yogic powers, the *cittis,* which distinguishes the siddhars. The correct preparation and consumption of muppu will make an ordinary person a siddhar: "No one in the four directions knows this method to prepare muppu. I will sing this openly to you. If you understand it with skill, you too will become a rishi-siddhar!"[19] The siddhars, to protect their preeminence, do not wish ordinary people to have this knowledge, so they hide Agastya's text.

What are these other texts that Agastya collected? They are his own works, general medical texts that were not specifically on muppu, the most potent of kaṟpam or rejuvenative medicines. This work of 100 verses is thus a compilation of prior texts attributed to Agastya, indicating that it is more recent than other texts ascribed to the siddhars. "I sang many great texts, noble one. I gathered the appropriate parts on kaṟpam that were in those texts, and I put them in this text without technical language (*paripāṣai*) for the immortal survival of the people of the world."[20] Agastya repeatedly contrasts his own openness and generosity to the jealousy of the other siddhars. In claiming that his text is free of paripāṣai, he contends that his text is superior to other texts, whose meaning is obscured by paripāṣai and which therefore cannot be properly understood. Indeed, Agastya claims to have facilitated the work of vaidyas who seek to manufacture muppu by assembling all the information about medicines that promote longevity and presenting it here in compact form.

In narrating the attempt of other siddhars to hide this clear, direct text outlining the recipe of muppu, the author suggests the superiority of all knowledge attributed to Agastya. Accordingly, the other siddhars cannot be trusted because they do not want ordinary people to become siddhars—this is why they tried to hide Agastya's text, and why they wrote their own texts in paripāṣai. Paripāṣai is generally attributed to the texts of other siddhars, not one's own. Agastya claims, "I have not hidden the formula of muppu, but the other siddhars have hidden it in tens of millions of texts."[21] Other siddhars have hidden their knowledge so effectively that no one will be able to decipher the formula. The implication is that even if another lineage has a text on muppu, they will not understand it because it is riddled with impenetrable paripāṣai. Agastya holds that "I have revealed fully all kinds of medicines. Those who have not studied this text don't know what medicine is, or what kaṟpam is, but they speak as if they know. Those good people who know the meaning of this text will prepare the proper kaṟpam."[22] Even though vaidyas of other lineages might pretend to have knowledge of rejuvenative medicines, in fact they do not, as their texts are so deeply obscure that no one can decipher them. Only those who have this text by Agastiyar, or his text on muppu in 205 verses, will have any chance at properly preparing muppu.

Although Agastya has revealed this knowledge to the vaidya who can read this text, he is also clear that the formula for muppu must be exclusively preserved within the paramparai, only passed to those who do not "revile the guru." This goes for many of the formulae he gives. "Don't reveal this method to prepare the *cavvīra paṟpam* called *veḷḷai* to the people of the world."[23] The vaidya reading the text is not one of the "people of the world," which would include both nonmedical people and vaidyas of other lineages. Another siddhar, Bhogar, defines "people of the world" as "those who die," distinguishing them from "those who serve the goddess Valai (Shakti)."[24] In light of contemporary assertions that the siddhars represent the interests of ordinary people, Agastya's admonition to keep this knowledge from "the people of the world" appears somewhat surprising. For the author of this text, the people who deserve benefit from his knowledge are vaidyas of Agastya's lineage and those who can afford their medicines, not a broader community conceived along Tamil ethnic lines.

Vaidyas maintain the secrecy of their medicines in order to preserve the exclusivity of their knowledge. This exclusivity suggests the preeminence of the lineage in its unique knowledge that is denied to others, and it also implies the potency of their medicines. The premodern texts further assert the moral superiority of the paramparai, because it is the moral rectitude of the student that earns him the right to learn rare medical formulae. Texts of the lineage, and the knowledge that originated with the siddhars, are only for "good people of the world." These texts often warn of the proliferation of charlatans: "Those people who speak about the qualities of a guru and techniques of medicine, without having read texts, they are blind. They know nothing of muppu, but they deceive the people of the world. Look! For these people, who know nothing of rock-salt, medical alchemy will have no effect. They roam around the streets like dogs. What sort of alchemy will work for those low-born people?"[25] Indeed, the only secret that these quacks possess is that they have no secret knowledge at all! They are "low born" (*ceṉmitta vacaṭar*), which is probably not a reference to particular castes but a metaphor to indicate immoral people. Unlike the philosophical siddhar literature, which contains often strident rejections of caste hierarchy, there are almost no references to caste in the premodern medical texts that I read. The view that the medical siddhars were against elitism, and indeed that Tamil medical practice has always been egalitarian, seems to be a modern invention. Indeed, these premodern texts exhibit elitism in their bias for textual knowledge, as in the passage above, where the authors distinguish vaidyas with knowledge from those who are ignorant on the basis of access to texts and the ability to read them. Access to proper knowledge indicates not just education but also a prior morality, while the possession of this secret knowledge is itself the primary sign that distinguishes them as moral. The possession of secret knowledge creates a community of knowledge, the paramparai, set apart in its mastery of medical preparations, in its access to textual knowledge, and in its superior morality.

Undermining the authority of other paramparais is only part of the effort required to establish the authority of a particular lineage. Contra current depictions of the siddhars as rational scientists, in premodern texts Agastya predicates his authority not on scientific research but on his extraordinary relationship to Shakti and Shiva. "Holding the feet of Shakti in my mind, I saw the way to prepare muppu which is the path to immortality."[26] Interestingly, indications that the compiler may have been an ordinary human and not Agastya himself come through, when he announces that he "worships the feet of the siddhars" in giving this method, a strange action for the siddhar who is the most prolific of the siddhars, and to many vaidyas the most authoritative of them all.[27]

The narration of these disputes among the siddhars usually portrays the attributive author of the text at hand as happy to reveal knowledge that all the siddhars possess, while the other siddhars try to hide this text. These disputes among siddhars are not over differences in their knowledge, and so these texts do not elevate the knowledge of one siddhar over another. Rather, they narrate differences in the willingness of siddhars to share knowledge that they all have, and thus they imply differences in the clarity and value of the texts that the siddhars have written. As these texts are now imbedded in human practice, these differences highlight that the arena of contested knowledge outlined by the texts is not in the imaginary world of the siddhars, but rather in the competitive medical world of ordinary vaidyas.

Such claims to transmit potent knowledge against the protests of other vaidyas are repeated in texts of siddhars less eminent than Agastya. Kailasa Sattamuni uses his lack of status to claim that he is an outsider among the siddhars, his marginal status his motivation for breaking rank and transmitting valuable knowledge. In his one-hundred-verse treatise on the formulation of kaṟpam, Sattamuni gives a formula for the revitalizing *centūram* and then speaks of his dispute with other siddhars that arose over this medicine.[28]

> Twenty days after taking it the old skin will fall off.[29] Once, all of the siddhars called me and spoke. When they said, "the way to formulate this magic pill must be that of the knowledgeable Tirumular," I told them "it is my method." They told me to give the pill to them and asked "whose method?" I told them it is the method of the great Sattamuni. (64)
>
> They were in a conference on Mount Kailasa with the three great gods and Janaka, etc.[30] They asked my name, and asked "what is the method set out in Sattamuni's text? Give the book to Konkanar and tell him to read it." (65)
>
> It was Machamuni who read the text and praised it to the assembly. . . . He said that I had written everything very directly, and in his arrogance he even tried to sing from my book of 200 verses. In a split second,

> Machamuni called me there. All of the siddhars, along with Janaka, etc., said, "Was the vow (*tīṭcai*) you spoke in the guru's right ear, the vow to observe [i.e., follow] his path, given in arrogance? Are you now a guru to the siddhars? Are you completely pushing aside those words? Are you arrogantly saying that all the siddhars are second-rate gurus?" (66–68)
>
> Hearing these words, as I stood stunned, Tirumular took my text of 200 verses and tore it, ruining it. Then he handed it to me along with the text I had sung in 2,500 verses, saying "it is only for good siddhars," and told me to hide it in a cave. Look, that text which the siddhars saw is the very same as this text [which you have in your hands]! (69)[31]

Sattamuni is an upstart siddhar, a student of Agastiyar and therefore a secondary transmitter of siddha knowledge.[32] The text depicts Machamuni and Tirumular as his primary rivals, although all of the siddhars scold him. This account of Tirumular's attempt to keep the text from being revealed to others is contrary to G. J. Parthasarathy's description of him as freely distributing medical knowledge, as Parthasarathy himself generously does. The attempt of other siddhars to hide Sattamuni's lucid text highlights the veracity of its formulae and the power of its knowledge. By claiming that his text is exclusive, rare, and secret, Sattamuni imbues his text, and the medicines it contains, with the aura of the extraordinary.

Each of these premodern texts signifies an exclusive connection between an extraordinary siddhar and ordinary vaidyas of his lineage. The effect of this descent of knowledge into the human realm is to make the primary division of knowledge not that between the siddhars and the human world, but that between paramparais. Or rather, as a paramparai claims unobscured siddhar knowledge that other lineages do not possess, the distinction between siddhars and ordinary people is effectively transformed into a difference between the paramparai and the rest of the world.

Esotericism, Miraculous Medicine, and the Possibility of Immortality

As we have seen, the siddhars generally celebrate their texts as being clear, without the paripāṣai that obscures the texts of other siddhars. However, for the siddha vaidya today who tries to formulate the most powerful medicines, either rejuvenative or alchemical, none of the premodern texts seems clear. In his preface to his collection of Agastya's texts on muppu (which as we have seen were themselves compilations of prior texts), S. P. Ramachandran speaks of the difficulty in understanding Agastya's writings, and also of the great promise these writings possess.

> One of the reasons that the siddhars used technical language (*paripāṣai*) is so that others could not understand, as each siddhar used his own coded words. It is also because of this that siddha medicine cannot be produced correctly by those who are not appropriate, and why it cannot be employed correctly, why there is confusion among people.
>
> However, we are astonished when we hear of the miraculous work that has been accomplished by a few siddha vaidyas. An amount of medicine equal to a grain of rice can cure leprosy. It can change wrinkles and gray hair, restore youthfulness, and liberate from the grip of death. All of this is not fantasy. We know that these things have truly occurred.[33]

According to vaidyas today who try to interpret the writings of the siddhars, paripāṣai is the key that controls access to esoteric medical knowledge. In principle, only those who have the proper training, that is, those who have studied under a guru, will know the exact referents of paripāṣai, assuming that each coded term has a precise and single correspondence to a specific substance. Ramachandran admits that the siddhars were so effective in their use of paripāṣai that they have created much confusion. Yet he also affirms that "we" (the emphatic, inclusive *nāmē*) hear of the miracles worked by some siddha vaidyas, joining himself and his audience in the conspiracy of being part of something beyond explanation. It is this sort of testimony of that sustains the hopes of siddha vaidyas that their medical premises and texts may one day bring them fame and fortune.

There is often an assumption among vaidyas that at some time in the past, the meanings of paripāṣai were clearly known but have been lost with the passage of time. A formula given in a text, no matter how poorly understood at present, is material evidence for a fantastic medicine that has been formulated in the past and that might, perhaps, be produced in the future. Although it is impossible to demonstrate (and it is just this very impossibility that makes these claims of the miraculous appear feasible), I argue that much, but not all, paripāṣai of the medical texts has never been known to anyone; that is, it has always been language that has no referent. If this is true, the secret has always been that which Agastya warned us with respect to other paramparais: that there is no secret, and that there are no miraculous medicines. The power of paripāṣai, then, has never been that of concealing true medical formulae, but of concealing the fact that there are no true medical formulae, inserting an obstacle between the vaidyas' comprehension and illusory substances that will produce gold out of mercury or cure all ills. The formulation of this illusory medicine, and all the wealth that it will bring, appear to be within the grasp of the vaidya if only the paripāṣai can be deciphered. Paripāṣai effects the proximity of the miraculous, tempting belief that it is only the proper interpretation of a single word that stands between ordinary vaidyas and extraordinary medicine. While obscure language makes comprehension impossible, and therefore appears to be the impediment to its formulation, it is the very same paripāṣai which enables vaidyas to imagine that the recipe given in the text that they have in their hands, if understood properly, will indeed produce medicines of almost limitless potency.[34]

As an example of the use of paripāṣai and its power to impart credence to the extraordinary, I will focus on the preparation called muppu. Muppu literally means "three salts." B. V. Subbarayappa holds these three to be "*pūnīṟu* (possibly a mixture of carbonates), *kalluppu* (rock salt) and *aṇṭakkal* (probably calcium carbonate)."[35] He also notes that muppu is absent in Sanskrit alchemical texts, and most vaidyas I spoke with specified muppu as a distinguishing characteristic of siddha medicine. Kundrathur Ramamurthy spoke of an "original" muppu which could be used to transform copper into gold. That same original muppu could be mixed with medicine to increase its potency, and when ingested, it rejuvenates the body and makes hair grow. He was skeptical that any vaidyas today are able to produce this original muppu, however. G. J. Parthasarathy spoke of alchemical (*vāta*) muppu and medical (*vaittiya*) muppu, but he did not discuss it further because he had been sworn to secrecy by a guru who taught him about it. Subbarayappa distinguishes four kinds of muppu: alchemical, medical, yoga, and wisdom (*ñāṉa*).[36] Vaidyas generally consider muppu to combine medical and alchemical qualities, so the same substance that will turn base metals into gold will also impart youth, strength, and vigor to the body.

Muppu, all siddha vaidyas know, will cure all ills and bestow immortality, and so it is probably the most sought after of all medicines. Because it is shrouded in secrecy, however, its successful formulation is elusive. In the May 1972 issue of the medical periodical *Nandhi,* Dr. Venugopal writes, "In speaking of muppu, it will be a matter that ordinary people should not elaborate upon. It is a thing that one cannot easily grasp. . . . The siddhars have explained the elucidation of muppu in pāripāṣai. . . . Thus, siddha practitioners have received the explanation either as a verbal account from generation to generation or by their individual tinkerings fully in the path of the siddhars, and the situation is such that other people cannot understand it fully."[37] The formula for the preparation of muppu is a curious sort of secret, in that it is not clear that anyone today knows it. M. Shanmukavelu, a siddha practitioner attempting to formulate muppu based on Agastya's texts, frustrated with his lack of success, disputes Agastya's proclamation that he has openly revealed the formula for muppu against the wishes of the other siddhars. "Purposely he [Agastya] concealed these important points on muppu because he was afraid that his colleagues or co-Siddhas would find fault with him or accuse him and get angry."[38] Andiappa Pillai, in an article written in connection with the World Tamil Conference held in 1983, concurs. "The Siddhars are unanimous in concealing the details of manufacture of the magic drug Muppu. Even those Siddhars who loudly proclaim that they would narrate everything about Muppu ultimately do not say anything significant about it."[39]

The major difficulty in producing muppu is confusion around the substance called *pūnīṟu,* or "earth water." M. Shanmukavelu calls it "the first ingredient of muppu," and most texts on muppu mention it as a key ingredient.[40] In *Agastiyar Cūṭca Muppu 32* (Agastya's 32 verses on subtle muppu), we find the following description of pūnīṟu.

> Listen to the details of pūnīṟu. It sprouts above ground, and is very concentrated like lime. Don't touch it with your hand, as the hand will become blistered. (15)
>
> Gather it with a margosa leaf and put it in a container. Go only to the place called Pōm. There the stuff called *ām* [probably pūnīṟu] was graciously available to us there on a full-moon night, hanging densely in clusters, just as the love of Parvati hangs densely in clusters. Listen to the details of pūnīṟu which is called *pūm.* Oh pure one, I'll tell you this for your [immortal] survival! (16)
>
> If one asks what are the names that others have used for pūnīṟu: *curuṅkāṉa ravipījam* [the condensed seed of the sun], *pūnākam, pūminātam, civaṉuppu, veṇṇīr,* . . . [gives ten more names]. I only know these words, not the endless tens of millions of others. Oh, they have sung countless names! (17–18)[41]

These are the only details that Agastya gives as to how to locate pūnīṟu, before he moves on to describe its proper preparation, that is, it must be dissolved in pure water, and so on. The most specific reference is a place called Pōm, a place with no clear geographic reference.

In his dictionary of the Tamil sciences, T. V. Sambasivam Pillai writes about pūnīṟu: "Efflorescence grows in clusters and bursts out into flower at new moon or full moon nights during dew seasons . . . on the soil of fuller's earth. When the sun rises it turns to fine powder."[42] B. V. Subbarayappa calls it "a natural exudate from the soil which has Fuller's earth. . . . It has a composition similar to that of Fuller's earth (over 50% of silica, 13% of aluminium oxide, about 10% of iron (ferric) oxide, 5% of calcium oxide, 2% magnesium oxide, less than 2% of alkalis, and 18% of water)." Subbarayappa also notes that it is collected "ritualistically in certain places of Tamil Nadu by Siddha practitioners, specially on four full-moon nights in the months of Jan–April. . . . According to some Siddha practitioners who collect it, they should offer worship to the soil from which it emanates."[43]

Elsewhere, Subbarayappa describes "tradition" as holding that there are thirty-five places in south India where pūnīṟu grows, and that it is formed when the rays of the moon, considered to be male, shine on particular types of soil, considered to be female, which then "gives birth" to the pūnīṟu.[44] M. Shanmugavelu writes, "There is a peculiar and seasonal influence between the Earth and Moon for the formation of Puneer [*pūnīṟu*] in certain selected areas fit for its growth. Puneer crops up ten days after New Moon (Amavaseii) or about the time of Paurnami (i.e., Full Moon). It crops up early in the morning and loses its life after sun-rise."[45] However, the author admits that it is difficult for ordinary people to find *pūnīṟu,* that "we invariably fail to secure first rate puneer." Such high-quality pūnīṟu can only be acquired by "Yogis and Sadhus."[46] Shanmukavelu concludes, "I must frankly admit that the success of muppu depends largely upon what quality of puneer we get," a pessimistic estimation given the elusiveness of pūnīṟu.[47]

The conditions in which pūnīṟu might be acquired are numerous and ephemeral. The physical location is uncertain, but it is clear that pūnīṟu will only grow in a particular type of soil. The time is very specific, just between dawn and sunrise. Its appearance is of a somewhat extraordinary crystallization on the earth. Furthermore, there are hundreds of different names given for pūnīṟu in the premodern texts. The problem is both too little information and too much. If one searches the corpus of available siddhar texts and catalogues for the qualities of pūnīṟu in all its names, the list would be extremely long and certainly contradictory, effectively nullifying the possibility of gleaning precise knowledge. Here we find continuity between premodern and modern Tamil medical discourse, in that both posit the extraordinary just beyond the limits of knowledge and accessibility, whether on ancient island called Lemuria or in a unknown place called Pōm.

This recognition of the difficulty of producing muppu, and the lack of any clear exposition of its manufacture, does not prevent many vaidyas from attempting to formulate it. In my interview with him in 2007, Kundrathur Ramamurthy, practicing on the outskirts of Chennai, blamed his failed efforts to produce muppu on the lack of sharing of knowledge among practitioners today. "I've put a lot of effort into preparing muppu. The problem is, those who have made it don't show us. They keep it inside and we can't do anything. Those who have done it should show us. If not, there's no way to know. It's a difficult process." In his February 9, 1991, speech at a meeting of the Kerala Siddha Sangam, Dr. Edison spoke of the necessity of manufacturing muppu powder (*muppu cuṇṇam*), announcing: "I have planned a scheme for our preparing muppu cuṇṇam in our ashram. If everyone will share, we can prepare the muppu cuṇṇam required."[48] The potential that muppu might be prepared, and the promise offered by its successful completion, overshadow the reality of failed attempts at production. Devasahayam, a siddha vaidya who runs a medical shop, states: "We have not prepared muppu. But we are not without the thought of doing preparation of muppu. Yes, we have made some attempts to prepare it. . . . If there is muppu, it is said that people will be without even gray hair and wrinkles. There will be no gray hair and wrinkles. No cancer. Now the AIDS which is here, they say that if there is muppu, treatment can be given to all."[49]

Although no one seems to know how to make muppu, everyone knows what it can do. The absence of muppu, and the elusiveness of a precise recipe for its formulation, is balanced by its overwhelming presence in siddha medical discourse, and by a clear sense of all that it will offer. When these contemporary vaidyas describe muppu's effectiveness, they continue a tradition evidenced by the siddhar texts, which also imbue muppu with great power: the body will become as hard as a diamond, camphor-scented, and golden in color.[50] One will become strong and beautiful, gray hair and wrinkles will vanish, and "the word *emaṉ* [the god of death] will itself die."[51] One will have the power to chase away ghosts (*pēy*), evil spirits (*picācu*), and demons (*pūtam*), and bring all wealth under one's control.[52] More recently, muppu has been touted as a cure for AIDS, cancer, asthma, and all other chronic illnesses that biomedicine cannot effectively cure.

Although it is the extravagance of the claims for muppu that captures the imagination of siddha practitioners, it is the secrecy in which it is shrouded that enables them to hold out hope for its future manufacture. As A. Shanmuga Velan paraphrases Paracelsus, "No science can be deservedly held in contempt by one who knows nothing about it."[53] What is true for science is true for specific medicines. The fact that no one has ever seen muppu, and that no one has achieved the immortality it bestows, does not deter those who pronounce its position at the apex of the world's medical preparations, and thereby assert the preeminence of siddha medical knowledge of which muppu is the greatest "achievement."

Conclusion

Georg Simmel, speaking of the obfuscation of knowledge, points out the "contradiction that what recedes before the consciousness of others and is hidden from them, is to be emphasized in their consciousness."[54] This is true as well, perhaps even more so, for knowledge that is secret even to the self. After all, the most extraordinary medical knowledge promised in the siddha texts is hidden from those very people who claim this knowledge as their own. To speak of this as a contradiction, however, is to leave it unexplained, and in fact I am arguing just the opposite: the value attributed to muppu can be magnified precisely because of its ephemerality. If the presence of muppu is to be found only in discourse, there is no contradiction between its physical absence and the fascination which many vaidyas display toward it. As Simmel points out, it is what is offered to the imagination but never fully delivered that captivates most wholly. In this sense, knowledge that a few know, that is, a secret, differs little from knowledge that no one knows, or that only the siddhars know. To the degree that this knowledge is expressed in textual references and personal testimony, it appears to be true, while to the degree that it is obscured, it can be filled with the extraordinary possibilities of a space that falls outside scrutiny.

This juxtaposition of clarity and obscurity is reflected in the language of the premodern medical texts, which is extremely familiar and informal on the one hand, and enigmatic and abstruse on the other. K. Kailasapathy has pointed to this characteristic of the literary writings attributed to the siddhars, noting that "The poetry of the Siddhas is sustained by the simple colloquial expressions and speech patterns of the common people. . . . And yet these poems are, to be sure, full of obscurities and peculiarities that baffle the best of literary minds."[55] Likewise, the paripāṣai of the siddhar texts is balanced by their informal, colloquial language. For example, many of the verb forms are informal commands (e.g., *kēḷ!* "Listen!"). These commands are often followed by *appā,* literally "father" but here, and in everyday usage also, this is a term of address of an elder to someone younger, a usage that generally entails a casual relationship and even affection. While these conventions reveal the hierarchy of the siddhar/human and guru/student relationship, both of which are implied in the transmission of these texts, they also express a degree of informality in this transmission. This is consistent with contemporary assertions of siddha medicine as a medicine for the common people, in contrast to ayurveda and biomedicine, which siddha vaidyas vilify as elitist, expensive, and transmitted in languages that most Tamils do not understand. At the same time, they admit their failure to successfully decipher the paripāṣai of the siddhars.

This conjunction of the accessible and the obscure is less a problem for vaidyas to solve than it is a powerful discursive formula through which they impute great potential to their medicines. The effect of juxtaposing obscure and familiar language does not highlight the gap between them, but it makes the obscure seem knowable and the familiar seem mysterious. When the medical texts say "listen, man, I'll tell you the formula for muppu," they use a register that the reader identifies as a highly informal level of social interaction, the banter of family and friends. When this familiar language contains obscure formulae, the effect is to make obscurity itself seem familiar, rendering the indecipherable recognizable. The proximity of the familiar and the arcane makes the arcane appear to be within the vaidya's grasp. The obverse is also true, as the familiar is imbued with the value offered by the obscure. Vaidyas can declare that these texts and the medicines they expound, so clearly theirs because they are in the language they use everyday, contain great mysteries. The siddha texts thus tempt ordinary people with extraordinary medicine.

7

The Loss and Recovery of Medical Knowledge

Although secrecy has been a central feature in the transmission of siddha medical knowledge for centuries, the morality of secrecy in south India has dramatically changed since the beginning of the twentieth century. In Tamil-speaking south India and in South Asia more generally, secrecy as a mode of disseminating knowledge has undergone a radical change in value, from its consideration as a moral duty that keeps powerful knowledge in the hands of the good, to its regard as a selfish act that has led to the disintegration of a unified Tamil community. At a seminar on siddha medicine held in 1983 at the International Institute of Tamil Studies in Madras, the keynote speaker R. Thyagarajan spoke not of the dangers of the open display of knowledge, nor of the privilege of the possession of secret knowledge, but of the disastrous effects of secrecy on the development of siddha medicine. "Reticence, secrecy and selfishness were the triple defects which stood in the way, this glorious system was not allowed to flourish, though it did not die out because of its innate strength based on truth."[1] Many vaidyas today reject secrecy on both moral and pragmatic grounds. In the following pages, I will document the historical trajectory of obfuscation in siddha medicine, a history that is just one instance of more general debates in India about whether the proper locus of knowledge is in public or private spheres, in the archive or in the home.

In suggesting a history of the value of secrecy in twentieth century India, I follow Nietzsche's admonition that "we need a critique of moral values, the value of these values should itself, for once, be examined."[2]

Although secrecy is not itself a moral value, a history of the changing value of secrecy raises many of the same questions that Nietzsche's pioneering studies of morality did over a century ago. What historical factors have transformed the morality of secrecy among south Indian vaidyas? In what contexts has secrecy undergone this change of value? As we will see, we must speak not of a history of secrecy but of histories, as it is in specific contexts, namely, within projects to develop a unified siddha medical system, that secrecy is particularly condemned. Finally, given the contemporary proscription of secrecy in certain contexts, what, if not secrecy, currently serves to validate the extraordinary claims still voiced on behalf of siddha medicine? I will argue that the function of secrecy as a strategy for garnering prestige is now served by another form of concealed knowledge, that is, Tamil medical knowledge that has been lost in the ravages of time. Again, we will find that the ends of scrutable knowledge mark the beginnings of the extraordinary claims for siddha medicine.

Critiques of Secrecy

In twentieth-century south India, critiques of secrecy have come from a variety of quarters. The first that I will examine, initially voiced by colonial administrators and biomedical doctors and later taken up by Indians, is a charge that secrecy and hereditary education provide an unregulated space in which charlatans can operate with impunity, out of the public eye and so out of public domains of control and discipline. These critics have further held that secrecy is an impediment to the accumulation of effective medical knowledge and techniques, arguing that the public display of knowledge is the most efficient way to advance medicine. A similar critique has been advanced from the inside, so to speak, by those who have sought to defend rather than discount traditional practices. Vaidyas have argued for the moral and pragmatic failings of secrecy while pursuing agendas that run counter to colonial and biomedical projects. Often involved in formulations of Tamil revivalism as well as in government projects to centralize and control indigenous medical practices, these traditional medical leaders seek to define a unified siddha medical system. They reject secrecy as a selfish act that divides a naturally coherent Tamil medical community. At the same time, many vaidyas maintain their support of the conduit of secrecy, the hereditary lineage, arguing that hereditary education provides an experience common to vaidyas that distinguishes them from their biomedical adversaries and unites them as a community.

The critiques that were raised by medical scientists and administrators, first in the imperial state and later in independent India, malign secrecy and hereditary education for sustaining arenas of medical practice that are not susceptible to official regulation and standardization. K. R. Krishnan, a qualified biomedical doctor, holds that because of traditional modes of hereditary education, "Examination, certification and licensing were not in vogue. This enabled many a self-styled doctor with meagre knowledge and qualification to indulge in medical practice, and much worse than that, to pass on his whims and fancies as the wisdom of ancient matters. With no way to prove or disprove that claim, such spurious knowledge too gained wide currency, eclipsing the wisdom of the original seers."[3] In 1957, A. Srinivasalu Naidu, an M.D. and also retired dean of the College of Integrated Medicine, wrote of hereditary modes of medical education, "In days of yore, medical education was imparted by unitary teachers, 'Gurus' in 'Gurukulas,' in indifferent schools, subject to whims, fancies, and patronage of teachers often earned by pupils under tutelage and personal service to the teachers and his family and uncontrolled by a standard authority. Sometimes, teachers of indifferent merit masqueraded as scholars to the detriment of pupils."[4] For these medical leaders, hereditary education is not only detrimental to the effective development of medical knowledge but also fails to provide moral control over medical practice. Private knowledge provides a concealed space for quacks to operate outside of public scrutiny. Although the premodern Tamil texts similarly warned of false vaidyas, they did not raise a critique of secrecy per se—indeed, the proliferation of charlatans was itself articulated as a primary reason to exercise control in the transmission of powerful knowledge that, in the hands of the immoral, would be used for pernicious ends.

The view that values public knowledge over esoteric knowledge is for many one of the cornerstones of the modern sciences.[5] This perception holds for many in India. In describing biomedical methods, S. Alagappan, a member of the governing body of the general course in Indian medicine, writes:

> Since our [biomedical] knowledge has been acquired by rational and not secret method we are open to criticism and thereby correction of our knowledge. Few people realise that knowledge is one commodity that increases in its quantity and improves its quality, by being given to others. Another feature of modern medicine is that it lends itself to team work of various types. . . . Such being the nature and extent of modern rational allopathic system of medicine, it would be a misnomer to style other methods, such as Ayurvedic, Homeopathic, etc., as systems of Medicine. But unfortunately, exaggeration and self-glorification are our national trait, irrespective of results attained thereby."[6]

Alagappan's view of knowledge as a commodity, a possession to be shared or kept secret, is a sentiment that Tamil vaidyas of hereditary training also hold. However, his plea for the open sharing of knowledge goes against centuries of medical practice in South Asia according to which secret knowledge is rare, unique, and therefore valuable.

One effect of secrecy within lineages has been that Tamil vaidyas have developed a variety of different medicines and techniques to treat a single illness. Kumaresan, a siddha practitioner in the Kanya Kumari district of southern Tamil Nadu, was trained in traditional fashion by his father and also studied at a siddha medical college. He traces the variety of medical techniques among Tamil vaidyas to the different redactions of knowledge that originated with the various siddhars: "Siddha medical system was not written by one sage. It was written by many siddhars, the 18 siddhars. . . . Since each siddhar has written separately in his own way, the government could not compile them together into one scheme. . . . For fever, one siddhar would have said one medicine, Agasthiar would have said another medicine, Pāmpāṭṭi siddha would have mentioned another medicine. . . . So here it is not one medicine for the same disease, as in allopathy."[7] For Kumaresan, this lack of systematization of medical knowledge does not give cause for alarm, and it does not reduce the effectiveness of medical practice.

In the twentieth century, however, a growing number of vaidyas have endeavored to synthesize traditional medical knowledge. They have served as the faculty and directors of schools and hospitals of traditional medicine modeled on colonial institutions established by the British. This group, not those educated by hereditary means, have increasingly set the agenda for the development of traditional medicine and have been especially influential in establishing government policies that regulate and fund traditional medical practices. Their objective has been to gather and systematize siddha medical knowledge, a goal that is radically opposed to the proliferation of knowledge in hereditary lineages. K. R. Krishnan criticizes traditional forms of education and knowledge transmission as haphazard and dangerous.

> The individualized master-pupil system of learning by rote and apprenticeship, and the preservation of knowledge in palmleaf-manuscripts over a few millennia had resulted in a great proliferation of independent practitioners of varied capabilities and honesty and a bewildering variety of prescriptions—effective, ineffective, mixed, shotgun, ritual, magical, etc. Medical schools and organized teaching were unknown. The medical knowledge lay scattered in myriads of palmleaf-manuscripts worshipped as heirlooms in professional as well as lay households. Comprehensive textbooks dealing methodically with pathogenesis, diagnosis, prognosis and treatment of diseased states in classified completeness were lacking. Most of the palmleaf-manuscripts were fragmentary and sectional.[8]

This view that Tamil medical knowledge is "scattered" must be viewed in its historical context. As we have seen, premodern Tamil medical texts did not speak of the different siddhars having a variety of medical techniques, but distinguished them according to their willingness to reveal their knowledge. According to the logic of those premodern texts, differences that would arise between paramparais were not of the nature of a plethora of true formulae, but reflected competition in seeking the singular truth which all the siddhars knew but which they transmitted differently.

Secrecy did not diminish or divide true knowledge, then, but kept it safe. To those who seek to systematize siddha knowledge, however, the variety of medical formulae no longer signals the competition over a singular truth but rather the dispersal of truth. This suggests a project that vaidyas have increasingly set for themselves: to gather together these partial truths in order to unify a siddha medical system that they presume was once coherent. While a hereditary vaidya might argue that his paramparai has deciphered the true knowledge of the siddhars, in contemporary discourse of this systematizing type, all knowledge that is not shared is partial and will not attain its full value until it is joined with the rest of its dispersed epistemic brethren. What emerges is a critique of secrecy as an impediment to truth, a pragmatic critique that is based on the conviction that the public sharing of siddha medical knowledge is the best way to improve the effectiveness of siddha medicine.[9]

Whereas the obscurity of paripāṣai provides siddha vaidyas with the fantasy of extraordinary power, it is simply a frustrating and irrational aspect of traditional medicine to those who seek to unify disparate practices into a single system. Srinivasalu Naidu writes,

> It is contended by the followers of Siddha and Ayurveda systems of Medicine, that the textual matter or words are to be explained or annotated according to their context and the erudition of the scholar and no fixed value can ever be placed on a passage, unlike the very definite and unchangeable meaning of scientific or medical words or terms or passages. Such inconstancy of word meanings is unscientific and highly misleading. I had attended a meeting on "Muppu" (what exactly Muppu is no one knows) and about a dozen scholars spoke, arriving at no finality of the substance, one contending it to be derived from human urine, another from rock-salt, a third from submarine crystals on rocks, a fourth as common-salt and so ad galore. The personal factor of textual interpretation has first to be remedied for the universal acceptance of the textual matter of Ayurveda or Siddha.[10]

For Srinivasalu Naidu and others who seek to systematize traditional medicine, the polysemy of paripāṣai does not fill these words with extraordinary potential but empties them of all value. Many of these vaidyas and administrators argue that the opening of esoteric knowledge to scrutiny is the only way to save indigenous medicine from irrelevance: "While the world is tending to have one authorised system of medicine, India with its ancient Siddha and Ayurveda systems of medicine (along with modern medicine) has yet to standardise the former systems and throw them open for the world to study them. . . . The surest way of killing Indigenous Medicine is isolation, parallelism, emotionalism, passion and vituperation. Co-operation is the best goal of survival."[11] This goal of cooperation is exemplified by the school on behalf of which Srinivasalu Naidu writes, the now defunct Government College of Integrated Medicine, which was founded in 1947 in the optimism of Indian independence, in order to develop not only a single Indian medical system but also a system that would incorporate biomedical knowledge and practices.

In addition to these negative evaluations of secrecy on pragmatic grounds, there is a further moral critique of secrecy as motivated by selfishness. For those who raise this critique, secrecy is a result of individual desires that emerged at some point in history and corrupted the altruism and harmony of a previously unified system. It led to divisions among siddha practitioners and so it also generated division within the Tamil community. The justification for recent attempts to systematize Tamil medical knowledge rests on a claim to an original state of coherence of siddha medical knowledge. This assumption of prior unity has been concomitant with shifting notions of what constitutes medical difference, where the primary others are no longer vaidyas practicing under the auspices of different paramparais, but rather allopathic doctors working under a radically different medical framework, and ayurvedic practitioners who have suddenly come to represent the traditional Indian doctor. With the possibility that their practices might be incorporated into ayurveda or rendered irrelevant by biomedicine, Tamil vaidyas today generally consider themselves to be part of a single system, even if they do not in practice share their secrets with the rest of their newfound community.

K. Parthasarathy, a registered Indian medical practitioner, laments the lack of unity among siddha practitioners. "When I repeatedly proclaim the need for unity among siddha vaidyas, this creates great distress. Why this pathetic state? . . . All siddha doctors do their service, uniformly following the methods instituted by the siddhars. This being the case, why is there not even a modicum of unity?" He goes on to decry the plethora of rival siddha medical associations that have been formed, urging cooperation among vaidyas. "Siddha vaidyas must not give room for the accusations that slander is rife among them, and that they live hiding their valuable medical techniques from one another. When siddha vaidyas think how much mutual concern and solidarity will develop if they share those truths that they know with one another, integration into a single system will flourish!"[12] Another vaidya compares his colleagues who keep their texts secret to dogs who will not share a coconut, considering the secrets between paramparais as a cause for shame.[13]

The equation of secrecy with selfishness is not only recent; as we have seen in premodern medical texts, other siddhars were generally viewed as selfish in hiding knowledge, even as this selfishness signaled the value of their medicines. At the same time, these texts implore the vaidyas who have inherited them to keep their contents secret from those outside the paramparai. In these texts, the exclusive possession of a unique, effective medicine does not indicate an attitude of selfish accumulation but rather signals both medical and moral superiority, as powerful knowledge would only be revealed and understood by good people. The authors of the siddhar texts viewed secrecy as both an ethical and a pragmatic strategy, attesting to the moral character of the vaidya and conferring value on his medicines. As with the esoteric language these texts contain, secrecy itself embodied a range of meanings and values.

What is new in these modern critiques of secrecy, then, is not the equation of secrecy with selfishness but the terms of this equation, as the communities of knowledge that are deprived by secrecy are no longer individual, competing lineages but the cooperative Tamil community. In his 1968 article called "The Needs of Siddha Medicine," C. Meykandar suggests that siddha medicine began to decline in the eighteenth century, citing the major cause, aside from British imperialism, to be its secret, hereditary character. The remedies for this decay, he suggests, all originate with government action, such as setting up a central research committee on siddha medicine, locating all siddha manuscripts and books in one library in Tamil Nadu, and publicizing this knowledge in other Tamil sources.[14] A similar sentiment was voiced fifteen years later by K. C. Uttamarayan, retired director of the Department of Indian Medicine: "A few Tamil doctors are prescribing good medicines for a few specific diseases. They don't give these medicines to others; nor do they teach others the method to prepare these medicines. They have created these medicines as their family wealth and have been using them for generations (*paramparai paramparaiyāka*). They need to reveal these medicines to others. Otherwise, in order to obtain these medicines, the government should give them adequate funds."[15] This appeal that the government acquire this hereditary wealth signals a shift in what many vaidyas consider to be the proper location of siddha medical knowledge, from the hereditary lineage to the public sphere, a public sphere defined by the boundaries of a specifically Tamil community. The proponents of centralized models of education urge practitioners to sacrifice their individual goals for the good of the greater community, a community of knowledge they define in ethnic and linguistic terms. However, this sacrifice can be mitigated if the government pays vaidyas for revealing their secrets.

When siddha vaidyas work to collect their knowledge into a single system, they assume a natural coherence of practices that have been splintered for as long as we know. This hope of the recovery of an original unity distinguishes traditional medicine in modern India from prior conceptualizations. With the unification and systematization of siddha medical knowledge, these vaidyas claim, the full potential of siddha practice will be realized and siddha medicine will regain its place at the pinnacle of the medical world. The damage wrought by secrecy is not permanent, most contend, as the scattering of siddha medicine has not reduced the value of each of its pieces. "The rare truths of Tamil medicine are like precious hoardings in the minds of many siddha practitioners. Now is the time to join these as one so that they will increase."[16]

Kundrathur Ramamurthy argued that there is more sharing of siddha medical knowledge now than in the past.

> There was a time when there was much secrecy. That is, medical procedures were all hereditary. That being the case, these medical procedures were told to the son, or to students. They were never revealed openly. They maintained secrecy. . . . Some processes were not in books at all. Take for example *cittiramūlam* [*plumbago indica*]. . . . Take its leaves, grind in water. . . . That very plant, at the village level, in some villages, if you ask how they use it there . . . they take its leaves and roots, put in oil and heat, take that oil and use it to heal long-lasting, difficult sores. . . . They did this from generation to generation. But now they've begun to divulge many processes openly. . . . 90 percent is spoken of openly.

Kundrathur Ramamurthy views this divulging of hereditary secrets, and the official collection of local data, as key to the development of siddha medicine. He himself worked on a government project to collect local knowledge about plants, traveling to the far reaches of south India searching for herbs and learning from vaidyas about the properties of local plants. Although he complains that the government did not act on his report, he is heartened by a research environment in which similar projects are being funded and their findings made public: "Previously, many people would be reluctant to speak about siddha plants. All that is not the case anymore. Many plants are now known. . . . Botanists are furiously engaged in research. At St. Joseph's College in Trichy, there are many plant collections. They have done a complete computer survey of these plants. . . . They have made an official record of everything: what are the medical uses of the plants, what are the names given by local people, etc. . . . There are a few mistakes in that record. Even so, that is development." At the same time, Ramamurthy admits the limits of openness, and maintains secrecy when it comes to some of his own medicines. In response to my question as to whether he would share the formula if he discovers a powerful medicine, he replied, "If I speak about it openly, you'll open a shop next to mine and sell it. . . . I have published a book. I've written fully about my many experiences, about plant usages, all of that. . . . But I kept to myself a few processes. I didn't reveal them openly." Thus, while many vaidyas admit the moral superiority of the open sharing of knowledge, the play of secrecy and openness continues to mark the transmission of siddha medical knowledge.

The effect of the opening up of siddha medical knowledge is encapsulated in the hope that even muppu might be within the grasp of the unified Tamil community. "A systematic approach to these Kalpa plants as described in ancient Siddha medical works may answer the problems of cancer, cardiovascular and other degenerated [sic] diseases, if not for rejuvenating the entire system."[17] After commenting that each vaidya has a few "rare medicines" that he secretly conceals, M. Shanmukavelu appeals to vaidyas to "exchange ideas," following which "a day may come, not far off, for any one of the Siddha physicians to achieve successful preparations of not only 'vaidya muppu' but also its allied compounds and various other rare specific medicines even for diseases which have no substantial cure discovered yet."[18] Kundrathur Ramamurthy spoke to me about the existence of a "muppu committee, a muppu sangam" that is working to formulate muppu. The promise for siddha vaidyas is not only the selfless healing of the people of the world but also the winning of fame and fortune. Shanmukavela appeals to his fellow vaidyas: "If this vaidya-muppu is successfully achieved, it is needless to point out that the standard of Siddha system of medicine in particular will reach a very high pitch and the whole world will look to you for guidance and appreciate."[19] The open dispersal of siddha medical knowledge in the global medical market may bring siddha vaidyas and Tamil civilization global renown.

In Defense of the Guru

In the early decades of the twentieth century, siddha practitioners were already lamenting the decline of hereditary modes of education with the ascendance of British-style education and institutions. In his contribution to the investigation into indigenous medical systems of the Madras state published in 1923, V. Ponnuswami Pillai of Kumbakonam writes, "Those who practice native medicine have more faith in experience and in guru-student education than they do in literary research and formal educational institutions. Therefore, medical reform in this country won't happen through school education as it does in the Western countries. . . . Those who skillfully practice medicine on the basis of traditional experience (*pāramparyamāṉa aṉupavam*) are no longer influential in the profession because of the singular prestige gained through modern medical institutions."[20] Traditional styles of education in India have been under attack and have lost ground over the past century. Ponnuswami Pillai might have been surprised, then, to learn that hereditary medical education continues into the twenty-first century. Why did the critiques that I have outlined not lead to the eradication of hereditary methods? Hereditary education has not only survived but it remains, in Bruce Lincoln's words, an "ideological warrant" for siddha medicine and Tamil tradition, a specific criterion that vaidyas invoke in their bid for authority.[21]

Siddha medicine today is a modern tradition, not in the way that Tamil vaidyas argue—as an ancient system that has always featured contemporary scientific ideals and techniques—but insofar as it is has maintained its vitality and popular appeal. Tradition defends the ancient from the demands of the modern, even as its rhetoric transforms the ancient into the modern. Yet this is not to say that the siddha tradition is only recently invented, or that its claim to represent the past is only pretension. As a space within which Tamils successfully authorize precolonial practices, siddha medicine today is not only new, not only a contemporary space in which history is organized, but is itself organized by the history that precedes it, a history that is not only colonial. The transformations that have occurred in medical practice and discourse in Tamil Nadu have not taken shape wholly in line with, nor entirely in opposition to, colonial and nationalist challenges. Even under the imperial British, vaidyas were agents in their formulation of a Tamil medical tradition. Thus, in responding to the critiques of secrecy raised above, many vaidyas have continued to support hereditary education.

These vaidyas often cite the experience of hereditary training as qualitatively different from book learning taught in schools. They emphasize the guru/student relationship as a feature of siddha medicine that is held in common across lineages. It distinguishes not only the content but the very nature of siddha medical knowledge from that of Western medicine, and it links siddha vaidyas, if not always in a collective community of knowledge, then at least in a collective community of experience. V. R. Madhavan holds that before the influence of the British in India, "Education itself was taken in its original sense as involving the educing of the latest capabilities and potentialities . . . and not as a mere mechanical process, operating on the basis of collective drill and training, as it is being done at the present day in the system of modern education. Mechanism is fatal to learning and spirituality where the mind and soul should be left free. . . . The process of individual growth (inner) can only be achieved by means of a constant and close relationship between the pupil and the teacher."[22] Although the details transmitted by different gurus may vary, Madhavan emphasizes the similarities in the experience of the guru/student relationship. He inverts prevalent notions of modern and traditional education, contrasting the creativity and dynamism of hereditary education, which offers "the latest capabilities and potentialities," to the lifeless knowledge transmitted in classrooms. His emphasis on form over content, and indeed his consideration of hereditary teaching as a distinct method of education among many possibilities, was only thinkable with the entry into south India of a radically different educational form, the "modern education" to which it is here, not coincidentally, juxtaposed.

Vaidyas caricature Western education as carried out solely through written works, devoid of personal contact. Kasturi contrasts the impersonal nature of biomedical knowledge to the oral nature of siddha knowledge: "A medical person can only know the methods of siddha medicine after sitting with a good guru and watching that guru prepare effective, unique medicines, even though those methods have been described at length in books. Only then will *ceypākam* [medical knowledge] and *kaipākam* [skill of hand in compounding medicines] be truly clear. In other medical systems, one can make medicines after simply reading and understanding books."[23] Consistently with their depiction of siddha medical knowledge as intuitive, grasped only by seeing beyond material nature, vaidyas hold that their medicine can only be learned through a mode of transmission that transcends the physicality of written texts. Writing in their view is at best a secondary transmission of a more primary and direct teaching, so texts need to be supplemented by the words of a guru in order to be understood properly. Indeed, orality fosters this sense of closeness because it demands a social relationship, something that is not compelled in the act of writing. The secrets of siddha medicine, Kasturi holds, are only available through the orality of traditional education.

Many vaidyas cite their common "experience" (*an̲upavam*) of siddha medical knowledge as a primary criterion for the authority of their practice. They assert that those without this experience, and those who try to learn about their system entirely through books, do not have true knowledge of siddha medicine. Thus, there is often tension between siddha practitioners who have been educated in schools and those who have hereditary training. Kundrathur Ramamurthy views the founding of schools and colleges of siddha medicine as a positive development, but criticizes this "official" mode of education as deficient both in its reliance on books and in its neglect of integrating the knowledge of "village vaidyas" into its curriculum.

> College study only is not enough; it's not useful. This siddha medicine began as home remedy.... Even today, in villages where [Western] doctors don't go, they're practicing medicine.... Like that, many of the hereditary doctors, all the village doctors, they continue to use many processes. These processes need to be studied, researched, and developed.... What is the use of book learning only? ... If one just reads reference books, graduates and begins work as in other fields, one's mind might go blank. If one wants, one can just buy IMPCOPS or patent drugs and use those.[24] But seeing directly what medicines have what effect, and how we prepare these, only then can one do medicine

> successfully. Then one can obtain full benefit. Every student should be able to prepare medicine.

Ramamurthy does not acknowledge the emphasis on textual learning that we observed in premodern Tamil medical works, and the "book learning" he speaks of does not refer to the modern study of these premodern texts, but to "reference books" that are used in colleges of both Western and traditional medicine. He goes on to distinguish siddha medicine from other disciplines of learning. "From books, you only learn the names of plants. But you can't learn about the plants themselves. . . . One needs to go to the field for that. . . . We can be successful only after we approach people with expertise in preparing medicine, and learn the processes of medical preparation. One can't just use books. Books are just a guide. In other fields a guide is enough. One can't do that in siddha medicine." Ramamurthy's critique here, one he shares with other hereditary practitioners, is not only of schools of siddha medicine but also of biomedical education, which has provided the model for teaching in siddha colleges. Further embedded in his critique is a broader claim that siddha medicine is unlike other disciplines of knowledge and practice, requiring personal study under an established vaidya. When he speaks of the origin of his practice in home remedies that use common ingredients like *rasam*, tamarind, salt, and pepper, he emphasizes that siddha medicine is founded on the food that every Tamil consumes in their midday meal. This highlights the Tamil nature of siddha medical experience, which comes in the homes and the villages of the common people, not in the classrooms and libraries of the educated elite.

In drawing a distinction between hereditary experience and book learning, vaidyas run the risk of dividing siddha vaidyas into two groups, those who have hereditary training and those who learned about siddha medicine in a school or college. Vaidyas address this potential rift by urging the government to incorporate hereditary knowledge into college teaching of siddha, as Ramamurthy emphasized above. Indeed, some see hereditary knowledge as the basis of current siddha college curriculums. G. J. Parthasarathy, like other hereditary practitioners, chides college-educated students for their lack of experience. "Those who have studied at colleges do not have the knowledge, ideas, or experience of hereditary practitioners like us. They don't have so much knowledge about things. Just theoretical knowledge. They do as they read in books." However, he downplays the distinction between these two forms of education, connecting classroom teaching with hereditary knowledge.

> There's the opinion that in general these with a BSMS degree don't really accept hereditary practitioners.[25] But those who are smart, they acknowledge that hereditary practitioners know many things. The syllabus which

> is used by students today, it is our hereditary practitioners themselves who have provided that. Those who have created the syllabus and everything, they are our old vaidyas. There still isn't a syllabus that is just for college students. I don't think it's a competition, me or you; I don't say that they are great, or we are great. For those who have finished their studies, there's an opportunity. They still need to learn many things. They need to do well. Particularly, they need to meet people. They need to do genuine service for them.

While distinguishing hereditary and classroom styles of education, G. J. Parthasarathy does not distinguish the content of teaching, holding that the college siddha syllabus was devised on the basis of hereditary knowledge. A college-educated student can still gain the experience necessary to become a successful and effective siddha vaidya, so formal education need not exclude a graduate from sharing in the community of siddha medical experience. He emphasizes that all siddha practitioners should share a common goal of serving people, and it is this shared responsibility to the larger community that finally must unite all siddha vaidyas.

When hereditary vaidyas in particular refer to their medical "experience," their usage of the term shares those qualities that Raymond Williams attributed to its English usage. That is, experience expresses an authority similar to that claimed by theological "witness," where "such experiences are offered not only as truths, but as the most authentic kind of truths."[26] Joan W. Scott similarly points to (and challenges) the consideration of experience as the acquisition of nondiscursive truth.[27] Colonial administrators and biomedical authorities have typified the experience of vaidyas differently, not as delineating an inscrutable and authoritative realm of activity, but in ways that reflect the eighteenth-century English usage that connects "experience" with "experiment" and "empiricism," which in turn retain the derogatory seventeenth-century medical usage of "empericks" as charlatans and quacks.[28] For these critics of traditional medical knowledge, hereditary experience offers not a realm of truth but its opposite, a refuge for the deceitful.

Already in 1923, Ponnuswami Pillai of Kumbakonam acknowledged and countered such critiques of the experience of vaidyas, asserting instead the incommensurability of experience: "It is entirely offensive to think lowly of the experiential knowledge of indigenous medicine, saying that it would not stand up to modern research. How can one say for certain that only those doctrines of medical science that are profitable for modern research are conclusive? Don't many doctrines change according to the opinions of distinguished researchers? So, it is unfair to emphasize that indigenous medical knowledge can only be accepted after it is tested by modern research."[29] Ponnuswami Pillai overstates the uniqueness of siddha medical experience, making a radical distinction between indigenous experience, on the one hand, and the doctrines and "modern research" of biomedicine on the other, neglecting the fact that clinical experience is an essential part of the training of biomedical doctors. He does not claim simply that siddha vaidyas and biomedical doctors have *different* experiences, but that siddha vaidyas learn through experience while biomedical doctors learn through impersonal and theoretical means. He thus naturalizes and essentializes distinctions between indigenous and Western disciplines of knowledge. He emphasizes difference by invoking the radical interiority of indigenous experience, whether it is individual, between a guru and student, or shared by a community, which makes it the exclusive domain of the Tamil community and provides a space in which its authority appears self-evident.

The interiority of experience that these vaidyas celebrate is usually that of the hereditary lineage or of an imagined community of all siddha vaidyas, not of the individual practitioner. They tend to downplay the authority of individual and original experience both because it is contrary to the notion that medicinal knowledge is best accumulated and preserved, not invented, and because it does not conform to their vision of a coherent medical system of selfless, cooperating vaidyas. In citing the commonality of their medical experience, they mark community boundaries, especially those which distinguish their medicine from Western medicine. In emphasizing that the experience of hereditary education is one that biomedical doctors do not share, siddha vaidyas pose a radical distance between their methods and the techniques, and critiques, of biomedicine. It is this relativity and inscrutability of the common experience of tradition that makes it a realm of activity, a site, from which external critique can be deflected and in which extraordinary claims appear feasible.

By emphasizing the shared experience of hereditary education, vaidyas locate the presumed decay of their system in nontraditional sources, scapegoating new methods of education that were institutionalized in colonial India. The siddhars had "practised and preached this great system and left a mass of literature in Tamil on Palmyra leaves. As the subject treated is a highly technical one with its own special meanings for the words employed, they came to be misunderstood, when the personal instruction and guidance of the Guru to the disciple was lost."[30] While vaidyas blame the British imperial government for the destruction of their educational system and for the decay of their knowledge, they appeal to contemporary state and national governments to help recuperate this knowledge. Kundrathur Ramamurthy spoke of his appreciation of government efforts to develop siddha medicine through medical colleges, but pointed to a lack of effort in supporting hereditary knowledge.

> If you ask about siddha medical colleges . . . the government is trying to do something. There those who have graduated are conducting all

> kinds of lessons. Many students have joined and are studying. But that is not enough. No matter how one looks at it, it's insufficient. There hasn't been enough development. The government still needs to do a lot. . . . This siddha medicine began as home remedy. . . . Hereditary doctors, village doctors . . . are practicing medicine like first aid. Government needs to learn about these processes, research and develop them. Now the work done is insufficient. Much still needs to be done.

Vaidyas even pleaded with the colonial British to support traditional education. In the 1923 *Report of the Committee on the Indigenous Systems of Medicine*, N. Veeraraghavaperumal Pillai urges novices to study under a "Tamil medical guru," assuring that only then will they become medical experts. "If these government officials support guruhood (*kuruttuvam*) in the name of Tamil medicine, without thinking too much or too little about their own objectives, there will be no obstacle to us, as Tamil doctors, attaining a praiseworthy position equal to that of Western doctors in some areas. If government officials attend to this matter, it is not due to partiality but justice."[31] In their calls for official support of hereditary education, vaidyas acknowledge the importance of government medical patronage, and they seek to transform the negativity of official perceptions of their modes of education.

The Official Authority of Obscure and Lost Knowledge

Government calls for the public and open display of medical knowledge has not meant that government bodies in India have been immune to the captivating effects of obscured knowledge. Take, for example, Government Order (GO) no. 1060 from the Government of Madras Education and Public Health Department, dated June 13, 1966. This GO traces the work of a committee convened to compile materials for the completion of siddha medical textbooks for use at the College of Indian Systems of Medicine, established in November 1964 at Palayamkottai. This work continued the efforts of an earlier committee that first met in 1962, also to collect information for official publications. The information gathered by the committee was of three sorts: (1) palm-leaf manuscripts, collected from hereditary practitioners; (2) research and collection of medicinal plants in mountainous and forest areas in Tamil Nadu state; (3) gathering of medical knowledge from hereditary practitioners.[32] The focus for their collection of texts, plants, and personal knowledge was the "districts of the Tamil Nad" and did not include non-Tamil-speaking regions, and thus was both ethnically and politically determined.[33] The collection of plants and manuscripts became the focus of the project, and the knowledge of practicing vaidyas was largely ignored.

The committee first toured the mountainous Salem District, where "rarer medical plants are abundantly found." They visited the many forests and mountains of the region, noting that the medicinal plants in these areas needed protection from the devastation of animals. These regions, where these "rare" plants are paradoxically found in abundance, "will be of much use if they were undertaken for the purpose of the growth, maintenance, collection and distribution of such rare medicinal plants."[34] The committee was most interested in finding those "medicinal plants and herbs described in ancient siddha literatures." After visiting "Kolli Hills, Yercaud (Sehrvaroy Hills), and Siddhar Malai [Mountain of the Siddhars]," where these "rare herbal plants are said to have a natural growth," they lamented the difficulty of the collection task. In such a short visit, "it is not physically possible to investigate, identify and collect those herbs. It requires a good amount of hiking waiting and perseverance and it is also essential to obtain assistance and co-operation from local inhabitants and physicians who have already personal knowledge of these tracts." They thus petitioned the government for more money to carry out this work, "in view of the fact that abundant useful knowledge may be available for the medical world by the proposed investigation of the committee into these rare herbs." The committee members predicated the potential medical value of plants on their rareness, and their rareness on their inaccessibility. On a trip to Kanjan Malai, they only made it to the "foot of the hill since time was short. The committee feels that a sufficient time should be spared to see the growth of the rarer medicinal plants at the top of the hill."[35] The higher one goes, and the farther one travels from the centers of human habitation, the rarer the plants and the more promising their potential to heal, even though the committee admits that they did not see, let alone evaluate, these "rarer medicinal plants."

Vaidyas invariably cite mountains and forests, and to a lesser degree villages, as the most productive places of siddha medical activity. G. J. Parthasarathy criticized students at siddha medical colleges for learning only in cities. "They need to go out to the villages and do fieldwork. They need to go to the forested mountains, stay and live there, as I have lived." Mountains and forests or, best, forested mountains, are the dwelling places of the siddhars, where they first developed siddha medicine and where the most potent medicinal plants are found. This location of the most powerful siddha medicine beyond the edges of civilization is not new, and I suspect that the search for nonlocal medical plants in places inaccessible to others has long been a way that vaidyas could distinguish themselves from competing vaidyas. For vaidyas today, even if the mountains and forests of siddha medicine fall within political borders determined by the modern state, their appeal is partly that they are far from the centers of cosmopolitan India. Vaidyas often hold that urban areas are corrupted by the mixing of cultures, both non-Tamil Indian cultures and most important Western culture that is embodied in modern civilization. The original siddha medical tradition must be located in a state of true nature, which is best realized in those areas least touched by modern civilization, that is, mountains, jungles, and to a lesser degree villages. The captivating appeal of rare, exotic plants also holds today, though this is seen in somewhat different terms in line with shift in medical competition. If previously, vaidyas would seek exotic herbs in distant places so they could claim to have medicines that neighboring vaidyas did not, today mountains and forests might yield plants that have so far eluded the acquisition, classification, analysis, and exploitation of botanists and the allied biomedical and phamaceutical industries.

After failing to collect valuable medical plants, the committee turned their attention to meeting vaidyas practicing throughout Tamil Nadu state. Consistently with their fascination with data that is imperiled and obscure, the committee members expressed far more interest in obtaining the palm-leaf manuscripts in the possession of vaidyas than they did in recording the knowledge that these vaidyas used in their everyday practices.[36] This was despite their stated goal, that the textbooks they produced would harmonize "the ancient and modern knowledge wherever possible. The best in the old and in the new on any topic or subject should be embodied in them [the textbooks] without any glimpse of deviation from the fundamental principles of Siddha medicine."[37] Their assumption that siddha medicine has basic principles that remain constant through all times, texts, regions, vaidyas, and practices is consistent with their representation of siddha medicine as a unified medical system. Their textbooks, and the school that would utilize them, would teach these eternal principles of siddha medicine. However, the committee clearly saw the premodern texts and rare medical plants as embodying these principles more accurately than the "modern knowledge" of contemporary vaidyas. The committee, "after meeting many traditional Vaidiars was able to collect a large volume of palm leaf manuscripts pertaining to Siddha medicine."[38] Their consultations with siddha vaidyas was primarily to ascertain whether they possessed palm-leaf manuscripts that they would be willing to part with, rather than to record the details of their daily medical practices.

The GO details meetings with dozens of traditional vaidyas throughout the state. Typical was the committee's meeting with "siddha physician Thiru M. Krishnayya" of Nagercoil in 1962. "He stated that he is having cudgeon leaves, nearly 10. Some of them have been written and they are now as manuscripts. He has got no idea of the list of the names of the cudgeon leaves. The manuscripts are written in Tamil and they are roughly 12 in number. He informed that he will co-operate with the committee."[39] They did not express any interest in his present practice, placing greater value on the manuscripts in his possession, which he did not understand, than on the medical knowledge he did possess. This preference for textual knowledge over practical experience bears out the critique posed by hereditary vaidyas, that official versions of siddha medicine emphasize texts over experience. Indeed, in the everyday practice of most vaidyas, textual authority is balanced by their own experiences and discoveries, and often palm-leaf manuscripts in their possession are unintelligible to them. The committee members also had difficulty reading these manuscripts, admitting that "the collected palm leaves from the Kanyakumari District were copied by the Epigraphist, and considerable difficulty was experienced by the Member-Secretary to compare the typed manuscript with cadjan leaves."[40] This official fascination with obscure knowledge, this abiding by the authority of the mysterious, challenges the tempting dichotomy between hereditary vaidyas as haphazard healers practicing in secrecy and obscurity, on the one hand, and cosmopolitan officials who seek to formulate a scientific traditional medicine, on the other.

Because of this official regard for textual knowledge, siddha vaidyas and scholars have been successful in winning support to preserve this textual knowledge in their appeals to both national and international bodies. The disintegration of these texts is the most literal manifestation of the decay of traditional medicine that all parties seem to agree upon, if for different reasons. Their motivations for preserving this knowledge is likewise disparate, from the hopes of some vaidyas that the systematic compilation of this substantial body of knowledge will lead to the rediscovery of extraordinary medicines, to nationalist projects to develop indigenous sciences, to global projects to preserve past civilizations. Yet they all are susceptible to the appeal of obscured knowledge.

Lost knowledge shares with secret knowledge the qualities of being inscrutable and thus mysterious, qualities that lead people to idealize it. Lost knowledge, insofar as it is not accessible to anyone, is perhaps concealed knowledge par excellence. Given the current ambivalence of the morality of secrecy, many vaidyas have shifted the focus of their extraordinary claims from the secrets of the paramparai to the knowledge that is perpetually lost with to ravages of history. They cite lost manuscripts as the treasure of their siddha medical system, making the curious claim that what they no longer possess testifies to the greatness of their tradition. That is, they celebrate knowledge that they admit they do not know, and manuscripts that no longer exist, thereby invoking loss as evidence for the value of their tradition. Their rhetoric is persuasive because they provide specific locations for this knowledge, either in the past, or in extant but decaying manuscripts, and in this way they make this knowledge visible. Furthermore, insofar as such knowledge is concealed, it is an empty template that vaidyas color in often extraordinary ways. Like secret knowledge, lost knowledge can offer fabulous potential, setting it apart from knowledge that can be tested and scrutinized. In their mysterious appeal, secrets that a few know differ little from secrets that no one knows.

Lost and Decaying Manuscripts

Siddha vaidyas advance the construction of a pure Tamil siddha medical system with palm-leaf manuscripts, which they view as tangible survivals of the ancient glory of their medicine. These manuscripts are viewed as evidence not only for a sophisticated medicine practiced by a refined civilization but also for the existence of the siddhars themselves, the attributive authors of these texts. In his *History of Agastya*, A. Chidambaranar responds to those who deny the existence of the siddhar Agastya. "Still today there are many siddha texts written by a siddhar named Agastya. How can one claim, then, that a siddhar named Agastya did not exist?"[41] Private organizations and regional and national government institutions have collected thousands of these manuscripts in the last century, housing them in archives and libraries throughout Tamil Nadu.[42] Some of these texts have been edited and printed for use by individual practitioners and medical colleges. The latter read them as recipe books for different medicines that might be formulated and tested, ignoring their overtly religious elements, such as those portions that depict the activities of the siddhars, or that urge the vaidya to worship the goddess in conjunction with the formulation of medicines. College textbooks on siddha medicine quote these texts as authoritative canon. However, when vaidyas invoke the extraordinary potential of their medicine, they are less likely to cite this readily available knowledge than they are texts that are decaying or have been lost in the vicissitudes of history. Even extant Tamil manuscripts are often unreadable in parts, an essential ingredient for a medical preparation consumed by a worm or termite, leaving a hole in the manuscript and a doubt in medical knowledge that is not only lamented by practitioners as the loss of a great medicine but that also creates an inscrutable space in which vaidyas express the glory of their medicine.[43]

The number of manuscripts that have been edited and published is small, while the vast majority lie unread, their contents disintegrating despite the best efforts and strongest chemicals applied by conservationists. Certainly, the number that has been lost is also large. V. R. Madhavan mourns this loss of palm-leaf texts: "Manuscripts on palmleaf or paper of the ancient works are the great treasures solely inherited by the Tamils. Many of Siddha medical manuscripts were destroyed by white ants, fire and water and some were taken away by foreigners. Even among those that have escaped the ravages of time the works which have so far been destined to see the light of day are only a few."[44] Just as the call to systematize the knowledge of individual paramparais assumes the naturalness of an encompassing, synchronic Tamil-speaking community, the notion that the loss of manuscripts signals a break with the ancient Tamil medical community assumes a natural temporal continuity, a proper inheritance of tradition. Vaidyas often speak of the loss of these manuscripts as death, not just of the manuscripts but also of Tamil tradition and community as a whole. In his autobiographical account of his collection and preservation of palm-leaf manuscripts, G. John Samuel depicts his recovery mission in terms of mortality: "Remembering those who have passed away, thinking of them with terrible mental anguish and deep hurt, people who live on suffer in so many ways on account of such losses. . . . How do people of a linguistic community face such great losses, the likes of which make individuals tremble? How do they bear those losses? My attempts to acquire and restore Tamil palm-leaf manuscripts were in part born out of these concerns."[45] It is a linguistic community that Samuel sees as helping individuals deal with the sorrow of death. Communities provide a locus of identity that transcends the mortality of individuals, preceding the birth of the individual and continuing after its death.[46] Insofar as an individual identifies with this greater self, communities offer individuals a way to imagine themselves as part of something immortal.

Continuity in the transmission of knowledge in South Asia has lent itself to biological metaphors of generation and death for millennia. From Vedic times, oral transmission of knowledge has been viewed as a new birth, as the initiation to Vedic study, effected through the *upanayana* investiture of the sacred thread, is the "second birth" of the student who becomes "twice born" (*dvija*). Transmission is thus a regeneration of knowledge that maintains continuity from one generation to the next, and any break in this chain will result in the death of that knowledge. Indeed, Samuel speaks of destroyed manuscripts as the lost, literary "children" of "mother Tamil," drawing on the symbol of *Tamiḻtāy*, the goddess of Tamil that has played a large role in the revivalist deification of the Tamil language.[47]

> Mother Tamil stands weeping and helpless, losing so many literary children (*ilakkiyap piḷḷaikaḷ*) to the cruel dance of time, to the fury of nature, to the heat of fire, and to the floods of swollen rivers. . . . How many of her artistic treasures have been lost because of the indifference and the superstitions of people on this soil? How many of her literary children were sacrificed in the name of the cruelty of men in times of religious conflict? How many of her creations of refined Tamil were lost in times of the invasion of others and the spread of outsiders? How many of these literary children of Tamil even today are caught in the creeping hands of death, slowly dying in all the unreachable corners of various foreign countries? This book resulted from my search for these lost texts.[48]

He considers these manuscripts as the products neither of individuals nor of the siddhars but of an ethnic, linguistic community unified in the symbol of a mother. Speaking in the language of Tamil revivalism, Samuel likens a break in the transmission of manuscripts to a death in the Tamil family. While the reasons for the loss of manuscripts are both natural and social, he gives primacy to the legacy of foreign impact, because it has not only resulted in the destruction or exportation of manuscripts but has also made Tamils indifferent to these texts.

Samuel portrays himself as a good son, a loyal member of a community that he conceives as a family. His conviction that Tamil language, culture, and literature are equal to any in the world came at a young age, flowing "in my blood" and "inscribing itself deeply in me."[49] He struggles to explain this physiological devotion to Tamil, especially given that he grew up in Neyur, a town in the southern district of Kanya Kumari that was a center of the anglicizing project of Christian missionaries. He contrasts himself not only to his family and childhood acquaintances but more important to Tamil scholars and local government ministers and authorities who declared that all the valuable Tamil manuscripts had already been published and that the rest are "rubbish." Samuel castigates these people, saying that they win the trust of the people with the words "my body is of the soil and my soul of Tamil," but they subsequently neglect their "mother tongue." Their "Tamil feeling" (*tamiḻuṇarvu*), Samuel concludes, is the "fake deceit of their work."[50]

Samuel describes his own "Tamil feeling" as emerging from his nostalgic visions of the traditional past: "My heart began to imagine the revolution in knowledge that occurred in past society through these palm-leaf manuscripts. Scenes that I had heard of kids in traditional schools writing with awls appeared often before my mental eye. Shadowy visions of great poets taking their awls and writing on manuscripts, nourishing the garden of Tamil literature, appeared to me. Every time I saw a palm-leaf manuscript, my mind was intoxicated with joy. But still, I was not able to read clearly the letters written on those manuscripts."[51] Samuel's evocative fantasy of the utopia that was traditional Tamil society is aroused by the mere sight of Tamil manuscripts, manuscripts whose content, he admits, were opaque to him. This juxtaposition of enchantment and ignorance is no coincidence, because the illegibility of the manuscripts to Samuel meant that he could read into them his own fertile visions. The ambiguity of concealed knowledge gives it the pliancy to accommodate a variety of shifting contexts and agendas.

If unreadable extant manuscripts evoke utopian visions, lost manuscripts do so even more, because they symbolize the loss of the original transmission of siddha medical knowledge. In his presentation at the Second World Tamil Conference in 1968, P. Muttukkaruppa Pillai laments the loss of siddha medical knowledge: "Many rare and precious texts of the great siddhars, which definitively prescribe the best way for everyone to achieve a good life, have been destroyed in many different ways and at many different occasions due to the neglect of our ancestors and to the changes of nature. Rich treasurehouses of the siddhars' ideas were lost, both when the Lemurian continent was submerged in the Indian Ocean at the time of the first academy, and when Kannaki, seeing the mistake of the Pandyan king, made Madurai city prey to fire during the last academy."[52] Tamil feeling compels the evaluation of the unknown in Tamil tradition as precious and valuable, arising in conjunction with visions of Tamil utopia. Vaidyas often read the history of palm-leaf manuscripts within Tamil revivalist history, considering the oldest texts to have contained the most effective medical knowledge. They hold that extant manuscripts are just the remnants of a vast number of ancient manuscripts, most of which have been lost.

Even as the extant manuscripts provide evidence for the existence of lost manuscripts, the assertion that much has been lost in turn makes what remains all the more valuable.

> Even though we know of countless texts that were written at the time of the last academy, only a few of those are still available to us. Through those few texts which have survived all these sorts of destruction and which we have in our hands, it is clear that our ancestors attained great expertise in wisdom, clarity, research and service, and rose to the foremost position as the greatest race in the world. With all the great texts written by the siddhars that we still have, is there any limit to the benefits we can obtain?[53]

Perfect in their original redaction, extant manuscripts have, however, become obscured through historical processes. V. R. Madhavan writes of the perfection of the system, a perfection that will be achieved only if the knowledge is recovered from obscurity. "Siddha system is a complete system. . . . It may be asked that while Siddha Medicine is a perfect, unique and superior system, why has it not become popular. The answer is, defective books as well as defective use of books which abound in Siddha Medical Literature."[54] Recent editions of the manuscripts have been published, yet Madhavan laments the quality of these editions. "All the books as they are now, are without any doubt, spurious works, mostly badly copied and printed. Though the books are spurious, a good percentage of them have got some proportion of stray valuable contents, which have come from the ages past."[55] Not only have thousands of the most valuable manuscripts been lost but even the manuscripts that are available today are full of mistakes. It is a testament to the brilliance of ancient Tamil society that anything of value remains.

What has been for the most part lost, then, is not only precious medical knowledge, and not only the continuity of the siddha medical legacy, but also an important link to the ancient Tamil community. But this connection has not been completely severed, and vaidyas hold out hope that the knowledge and luster of ancient Tamil culture can be recovered. Kasturi writes,

> There are still thousands of siddha medical manuscripts that have not been printed. Skillful siddha doctors are decreasing. Diagnosis by pulse reading is not explained well, not taught, and not practiced. Important siddha medical truths lie buried as archeological material, needing to be researched and revealed. Thousands of texts have been destroyed. They are still decaying. Some excellent siddha medicines have not been prepared or used for about two thousand years. This medical system has been crushed by other medical systems for 2,000 years. Now is the time to give it a measure of new life. We urge our Tamil Nadu government to nurture and encourage this great medical system.[56]

The goal, most agree, is to systematize the texts. Manuscripts must be collected from private homes and foreign countries, and gathered together in Tamil Nadu, their place of origin, and their contents compared. They must be edited and published so that they are available to the public. This is one of the motivations behind S. Chidambarathanu Pillai's founding of the Siddha Medical Literature Research Centre. The original charter of the center gives fourteen objectives, of which the first is: "The truths of siddha medicine, contained in thousands of manuscripts, are decaying. These great and rare siddha medical texts which have yet to be published must be collected, researched and published in a proper manner and within a specified time."[57] Research here is primarily textual and does not yield new discoveries but aims to rediscover ancient knowledge. Research in this sense bridges the gap between the present Tamil community and the ancient Tamil community that it imagines, attempting to reconstitute a Tamil community not limited to, or by, the modern world.

Most vaidyas appeal to the government to do this work, assuring that if these texts are collected and the knowledge contained in them recovered, siddha medicine will rise to its prior position as the preeminent medical system in the world.

> So many manuscripts are decaying with families. These are old and worn and are deteriorating, of no use to those who possess them nor to others. In those very texts, many rare treasures lie hidden. Tamils themselves must come forward and donate these. The government must also establish separate committees for this, which will go to every corner of the Tamil land, collect these rare treasures, examine all the medicines in them, and organize them so that they are useful for the people of the world. . . . If basic steps such as these are taken, Tamil medicine will flourish forever.[58]

The recuperation of siddha medical knowledge will reestablish the link with the utopian Tamil past, thereby reuniting a timeless, unnaturally divided community.

Tamil medicine can bestow immortality because it is itself part of an immortal tradition.

Conclusion

The ideals of open knowledge, systematization, and publication have, in the practice of siddha medicine, been the grounds for a critique of secrecy. Siddha vaidyas thus claim the prestige offered by secrecy through different means, by positing glory in medical knowledge that has been destroyed by the furies of nature and the invasions of foreigners. This not only enables them to continue to imbue their medicine with extraordinary potential but it also accords with international efforts to preserve histories and cultures. For example, Samuel's Institute of Asian Studies, which collects, edits, and publishes palm-leaf manuscripts, receives Japanese funding and is part of UNESCO's "Memory of the World Project." The interests of this UNESCO project are similar to those voiced by Andrew Cardew in August 1918, when he asserted that any colonial interest in ayurveda was for "antiquarian" purposes.[59] Siddha medical manuscripts, according to the language of UNESCO, are part of the "memory" of the world, not its present or its future. The goals of siddha vaidyas in preserving their texts and practices are far more urgent, consisting of the preservation of their tradition, their community as they conceive it, and their livelihoods. That these objectives only vaguely correspond to those of international concerns matters little, as vaidyas will accept whatever financial support is available to them.

Many, like S. P. Ramachandran, note the irony of the fragility of the medical system that discovered the formulae for immortality. "Isn't it pitiful to think that today siddha medicine, which discovered medicines that bestow immortality, today has to be rescued from a state of dying!"[60] Vaidyas lament their losses, but they temper their sorrow with the hope that not all has been lost. The current state of siddha medical knowledge, they say, is just a pale reflection of its former glory, yet this reflection contains the seeds for a reconstruction of the original, evidenced in the thousands of manuscripts that are in desperate need of preservation. Although they cite these disintegrating texts as evidence of lost glory, they posit that the reintegration of these texts, their collection from selfish vaidyas and foreign archives and relocation into public, Tamil spaces, will initiate the recovery of this perfect medicine. They equate the revival of this lost tradition with the conquest of death, because it will reestablish links with a timeless community, and more concretely, because it may result in the rediscovery of medicine that can bestow immortality. This project might restore siddha medicine to the apex of the world's medical systems, immortalizing the knowledge that is currently in peril of disappearing.

8

Conclusion

The Holy Science of Siddha Medicine

Two Recipes, One for Immortality

Dr. A. Shanmuga Velan, whose eulogy to siddha medicine we saw in the introduction, became interested in the possibility of significantly extending the human life span in his "college days," and he established the Tirumular Siddha Medical Academy in Madras in 1959 to pursue knowledge of this "fundamental principle of siddha medicine." He published the results of his research in 1963 in English, in a book entitled *Siddhar's Science of Longevity and Kalpa Medicine of India*. He carried out this research with his own funding, as none was forthcoming from any government or private organization.[1] In this book, Shanmuga Velan reveals details of the production of muppu. It is made of three salts, "pooneeru," "kalluppu," and "vediyuppu." Pooneeru is born from fuller's earth deposits, kalluppu refers to either mined rock salt or sea salt, and vediyuppu is potassium nitrate. Following a text of the siddhar Yugi Muni, Shanmuga Velan gives the following instructions for preparation. These three salts are purified with the juice of a few of the 108 kalpa or longevity plants, and also with *amuri*, usually urine but what Velan describes as the "quintessence of all the waters of Seven Seas which has no taste of salt . . . the genuine magna mater."[2] These salts are purified with nitric acid and then calcinated. Mercury, sulphur, arsenic, and other inorganic substances are purified with "suitable medicinal plants and rendered as non-volatile substances." These are then calcinated, and the resultant powder is mixed with the calcinated three salts to complete the formulation of muppu. This muppu has the power "to conquer everything and can penetrate every solid." It is used to prepare medicines that can "be used as a panacea for degenerative diseases like cancer, etc." This muppu is "highly regarded as the Elixer of life which can be safely administered to the system to rejuvenate the degenerated cellular organisms for living a longer and useful life."[3] Shanmuga Velan goes on to announce the formulation of a medicine he calls "Anti-Cancer Elixir Guru 5," and he gives a number of kalpa plants that prolong life, such as "Sarkarai vembu—Sweet margosa" and "Kodi nelli—Creeper goose-berry."[4]

Although Velan's search for rejuvenative medicines is not unusual among vaidyas, more common are medicines that promise much less, and that are formulated with less exotic materials. An article in *Mūlikaimaṇi*, "Nalla Nalla Nāṭṭu Maruntukaḷ" (Very good country medicines), gives the medical benefits of a number of common plant substances. For example, if one takes the herb called *ōmam* (bishop's weed) and fries it with equal portions of black pepper, long pepper (*tippili*), and cardamom, grinds it into a powder, and mixes it with an equal portion of sugar, the resulting medicine is good for indigestion, pleurisy, and flatulence. One should take two or three pinches of it with water.[5] Another organic product, *kuṅkiliyam*, the sap of a shorea tree, is widely available at country medicine shops. It is either white or dusty white in color. The author recommends the pure white *kuṅkiliyam*, which should be added to boiling coconut water. It will melt in the hot water, and the resulting broth should be left to evaporate, leaving just the "purified" *kuṅkiliyam*. This residue should be pulverized, and one-quarter spoon of the powder should be taken with coconut water. This will cure indigestion and any urinary problems, and it will alleviate the burning of sores in the urinary tract. It is also an excellent preventative medicine for strangury in the hot season, and it can even be used as a kind of incense to remove foul air from the home.[6]

Why a Holy Science?

The daily work of siddha vaidyas is not the pursuit of immortality, but the healing of common ailments, most of which are not life-threatening. Vaidyas earn their living by giving advice and medicines to patients who come to them with asthma, sexual dysfunction, or joint pain; their clients do not come expecting their youth to be restored or their body made golden in color and hard as a diamond. How, then, do we understand the consistency with which siddha vaidyas juxtapose the banal and the extraordinary, a medicine for indigestion with the elixir of life?

To clarify some of the specific features of this juxtaposition, it is helpful to compare modern siddha medicine with modern yoga. In the last century, the discursive space that siddha vaidyas have constructed for their knowledge and practices shares much with that carved out by leading figures in modern yoga. In *Yoga in Modern India*, Joseph Alter examines the ways that leading figures in the promotion of modern yoga have worked to establish yoga as a science. He focuses on "physiology and physical fitness rather than on metaphysics, meditation, and soteriology." At the same time, he recognizes the importance of the supernatural in yoga, and he considers at length the "complex intersection of at least two powerful myths—the metaphysics of Yoga, and yogic physiology in particular, and the methods of science and scientific knowledge." In an especially pithy and powerful phrase, he notes that the early leaders of modern yoga used science as it suited them: yoga "has absorbed, and not just withstood, the harsh light of science."[7] Elsewhere Alter reflects on what he sees as a disjunction between the materialist features and scientific claims of yoga, on the one hand, and its alchemical, magical aspects on the other.[8] The authors of modern yoga work within a framework that he calls "secularised spiritualism," according to which they try to purge yoga of some of its more extraordinary features and claims. Alter argues that there is "a degree of profound ambivalence if not explicit contradiction between a secularised, 'sanitised' scientific ideal of medicalised practice, and the 'other history' of sex, magic, and alchemy." He attributes this tension to the convergence of two histories, an alchemical, magical, tantric tradition of yoga that dates to the tenth and eleventh centuries, and the modern incorporation of the language of science.[9]

Alter's work is fascinating, both for its provocative style and more specifically here for its analysis of features similar to those in which siddha vaidyas today define their practice. The "secularised spiritualism" that frames twentieth-century formulations of yoga shares much with the way that siddha vaidyas consider their knowledge as, in T. V. Sambasivam Pillai's words, a "holy science." Both yoga and siddha have been able to more or less effectively claim status as a science by citing the materialist, bodily focus of their knowledge and practices. Alter highlights the recent "medicalisation" of yoga practice, which positions yoga as a form of therapy, and yoga has a strong presence in siddha medicine, both in the siddhars' texts and in contemporary conceptions of the body, health, and so on. However, apart from the obvious difference that siddha medicine has, from the earliest Tamil medical texts to the present, devoted much of its energy to the formulation and administering of medicines, the relationship between siddha and science has been much more ambivalent than that between yoga and science. As a result, siddha vaidyas have far more readily retained the metaphysical features of their past practices, and they have launched a much stronger critique of science than yoga seems to have done.

Alter is right to point to the alchemical history of yoga, and also to its prior metaphysics, especially present in the claim that a yogi can attain the siddhis. However, the tensions that Alter outlines between this past metaphysics and present attempts to modernize are largely absent for most siddha vaidyas, who promote alchemy and immortality as the centerpieces of their medical science. The authority of modern siddha medicine derives not only from its recent incorporation of a discourse of science, and not just from the work of rationalizing medical practice in line with this discourse, but also from its consistent insistence on the extraordinary wisdom of the past, and its use of material from this past to formulate a new tradition. This is to say that the juxtaposition of the scientific and the extraordinary in siddha medicine is not an awkward embarrassment for siddha vaidyas; this is more than a result of residing at the crossroads of history, because it has been actively forged by vaidyas and their defenders over the past century.

Vaidyas have retained many of the extraordinary claims of their tradition by making the mystical attributes of their medicine more amenable to their modern world. The metaphysics of siddha medicine today is eminently contemporary. Vaidyas explain the extraordinary power of the siddhars as adhering to the laws of nature; they shift accounts of the origins of their medicine from divinity to intuitive, ancient scientists; the focus of obfuscation moves, in official circles especially, from secrecy to lost manuscripts; and vaidyas align a narrative of utopian medical beginnings with archeology and geology. There is much new in modern siddha medicine, and it is tempting to think that it is all new, that it is all invented tradition. However, the continuity with the past that siddha tradition claims is not only imagined. The extraordinary powers of the siddhars retain some of their prior anti-authoritarian character, challenging the hegemony of science as they earlier challenged the ritual hegemony of brahmans. Vaidyas assign healing efficacy to the Tamil language that recalls earlier recourse to mantras, while a history of degeneration of knowledge and health is consistent with traditional considerations of the transmission of knowledge and the cycles of the yugas. The notion of the three humors suggests a natural conjunction of Tamil medicine, knowledge, and bodies. Even critiques of secrecy and lamentation over the loss of manuscripts are not new, though their justifications and meanings have changed. Indeed, it is difficult to somehow "untangle" the new and the old, nor can one easily assign the metaphysics of siddha to its past features and its rational features to modern influences. This has not in any case been my goal here; I have instead sought to show the complexity of the relations between past and present, and between self and other, and to reflect on the rhetorical power of a holy science.

Siddha vaidyas emphasize the extraordinary character of their medicine in part to challenge biomedicine as a limited, banal science. While authors of modern yoga invoke notions of science that incorporate metaphysics, siddha vaidyas have engaged in much greater contestation of the criteria by which particular practices may be considered scientific. This is largely because science, in its specific colonial and postcolonial institutional forms and especially in biomedicine, has directly challenged the structuring models and efficacy of siddha medicine. Unlike yoga, medicine has been a matter of great official concern, both for the colonial state and for the independent Indian government, and so it has often been a site of competition and conflict, as I have highlighted. The modern formulation of siddha medicine, far more than modern yoga, has therefore been a form of social protest. The strategies that vaidyas employ in constructing authority for their practices, such as the narration of utopia, the articulation of a holy science, and the assertion that their medicine can cure all diseases, all accomplish the work of critique, questioning dominant notions of history, truth, and community boundaries. Their targets have been as varied as the discourses they engage in: Aryan nationalists, biomedical doctors, colonial administrators, Indian scientists, and disloyal Tamils have all been singled out for criticism at particular times and in specific contexts. In the discourses that I have outlined, vaidyas seek to rescue siddha medicine, Tamil tradition, and the non-brahman Tamil people from irrelevance in the modern world. Their reformulation of an extraordinary medicine, in its most ambitious moments, seeks to liberate non-brahman Tamils from their status as subjects to north Indians, to brahmans, to the British, and to "the West."

In thinking about the relationship between the material and the extraordinary in siddha medicine, it is useful to revisit one of Georg Simmel's remarks about secrecy: "The secret offers, so to speak, the possibility of a second world alongside the manifest world; and the latter is decisively influenced by the former."[10] For siddha vaidyas, this manifest world is contemporary Tamil society, a world in which they vie for medical authority and clientele in a competitive medical market. It is a world of simple medicines for common ailments that are available to ordinary people, a world of extant manuscripts that can be edited and published, of historical and archeological data that can be scrutinized. This is the place that science can explain. Vaidyas also imagine a second world that exceeds the possibilities of a limited science. They create this world not only through secrecy but also by narrating a utopian past, by delineating a unique space of tradition, by positing the origins of their knowledge with evasive yogis and a Tamil god, and by invoking lost texts. Their imagined nether-world is the location of a glorious Tamil medical system that can cure all ills, and that even offers the holy grail of medical potential—the achievement of bodily immortality. Siddha medicine as it is apprehended in the contemporary manifest world is a pale shadow of this sublime second world, retaining only vestiges of its former glory.

As I have shown, the extraordinary aspects of siddha medicine have been actively reworked in contemporary times to more closely conform to shifting bases of authority in modern Tamil Nadu. But as Simmel suggests, the "second world" does not just emerge as a epiphenomenon of the manifest world, as it has significant influence over that manifest world. This imagined world is not idle reverie, because the experiences of vaidyas, their perceptions of their medicine, and especially their sense that much has been lost, emerge from discordance between their idealizations of tradition and their estimation of the present state of their knowledge. Their utopian formulations are themselves primary modes through which vaidyas construct their world, modes that are irreducible to other sorts of human activity. Furthermore, the contrast between these two worlds forges a relationship between them. The character vaidyas ascribe to this concealed second world suggests the work that those with the proper "Tamil feeling" should set for themselves in the manifest world: the recuperation and revelation of this obscure world through collecting and systematizing its scattered remains. In this way vaidyas hope to merge these two worlds, to recover the traditional world for modernity, to make siddha medical knowledge available to public scrutiny. Such a merger, they suggest, will revive the glory of Tamil medicine and culture that at this point exists most forcefully in the hopeful writings of Tamil revivalism.

If for heuristic reasons it is useful to think of vaidyas as engaging in two worlds, the utopian and mundane, or the extraordinary and the ordinary, this does not mean that the practices, experiences, and hopes of vaidyas are bifurcated or contradictory. After all, the distinction between religion and science is not absolute, as we now understand that religion is not a phenomenon distinct from other arenas of human activity, nor is science purely materialist and rational. Conceptions of the extraordinary are subject to political, economic, and material concerns, and science is likewise transformed by politics, consumerism, nationalist objectives, and fancies of the imagination. This is borne out in siddha medicine, in which science and religion have both become signs and sites of contestation, used as much for their rhetorical force as for their descriptive and methodological value. Vaidyas claim that their medicine is both eminently practical and potentially liberating, useful for common ailments but capable of curing even the most chronic and deadly diseases. Indeed, among the most common siddha medicines are those that use widely available ingredients and that promise something between immortality and remedy.

For example, the *Mūlikaimaṇi* article on country medicines describes sandalwood as "well-known for its use as a decorative substance," yet it also has "medical greatness." Red sandalwood is particularly powerful. If one soaks a chunk of sandalwood in water and drinks the water, "body heat and bile will decrease. Painful urination and chest palpitations will disappear. It will give the body strength and youth." If one grinds high-quality sandalwood root into a powder, mixes it with milk, and drinks it, diabetes will be brought under control.[11] The simple and the extraordinary reside comfortably together. G. J. Parthasarathy gave me a flyer that announces the recipe for an oil bath, with the heading "apply oil and then bathe, and get rid of all diseases!" His simple medicated oil is prepared with sesame oil, the leaves of a drumstick tree, parboiled rice, cumin, black pepper, garlic, dried pepper, and turmeric. When applied twice a week under specific conditions, it will cure forty ailments, including varicose veins, insomnia, skin diseases, diabetes, and problems with vision. This is the "technique of good living of our ancestors, on account of which they lived 'lives without disease.'" Parthasarathy told me that he had ten thousand of these fliers printed and posted as part of his public service. He insisted that oil baths are necessary in Tamil Nadu because of the hot weather, and that I should also take oil baths when I am in Tamil Nadu. "Only then can you be without disease. If you don't, then some disease will come." He told me that oil baths cool the body and reduce bile, and so are necessary to compensate for the hot climate. "If there's too much heat, cancer, diabetes, all diseases will come. To level that, always oil bath."

The extraordinary promise imbedded in the medicine of ordinary Tamils provides its captivating appeal. This mysterious character of siddha medicine is more than a historical curiosity, and more even than a tool with which to critique aggressive competitors. The possibility that one's local environment has the potential to bring beauty, youth, and eternal life, if only manipulated in the right way, continues to entice vaidyas and patients as it has for centuries. By emphasizing that the components of siddha medicine are both accessible and obscure, both ordinary and fabulous, vaidyas make the extraordinary appear within reach. They attribute great power to local histories, ingredients, and yogis, revealing to Tamils the greatness of their past, their traditions, and their community. Insofar as vaidyas and patients identify siddha medicine as theirs, the healing it offers is not only physical but also addresses the very conception of Tamil selfhood.

Siddha Medicine and the World

As we spoke in his house/clinic/laboratory, Kundrathur Ramamurthy told me about the siddhars: "In siddha medicine, Ramadevar was a siddhar. He went to Arabia under the name of Yacob and healed Muhammad Nabigal Nayagam. Bhogar flew in the air and went to China and did all sorts of things there. They all are 'worldish,' we can say. We talk about them in Tamil Nadu, as Tamils. . . . They are public figures for the world." The siddhars' position on the margins of society has also always seemed to place them on the cutting edge of society and culture. Throughout the history of their representations, they consistently challenge the boundaries of possibilities as conceived in specific contexts, whether caste, ritual, the limits of the body and health, or in recent times Indian nationalism and the dominance of science and biomedicine. They have also pushed the boundaries of the global imaginary of siddha medical activity. Most recently this has been accomplished through the Lemuria narrative and its implication that siddha medicine is the mother of all medicines, but this is not the first time the siddhars have been described as traveling to the limits of the known world. Agastya and Tirumular came from the Himalayas in the north, and more recently, as Ramamurthy mentions above, Yacob is said to have gone to Arabia and Bhogar to China. I will look at the far-reaching adventures of Yacob and Bhogar before discussing more generally the global character of siddha medicine.

Kanchana Natarajan dates the texts of Yacob to some point between the fifteenth and seventeenth centuries. These works describe Yacob as being born as Iramadevar and later converting to Islam after a trip to Mecca, and there are texts ascribed to both names. Iramadevar, of a warrior (*maravar tevar*) caste, lived in Nagapattinam, a center of maritime trade, and learned from Arab traders that there was alchemical knowledge among the *nabis* of Mecca. The texts recount that he traveled to Mecca in two different ways, by sea and also by taking a *kuḷikai* pill and flying there. While in Mecca, he converted to Islam, was circumcised, and took the name Yacob. He learned a variety of alchemical processes from the *nabis*, and taught them an alchemical salt preparation.[12] In his *Pañcāmirtam,* Yacob ridicules "the foolish" who "live with superstition, cover their bodies with ash and worship images made of copper." It is not clear, however, whether he is speaking as an iconoclastic Muslim or an iconoclastic siddhar, because he still holds the siddhars to have great knowledge and continues to worship Valai, a goddess associated with alchemy. He also engages with Sanskrit sources: "I have seen the texts in Sanskrit and have adapted that material in this work."[13] Yacob's Tamil texts contain Sanskrit, Arabic, Persian, and Urdu phrases. In addition to presenting alchemical knowledge, he urges his readers to "think of Allah and worship him three times a day. Read the Holy Qur'ān and learn to chant well . . . always hide your discoveries. Do not drink alcohol." On account of Yacob's liberal invocation of the siddhars, Allah, and Valai, Natarajan comments that "it is clear that alchemy was his main focus; religion was subordinated to alchemy."[14]

When people today mention Bhogar, they almost always say that he traveled to China. Most ascribe antiquity to his texts, the most important being *Pōkar 7000*. Layne Little points to features of the text, such as its references to technology, modern language, and even English words, that suggest its composition just before its initial publication in 1888. It describes technology such as steamboats, trains, parachutes, and telescopes. Bhogar travels to Rome via a *kuḷikai* pill, discovers the "Well of Mercury," procures mercury after meditating on Manonmani and Shiva, and returns by flight to Potigai Mountain.[15] When Bhogar is in China he constructs a steam engine and teaches the people of China how to run it. He also gives a fairly detailed description of the workings of the engine: "You put the fire in the baking pan, on the side of which water is placed and this will be turned to gas." The five elements work together to drive the engine, and with these five, "I have established this divine chariot. No Nātha has uncovered this. Having searched to exhaustion in text after text, I [alone] have discovered it." Bhogar then travels the globe with this train, going to Rome where he saw the "beautiful disciples of Jesus," and then to Jerusalem to see the "Great Mother," where he encountered Muslims and Jews. He gathered together the "great Siddhas, Munis and Ṛṣis of the world and took them to China, batch after batch, and led them all over the world." He even meets the siddhar Yacob and takes him to China in his train.[16]

What is interesting about these accounts of siddhars is that they incorporate far-flung places, and engage with new ideas and technologies, in premodern and early modern times. Mythologies of the siddhars, from the early ñāṉasiddhar writings to the present day, have placed them at the cutting edge of knowledge acquisition and teaching. They are therefore apt figures to serve as medical leaders: because of the urgency of health, illness, and death, medical practitioners, and perhaps patients first and foremost, are quick to integrate new technologies and possibilities. An example of this is the rapid globalization of "alternative medicines," which is one of the most dynamic arenas of recent global cultural exchange. This search for new knowledge has been pursued in siddha medicine and alchemy for centuries, contrary to a rhetoric that emphasizes the enduring, unchanging character of siddha medical tradition. Mythologies of the siddhars, Tamil medical manuscripts, and modern siddha medicine have been particularly receptive to engaging with the newest technologies, geographical hotspots, and the latest, most destructive diseases. This engagement has often been rhetorical and imaginative rather than material—that is, Bhogar did not invent the locomotive steam engine. But vaidyas have also sometimes used these technologies despite limitations in material resoures and expertise, by testing their medicines on laboratory rats, for example, or when isolating chemical compounds in local medical plants. Perhaps the most enduring element of siddha medical practice that highlights this pursuit of new knowledge is alchemy, which contemporary vaidyas continue to use in their search for rejuvenative medicines.

Most scholarship on the introduction of biomedicine into India has rightly focused on the imperialist intentions of this introduction and on the institutions of discipline and control in which biomedicine is embedded. I have likewise discussed at length here the challenges that biomedicine poses to ordinary vaidyas. Without meaning to downplay the negative impact of colonial medicine on the authority and vocations of traditional practitioners, I would also suggest that certain opportunities emerged out of this encounter. Alasdair MacIntyre speaks of a "vital" tradition as one in which the contents of tradition are up for debate, and indeed, the introduction of radically different notions of the body, health, and authority have provided siddha practitioners with ample material for reworking their traditions.[17] This reformulation of their knowledge must not be viewed as only a "response" to the intrusion of colonialism or of biomedicine. The changes to Tamil tradition wrought by colonialism were not simply forced upon Tamils as passive actors, but were to a degree chosen by them in response to changing circumstances. Siddha vaidyas have not only situated their medicine in objective, foreign, or other worlds but they also situate the external world in relation to their tradition. Therefore, in promoting siddha medicine, vaidyas both reject and appropriate features of the institutions and discourses of their primary competitors. This reformulation has resulted in a medicine that is competitive in the modern world, in a medical market that is increasingly global and diverse. Vaidyas have incorporated a range of rhetorical strategies, signs, and terms drawn from non-Tamil sources to speak to Tamil audiences, and they increasingly seek to develop the rhetorical tools to effectively reach audiences outside of Tamil Nadu.

For the most part, though, at present the outreach aspects of siddha medicine are not well developed. Here it differs from modern yoga, which has been more global from its incipience in the early decades of the twentieth century. Alter notes that much early writing on modern yoga is in English, and suggests that "Eugene Sandow, the father of modern body building, has had a greater influence on the form and practice of modern yoga—and most modern Hatha Yoga—than either Aurobindo or Vivekananda."[18] Alter speaks of the shift of yoga from a nationalist to a transnationalist phenomenon, made possible by Kuvalayananda's attempts to take "the 'culture' out of Yoga, so to speak."[19] Kuvalayananda and other early leaders of modern yoga presented Yoga as a science of the human body, a focus that "enabled a translation of a branch of Indian philosophy into a form of practice that is, like Modern Science itself, putatively free of cultural baggage while clearly linked to the history of a particular part of the world."[20] Siddha vaidyas, however, have not been quick to relinquish their emphasis on the Tamil nature of their knowledge, which remains a cornerstone in their characterization of their medicine. This is partly due to the monolingual character of siddha medicine: although there are some resources in English, nearly all literature on siddha is in Tamil, and vaidyas consistently told me that without knowledge of Tamil, one could not engage in a study of siddha medicine.

The clients for siddha vaidyas, and the target audience of their histories and discourses about their medicine, are still overwhelmingly Tamil. Tamil society today, however, is not the Lemurian utopian society of unanimous compliance to a single pure tradition, and the majority of Tamils use Western medicine. Neither is the Tamil medical landscape simply one of competing medical systems, because there is not a single siddha medicine. The primary division within siddha is that between hereditary and college-educated practitioners, and siddha vaidyas are Muslims, Christians, women, men, Shaivas, tantrics, non-brahmans, brahmans, atheists, Indian separatists, and Indian nationalists, to name a few. It is important to note, then, that while the expansionary aspirations of siddha vaidyas target the world, they just as importantly target Indians, Tamils, and other siddha vaidyas, as the future shape of siddha medicine is a matter of heated debate. Much recent scholarship has focused on issues of competition between "alternative" medicine and biomedicine, but little has examined the competition between nonbiomedical practices. As I have shown, the Indian nationalist promotion of ayurveda was itself imperial in nature. In reworking their tradition, siddha vaidyas too seek not only to compete with biomedical doctors but also, in their own imperial way, to gain an advantage over other medical practices in Tamil Nadu. They suggest that theirs should be the only medicine of the Tamil people, against the claims of those who have more resources at their disposal, biomedicine and ayurveda, about whom siddha vaidyas have much to say. The advances they seek are also at the expense of those about whom they say little, those engaged in various forms of healing such as temple healings and exorcisms, for example. Tamil revivalists considered these healing practices to lack the credentials to serve as an authorized medicine of a distinct, civilized people: an institutional basis; a textual tradition; nonritual means of healing, especially the formulation of medicines; and an established set of categorizations about the human body and disease.

Among the most important historical changes in siddha medicine have been shifting conceptions of the community of siddha medicine, that is, who authored it, who owns it, who can effectively practice it, and who can be healed by it. These shifts correspond to changing identities and new conceptions of the scope of an internal community and the vastness of external communities. In reformulating their medicine, vaidyas have shaped their local and national worlds, and they have also transformed themselves in significant ways. In demarcating clear divisions between Tamil, Sanskrit, and Western medicines, Tamil vaidyas conceive their medical practices as composing a distinct system of the Tamil people, designating a much broader community of knowledge than was imagined before. At the same time, vaidyas have also developed the somewhat contrary sense that this large linguistic community is fundamentally local. Stepping back to view the effects of these changes on the vaidya as a historical subject, it becomes clear that shifting notions of community identity mark not only changes in the way autonomous, stable individuals view their practices but also that these notions have transformed the very ways that vaidyas view themselves. New articulations of Tamil tradition mark a transformation of the individual medical practitioner from simply vaidya to siddha vaidya (*citta vaittiyar*), to Tamil vaidya (*tamiḻ vaittiyar*), and to traditional vaidya (*pāramppariya vaittiyar*). The future expansion of the community of siddha medicine is not clear, and whether siddha vaidyas succeed in becoming global vaidyas (*ulaka vaittiyar*) will depend on how effectively they develop the tools to compete on a global market.

The integration of pharmacopea products from outside Tamil-speaking areas and the ever-expanding geographical range of the mythological adventures of the siddhars are just two ways in which Tamil vaidyas have been "globalizing" their medicine for centuries, even if their conception of the boundaries of the globe and the resources for delivering their rhetoric and medicines to these boundaries have increased considerably in recent times. The global project of vaidyas thus far has been less to take siddha medicine to the world than it has been to bring the world to siddha medicine. When I asked Kundrathur Ramamurthy what his relationship is to the siddhars, he replied, "I'm like dust at the feet of the siddhars. Knowing all that the siddhars taught is itself a great fortune. You've come here from overseas, doing research on the siddhars. . . . You've come now in the line of the siddhars, that's a great gift. . . . This won't come for everyone." This, in many ways, encapsulates the project of siddha vaidyas, to bring the world into their tradition, to bring the lucky few into the line of the siddhars. Perhaps siddha medicine, like the siddhars, is destined to remain at the margins of the world for some time to come, invisible to most while seeing it all.

Notes

CHAPTER 1

1. *Tiṉa Karaṉ* [The sun], December 10, 1999.

2. *Tiṉattanti* [The daily telegraph], November 11, 1998.

3. *Maruttuvar,* July 1999, 19.

4. *Maruttuvar,* July 1999, 3.

5. Central Council of Indian Medicine, "Status of Siddha Colleges for the Year 2007–2008."

6. Department of Ayurveda, Yoga and Naturopathy, Unani, Siddha and Homoeopathy (AYUSH), "State-wise Statistics of Siddha as on April 1, 2007."

7. Department of Ayurveda, Yoga and Naturopathy, Unani, Siddha and Homoeopathy, "Summary of Infrastructure Facilities under Ayurveda, Yoga and Naturopathy, Unani, Siddha and Homoeopathy (AYUSH) as on April 1, 2007."

8. Two recent books on south Indian temples and temple priests indicate that the strength of tradition in India extends beyond medicinal practice. See Fuller, *The Renewal of the Priesthood,* and Waghorne, *Diaspora of the Gods.*

9. *Tiṉa Karaṉ*, December 10, 1999.

10. *Tiṉattanti*, November 11, 1998.

11. *Maruttuvar*, November 1998, 28.

12. Here I translate the Tamil *nāṭṭu maruntu* as "country medicine," which would be more commonly rendered as folk medicine. There are shops set up throughout Tamil Nadu that sell medicines produced from organic products found in the country or *nāṭu.*

13. For studies of colonialism and medicine in India, see Arnold, *Colonizing the Body*, and A. Kumar, *Medicine and the Raj.* Two notable monographs that do address the response of indigenous practitioners are Langford, *Fluent Bodies,* and Sivaramakrishnan, *Old Potions, New Bottles.*

14. Fuller, *The Renewal of the Priesthood*, 164.

15. I have not used pseudonyms here. The vaidyas I worked with are well-known public figures, and each has a number of publications, which I use in addition to interview materials. These vaidyas without exception asked that I use their names in the book.

16. Venkatachalapathy, "Maruttuva Akarāti Tanta Mētai: Oru Tuṉpiyal Nāṭakam." Pillai or Piḷḷai is a caste name, designating members of Vellalar, land-owning castes. They have been Tamil scholars and siddha vaidyas for centuries, and have been particularly influential in the revival of Tamil tradition and dominate much of the contemporary literature on siddha medicine.

17. Ibid., 73–76. Venkatachalapathy goes into some detail about the publishing history of the dictionary.

18. The Tamil term is *cittar*, and the Sanskrit is *siddha*. The Tamil term has most often been transcribed into English as *siddhar*, which is the form I will use here.

19. Sambasivam Pillai, *Introduction to Siddha Medicine*, 8.

20. See, for example, Arnold, ed., *Imperial Medicine and Indigenous Societies.* On imperialism and medicine in India, see Arnold's excellent *Colonizing the Body*; also, A. Kumar, *Medicine and the Raj*; Harrison, *Public Health in British India*; and Buckingham, *Leprosy in Colonial South India.*

21. Arnold, *Colonizing the Body,* 293.

22. On these processes in Africa, see Comaroff and Comaroff, "Medicine, Colonialism and the Black Body."

23. Thus siddha practitioners today speak of *muppu,* a preparation that will bestow the eternal life that eludes biomedicine.

24. For example, O. P. Jaggi mistakenly asserts that the Tamil siddha system of medicine is simply ayurveda translated into Tamil. See Jaggi, *Yogic and Tantric Medicine,* 127.

25. On ayurveda and the culture of Indian nationalism, see Langford, *Fluent Bodies,* especially chapter 3.

26. Chatterjee, *The Nation and Its Fragments: Colonial and Postcolonial Histories.*

27. For example, Wilber Theodore Elmore distinguished Hinduism from Dravidian religion. He considered Hinduism to be the creation of Aryan brahmans, and characterized it as primarily theistic and philosophical, while Dravidian religion contains rites that he termed "Dravidian devil worship" (8). Contemporary Dravidians, he said, "stand where their ancestors did when they worshiped devils in the gloomy forests at the time of the Aryan invasion" (114). Elmore, *Dravidian Gods in Modern Hinduism.*

28. Ohnuki-Tierney, *Illness and Culture in Contemporary Japan*, 123.

29. For a Western participant's observations of the Fifth International Tamil Conference, held in Madurai, Tamil Nadu in 1981, see Cutler, "The Fish-eyed Goddess Meets the Movie Star."

30. I refer to several of Shanmuga Velan's works in the following chapters, including a book he wrote in English, *Siddhar's Science of Longevity and Kalpa Medicine of India.*

31. Shakti is the consort of Shiva. Tamil revivalists emphasize the Tamil loyalties of this divine "family" of Shiva as husband, Shakti as wife, and Murugan or Skanda as son.

32. This reference is to the siddhar Agastya, the most prolific of the medical siddhars. Myths of Agastya hold that he resided, or still resides, on Potigai Mountain in southern Tamil Nadu state. I will discuss Agastya at greater length in chapter 4.

33. *Muppū kuru* and *kaṟpa* are siddha medical preparations that are said to restore youth. Muppū is more commonly rendered "muppu."

34. Shanmuga Velan, "Vāḻka Citta Maruttuvam," 1.

35. On tradition as imitation, see Max Weber's influential discussion of authority in *Economy and Society*, 212–54. On tradition as invention, see Hobsbawm and Ranger, eds., *The Invention of Tradition.* For a fuller discussion of tradition, consciousness, and ideology, see my chapter authored with Gregory Grieve, "Illuminating the Half-life of Tradition."

36. Comaroff and Comaroff, *Of Revelation and Revolution* 1: 24.

37. Althusser, *For Marx*, 234.

38. Marx's famous and poignant formulation: "Men make their own history, but they do not make it just as they please; they do not make it under circumstances chosen by themselves, but under circumstances directly found, given and transmitted from the past. The tradition of all the dead generations weighs like a nightmare on the brain of the living." Marx, "The Eighteenth Brumaire of Louis Bonaparte," 595.

39. Anderson, *Imagined Communities.*

40. Zizek, *The Sublime Object of Ideology.*

41. Apte, *The Practical Sanskrit-English Dictionary.*

42. Advertisement in *Maruttuvar*, July 1999, 37.

43. For more on this debate between medical purists and innovators, see Leslie, "Interpretations of Illness: Syncretism in Modern Ayurveda." In his article "Science, Experimentation, and Clinical Practice in Ayurveda" in the same volume, Gananath Obeyesekere studies the innovative "science" of an ayurvedic practitioner in Sri Lanka.

44. On *Tamiḻppaṟṟu*, see Ramaswamy, *Passions of the Tongue*, 6.

45. Prakash, *Another Reason*, 7.

CHAPTER 2

1. A notable exception is the work of Partha Chatterjee. See his "The Nationalist Resolution of the Women's Question" and *The Nation and Its Fragments.*

2. The scope of this pan-Indian medical community is larger than any that was possible for Tamil vaidyas prior to the twentieth century, before the expansion of modern forms of media and communication. On media, community, and nationalism, see Anderson, *Imagined Communities.*

3. The challenges that biomedicine has posed to traditional techniques did not disappear with Indian independence, but have increased over the last half century. The independent Indian state continues to heavily subsidize biomedicine, and ever-expanding education in rural schools brings Western sciences to new areas.

4. On the *śudd* (pure) ayurveda versus *miśra* (mixed) ayurveda debate, see Langford, *Fluent Bodies*, 108–16. See also Leslie, "Interpretations of Illness."

5. See *The Government College of Integrated Medicine Decennial Souvenir.*

6. This is not to say that these practitioners did not make the further move of insisting on the universality of their knowledge. Like a one-way mirror, they affirmed their impunity from the external gaze while celebrating the transparency of the errors of biomedicine.

7. *Report of the Committee to Assess and Evaluate the Present Status of Ayurvedic System of Medicine*, 25; A. Kumar, *Medicine and the Raj*, 19; Gupta, "Indigenous Medicine in Nineteenth and Twentieth Century Bengal."

8. Khaleeli, "Harmony or Hegemony?," 82.

9. This was not, however, the first time traditional medicine had been taught in an institutional setting in South Asia. Epigraphical evidence from the eleventh and twelfth centuries indicates that ayurveda was taught at Vedic schools adjacent to hospitals, and at the Thiruvavadudurai monastery. See C. Madhavan, *History and Culture of Tamil Nadu*, 126–28.

10. A. Kumar, *Medicine and the Raj*, 18–19.

11. Quoted in ibid., 19.

12. Ibid., 20.

13. Williams, *Keywords*, 278.

14. Macaulay, "Minute on Education," 596, 597. Later scholars of Indian medicine note the damaging effects of Macaulay's attitude to indigenous sciences. See Samuel, ed., *Citta Maruttuvac Cuvaṭikuḷ*, 29.

15. *Report of the Committee to Assess and Evaluate the Present Status of Ayurvedic System of Medicine*; Arnold, *Colonizing the Body*, 13; A. Kumar, *Medicine and the Raj*, 22; Gupta, "Indigenous Medicine," 370; D. Kumar, *Science and the Raj, 1857–1905*, 48–49.

16. Khaleeli, "Harmony or Hegemony?" 83.

17. Quoted in A. Kumar, *Medicine and the Raj*, 20.

18. D. Kumar, *Science and the Raj*, 53.

19. On colonial policies of noninterference and sati, see Mani, *Contentious Traditions*. For hook-swinging, see Dirks, *Castes of Mind*, chapter 8.

20. Arnold, *Colonizing the Body*.

21. Gary J. Hausman, "Siddhars, Alchemy and the Abyss of Tradition," 116.

22. Ibid., 117, 119.

23. Ibid., 165, 155.

24. "Is Ayurveda to Be encouraged? Or the British Pharmacopea to Be Enlarged?" 1–4.

25. *Report of the Special Committee Appointed by the Joint Board of the Dravida Vaidya Mandal and the Madras Ayurveda Sabha in Reply to the Report on the Investigation into the Indigenous Drugs* (cited hereafter as *Dravida Vaidya Mandal and Madras Ayurveda Sabha*), 2–3, 7–8.

26. Ibid., 20.

27. Ibid., 95.

28. Ibid., 4.

29. Ibid., 72.

30. *Dravida Vaidya Mandal and Madras Ayurveda Sabha*, 79–80.

31. Ibid., 80.

32. Ibid., 9–10.

33. Ibid., 12.

34. *Dravida Vaidya Mandal and Madras Ayurveda Sabha*, 27–28. In 1833, a group of administrators led by Alexander Duff, the head of the Scottish Free Church Institution, questioned the capability of South Asian languages to represent scientific notions and so also dismissed the utility of the Native Medical Institution. They advocated "a knowledge of the English language which we consider as a *sine quanon*, because that language contains within itself the circle of all the sciences and incalculable wealth of printed works and illustrations, circumstances which give it obvious advantage over oriental languages in which are only to be found the crudest elements of science or the most irrational substitutes for it." A. Kumar, *Medicine and the Raj*, 22.

35. Chatterjee, *The Nation and Its Fragments*, 7. Contrary to my argument that vaidyas considered their traditions to be eminently scientific, Chatterjee considered science to be part of the "outer world," dominated by the West, to which Indians must submit. For further criticisms on this point, see Fuller, *The Renewal of the Priesthood*, 158; and Prakash, *Another Reason*, 201–2.

36. MacIntyre, *Three Rival Versions of Moral Enquiry*, 4–5.

37. MacIntyre, *After Virtue*, 222.

38. Nijalangappa, "Preface."

39. On colonialism and Orientalist disciplines of knowledge, see Said, *Orientalism*, and Inden, *Imagining India*. Although this delineation of a particular arena of Indian expertise is new, South Asian medical writings have long posited the influence of nonphysical forces on health.

40. *Tamiḻ (Citta) Maruttuvak Kōṭpāṭu*, 8.

41. Sambasivam Pillai, *Tamil-English Dictionary of Medicine*, 3: 2110.

42. Shanmuga Velan, *Siddhar's Science of Longevity*, 38.

43. Kasturi, "Citta Maruttuvam," 7.

44. Sambasivam Pillai, *Tamil-English Dictionary of Medicine*, 3: 2106.

45. *Report of the Committee on the Indigenous Systems of Medicine*, Part 2, 234.

46. Ibid., 232.

47. Pandian, "Exhibition of Indian Medicines: Opening Address," 32.

48. Jean Langford cites an ayurvedic vaidya's argument about the suitability of local medicines for local bodies. See Langford, *Fluent Bodies*, 79.

49. On the *tridoṣa* in classical ayurveda, see Wujastyk, *The Roots of Ayurveda*. On the *tiridōca* or *muppiṇi* in siddha, see Sambasivam Pillai, *Introduction to Siddha Medicine*. Wujastyk discusses at some length the difficulty of translating *doṣa*. I follow him in using the convention of rendering *doṣa* as "humor." See Wujastyk, 30–36, 281. On the humors in unani, see Rahman, "Unani Medicine in India."

50. Hausman, "Siddhars, Alchemy, and the Abyss of Tradition," 126.

51. *Report of the Committee on the Indigenous Systems of Medicine*, Part 2, 356.

52. On myth, nature, and history, see Barthes, *Mythologies*.

53. *Dravida Vaidya Mandal and Madras Ayurveda Sabha*, 9.

54. On the *yugas*, see O'Flaherty, *The Origins of Evil in Hindu Mythology*, and Biardeau, *Hinduism*, 100–4. Although ayurvedic doctors and many siddha practitioners

anticipated greater support for their practices in an independent Indian state, other siddha vaidyas felt that siddha medicine could only thrive in an independent south Indian, Dravidian, or Tamil state. I will detail the work of siddha vaidyas to distinguish their medicine from ayurveda in subsequent chapters.

55. This notion that traditional medical practice was in a state of decay by colonial times has been accepted not only by biomedical doctors, traditional doctors, and colonial authorities but also by scholars and historians of medicine in India. Historical data for this degeneration, however, is absent from these accounts. For a recent example, see Jaggi, *Medicine In India*, 311.

56. Quoted in Hausman, "Siddhars, Alchemy, and the Abyss of Tradition," 163.

57. *Dravida Vaidya Mandal and Madras Ayurveda Sabha*, 21–22.

58. Ibid., 64.

59. Ibid., 24.

60. Indigenous practitioners here parody the Western sciences, ignoring that scientific knowledge evolves subject to peer review, that is, with the authority of a scientific *community*, and that it accumulates in "traditional" ways.

61. *Dravida Vaidya Mandal and Madras Ayurveda Sabha*, Appendix 3, vii. It is important to note, however, that the freedom to innovate is valued by many indigenous practitioners. This has probably been true for centuries, as premodern Tamil texts speak of knowledge gained through one's own experience (*kaipākam*). The call for purity has been hotly debated in the twentieth century. The leadership of the Government College of Indigenous Medicine in Columbo, Sri Lanka, in the late 1950s and early 1960s was strongly divided between ayurvedic purists and those who wanted to develop ayurveda along the lines introduced by biomedicine. The conflict was so heated that the minister of health and a faculty member of the college were arrested in connection with the 1959 assassination of Prime Minister Bandaranaike, who had sympathy with the innovators and was killed by a purist. Leslie, "Interpretations of Illness."

62. *Dravida Vaidya Mandal and Madras Ayurveda Sabha*, 40. Gananath Sen was a hereditary Bengali ayurvedic practitioner who was, somewhat counter to the statement quoted above, dedicated to the explication of ayurveda in the terms of Western science, founding an institution in 1932 in which ayurveda and allopathy were taught side by side. For more on hereditary ayurvedic lineages in nineteenth- and twentieth-century Bengal, see Gupta, "Indigenous Medicine," 368–78.

63. Narayanaswami, "Systematic Development of Ayurveda," 79. The categories of nature and divinity are often elided in siddha discourses. See chapter 5.

64. *Report of the Committee on the Indigenous Systems of Medicine*, Part 2, 249.

65. This notion of the perfection of texts and tradition has precedence in the consideration of the Sanskrit Vedas as *śruti*, i.e., as heard from an original, divine source. Classical Sanskrit medical treatises display this veneration of hereditary knowledge as of cosmic, not human origin. In one of the canonical texts of ayurveda, for example, Suśruta wrote about medicinal plants: "No need to examine them, no need to reflect on them, they will make themselves known, the remedies that the clear-sighted must prescribe in accordance with tradition. . . . Were there a thousand reasons to do so, the ambaṣṭhā group will never set itself to purging! The wise must therefore adhere to tradition,

without arguing." *Suśruta*, sūtra XL, 19–21, quoted in Zimmerman, *The Jungle and the Aroma of Meats*, 158.

66. A vast ethnographic literature attests to this. For two south Indian examples, see G. Djurfeldt and S. Lindberg, *Pills against Poverty*, and Beals, "Curers in South India."

67. Leslie, "Ambiguities of Revivalism in Modern India," 362–63.

68. *Dravida Vaidya Mandal and Madras Ayurveda Sabha*, 96.

69. Ibid., 96.

70. Nehru, "Preface."

71. Srinivasalu Naidu, "Medical Education and Medical Relief," 41.

72. *Report of the Committee on the Indigenous Systems of Medicine*, Part 2, 363.

73. Subramaniam, *Cittavaittiyattiṉ Muṉṉēṟṟam*, 50.

74. *Dravida Vaidya Mandal and Madras Ayurveda Sabha*, 27, 65, 84, 35.

75. Meykandar, "Citta Vaityattiṉ Tēvai," 48.

76. *Report of the Committee on the Indigenous Systems of Medicine*, Part 1, 2.

77. Perumal, "Citta Maruttuvattiṉ Māṇpu," 72.

78. Levinas, *Totality and Infinity*, 33.

79. Ibid., 37–38.

80. Indeed, colonial authorities and institutions, and British culture, were rarely hegemonic in India, in Gramsci's sense of hegemony. See Guha, *Dominance without Hegemony*.

CHAPTER 3

1. Some traditional medicines, most notably "Chinese" medicine and ayurveda, have been successfully globalizing their knowledge and practices. There is a burgeoning literature on this globalization; see especially Alter, ed., *Asian Medicine and Globalization*. It should be recognized, however, that most traditional medical practices are still local.

2. Little, "Bowl Full of Sky," 6.

3. Kalai Arasu, *Cittarkaḷ Collum Tirāviṭa Āṉmīkam*, 13.

4. Ramachandran, *Cittarkaḷ Varalāṟu*, iii.

5. One of the lead actresses of the series, Radhika, describes the series: "It's about Siddhars. . . . I wanted to relate to religion in a different way . . . we did a lot of analysis and in depth study." See Rangarajan, "Managing a Mega Show."

6. Muttukkaruppa Pillai, "Cittarkaḷiṉ Vayatu," 36.

7. Good, *Medicine, Rationality, and Experience.*

8. Donald S. Lopez, Jr., "Belief," in Taylor, *Critical Terms for Religious Studies*, 22.

9. Good, *Medicine, Rationality, and Experience*, 54–55; Geertz, *The Interpretation of Cultures*, 5. Note that Geertz in turn was paraphrasing Max Weber.

10. As Sheldon Pollock and colleagues have argued, globalization and increasing cosmopolitanism have often been accompanied by countervailing claims to cultural essences and purity. See Pollock et al., "Cosmopolitanisms," 11–12.

11. There is a large literature on technology, science, and imperialism. For seminal works, see Headrick, *The Tools of Empire*, and Adas, *Machines as the Measure of Men.*

12. Others have noted the difficulty in accounting for historical change with a Geertzian approach. See, for example, Sewell, "Geertz, Cultural Systems, and History."

13. Burke, *A Rhetoric of Motives*, 43.

14. See Apte, *The Practical Sanskrit-English Dictionary.*

15. White, *The Alchemical Body.* A Purāṇa is a text that recounts myths of divine beings. There are thousands of Purāṇas written in Sanskrit, Tamil, and other South Asian languages.

16. Venkatraman, *A History of the Tamil Siddha Cult*, 7–9, 50–90.

17. The *Encyclopaedia of Tamil Literature* holds to this twofold categorization, equating *ñāṉa cittar* with *yoga cittar* as distinct from *kāya cittar*. See "Tamil Cittar," in *Encyclopaedia of Tamil Literature*, 1: 335. Kamil V. Zvelebil distinguishes three groups: (1) alchemists and physicians; (2) thinkers and poets; and (3) "A few 'Siddha-like' poets who have been 'appended' to the Siddha school by posterior generations." Zvelebil, *The Poets of the Powers*, 17–18.

18. *Cittar Pāṭalkaḷ*, ed. Ramanathan.

19. Sambasivam Pillai, *Tamil-English Dictionary of Medicine*, 2: 1871.

20. Samuel, ed., *Citta Maruttuvac Cuvaṭikaḷ*, 30.

21. Arangarajan, "Potu Maruttuvac Cuvaṭikaḷ," 115.

22. For example, *Kailāca Caṭṭamuṉināyaṉār Aruḷicceyta Kaṟpaviti 100*, verse 12, in *Patiṉeṉ Cittarkaḷ Vaittiya Cillaṟaik Kōvai, Iraṇṭām Pākam*, 464.

23. *Cittar Pāṭalkaḷ*, ed., Manikkavasagam, viii–ix; Madhavan, *Siddha Medical Manuscripts in Tamil*, 57–85.

24. *Report of the Committee on the Indigenous Systems of Medicine*, Appendix 1, 139–47; *Encyclopaedia of Tamil Literature*, 1: 329; Ganapathy, *The Yoga of Siddha Boganathar*, 1: 243–44.

25. Madhavan, *Akattiyar Vaittiya Kāviyam 1500*, 10.

26. Ibid., 11.

27. Venkatraman, *A History of the Tamil Siddha Cult*, 115.

28. *Encyclopaedia of Tamil Literature*, 1: 360.

29. Natarajan, "'Divine Semen' and the Alchemical Conversion of Iramatevar," 257.

30. Scharfe, "The Doctrine of the Three Humors in Traditional Indian Medicine and the Alleged Antiquity of Tamil Siddha Medicine," 611.

31. On the dating of the *Tirumantiram*, see the section "A History of Tirumular" below.

32. See O'Flaherty, trans., *The Rig Veda*, 167–72, 250–52.

33. Venkatraman, *A History of the Tamil Siddha Cult*, 40–41.

34. This text, as Agastya himself describes it, is a collection of verses on rejuvenative medicines taken from other texts attributed to Agastya. It is therefore somewhat later than the earliest siddha medical texts.

35. The divine couple of Shakti and Shiva, along with their devoted bull Nandi and son Murugan, are the deities most often linked to siddha medical knowledge.

36. Kaṟpam is a class of rejuvenative medicines.

37. Centūram is a red chemical preparation, and paṟpa is a white powder of metallic oxides. Sambasivam Pillai, *Tamil-English Dictionary of Medicine.*

38. *Akastiya Muṉivar Aruḷiya Kaṟpa Muppu Kuru Nūl 100*, verses 1–6, in *Akastiyar Muppu Cūttiraṅkaḷ*, ed. Ramachandran, 9–12.

39. Chidambarathanu Pillai, *Citta Maruttuva Amutu*, 5.

40. For more on the uyir and the inability of Westerners to account for it, see chapter 5.

41. Note, however, that the *Tirumantiram* speaks of preserving the body as an instrument to develop wisdom (verse 704). The medical texts attributed to the siddhars, on the other hand, tend to consider the retention of the body an end in itself.

42. Tangavel, "Tamiḻakamum Citta Vaittiyamum," 19.

43. Kandaswamy Pillai, *History of Siddha Medicine*, 406.

44. See the third section of the *Yoga Sutras*, and *Yoga Sutra* 4.1, Miller, trans., *Yoga: Discipline and Freedom.* Miller cites a scholarly majority who date the *Yoga Sutras* to the third century C.E. (p. 6), and Ian Whicher dates the text to the second or third century C.E. Whicher, "Yoga and Freedom: A Reconsideration of Patanjali's Classical Yoga," 272.

45. Eliade, *Yoga, Immortality and Freedom*, 318.

46. Kandaswamy Pillai, *History of Siddha Medicine*, 2.

47. On the need of scholars to attend to the history of yogas, see Alter, *Yoga in Modern India.*

48. R. Manikkavasagam, *Nam Nāṭṭu Cittarkaḷ*, 213.

49. Madhavan, *Akattiyar Vaittiya Kāviyam 1500*, 37.

50. Subramaniam, *Cittarkaḷ Iracavātakkalai*, 7.

51. Sambasivam Pillai, *Tamil-English Dictionary of Medicine*, 3: 2083.

52. Shanmuga Velan, *Siddhar's Science of Longevity*, 78–91.

53. Srirangam Siddhar, *Siddhar's Yogic Experiences*, 4.

54. Srirangam Siddhar, *You Can also Become a Siddhar.*

55. Little, "Bowl Full of Sky."

56. Sambasivam Pillai, *Tamil-English Dictionary of Medicine*, 3: 2089.

57. Subramaniam, *Cittarkaḷ Iracavātakkalai*, 8.

58. Kalimuttu Pillai, "Cittar Tiṟaṅkaḷ," 64.

59. Urban, *The Economics of Ecstasy*, 203.

60. Shanmuga Velan, "Tirumūlar Aruḷiya Maruttuvat Tirumantiram 8000," 49. On north Indian siddha traditions, see White, *The Alchemical Body.*

61. Charangapani, *Citta Neṟi* 1: 3.

62. Parvati, "Citta Vaittiyamum Makaḷir Maruttuvamum," 86.

63. *Tamiḻ (Citta) Maruttuvak Kōṭpāṭu*, 4–5.

64. *Tirutoṇṭattokai* 5. See Shulman, trans., *Songs of the Harsh Devotee*, 240.

65. *Tiruttoṇṭar Tiruvantāti*, verse 36, in *Patiṉōrām Tirumuṟai, Mūlamum Uraiyum*, 751.

66. Zvelebil, *Lexicon of Tamil Literature*, 473; Monius, "Love, Violence, and the Aesthetics of Disgust," 118; Vaiyapuripillai, *History of the Tamil Language and Literature*, 77–8; Goodall, ed. and trans., *Bhaṭṭa Rāmakaṇṭha's Commentary on the Kiraṇatantra*, xxxvii–xxix.

67. Venkatraman, *A History of the Tamil Siddha Cult*, 77, 82–83.

68. For a brief account of the *Tirumuṟai*, see Peterson, *Poems to Śiva*, 12–18. On the *Tirumantiram* in the *Tirumuṟai*, see Vellaivaranan, *Paṉṉirutirumuṟai Varalāṟu*, 2: 512–655.

69. The editions I employed are: *Tirumūla Nāyaṉār Aruḷic Ceyta Tirumantiram* with commentary of P. Ramanatha Pillai (Shaiva Siddhanta edition); *Tirumūlanātar Aruḷiya Tirumantiram* with explanatory notes by Dr. Cupa Annamalai; *Tirumantiram: A Tamil Scriptural Classic,* trans. B. Natarajan (Ramakrishna Math edition); and *Tirumantiram*, with commentary of G. Varadarajan. The Ramakrishna Math edition and the Varadarajan edition agree in their numbering of verses. The translations into English are my own.

70. For a brief overview of the Shaiva Āgamas, see Davis, *Ritual in an Oscillating Universe.*

71. This line is presented in the Shaiva Siddhanta edition as a prologue to the text as a whole, while the other two editions include it in the body of the text. Shaiva Siddhanta edition, prologue, p. 87; Ramakrishna Math edition, verse 101.

72. Shaiva Siddhanta edition, prologue, p. 88; Ramakrishna Math edition, verse 99.

73. Here the text follows lists of types of beings common to Sanskrit epics, where siddhas are simply one type of divine being. See Hopkins, "The Hosts of Spirits," in his *Epic Mythology*, 152–76.

74. This is the verse number in the Ramakrishna Math edition and in the G. Varadarajan edition.

75. Verse number in the Ramakrishna Math edition.

76. I will explore these processes in more detail in chapter 5.

77. The translations here are my own. For a translation of the entire episode, see McGlashan, *The History of the Holy Servants of the Lord Siva,* 298–300.

78. *Periya Purāṇam eṉṉum Tirutoṇṭar Purāṇam*, with commentary by C. K. Subramanya Mudaliyar, 6: 462.

79. *Periya Purāṇam eṉṉum Tiruttoṇṭar Purāṇam*, 6: 472–78.

80. *Periya Purāṇam eṉṉum Tiruttoṇṭar Purāṇam*, 6: 485.

81. This is a reference to the four paths described in the *Tirumantiram*: knowledge or wisdom (*ñāṉam*), yoga (*yōkam*), rites prescribed by the Shaiva Āgamas (*kiriyai*), and worship (*cariyai*).

82. This repeats the first verse of the *Tirumantiram*, which begins, "Oṉṟavaṉ tāṉē . . ." "Indeed there is just him . . ."

83. *Periya Purāṇam eṉṉum Tiruttoṇṭar Purāṇam*, 490.

84. Dandapani Desikar, *Tirumantira Muṉṉurai*; Vengatasubramanian, ed., *Tirumantiram Vaittiyappakuti*. Kathleen Iva Koppedrayer notes that this goal of public outreach is shared by other monastic orders in south India. See her dissertation, "The Sacred Presence of the Guru," 3.

85. Koppedrayer, "The Sacred Presence of the Guru," 5.

86. Ibid., 167.

87. Dandapani Desikar, *Tirumantira Muṉṉurai*, xv.

88. Ibid., 75.

89. Ibid., 76–77.

90. Ibid., 75–76. It is not clear to whom Dandapani Desikar is referring as "false prophets."

91. Ibid., 76–77.

92. N. Manikkavasagam, *Cittar Pāṭalkaḷ,* 321. Likewise, in his introduction to verses of Agastya, Manikkavasagam does not mention Agastyar's northern mythological references, which are even more significant than those of Tirumular.

93. Ibid., iii.

94. This assertion that his original name was Sundarar rests on a questionable reading of *Tirumantiram,* verse 101 of the Ramakrishna Math edition, and in the prologue of the Shaiva Siddhanta edition, p. 87. For a good overview of the dispute, see K. R. Arumugam's introduction in Ganapathy and Arumugam, *The Yoga of Tirumular,* 13–16.

95. A. Chidambaranar, "Kuṟippukkaḷ" [Notes], in *Periya Purāṇam eṉṉum Tirutoṇṭar Purāṇam* 6: 1.

96. Ramaswamy, *The Lost Land of Lemuria,* 115–17.

97. Sambasivam Pillai, *Tamil-English Dictionary of Medicine,* 4: 1116.

98. A. Chidambaranar, "Tirumūlanāyaṉār Varalāṟu," 70, 80–84.

99. Ramachandran, *Cittarkaḷ Varalāṟu,* 30.

100. Shanmuga Velan, "Tirumūlar Aruḷiya Maruttuvat Tirumantiram 8000," 49.

101. Naranjana Devi, *Teṉṉintiya Maruttuva Varalāṟu,* 162.

102. Shanmuga Velan, "Tirumūlar Aruḷiya Maruttuvat Tirumantiram 8000," 49–50.

103. Kuppusami Mudaliyar, *Citta Maruttuvam,* lxv.

104. G. J. Parthasarathy, "Cittar Varalāṟu: Tirumūlar," 8.

105. Several of these medical texts have been published by Tamarai Nulakam, such as: *Tirumūlar Vaittiyam 1000,* ed. S. P. Ramachandran, and *Tirumūlar Karukkiṭai Vaittiyam 600.*

106. Venkatesan, *Tamiḻ Ilakkiyattil Citta Maruttuvam,* 223.

107. Madhavan, *Siddha Medical Manuscripts in Tamil,* 29.

108. Kuppusami Mudaliyar, *Citta Maruttuvam,* lxv.

109. Shanmuga Velan, "Tirumūlar Aruḷiya Maruttuvat Tirumantiram 8000," 50.

110. Ramachadran, "Introduction," in *Tirumūlar Vaittiyam 1000,* 4, 9.

111. Ibid., 5–8, esp. 7.

112. Verse 1000, *Tirumūlar Vaittiyam 1000,* 295.

113. Joseph Alter applies uses this term to describe popular literature on modern yoga: *Yoga in Modern India,* xix.

114. Ramachandran, *Cittarkaḷ Varalāṟu,* 23, 27.

115. Sambasivam Pillai, *Tamil-English Dictionary of Medicine,* 3: 2083–84.

116. Shanmuga Velan, *Siddhar's Science of Longevity,* 38.

117. "Mental eye," *maṉakkaṇ*: Kasturi, "Citta Maruttuvam," 7. "Wisdom eye": Shanmuga Velan, *Siddhar's Science of Longevity,* 38.

118. Sambasivam Pillai, *Introduction to Siddha Medicine,* 8, 4, 42–43.

119. *Pōkanāyaṉār Aruḷicceyta Pūjāviti* 37, verse 31, in *Patiṉeṉ Cittarkaḷ Vaittiya Cillaṟaik Kōvai, Iraṇṭām Pākam,* 380.

120. *Akastiya Muṉivar Aruḷiya Kaṟpa Muppu Kuru Nūl 100,* verses 4–6, in *Akastiyar Muppu Cūttiraṅkaḷ,* 10–12.

121. *Agastiyar Cūṭca Muppu* 32, verses 29–30, in *Akastiyar Muppu Cūttiraṅkaḷ,* 122.

122. *Akastiya Muṉivar Aruḷiya Kaṟpa Muppu Kuru Nūl 100,* verse 4.

123. *Kailāca Caṭṭamuṇināyaṉār Aruḷicceyta Kaṟpaviti 100*, 479.

124. Sambasivam Pillai, *Tamil-English Dictionary of Medicine*, 3: 2083. By "original ayurveda" Sambasivam Pillai probably means classical ayurveda, not that ayurveda is prior to siddha.

125. Contrary to this representation of ayurveda and also to Indian nationalist formulations of ayurveda, the classical Sanskrit medical texts themselves are often in tension with the dictates of orthodoxy. See Zimmermann, *The Jungle and the Aroma of Meats*, and Zysk, *Asceticism and Healing in Ancient India.*

126. Sambasivam Pillai, *Tamil-English Dictionary of Medicine*, 3: 2090.

127. Kandaswamy Pillai, *History of Siddha Medicine*, 313.

128. Ibid., 315.

129. Subramaniam, *Cittarkaḷ Iracavātakkalai*, 10.

130. Muttukkaruppa Pillai, "Cittarkaḷiṉ Vayatu," 36.

131. Sambasivam Pillai, *Tamil-English Dictionary of Medicine*, 3: 2108.

132. Ibid., 2111.

133. Ibid., 2106.

134. Shanmuga Velan, "Tirumūlar Aruḷiya Maruttuvat Tirumantiram 8000," 53. On iracamaṇi and its contemporary commercialization, see chapter 1. The kavaṉa pill is one that transports the consumer to aerial regions.

135. Sambasivam Pillai, *Tamil-English Dictionary of Medicine*, 3: 2123.

136. Francis Bacon, "In Praise of Human Knowledge," quoted in Horkheimer and Adorno, *Dialectic of Enlightenment*, 3.

137. Horkheimer and Adorno, *Dialectic of Enlightenment*, 4.

CHAPTER 4

1. For a historical account of the idea of Lemuria, see Ramaswamy, *The Lost Land of Lemuria.*

2. The following are the books that I have found most useful: Hardgrave, *The Dravidian Movement;* Barnett, *The Politics of Cultural Nationalism in South India*; Irschick, *Politics and Social Conflict in South India;* Nambi Arooran, *Tamil Renaissance and Dravidian Nationalism, 1905–1944*; Ramaswamy, *Passions of the Tongue*; N. Subramanian, *Ethnicity and Populist Mobilization;* Ramaswamy, *The Lost Land of Lemuria*; and Venkatachalapathy, *In Those Days There Was No Coffee.*

3. Ricoeur, *Lectures on Ideology and Utopia*, 16–17.

4. Foucault, "Nietzsche, Genealogy, History," 82.

5. V. R. Madhavan, *Siddha Medical Manuscripts in Tamil.*

6. See, for example, Masilamani, "Cittarkaḷ Ārātaṉai Muṟaiyum Payaṉum," 19.

7. Venkatraman, *A History of the Tamil Siddha Cult*, 41; W. S. Davis, "Agastya."

8. Buck and Paramasivam, trs., *The Study of Stolen Love*, 4–5.

9. Verses 323–24. *Tirumūla Nāyaṉār Aruḷic Ceyta Tirumantiram.*

10. Quoted in W. S. Davis, "Agastya," 251.

11. Nilakanta Sastri, *A History of South India*, 70.

12. Shulman, *Tamil Temple Myths*, 8.

13. Kuppusami Mudaliyar, *Citta Maruttuvam,* lxv–lxvi.

14. T. V. Sambasivam Pillai, *Tamil-English Dictionary of Medicine,* 3: 2089.

15. Ibid., 2089. On the Vellalars and Tamil revivalism, see A. R. Venkatachalapathy, *Tirāviṭa Iyakkamum Vēḷāḷarum,* and also his "The Dravidian Movement and the Vellalars, 1927–1944," in his *In Those Days There Was No Coffee,* and Maraimalai Adigal, *Vēḷāḷar Nākarikam.*

16. Chidambaranar, *Akattiyar Varalāṟu,* 13, 20.

17. Ibid., 21, 22, 24.

18. Ibid., 96.

19. There is a number of works in both English and Tamil that set out the basic principles of siddha medicine. For English works, see especially Narayanaswami, *Introduction to the Siddha System of Medicine;* Sambasivam Pillai, *Introduction to Siddha Medicine;* Thirunarayanan, *An Introduction to Siddha Medicine;* Thottam, *Siddha Medicine;* and B. V. Subbarayappa, "Siddha Medicine," in Subbarayappa, ed., *Medicine and Life Sciences in India.* In Tamil, see Kuppusami Mudaliyar, *Citta Maruttuvam,* and R. Madhavan, *Akattiyar Vaittiya Kāviyam 1500.*

20. Scharfe, "The Doctrine of the Three Humors."

21. For issues related to translation of these terms that describe the structure of the body, see Wujastyk, *The Roots of Ayurveda,* 30–36.

22. On alchemical traditions and ayurveda, see White, *The Alchemical Body,* especially 184–88. For a history of alchemy in India, see Subbarayappa, "Chemical Practices and Alchemy."

23. Joshi, "Rasaśāstra."

24. White, *The Alchemical Body,* 52.

25. Government Order 1267, March 26, 1941. Government of Madras, Education and Public Health Department, 1.

26. *The Report of the Committee on the Indigenous Systems of Medicine,* Part 2, 366.

27. Ibid., 340, 219, 238.

28. Ibid., 354.

29. Thirunarayanan, *An Introduction to Siddha Medicine,* 2–3.

30. Srinivas Iyengar, *History of the Tamils,* 1.

31. The similarity between these narratives and those of German Romanticism are striking. Both assert a natural relationship between the people and the soil, racial purity, a rationalized religion; both emphasize the harmony of the people with nature; and indeed, both have a notion that the character of the people was formed by the natural and climatic environment. Both also similarly characterize an "other," a people with no homeland, a diasporic race whose lack of native soil reflected their shifty, crafty, untrustworthy, indeed "parasitic" nature. A detailed comparison with the German romantic narratives, and a more thorough examination of sources for the Tamil narratives, while fascinating, are beyond the scope of this book. For an account of these European narratives, see Bruce Lincoln, *Theorizing Myth,* 47–75.

32. Harvey, *Spaces of Hope,* 160.

33. Ramaswamy, *The Lost Land of Lemuria,* 21–22; de Camp, *Lost Continents,* 51–52.

34. Ramaswamy, *The Lost Land of Lemuria,* 35.

35. Ibid., chapter 3; de Camp, *Lost Contitnents*, 56. Blavatsky and Besant attempted to synthesize their cosmological vision with Sanskrit learning and the Vedas, and so they had an active program to promote what they considered to be these most ancient pillars of Aryan culture. Tamil separatism, on the other hand, fashioned its social vision and political agenda partly against the Theosophical Vedic revivalist project. Ironically, then, in their propagation of the Lemurian theory, the Theosophists popularized a symbol that was to play a central role in the Tamil critique of Aryan civilization.

36. Ramaswamy, *The Lost Land of Lemuria*, 103.

37. Somasundara Bharathiar, in *The Papers of Dr. Navalar Somasundara Bharathiar*, 27.

38. Ramaswamy, "Lemuria in Tamil Spatial Fables," 582.

39. Mahalingam, *Concept of Kumari Kandam*, 54.

40. Ibid., 8–14.

41. Devaneyan, *The Primary Classical Language of the World*, 300.

42. Hart, *The Poems of Ancient Tamil*, 9. Dating this literature is difficult and has given rise to much debate. Herman Tieken dates sangam literature much later. See Tieken, *Kāvya in South India.*

43. Chidambaranar, "Tirumūlanāyaṉār Varalāṟu," 73–75.

44. Ibid., 75–76.

45. Ramaswamy, *Passions of the Tongue*, 92.

46. Quoted in Ramaswamy, *The Lost Land of Lemuria*, 116–17.

47. Muttukkaruppa Pillai, "Cittarkaḷiṉ Vayatu," 37–38.

48. Anbazhagan, "Foreword," iii.

49. Narayanaswami, *Introduction to the Siddha System of Medicine*, 1–3.

50. Subramaniam, *Cittavaittiyattiṉ Muṉṉēṟṟam*, 1–2.

51. This notion of an early period of perfect health is also found in classical ayurvedic texts. The *Carakasaṃhitā*, parts of which may have been composed as early as the third century B.C.E., narrates a history of degeneration of health from an original "golden age," in which human lifespans were without limit, and their bodies were "as solid as the condensed essence of mountains." See Wujastyk, *The Roots of Ayurveda*, 85–86.

52. Subramaniam, *Cittavaittiyattiṉ Muṉṉēṟṟam*, 1–5.

53. Kandaswamy Pillai, *History of Siddha Medicine*, 283.

54. Circapai, "Citta Vaittiyattiṉ Ciṟappum Ataṉ Tēvaiyum," 78.

55. Renganathan, "Mutal Paricu Peṟṟa Kaṭṭuraikaḷ," 31.

56. Kalimuttu Pillai, "Cittar Tiṟaṅkaḷ," 64.

57. Ibid., 66.

58. Somasundara Bharathiar, *The Papers of Dr. Navalar Somasundara Bharathiar*, 27, 106.

59. Thottam, *Siddha Medicine*, 3–5.

60. Nathan, "Cintuveḷi Nākarikam Paṟṟiya Varalāṟṟu," 64.

61. Kasinathan, "Tamiḻakamum, Harappaṉ Nākarikamum," 17.

62. Nathan, "Cintuveḷi Nākarikam Paṟṟiya Varalāṟṟu," 66, 64.

63. Ibid., 64.

64. *Kriyāviṉ Taṟkālat Tamiḻ Akarāti*, 616.

65. Daniel, *Fluid Signs*, 88.

66. Somasundara Bharathiar, *The Papers of Dr. Navalar Somasundara Bharathiar*, 36.

67. Dharmaniti, *Kumarikkaṇṭattu Nākarikam*, 14.

68. Ibid., 15.

69. Ibid., 202, 223.

70. Ibid., 16, 17.

71. As Levinas speaks of the wistfulness of human discontent, "The 'otherwise' and the 'elsewhere' they wish still belong to the here below they refuse." Levinas, *Totality and Infinity*, 41.

72. Probably the greatest modern figure of Tamil scholarship is Dr. U. V. Swaminathaiyer, a brahman who was almost single-handedly responsible for bringing Tamil sangam literature to public attention. For an English account of his work in Tamil literature, see Swaminathaiyar, *The Story of My Life.*

73. Pollock, "The Cosmopolitan Vernacular," 29.

74. Indeed, in some narratives of Tamil identity, the historical record has been interpreted in ways that counter the narrative of brahman as other, instead telling the story of brahman integration in Tamil society, celebrating the synthesis of Sanskrit and Tamil, and asserting the essential role of brahmans in the formation of modern Tamil culture.

75. Barnett, *The Politics of Cultural Nationalism*, 16. By "caste groupings" here I refer to *varṇa*, which is a more general rubric than *jāti*. Caste identities have two layers, the first being varṇa, which is less relevant "on the ground" than the second, jāti, the actual community that is the basis of marriage and other ritual and social relations.

76. Irschick, *Politics and Social Conflict*, 14.

77. For this reason, varṇa classification does not accurately describe relations and hierarchy in Tamil Nadu.

78. Barnett, *The Politics of Cultural Nationalism*, 16–17.

79. Burton Stein writes of the cooperation between Vellalars and brahmans, and the integral part brahmans have played in Tamil society, in his *Peasant, State, and Society in Medieval South India.* For a more pointed discussion of this relationship in Shaivism, see Peterson, *Poems to Śiva*, and her "Śramaṇas against the Tamil Way: Jains as Others in Tamil Śaiva Literature."

80. Nicholas Dirks convincingly argues that Caldwell's conversion agenda played a significant role in his his linguistic and racial theories. See Dirks, *Castes of Mind*, 134–44.

81. Robert Caldwell, *A Comparative Grammar of the Dravidian or South-Indian Family of Languages.* On Ellis and others who contributed to the Dravidian debate, see Trautmann, *Languages and Nations.*

82. *Tolkāppiyam* 884, 885. See *Tolkāppiyam*, with commentary of S. Singaravelan.

83. *Tēvāram*, Appar VI.301.1, in Peterson, *Poems to Śiva*, 69–71.

84. *Cilappatikāram* of Iḷaṅkō Aṭikaḷ, trans. R. Parthasarathy, *The Tale of an Anklet*, 227–48.

85. See, for example, Max Mueller, *Chips from a German Woodshop*, 1: 63–64.

86. Irschick, *Politics and Social Conflict*, 14, 18.

87. Barnett, *The Politics of Cultural Nationalism*, 25.

88. Nambi Arooran, *Tamil Renaissance and Dravidian Nationalism*, 45–47.

89. *New India*, August 15, 1919. Quoted in Hausman, "Siddhars, Alchemy, and the Abyss of Tradition," 182.

90. For more on the promotion of ayurveda in nationalist contexts, see Langford, *Fluent Bodies*.

91. *Report of the Committee on the Indigenous Systems of Medicine,* Part 2, 247.

92. *Report of the Committee on the Indigenous Systems of Medicine,* Part 1, 1.

93. Nationalist concerns are not the only reason for siddha practitioners to assert the uniqueness of a Tamil medical practice. Market concerns have also been a major factor, as various medical practitioners compete for clientele in a tight market for indigenous medicines.

94. *Report of the Committee on the Indigenous Systems of Medicine,* Part 2, 341.

95. Government Order 53, Health, Education, and Local Administration Department, January 6, 1960, 133.

96. Ibid., 143, 149.

97. Kasturi, "Citta Maruttuvam," 3.

98. Purnalingam Pillai, *Tamil Literature,* 265–66.

99. Sambasivam Pillai, *Tamil-English Dictionary of Medicine,* 3: 2104.

100. V. R. Madhavan, *Siddha Medical Manuscripts in Tamil,* 34, 35, 52.

101. Ricoeur, *Lectures on Ideology and Utopia,* 17.

102. Levinas, *Totality and Infinity,* 156.

103. Slavoj Zizek, "Is It Possible to Traverse the Fantasy in Cyberspace?" 114.

104. Ibid., 116.

105. Here I disagree with Karl Mannheim, who holds that what is "truly utopian" is realizable in the future. Mannheim, *Ideology and Utopia,* 204.

106. Thanks to Bruce Lincoln for clarifying this point.

107. Although, I choose to emphasize the structural correspondences of the Tamil identity narratives and the Oedipus narrative, their narrative elements are also strikingly similar. The Tamil language, Tamil civilization, and the Tamil nation coalesce in the metaphor of "Tamiḻttāy," or Mother Tamil, an embodied ideal that lies at the core of the perfect, natural Tamil society. The Tamil people are generally considered to be the "devotees," or more commonly the "sons," of Mother Tamil, and her blood runs through their veins. The Aryan, though not characterized as the father, is a patriarchal, aggressive figure who has destroyed the purity of the Tamil mother and who stands between the final union of mother and son. His presence is unnatural, as he does not share the blood of either the son or the mother—so his position is not as the father but as the rapist of Mother Tamil. See Ramaswamy, *Passions of the Tongue*.

CHAPTER 5

1. *The Hindu* (Chennai), March 8, 2000.

2. This school is the descendent of the College of Indian Medicine, which was founded on the recommendation of the 1923 *Report of the Committee on the Indigenous Systems of Medicine*.

3. Ranga et al., "Rasagenthi Lehyam (RL)."

4. Abirami, "Stala Viruṭcaṅkaḷum Ārōkkiyamum!" 8. The linking of siddha medicine to Hindu temples, such as the medical use of the *navapāśāṇam* (nine minerals) scrapings of Bhogar's icon at Palani, or the highlighting of siddha medical uses of temple trees, seems to be a new development and parallels a growing trend that connects the siddhars to specific temples. Layne Little discusses the healing powers of the navapāśāṇam at Palani, and also the location in temples of siddhar *camātis* (*samādhis*), places where the siddhars transcended their bodies in a deep meditative state. See Little, "Bowl Full of Sky," chapter 2.

5. Abirami, 8.

6. Lincoln, "Theses on Method," 225.

7. It is not only non-brahman leaders who emphasize the scientific genius of the Tamils. Even those who celebrate the synthesis of Tamil and Sanskrit culture agree. Thus, P. T. Srinivasa Aiyangar writes, "The genius of Tamil is marked by the scientific temperament; concrete ideas and images appeal to the Tamil people and hence Tamil is peculiarly fitted to be the vehicle of scientific knowledge. The genius of Sanskrit is marked by the philosophical temperament." Srinivasa Aiyangar, *Pre-Aryan Tamil Culture*, 85.

8. See Kailasapathy, "The Writings of the Tamil Siddhas," 391.

9. Zvelebil, *The Smile of Murugan*, 218.

10. Varadarajan, *A History of Tamil Literature*, 184–85.

11. Purnalingam Pillai, *Tamil Literature*, 263.

12. Varadarajan, *Tamiḻ Ilakkiya Varalāṟu*, 190.

13. Tamilpriyan, *Patiṉeṭṭu Cittarkaḷiṉ Mukkiya Pāṭalkaḷum Viḷakkaṅkaḷum*, 9.

14. Government Order 3318, Health Department, October 24, 1952, 21.

15. Thottam, *Siddha Medicine*, 14–17.

16. *Cittar Ulakam*, January 2007, 1.

17. *Cittar Ulakam*, July 2006, 1.

18. *Cittar Ulakam*, December 2006, 1.

19. *Cittar Ulakam*, July 2006, 1.

20. Visswanathan, *The Political Career of E. V. Ramasami Naicker: A Study in the Politics of Tamilnadu, 1920–1949*, 20–23.

21. Barnett, *The Politics of Cultural Nationalism*, 37.

22. Ramasami, *Tamiḻar Tamiḻnāṭu Tamiḻarpaṇpāṭu*, 45–46.

23. Anita Diehl, *E. V. Ramaswami Naicker-Periyar*, 41, 55, 56.

24. Ramasami, *Is There a God?* 39, 49, 45. For more on the atheism of E.V.R., see Anaimuthu, *Contribution of Periyar E.V.R. to the Progress of Atheism*.

25. Ramasami, *The Ramayana (A True Reading)*, iv.

26. Ramasami, *The Revolutionary Sayings of Periyar*, 15.

27. Ramasami, *Tamiḻar Tamiḻnāṭu Tamiḻarpaṇpāṭu*, 13.

28. Ramasami, *Revolutionary Sayings*, 18–19.

29. Ramasami, *Is There a God?* 62.

30. See Arooran, *Tamil Renaissance and Dravidian Nationalism*, 166. Sami (Cāmi) Chidambaranar is not to be confused with A. Chidambaranar, who wrote revivalist histories of Tirumular and Agastya.

31. Chidambaranar, *Tamiḻar Talaivar Periyār I. Ve. Rā. Varalāṟu*.

32. Thambidurai, "Policy Note 2001–2002."

33. Chidambaranar, *Cittarkaḷ Kaṇṭa Viññāṉam Tattuvam.*

34. Ibid., 6.

35. Ibid., 9–11.

36. Ibid., 7–8.

37. Ibid., 18–19.

38. Ibid., 26–28.

39. Ibid., 30.

40. Ibid., 30–31, 28.

41. Ibid., 9.

42. Ibid., 13–14.

43. Kalai Arasu, *Cittarkaḷ Collum Tirāviṭa Āṉmīkam*, 9–13, 21.

44. Ibid., 25–26.

45. Ibid., 7, 10, 26, 15.

46. For more on this tension, see Kailasapathy, "The Writings of the Tamil Siddhas," 385–411; and Little, "An Introduction to the Tamil Siddhas."

47. Zvelebil, *The Poets of the Powers*, 80–81.

48. Sivavakkiyar 33, ibid., 83.

49. Sivavakkiyar 496, ibid., 87.

50. Ñānaveṭṭiyāṉ 527. The *linga* is a phallus that represents Shiva; the *atmalinga* is a concept in which the internal source of life is conceived as a *linga*. Quoted in Venkatraman, *A History of the Tamil Siddha Cult*, 151.

51. Ibid., 150.

52. Ramachandran, *Cittarkaḷ Varalāṟu*, 23–24.

53. Subramania Iyer, *The Poetry and Philosophy of the Tamil Siddhars*, 7–8.

54. Subramanian, *Nellai Māvaṭṭac Cittarkaḷ*, 2–3.

55. See, for example, Thomas Wise, *Commentary on the Hindu System of Medicine*, first published in 1845, parts of which were recently published as *Ayurveda, or, Hindu System of Medical Science*. See also Tirumurti, "Presidential Address," 16; and Ramaswami Reddiar, "Hindu System of Medicine and the Spirit of Service." Tirumurti cites Wise as an authority.

56. Zimmermann, *The Jungle and the Aroma of Meats.*

57. Langford, *Fluent Bodies*, 94. See also Sivaramakrishnan, *Old Potions, New Bottles*, 7, 11.

58. Zvelebil, *Poets of the Powers*, 20. Italics in original.

59. Barnett, *The Politics of Cultural Nationalism*, 32–34.

60. Quoted in Sivathamby, "The Politics of a Literary Style," 30.

61. *Sentamil Selvi*, July–August, 1928, quoted in Venkatachalapathy, "The Dravidian Movement and the Vellalars, 1927–1944," in his *In Those Days There Was No Coffee*, 116–17. Venkatachalapathy gives an excellent historical account of the relationship between the Shaiva Siddhantin and the Self-Respecters, with a particular focus on Maraimalai Adigal.

62. Ibid., 130.

63. Ibid., 117.

64. On Maraimalai Adigal, see Ramaswamy, *Passions of the Tongue*; Venkatachalapathy, "The Dravidian Movement and the Vellalars, 1927–1944"; and Vaitheespara, "Caste, Hybridity and the Construction of Cultural Identity in Colonial India."

65. Maraimalai Adigal, English preface to *Tamiḻar Matam*, 13–14.

66. Thottam, *Siddha Medicine*, 157.

67. Uttamarayan, *Tōṟṟakkirama Ārāycciyum Cittamaruttuva Varalāṟum*, 285. In Sanskrit, *linga* means "phallus," and also "sign." Both meanings are salient here, as the linga is a phallic image that represents Shiva.

68. Sambasivam Pillai, *Tamil-English Dictionary of Medicine*, vol. 3, 2219–2220.

69. Maraimalai Adigal, *Tamiḻar Matam*, 33–36; see also K. R. Subramanian, *The Origin of Saivism and its History in the Tamil Land*, 24.

70. Verse 1619, *Tirumūla Nāyaṉār aruḷic ceyta Tirumantiram*, 635. P. M. Venugopal, chief lecturer in siddha at the Government College of Integrated Medicine, gives a similar argument on the basis of the global distribution of Shivalingas. See Venugopal, "Siddha System of Medicine Based on Saiva Siddhanta Doctrine."

71. Government Order 53, Health, Education, and Local Administration Department, January 6, 1960, 107.

72. Ibid., 149.

73. Maraimalai Adigal, *Tamiḻar Matam*, 14, 17–18.

74. Maraimalai Adigal, English preface to *Māṇikkavācakar Varalāṟum Kālamum*, 16.

75. Maraimalai Adigal, *Tamiḻar Matam*, 20.

76. Ramasami, *Irāmāyaṇap Pāttiraṅkaḷ*, 68

77. Sivathamby, "Politics of a Literary Style," 23.

78. In this they diverge from the strict materialism of *lokāyata*, a doctine of the Cārvāka school that dates to the time of the *Mahābhārata*. The Cārvākas only accepted the authority of *pratyakṣa*, literally, what is "before the eyes," as a means (*pramāna*) to knowledge, denying the validity of spoken authority (*śabda*), analogy (*upamāna*), and even inference (*anumāna*).

79. Verse 23, *Urōmariṣi Muppucūttiram* 30, in *Patiṉeṇ Cittarkaḷ Vaittiya Cillaṟaik Kōvai*, 526.

80. *Tamiḻ (Citta) Maruttuvak Kōṭpāṭu*, 5.

81. Maraimalai Adigal, *Mānikkavācakar Varalāṟum Kālamum*, 16.

82. Maraimalai Adigal, *Can Hindi be the Lingua Franca of India?*, 18.

83. Maraimalai Adigal, *Tamiḻar Matam*, 24.

84. Maraimalai Adigal, *Vēḷāḷar Nākarikam*, 11.

85. Maraimalai Adigal, *Tamiḻar Matam*, 34, 33.

86. Ibid., 47. Although it is tempting here to read this emphasis on monotheism as simply a response to missionary critiques of a polytheistic, superstitious Hinduism, the singular, zealous worship of Shiva is advocated by texts that form the canon of Tamil Shaiva Siddhanta, such as Cekkilar's *Periyā Purāṇam*, which was written during the reign of the Chola king Kulotunga II (1133–1150 C.E.).

87. Maraimalai Adigal, *Tamiḻar Matam*, 16.

88. Dr. Circapai, "Citta Vaittiyattiṉ Ciṟappum Ataṉ Tēvaiyum," 78.

89. Kuppusami Mudaliyar, *Citta Maruttuvam*, vi.

90. Ibid., vi.

91. Ibid., vii–xiii, xxii–xxiii, lxxii, lxv–lxvi.

92. Ibid., lxvii–lxx, lxxviii–lxxix, xcii–xcviii.

93. Ibid., ciii, cvi.

94. Subramania Pillai, "Introduction and History of Saiva Siddhanta," 20. A *tatva* or more commonly *tattva* is an essential element or principle of the cosmos.

95. Ibid., 13.

96. Rama Dharmaniti, *Kumarikkaṉṭattu Nākarikam*, 219–20.

97. Ibid., 16–17.

98. Kuppusami Mudaliyar, *Citta Maruttuvam*, iii–v.

99. Ibid., lxxvii.

100. Kailasapathy, "The Tamil Purist Movement," Sivathamby, "The Politics of a Literary Style," 16; 29. On the Pure Tamil Movement, in addition to Sivathamby and Kailasapathy, see Venkatachalapathy, "Coining Words: Language and Politics in Late Colonial Tamil Nadu," in his *In Those Days There Was No Coffee*.

101. Arooran, *Tamil Renaissance and Dravidian Nationalism*, 166, 167.

102. Kailasapathy, "The Tamil Purist Movement," 34.

103. Maraimalai Adigal, *Can Hindi be the Lingua Franca of India?* 31.

104. Ibid., 8–9.

105. Ibid., 31.

106. Two fascinating controversies quickly arose over this decision. One was uncertainty over the release of a film in 2007 starring Rajnikanth, who plays the protagonist, Sivaji, after whom the film was named. After some debate over whether Sivaji is a Tamil title, the Tamil state government ruled that it was a Tamil name and gave the film tax-exempt status. See Shankar, "Tax Exemption for Shivaji." The second controversy emerged after several Tamil films gained tax-exempt status but used sexually provocative Tamil words in their titles. In August 2007, the state government ruled that to receive tax-exempt status, film titles must be in Tamil and must also adhere to the values of Tamil culture. See "Panel to Scrutinise Tamil Film Titles."

107. "Tamiḻil Peyar Vaittāl Atirṣṭam Atikarikkum."

108. Manickam Naicker, *The Tamil Alphabet and Its Mystic Aspect*, 18–19.

109. Ibid., 21, 24, 29–34, 41.

110. Ibid., 49–59. Manickam Naicker's claim that *ōm* was discovered by Tamils runs counter to literary evidence, which attests to the importance of this sound in Sanskrit literature that predates the earliest extant Tamil texts, and his theory of language reflects classical Sanskritic theories of the creative power of mantras.

111. Maraimalai Adigal, *Tamiḻiṉ Taṉic Ciṟappu*, 12–13.

112. Ibid., 23–24.

113. Ibid., 21.

114. N. Manikkavasagam, *Cittar Pāṭalkaḷ*, v, vi.

115. Kalimuttu Pillai, "Cittar Tiṟaṅkaḷ," 64–65.

116. Madhavan, *Siddha Medical Manuscripts in Tamil*, 2–3.

117. Scharfe, "The Doctrine of the Three Humors."

118. Venkatesan, *Tamiḻ Ilakkiyattil Citta Maruttuvam*, 160.

119. On the emergence of the Tamil literary canon and the criteria that contributed to its construction, see A. R. Venkatachalapathy, "'Enna Prayocanam?' Constructing the Canon in Colonial Tamil Nadu."

120. Zvelebil, *Lexicon of Tamil Literature*, 669.

121. Ramasami, *Revolutionary Sayings*, 50–51.

122. Blackburn, "Corruption and Redemption."

123. Madhavan. *Siddha Medical Manuscripts in Tamil*, 10.

124. Manikkavasagam, *Cittar Pāṭalkaḷ*, 325.

125. Kasturi, "Citta Maruttuvam," 1.

126. Murukaiyan, *Tiruvaḷḷuvam*, 68.

127. Chidambarathanu Pillai, *Citta Maruttuva Amutu*, 27.

128. Zvelebil, *Tamil Literature*, 117.

129. Venkatesan, "Tamiḻarp Paṇpāṭṭil Ārōkkiyam."

130. Ibid., 36.

131. Maraimalai Adigal, *Can Hindi be the Lingua Franca of India?* 4.

132. Venkatesan, "Tamiḻarp Paṇpāṭṭil Ārōkkiyam," 40.

133. Maraimalai Adigal, *Tamiḻiṉ Taṉic Ciṟappu*, 20.

134. Ramamurthy and Devi, *Uṭal Nalam Uṅkaḷ Kaikaḷil.*

135. Ramamurthy, *Mūlikai Pēcukiṟatu*, 17.

136. Ibid., 17–21.

137. Langford also notes this tendency of patients in Indian to criticize Western medicines for their side effects. Langford, *Fluent Bodies*, 56.

138. Venkatesan, "Alōpatiyil 'Side Effects' Atircci Rippōrṭ," 9, 12.

139. Ibid., 11.

140. Manian, *Cittar Kaṇṭa Mūlikai Maruttuvam (Iranṭām Pākam)*, 3.

141. Singaravelu Vaittiyar, *Ārōkkiyam Tarum Cittarkaḷiṉ Kīraikaḷ, Mūlikaikaḷ*, 3–5.

142. Chengalpattu Siddha Medical Association, "Vallamai Tarum Vajjiravalli," 15.

143. Ibid., 16–19.

144. Sanguppulavar, *Cittarkaḷ Kaṇṭa Uṇavu Maruttuvam*, 3, 29.

145. *Simple Home Remedies in Indian Medicine.*

146. Chidambarathanu Pillai, *Citta Maruttuva Amutu*, 1.

147. Ibid., 4.

148. Ibid., 19.

149. In this sense, the rhetoric of Tamil nationalism resembles the rhetoric of the Sanskrit dharmaśastric literature, in which dharma dictates human action and duty only because it is the very nature of things.

150. Kasturi, "Citta Maruttuvam."

151. Ibid., 4–6.

152. Krishnamurthy, "Citta Maruntum Iṉṟaiya Ulakum," 98.

153. Ibid., 98–100.

154. Madhavan, *Siddha Medical Manuscripts in Tamil*, v.

155. *Report of the Committee on the Indigenous Systems of Medicine*, Part 2, 337.

156. B. Anandaraman, "Nalivuṟṟa Citta Maruttuvarkaḷ Vāḻa Vaḻimuṟaikaḷ."

157. Quoted in Subramanian and Madhavan, eds. *Heritage of the Tamils: Siddha Medicine*, vii. On Srinivasamurthi, see Ashis Nandy and Shiv Visvanathan, "Modern Medicine and Its Non-modern Critics," 175–78. As we saw earlier, baspams (medicines of calcinated powder) and chendoorams (any metallic compound used as medicine) are often cited as distinguishing features of siddha medicine.

158. The modern character of this process of identification does not lie in the act of identification itself, since the linking of knowledge, practices, and vocations to particular communities has taken place in South Asia for millennia. What is new in this process are the contours of the articulated communities and the ways in which knowledge and practice are conceived to be both traditional and scientific.

159. Barthes, *Mythologies*, 129–41.

160. Zizek, *The Plague of Fantasies*, 7.

161. Circapai, "Citta Vaittiyattiṉ Ciṟappum Ataṉ Tēvaiyum," 80.

CHAPTER 6

1. On siddha and ayurvedic claims to have discovered cures for HIV/AIDS, see van Hollen, "Nationalism, Transnationalism, and the Politics of 'Traditional' Indian Medicine for HIV/AIDS."

2. Simmel, *The Sociology of Georg Simmel*, 332. Italics in original.

3. Ibid.

4. See Luhrmann, "The Magic of Secrecy," 144.

5. These global processes have had an impact on the content of traditional medical practices, the value of these practices within the Tamil community, and perhaps most significantly, the very idioms in which vaidyas consider their knowledge and advertise it to those outside Tamil Nadu.

6. Urban, *The Economics of Ecstasy*, 101.

7. Simmel, *The Sociology of Georg Simmel*, 332.

8. Urban, *The Economics of Ecstasy*, 12.

9. Khaleeli, "Harmony or Hegemony?," 85.

10. For a detailed discussion of the registration of siddha vaidyas, see Hausman, "Siddhars, Alchemy, and the Abyss of Tradition," chapter 7.

11. Agastya, for example, "saw" the method to prepare muppu after focusing his mind on Shakti's feet. *Akastiya Muṉivar Aruḷiya Kaṟpa Muppu Kuru Nūl 100*, verse 3, 10.

12. Krishnan, "Siddha Medicine during the Period of the Marattias," 55.

13. Obeyesekere, "Science, Experimentation," 160.

14. V. R. Madhavan, "Medical Education of the Tamils," 227.

15. Krishnan, "Siddha Medicine during the Period of the Marattias," 56.

16. Samuel, *Kumari Mutal Vārcā Varai*, 3–4.

17. Velan, *Siddhar's Science of Longevity*, 96.

18. *Akastiya Muṉivar Aruḷiya Kaṟpa Muppu Kuru Nūl 100*, verses 66–67, 41–42.

19. Ibid., verse 4, 11.

20. Ibid., verse 2, 9–10.

21. *Akastiya Muṉivar Aruḷiya Kuru Nūl Muppu 50*, verse 18, in *Akastiyar Muppu Cūttiraṅkaḷ*, 69.

22. *Akastiya Muṉivar Aruḷiya Kaṟpa Muppu Kuru Nūl 100*, verse 100, 58.

23. *Akastiya Muṉivar Aruḷiya Kaṟpa Muppu Kuru Nūl 100*, 19. It is somewhat unclear what cavvīra paṟpam is, though it may be calcinated bisulphate of mercury. For different possibilities and one method of preparation as set out in Agastya's "Poorna Sootram," see Sambasivam Pillai, *Tamil-English Dictionary of Medicine*, 3: 1962.

24. *Pōkanāyaṉār Aruḷicceyta Pūjāviti 37*, verse 11, 375. Venkatraman speaks of Valai as a "benign girl, 5 years old." Venkatraman, *A History of the Tamil Siddha Cult*, 93.

25. *Akastiya Muṉivar Aruḷiya Kuru Nūl Muppu 50*, verse 16, 68.

26. *Akastiya Muṉivar Aruḷiya Kaṟpa Muppu Kuru Nūl 100*, verse 3, 10.

27. *Akastiya Muṉivar Aruḷiya Kaṟpa Muppu Kuru Nūl 100*, verse 6, 12.

28. Centūram is red chemical preparation.

29. This is a good thing, as the old skin will be replaced by a new, younger one, or perhaps even a golden skin. This is one of the effects of *kaṟpam*. See Sambasivam Pillai, *Tamil-English Dictionary of Medicine*, 3: 1790.

30. The three gods are Brahma, Shiva, and Vishnu. Janaka, etc. refers to the four mind-born sages of Brahma.

31. *Kailāca Caṭṭamuṉināyaṉār Aruḷicceyta Kaṟpaviti 100*, verses 63–69, 476–77. R. Venkatraman looks at this passage as well, remarking that this episode appears in works by several other siddhars. Venkatraman, *A History of the Tamil Siddha Cult*, 51.

32. Sambasivam Pillai, *Tamil-English Dictionary of Medicine*, 3: 1790.

33. The editor's preface to *Akastiyar Muppu Cūttiraṅkaḷ*, 4–5.

34. This is not to say that the medical texts of the siddhars and the current practice of siddha vaidyas are empty of content. Many people continue to be healed by the medicines that vaidyas produce. I have focused here on the medicines for which the most extraordinary claims are made, and I suspect that these medicines are the most "empty" of all siddha medicines, in accordance with the grandeur of the claims made for them.

35. Subbarayappa, "Chemical Practices and Alchemy," 335.

36. Ibid., 339.

37. *Nandhi [Nanti]*, mālai 9, maṇi 7, May 1972, 13. Quoted in Hausman, "Siddhars, Alchemy, and the Abyss of Tradition," 410.

38. Shanmukavelu, *A Study of Siddha Vaidya Muppu*, 46.

39. Quoted in Hausman, "Siddhars, Alchemy, and the Abyss of Tradition," 408.

40. Shanmukavelu, *A Study of Siddha Vaidya Muppu*, 35.

41. *Agastiyar Cūṭca Muppu 32*, verses 15–18, 118–19.

42. Sambasivam Pillai, *Tamil-English Dictionary of Medicine*, 5: 543.

43. Subbarayappa, "Siddha Medicine," 437.

44. Subbarayappa, "Chemical Practices and Alchemy," 336–37.

45. Shanmukavelu, *A Study of Siddha Vaidya Muppu*, 59.

46. Ibid., 36.

47. Ibid., 129.

48. Quoted in Hausman, "Siddhars, Alchemy, and the Abyss of Tradition," 412.

49. Quoted in ibid., 413.

50. *Akastiya Muṉivar Aruḷiya Kaṟpa Muppu Kuru Nūl 100*, verses 26, 29, 25–27.

51. Ibid., verse 54, 35.

52. *Agastiyar Cūṭca Muppu 32*, verse 27, 121–22.

53. Shanmuga Velan, *Siddhar's Science of Longevity,* 105.
54. Simmel, *The Sociology of Georg Simmel,* 337.
55. Kailasapathy, "The Writings of the Tamil Siddhas," 394–95.

CHAPTER 7

1. Thyagarajan, "Key Note Address," vii.
2. Nietzsche, *On the Genealogy of Morality,* 8.
3. Krishnan, "Siddha Medicine during the Period of the Marattias," 58.
4. Srinivasalu Naidu, "Medical Education and Medical Relief," 43.
5. I do not mean to imply that there is no secrecy in science, nor is the practice of science an entirely demystified discipline. But I do agree with David Himrod that science is characterized more by openness than by secrecy. David K. Himrod, "Secrecy in Modern Science," 103.
6. Alagappan, "Medical Education," 38.
7. Quoted in Hausman, "Siddhars, Alchemy and the Abyss of Tradition," 387–88.
8. Krishnan, "Siddha Medicine during the Period of the Marattias," 57–58.
9. The critique of esoteric education in India is not new. However, it generally has been elaborated in terms of the monopolization of knowledge by particular groups, rather than being based on a general, formal principle that the public development of knowledge is superior.
10. Srinivasalu Naidu, "Medical Education and Medical Relief," 45.
11. Ibid., 43.
12. K. Parthasarathy, "Kaṭṭiḻanta Citta Maruttuvarkaḷ Orumaippāṭu," 26, 27.
13. Muttukkaruppa Pillai, "Cittarkaḷiṉ Vayatu," 37.
14. Meykandar, "Citta Vaityattiṉ Tēvai," 44–47.
15. Uttamarayan, "Tamiḻ Maruttuvam Uyvaṭaiya Vaḻimuṟai," 42.
16. N. Subramaniam, *Cittavaittiyattiṉ Muṉṉēṟṟam,* 51.
17. Shanmuga Velan, *Siddhar's Science of Longevity,* 143.
18. Shanmukavelu, *A Study of Siddha Vaidya Muppu,* 3–4. Here he distinguishes "vaidya muppu," as muppu specifically targeted for healing ailments, from muppu used for alchemical processes, such as transforming mercury into gold.
19. Ibid., 5–6.
20. *The Report of the Committee on the Indigenous Systems of Medicine,* Part 2, 363.
21. Lincoln, *Authority,* 117.
22. Madhavan, "Medical Education of the Tamils," 227–28.
23. Ibid. On ceypākam and kaipākam, see chapter 1, 16.
24. IMPCOPS stands for the Indian Medical Practitioners Co-operative Pharmacy and Stores Limited. Located in Chennai and with branches in other centers in Tamil Nadu, it is a major producer of siddha, ayurveda, and unani medicines.
25. The BSMS degree is a Bachelor of Siddha Medicine and Surgery degree, awarded after completion of a five-year course.
26. Williams, *Keywords,* 128.
27. Scott, "The Evidence of Experience."

28. Williams, *Keywords*, 128, 115.

29. *Report of the Committee on the Indigenous Systems of Medicine*, Part 2, 359.

30. Shanmuga Velan, *Siddhar's Science of Longevity*, preface.

31. *Report of the Committee on the Indigenous Systems of Medicine*, Part 2, 371.

32. Government Order 1060, Government of Madras Education and Public Health Department, June 13, 1966, 16.

33. At this time, the official political name of the Tamil-speaking region was "Madras," though in communications internal to the state, and in communications in the Tamil language, the name "Tamil Nad" could be used. The name was officially changed to "Tamil Nadu" on January 14, 1969. On the fascinating debate over the name of the region, see Ramaswamy, *Passions of the Tongue*, 154–61.

34. Government Order 1060, 34.

35. Ibid., 36, 48.

36. This promotion of textuality over conventional practice is consistent with broader patterns in the formulation of official knowledge about tradition in South Asia. For these debates vis-à-vis *sati* in the early colonial era, see Lata Mani, *Contentious Traditions*.

37. Government Order 1060, 10.

38. Ibid., 14.

39. Ibid., 32.

40. Ibid., 30.

41. Chidambaranar, *Akattiyar Varalāṟu*, 14–15.

42. For a list of siddha medical manuscripts and the various libraries in which they are housed, see Madhavan, *Siddha Medical Manuscripts in Tamil*, appendix.

43. Anguish over lost manuscripts is nothing new in South Asia. The *Tirumuṟaikaṇṭa Purāṇam* (The story of the recovery of the Tirumuṟai), narrates the partial recovery of the *Tēvāram* hymns, most of which were were ruined after an extended period under an anthill. See Shulman, trans., *Songs of the Harsh Devotee*, xix–xx.

44. Madhavan, *Siddha Medical Manuscripts in Tamil*, 52.

45. Samuel, *Kumari Mutal Vārcā Varai*, preface.

46. See Anderson, *Imagined Communities*, 9–12; and MacIntyre, *After Virtue*, 221.

47. On Mother Tamil and language devotion, see Ramaswamy, *Passions of the Tongue*.

48. Samuel, *Kumari Mutal Vārcā Varai*, muṉṉurai.

49. Ibid., 1.

50. Ibid., 13–14.

51. Ibid., 4–5.

52. Muttukkaruppa Pillai, "Cittarkaḷiṉ Vayatu," 36–37. The reference to Kannaki and the Pandyan king is to the epic *Cilappatikāram*, in which the Pandyan king, reigning in Madurai, mistakenly blames Kannaki's husband Kovalan for stealing an anklet and puts him to death. Kannaki, in retaliation for this injustice, burns the city, which is said to have been the site of the third, and last, literary Tamil academy.

53. Ibid., 37.

54. Madhavan, *Siddha Medical Manuscripts in Tamil*, v–vi.

55. Ibid., 53.

56. Kasturi, "Citta Maruttuvam."
57. "Citta Maruttuva Ārāycci Nilaiya Kuṟikkōḷ," 8.
58. Uttamarayan, "Tamiḻ Maruttuvam Uyvaṭaiya Vaḻimuṟai," 42.
59. See chapter 2 above.
60. In his editor's introduction to *Akastiyar Muppu Cūttiraṅkaḷ*, 4.

CHAPTER 8

1. Shanmuga Velan, *Siddhar's Science of Longevity*, 9.
2. Ibid., 108.
3. Ibid., 114–15.
4. Ibid., 165, 186.
5. "Nalla Nalla Nāṭṭu Maruntukaḷ," 42.
6. Ibid., 43.
7. Alter, *Yoga in Modern India*, 26, 30–31, 105.
8. Alter, "Modern Medical Yoga," 119.
9. Alter, "Modern Medical Yoga," 119. I would put some of the older ideas much earlier, dating back to the *Yoga Sutras* (third century) with its well-known chapter on the siddhis, though the detailed tantric views of the body and liberation emerge only in the medieval period, as Alter suggests.
10. Simmel, *The Sociology of Georg Simmel*, 330.
11. "Nalla Nalla Nāṭṭu Maruntukaḷ," 43.
12. Natarajan, "Alchemical Conversion of Iramatevar," 257, 263, 265–66.
13. Quoted ibid., 271.
14. Ibid., 262, 270, 276.
15. Little, "Bowl Full of Sky," 39, 68, 88–89.
16. Ibid., 100–4.
17. MacIntyre, *After Virtue*, 222.
18. Alter, *Yoga in Modern India*, 28.
19. Ibid., 102.
20. Ibid., 77.

Bibliography

Abirami, K. V. "Stala Viruṭcaṅkaḷum Ārōkkiyamum!" [Temple trees and health!]. *Mūlikaimaṇi* 29.9 (March 2002): 8–11.

Adas, Michael. *Machines as the Measure of Men: Science, Technology, and Ideologies of Western Dominance*. Ithaca, NY: Cornell University Press, 1989.

Akastiya Muṉivar Aruḷiya Kaṟpa Muppu Kuru Nūl 100 [Agastya's 100 verses on the regenerative compound muppu]. In *Akastiyar Muppu Cūttiraṅkaḷ* [Agastya's texts on muppu], edited by S. P. Ramachandran, 9–59. Chennai: Tamarai Nulakam, 1994.

Akastiya Muṉivar Aruḷiya Kuru Nūl Muppu 50 [Agastya's text in 50 verses on muppu]. In *Akastiyar Muppu Cūttiraṅkaḷ* [Agastya's texts on muppu], edited by S. P. Ramachandran, 60–85. Chennai: Tamarai Nulakam, 1994.

Akastiyar Cūṭca Muppu 32 [Agastya's 32 verses on subtle muppu]. In *Akastiyar Muppu Cūttiraṅkaḷ* [Agastya's texts on muppu], edited by S. P. Ramachandran, 115–23. Chennai: Tamarai Nulakam, 1994.

Akastiyar Muppu Cūttiraṅkaḷ [Agastya's texts on muppu], edited by S. P. Ramachandran. Chennai: Tamarai Nulakam, 1994.

Alagappan, S. "Medical Education." In *The Government College of Integrated Medicine Decennial Souvenir*, 37–40. Chennai: 1957.

Alter, Joseph S., ed. *Asian Medicine and Globalization*. Philadelphia: University of Pennsylvania Press, 2005.

———. "Modern Medical Yoga: Struggling with a History of Magic, Alchemy and Sex." *Asian Medicine* 1.1 (2005): 119–46.

———. *Yoga in Modern India: The Body between Science and Philosophy*. Princeton, NJ: Princeton University Press, 2004.

Althusser, Louis. *For Marx*. Translated by Ben Brewster. New York: Verso, 1996 [1965].

Anaimuthu, Tiruchi V. *Contribution of Periyar E.V.R. to the Progress of Atheism.* Madras: Periyar Nul Veliyittakam, 1980.

Anandaraman, B. "Nalivuṟṟa Citta Maruttuvarkaḷ Vāḻa Vaḻimuṟaikaḷ" [Ways for siddha doctors to survive their decline]. In *Citta Maruttuva Nūl Ārāycci Nilaiyam Mupperum Viḻā Malar* [Souvenir of the conference of the Siddha Medical Literature Research Centre], 69–73. Chennai: Siddha Medical Research Centre, 1983.

Anbazhagan, K. "Foreword." In V. Narayanaswami, *Introduction to the Siddha System of Medicine*, iii–iv. Madras: Anandam Research Institute of Siddha Medicine, 1975.

Anderson, Benedict. *Imagined Communities: Reflections on the Origin and Spread of Nationalism.* Revised ed. New York: Verso, 1991.

Andra Medical Journal (1922).

Apte, V. S. *The Practical Sanskrit-English Dictionary.* 3 volumes. Poona: Prasad Prakashan, 1959.

Arangarajan, C. "Potu Maruttuvac Cuvaṭikaḷ" [Public medical manuscripts]. In *Citta Maruttuvac Cuvaṭikaḷ* [Siddha medical manuscripts], edited by G. John Samuel, 115–50. Chennai: Institute of Asian Studies, 1999.

Arnold, David, ed. *Colonizing the Body: State Medicine and Epidemic Disease in Nineteenth-Century India.* Berkeley: University of California Press, 1993.

———. *Imperial Medicine and Indigenous Societies.* New York: St. Martin's Press, 1988.

Barnett, Marguerite Ross. *The Politics of Cultural Nationalism in South India.* Princeton, NJ: Princeton University Press, 1976.

Barthes, Roland. *Mythologies.* New York: Hill and Wang, 1972.

Beals, Alan. R. "Curers in South India." In *Asian Medical Traditions: A Comparative Study*, edited by Charles Leslie, 184–200. Delhi: Motilal Banarsidass, 1998.

Biardeau, Madeleine. *Hinduism: The Anthropology of a Civilization.* Translated by Richard Nice. Delhi: Oxford University Press, 1994.

Blackburn, Stuart. "Corruption and Redemption: The Legend of Valluvar and Tamil Literary History." *Modern Asian Studies* 34.2 (2000): 449–82.

Bolle, Kees W., ed. *Secrecy in Religions.* Studies in the History of Religions Series 49. New York: E. J. Brill, 1987.

Buck, David C. *Dance, Snake, Dance: A Translation with Comments of the Songs of Pāmpāṭṭi-cittar.* Calcutta: Writers Workshop, 1976.

Buck, David C., and K. Paramasivam, trans. *The Study of Stolen Love: A Translation of Kaḷaviyal eṉṟa Iṟaiyaṉār Akapporuḷ with Commentary by Nakkīraṉār.* Atlanta: Scholars Press, 1997.

Buckingham, Jane. *Leprosy in Colonial South India: Medicine and Confinement.* New York: Palgrave, 2002.

Burke, Kenneth. *A Rhetoric of Motives.* Berkeley: University of California Press, 1969.

Caldwell, Robert. *A Comparative Grammar of the Dravidian or South-Indian Family of Languages.* Madras: Asian Educational Services, 1998 [1856].

Central Council of Indian Medicine, Ministry of Health and Family Welfare, Government of India. "Status of Siddha Colleges for the Year 2007–2008." http://www.ccimindia.org/colleges_3.htm, accessed January 13, 2008.

Charangapani, A. R. *Citta Neṟi* [Path of the siddhars]. 2 vols. Chennai: Manivacakar Patippakam, 1997.

Chatterjee, Partha. *The Nation and Its Fragments: Colonial and Postcolonial Histories.* Princeton Studies in Culture/Power/History. Princeton: Princeton University Press, 1993.

———. "The Nationalist Resolution of the Women's Question." In *Recasting Women: Essays in Indian Colonial History*, edited by Kumkum Sangari and Sudesh Vaid, 233–253. New Brunswick, NJ: Rutgers University Press, 1990.

Chengalpattu Siddha Medical Association. "Vallamai Tarum Vajjiravalli" [The vajjiravalli plant which gives strength]. *Cittar Ulakam* 2.7 (February 2003): 15–19.

Chidambaranar, A. *Akattiyar Varalāṟu* [The history of Agastya]. Chennai: South Indian Shaiva Siddhanta Works Publishing Society, 2002 [1950].

———. "Tirumūlanāyaṉār Varalāṟu" [The history of Tirumular Nayanar]. In *Tirumūla Nāyaṉār aruḷic ceyta Tirumantiram* [Tirumantiram of Tirumular Nayanar], with commentary of P. Ramanatha Pillai, 63–86. Tirunelveli, Tamil Nadu: South Indian Shaiva Siddhanta Works Publishing Society, 1994 [1942].

Chidambarathanu Pillai, S. *Citta Maruttuva Amutu* [The nectar of siddha medicine]. Chennai: Siddha Medical Literature Research Centre, 1991.

———. *Siddha System of Diseases.* Madras: Siddha Medical Literature Research Center, 1992.

———. *Siddha System of Life.* Madras: Siddha Medical Literature Research Center, 1991.

Circapai, Dr. "Citta Vaittiyattiṉ Ciṟappum Ataṉ Tēvaiyum" [The excellence of siddha medicine and its importance]. In *Iraṇṭām Ulakattamiḻ Mānāṭu Citta Maruttuva Karuttaraṅku Ciṟappu Malar* [Second World Tamil Conference, siddha medicine seminar special souvenir], 78–80. Chennai: Second World Tamil Conference, 1968.

"Citta Maruttuva Ārāycci Nilaiya Kuṟikkōḷ" [The goals of the Siddha Medical Literature Research Centre]. In *Citta Maruttuva Nūl Ārāycci Nilaiyam Mupperum Viḻā Malar* [Souvenir of the conference of the Siddha Medical Literature Research Centre], 15. Chennai: Siddha Medical Literature Research Centre, 1983.

Citta Maruttuva Nūl Ārāycci Nilaiyam Mupperum Viḻā Malar [Souvenir of the conference of the Siddha Medical Literature Research Centre]. Chennai: Siddha Medical Literature Research Centre, 1983.

Cittar Pāṭalkaḷ [Verses of the siddhars]. Edited by N. Manikkavasagam. Chennai: Uma Patippakam, 1995.

Cittar Pāṭalkaḷ [Verses of the siddhars]. Edited by I. Ramanathan. 2 vols. Chennai: Prema Pirasuram, 1995.

Cittar Ulakam [Siddhar world]. Edited by G. J. Parthasarathy. Chennai: G. J. Parthasarathy, 2002–2008.

Comacuntaram, M. P. *Cittar Ilakkiyam* [Siddhar literature]. 2 vols. Chidambaram, Tamil Nadu: Annamalai University Press, 1989.

Comaroff, Jean, and John Comaroff. "Medicine, Colonialism and the Black Body." In their *Ethnography and the Historical Imagination*, 215–233. Boulder, CO: Westview Press, 1992.

———. *Of Revelation and Revolution: Christianity, Colonialism, and Consciousness in South Africa*, vol. 1. Chicago: University of Chicago Press, 1991.

Cutler, Norman. "The Fish-eyed Goddess Meets the Movie Star: An Eyewitness Account of the Fifth International Tamil Conference." *Pacific Affairs* 56.2 (Summer 1983): 270–287.

Dandapani Desikar, C. *Tirumantira Muṉṉurai* [Introduction to Tirumantiram]. Third ed. Thiruvavadudurai, Tamil Nadu: Thiruvavadudurai Adinam, 2004 [1956].

Daniel, E. Valentine. *Fluid Signs: Being a Person the Tamil Way.* Berkeley: University of California Press, 1984.

———. "The Pulse as an Icon in Siddha Medicine." In *Contributions to Asian Studies* 18, edited by E. Valentine Daniel and Judy F. Pugh, 115–26. Leiden: E. J. Brill, 1984.

Davis, Richard. *Ritual in an Oscillating Universe: Worshiping Shiva in Medieval India.* Princeton, NJ: Princeton University Press, 1991.

Davis, William Spencer. "Agastya: The Southern Sage from the North." PhD dissertation, University of Chicago, 2000.

de Camp, L. Sprague. *Lost Continents: The Atlantis Theme in History, Science, and Literature.* New York: Dover, 1970.

Department of Ayurveda, Yoga and Naturopathy, Unani, Siddha and Homoeopathy (AYUSH), Ministry of Health and Family Welfare, Government of India. "State-wise Statistics of Siddha as on April 1, 2007." http://www.indianmedicine.nic.in/Statewise-siddha.adp, accessed January 13, 2008.

Department of Ayurveda, Yoga and Naturopathy, Unani, Siddha and Homoeopathy (AYUSH), Ministry of Health and Family Welfare, Government of India. "Summary of Infrastructure Facilities under Ayurveda, Yoga and Naturopathy, Unani, Siddha and Homoeopathy (AYUSH) as on April 1, 2007." http://www.indianmedicine.nic.in/summary-of-infrastructure.asp, accessed January 13, 2008.

Devaneyan, G. *The Language Problem of Tamil Nad and Its Logical Solution.* Madras: G. Devaneyan, 1967.

———. *The Primary Classical Language of the World.* Madras: Nesamani Publishing House, 1966.

Dharmaniti, Rama. *Kumarikkaṇṭattu Nākarikam* [The Kumari Kandam Civilization]. Viluppuram, Tamil Nadu: Muttu Patippagam, 1987.

Dhavamony, Mariasusai. *Love of God According to Śaiva Siddhānta: A Study in the Mysticism and Theology of Śaivism.* Oxford: Oxford University Press, 1971.

Diehl, Anita. *E. V. Ramaswami Naicker-Periyar: A Study of the Influence of a Personality in Contemporary South India.* Lund Studies in International History 10. Stockholm: Scandinavian University Books, 1977.

Dirks, Nicholas. *Castes of Mind: Colonialism and the Making of Modern India.* Delhi: Permanent Black, 2003.

Djurfeldt, G., and S. Lindberg. *Pills against Poverty: A Study of the Introduction of Western Medicine in a Tamil Village.* Scandanavian Institute of Asian Studies. New Delhi: Macmillan, 1980.

Eliade, Mircea. *Yoga, Immortality, and Freedom.* Translated by Willard R. Trask. Bollingen Series LVI. Princeton, NJ: Princeton University Press, 1973 [1958].

Elmore, Wilber Theodore. *Dravidian Gods in Modern Hinduism: A Study of the Local and Village Deities of Southern India.* Madras: Christian Literature Society for India, 1925.

Encyclopaedia of Tamil Literature. Vol. 1. Edited by Dr. G. John Samuel. Madras: Institute of Tamil Studies, 1990.

Foucault, Michel. *The Birth of the Clinic: An Archaeology of Medical Perception.* Translated by A. M. Sheridan Smith. New York: Vintage, 1994.

———. *Madness and Civilization: A History of Insanity in the Age of Reason*. New York: Pantheon, 1965.
———. "Nietzsche, Genealogy, History." In *The Foucault Reader*, edited by Paul Rabinow, 76–100. New York: Pantheon, 1984.
Fuller, C. J. *The Renewal of the Priesthood: Modernity and Tradition in a South Indian Temple*. Princeton, NJ: Princeton University Press, 2003.
Ganapathy, T. N. *The Philosophy of the Tamil Siddhas*. New Delhi: Indian Council of Philosophic Research, 1993.
———. "The Twilight Language of the Siddhas." In *India Philosophical Annual* 17, edited by R. Balasubramanian, 201–209. Madras: University of Madras, 1985.
———. *The Yoga of Siddha Boganathar*. Vol. 1. Eastman, QC: Babaji's Kriya Yoga and Publications, 2003.
Ganapathy, T. N., and K. R. Arumugam. *The Yoga of Tirumular: Essays on the Tirumantiram*. Eastman, QC: Babaji's Kriya Yoga Publications, 2004.
Geertz, Clifford. *The Interpretation of Cultures*. New York: Basic Books, 1973.
Geetha, V., and V. Rajadurai. *Towards a Non-brahmin Millennium: From Jyothee Thass to Periyar*. Calcutta: Samya, 1998.
Goldman, Robert P., and Sally J. Sutherland. *Devavāṇīpraveśikā: An Introduction to the Sanskrit Language*. Berkeley, CA: Center for South and Southeast Asia Studies, 1987.
Good, Byron J. *Medicine, Rationality, and Experience: An Anthropological Perspective*. Lewis Henry Morgan Lecture Series. Cambridge: Cambridge University Press, 1994.
Goodall, Dominic, ed. and trans. *Bhaṭṭa Rāmakaṇṭha's Commentary on the Kiraṇatantra*. Pondicherry: Institut Français de Pondichéry, 1998.
The Government College of Integrated Medicine Decennial Souvenir. Chennai, 1957.
Guha, Ranajit. *Dominance without Hegemony: History and Power in Colonial India*. Cambridge, MA: Harvard University Press, 1997.
Gupta, Brahmananda. "Indigenous Medicine in Nineteenth and Twentieth Century Bengal." In *Asian Medical Systems: A Comparative Study*, edited by Charles Leslie, 368–78. Delhi: Motilal Banarsidass, 1998.
Hardgrave, Robert L. *The Dravidian Movement*. Bombay: Popular Prakashan, 1965.
Harrison, Mark. *Public Health in British India: Anglo-Indian Preventative Medicine, 1859–1914*. Cambridge: Cambridge University Press, 1994.
Hart, George L. III. *The Poems of Ancient Tamil: Their Milieu and Their Sanskrit Counterparts*. Berkeley: University of California Press, 1975.
Harvey, David. *Spaces of Hope*. Berkeley: University of California Press, 2000.
Hausman, Gary J. "Siddhars, Alchemy, and the Abyss of Tradition: 'Traditional' Tamil Medical Knowledge in 'Modern' Practice." PhD dissertation, University of Michigan, 1996.
Headrick, Daniel R. *The Tools of Empire: Technology and European Imperialism in the Nineteenth Century*. New York: Oxford University Press, 1981.
Himrod, David. K. "Secrecy in Modern Science." In *Secrecy in Religions*, edited by Kees W. Bolle, 103–150. New York: E. J. Brill, 1987.
The Hindu. Chennai.
Hobsbawm, Eric, and Terence Ranger, eds. *The Invention of Tradition*. New York: Cambridge University Press, 1983.
Hopkins, E. Washburn. *Epic Mythology*. New York: Biblo and Tannen, 1969 [1915].

Horkheimer, Max, and Theodor W. Adorno. *Dialectic of Enlightenment*. Translated by John Cumming. New York: Continuum, 1972 [1944].

Inden, Ronald. *Imagining India*. Cambridge, MA: Blackwell, 1990.

Iranṭām Ulakattamiḻ Mānāṭu Citta Maruttuva Karuttaraṅku Ciṟappu Malar [Second World Tamil Conference, siddha medicine seminar special souvenir]. Chennai, Second World Tamil Conference, 1968.

Irschick, Eugene F. *Politics and Social Conflict in South India: The Non-Brahman Movement and Tamil Separatism, 1916–1929*. Berkeley: University of California Press, 1969.

———. *Tamil Revivalism in the 1930s*. Madras: Cre-A Publishers, 1986.

"Is Ayurveda to Be Encouraged? Or the British Pharmacopea to Be Enlarged?" *Andhra Medical Journal* 1.4 (November 1922): 1–4.

Jaggi, O. P. *Medicine In India: Modern Period*. History of Science, Philosophy, and Culture in Indian Civilization 9.1. New Delhi: Oxford University Press, 2000.

———. *Yogic and Tantric Medicine*. History of Science and Technology in India 5. Delhi: Atma Ram and Sons, 1973.

Joshi, Damodar. "Rasaśāstra: Its Principles and Medicinal Aspects." In *Medicine and Life Sciences in India*, edited by B. V. Subbarayappa, 270–291. Delhi: Centre for Studies in Civilization, 2001.

Journal of Indian Medicine. Chennai.

Kailāca Caṭṭamuṉināyaṉār Aruḷicceyta Kaṟpaviti 100 [Kailāca Caṭṭamuṉi's 100 verses on rejuvenative medicine]. In *Patiṉeṉ Cittarkaḷ Vaittiya Cillaṟaik Kōvai, Iranṭām Pākam* [A collection of medical tidbits of the eighteen siddhars, vol. 2], edited by S. P. Ramachandran, 461–485. Chennai: Tamarai Nulakam, 1996.

Kailasapathy, K. "The Tamil Purist Movement: A Re-evaluation." *Social Scientist* 7.10 (May 1979): 23–51.

———. "The Writings of the Tamil Siddhas." In *The Sants: Studies in a Devotional Tradition of India*, edited by Karine Schomer and W. H. McLeod, 385–411. Delhi: Motilal Banarsidass, 1987.

Kalai Arasu. *Cittarkaḷ Collum Tirāviṭa Āṉmīkam* [The Dravidian spirituality of the siddhars]. Coimbatore: Arun Pathippagam, 2005.

Kalimuttu Pillai, S.K.S. "Cittar Tiṟaṅkaḷ" [The powers of the siddhars]. In *Iranṭām Ulakattamiḻ Mānāṭu Citta Maruttuva Karuttaraṅku Ciṟappu Malar* [Second World Tamil Conference, siddha medicine seminar special souvenir], 64–68. Chennai: Second World Tamil Conference, 1968.

Kandaswamy Pillai, N. *History of Siddha Medicine*. Second ed. Chennai: Tamil Nadu Government, 1998 [1978].

Kasinathan, Nadan. "Tamiḻakamum, Harappaṉ Nākarikamum" [The Tamil land, and the Harrapan Civilization]. In *Kumarikkaṇṭam Maṟṟum Cintuveḷi Mānāṭṭu Malar: Tamiḻ Aṉṉaikkum Maṟṟum Uṇmai Āyvaip Pōṟṟupavarkaḷukkum Kāṇikkai* [Kumari Kantam and the Indus Valley conference souvenir: A devotional offering to the Tamil mother and to those who treasure true research]. Madras: Pannattu Molimaiyam, 1994.

Kasturi, R. "Citta Maruttuvam" [Siddha medicine]. In *Tiruvaḷḷuvar Īrāyiramāṇṭu Niṟaivu Viḻā Malar* [Commemorative volume of the celebration of two thousand years of Tiruvalluvar], 1–9. Kovai, Tamil Nadu: Pavendar Bharatidasan Mandram, 1970.

Khaleeli, Zhaleh."Harmony or Hegemony? The Rise and Fall of the Native Medical Institution, Calcutta; 1822–35." *South Asia Research* 21.1 (2001): 77–104.

Koppedrayer, Kathleen Iva. "The Sacred Presence of the Guru: The 'Velala' Lineages of Tiruvavatuturai, Dharmapuram, and Tiruppanantal." PhD dissertation, McMaster University, 1990.

Krishnamurthy, L. "Citta Maruntum Iṉṟaiya Ulakum" [Siddha medicine and the world today]. In *Iraṇṭām Ulakattamiḻ Mānāṭu Citta Maruttuva Karuttaraṅku Ciṟappu Malar* [Second World Tamil Conference, siddha medicine seminar special souvenir], 98–100. Chennai, Second World Tamil Conference, 1968.

Krishnan, K. R. "Siddha Medicine during the Period of the Marattias." In *Heritage of the Tamils: Siddha Medicine*, edited by S. V. Subramanian and V. R. Madhavan, 54–86. Madras: International Institute of Tamil Studies, 1983.

Kriyāviṉ Taṟkālat Tamiḻ Akarāti, Tamiḻ-Tamiḻ-Āṅkilam [Kriya contemporary Tamil dictionary, Tamil-Tamil-English]. Madras: Cre-A Publishers, 1992.

Kumar, Anil. *Medicine and the Raj: British Medical Policy in India, 1835–1911*. New Delhi: Sage, 1998.

Kumar, Deepak. *Science and the Raj, 1857–1905*. Delhi: Oxford University Press, 1997.

Kumarikkaṇṭam Maṟṟum Cintuveḷi Mānāṭṭu Malar: Tamiḻ Aṉṉaikkum Maṟṟum Uṇmai Āyvaip Pōṟṟupavarkaḷukkum Kāṇikkai [Kumari Kantam and the Indus Valley conference souvenir: A devotional offering to the Tamil mother and to those who treasure true research]. Madras: Pannattu Molimaiyam, 1994.

Kuppusami Mudaliyar, K. N. *Citta Maruttuvam* [Siddha medicine]. Second ed. Chennai: Department of Indian Medicine and Homoeopathy, 1987 [1954].

Langford, Jean M. *Fluent Bodies: Ayurvedic Remedies for Postcolonial Balance*. Durham, NC: Duke University Press, 2002.

Latour, Bruno. *Science in Action: How to Follow Scientists and Engineers through Society*. Cambridge, MA: Harvard University Press, 1987.

Leslie, Charles. "Ambiguities of Revivalism in Modern India." In Leslie, *Asian Medical Systems: A Comparative Study*, 356–367. Delhi: Motilal Banarsidass, 1998.

———, ed. *Asian Medical Systems: A Comparative Study*. Delhi: Motilal Banarsidass, 1998.

———. "Interpretations of Illness: Syncretism in Modern Ayurveda." In *Paths to Asian Medical Knowledge*, edited by Charles Leslie and Allan Young, 177–208. New Delhi: Munshiram Manoharlal, 1993.

Leslie, Charles, and Allan Young, eds. *Paths to Asian Medical Knowledge*. New Delhi: Munshiram Manoharlal, 1993.

Levinas, Emmanuel. *Time and the Other [and Additional Essays]*. Translated by Richard Cohen. Pittsburgh, PA: Duquesne University Press, 1987.

———. *Totality and Infinity: An Essay on Exteriority*. Translated by Alphonso Lingis. Pittsburgh, PA: Duquesne University Press, 1969.

Lincoln, Bruce. *Authority: Construction and Corrosion*. Chicago: University of Chicago Press, 1994.

———. *Theorizing Myth: Narrative, Ideology, and Scholarship*. Chicago: University of Chicago Press, 1999.

———. "Theses on Method." *Method and Theory in the Study of Religion* 8.3 (1996): 225–227.

Little, Layne Ross. "Bowl Full of Sky: Story-making and the Many Lives of the Siddha Bhogar." PhD dissertation, University of California, Berkeley, 2004.

———. "An Introduction to the Tamil Siddhas: Tantra, Alchemy, Poetics and Heresy within the Context of Wider Tamil Shaiva World." *Indian Folklife* 2.4 (2003): 14–19.

Luhrmann, T. M. "The Magic of Secrecy." *Ethos* 17.2 (June 1989): 131–65.

Macaulay, Thomas. "Minute on Education." In *Sources of Indian Tradition*, compiled by Wm. Theodore de Bary et al., 596–601. New York: Columbia University Press, 1958.

MacIntyre, Alasdair. *After Virtue: A Study in Moral Theory*. Second ed. Notre Dame, IN: University of Notre Dame Press, 1984.

———. *Three Rival Versions of Moral Enquiry: Encyclopaedia, Genealogy, and Tradition.* Gifford Lectures delivered in the University of Edinburgh in 1988. Notre Dame, IN: University of Notre Dame Press, 1990.

———. *Whose Justice? Which Rationality?* London: Duckworth, 1988.

Madhavan, Chithra. *History and Culture of Tamil Nadu: As Gleaned from the Sanskrit Inscriptions*. Vol. 1. New Delhi: D. K. Printworld, 2005.

Madhavan, V. R. *Akattiyar Vaittiya Kāviyam 1500* [1500 medical verses of Agastya]. Thanjavur, Tamil Nadu: Tamil University Press, 1994.

———. "Medical Education of the Tamils." In *Heritage of the Tamils: Education and Vocation*, edited by S. V. Subramanian and V. R. Madhavan, 222–232. Madras: International Institute of Tamil Studies, 1986.

———. *Siddha Medical Manuscripts in Tamil*. Madras: International Institute of Tamil Studies, 1984.

Mahadevan, C. S. "Kumari Kandam—Land of Gold Mines." In *Kumarikkaṇṭam Maṟṟum Cintuveḷi Mānāṭṭu Malar: Tamiḻ Aṉṉaikkum Maṟṟum Uṇmai Āyvaip Pōṟṟupavarkaḷukkum Kāṇikkai* [Kumari Kantam and the Indus Valley conference souvenir: A devotional offering to the Tamil mother and to those who treasure true research]. Madras, 1994.

Mahalingam, N. *Concept of Kumari Kandam*. Madras: International Linguistic Centre, 1991.

Mani, Lata. *Contentious Traditions: The Debate on Sati in Colonial India*. Berkeley: University of California Press, 1998.

Manian, P. C. *Cittar Kaṇṭa Mūlikai Maruttuvam (Iraṇṭām Pākam)* [The herbal medicine of the siddhars (part 2)]. Chennai: Pilot Publications, 1993.

Manickam Naicker, P. V. *The Tamil Alphabet and Its Mystic Aspect*. Chennai: Asian Educational Services, 1985 [1917].

Manikkavasagam, I. *Nam Nāṭṭu Cittarkaḷ* [Our country's siddhars]. Chennai: Mulikai Mani Publishers, 1978.

Manikkavasagam, N. *Cittar Pāṭalkaḷ* [Verses of the siddhars]. Chennai: Uma Publishers, 1995.

Mannheim, Karl. *Ideology and Utopia: An Introduction to the Sociology of Knowledge*. Translated by Louis Wirth and Edward Shils. New York: Harcourt Brace, 1985 [1936].

Maraimalai Adigal. *Can Hindi Be the Lingua Franca of India?* Madras: South India Shaiva Siddhanta Works, 1969.

———. *Māṇikkavācakar Varalāṟum Kālamum* [The history and times of Manikkavacakar]. Tirunelveli, Tamil Nadu: South Indian Shaiva Siddhanta Works Publishing Society, 1957 [1930].

———. *Tamiḻar Matam* [Tamil religion]. Tirunelveli, Tamil Nadu: South Indian Shaiva Siddhanta Works Publishing Society, 1965.

———. *Tamiḻiṉ Taṉic Ciṟappu* [The unique greatness of Tamil]. Chennai: Pari Nilaiyam, 1959 [1951].

———. *Tirukkuṟaḷ Ārāycci* [Research on the Tirukkural]. Chennai: Pari Nilaiyam, 1977 [1957].

———. *Vēḷāḷar Nākarikam* [Vellalar civilization]. Tirunelveli, Tamil Nadu: South Indian Shaiva Siddhanta Works Publishing Society, 1963 [1923].

Maruttuvar: Kuṭumpanala Citta Maruttuva Māta Itaḻ [The medical doctor: A siddha medicine monthly for the health of the family]. Chennai: P. M. Selvarasu, 1998–1999.

Marx, Karl. "The Eighteenth Brumaire of Louis Bonaparte." In *The Marx-Engels Reader*. Second ed., edited by Robert C. Tucker, 594–617. New York: W. W. Norton, 1978.

Masilamani, B. "Cittarkaḷ Ārātaṉai Muṟaiyum Payaṉum" [The ways and uses of worship of the siddhars]. In *Citta Maruttuva Nūl Ārāycci Nilaiyam Mupperum Viḻā Malar* [Souvenir of the conference of the Siddha Medical Literature Research Centre], 43–45. Chennai: Siddha Medical Literature Research Centre, 1983.

McGlasham, Alastair. *See Periya Purāṇam.*

Meykandar, C. "Citta Vaityattiṉ Tēvai" [The needs of siddha medicine]. In *Iraṇṭām Ulakattamiḻ Māṉāṭu Citta Maruttuva Karuttaraṅku Ciṟappu Malar* [Second World Tamil Conference, siddha medicine seminar special souvenir], 44–48. Chennai: Second World Tamil Conference, 1968.

Miller, Barbara Stoler, trans. *Yoga: Discipline and Freedom: The Yoga Sutra Attributed to Patanjali.* Berkeley: University of California Press, 1996.

Monius, Anne. "Love, Violence, and the Aesthetics of Disgust: Śaivas and Jains in Medieval South India." *Journal of Indian Philosophy* 32 (2004): 113–172.

More, Thomas. *Utopia.* New York: E. P. Dutton, 1935.

Mueller, Max. *Chips from a German Woodshop,* vol. 1. *Essays in the Science of Religion.* Chico, CA: Scholars Press Reprint, 1985 [1869].

Murukaiyan, P. *Tiruvaḷḷuvam.* Iracapuram, Tamil Nadu: Muttu Illam, 1990.

Muthian, S. M. *Saiva Sithantham in Relation to Science.* Jaffna: P. Mahadevan Urunavalai, 1967.

Muttukkaruppa Pillai, P. "Cittarkaḷiṉ Vayatu" [The age of the siddhars]. In *Iraṇṭām Ulakattamiḻ Māṉāṭu Citta Maruttuva Karuttaraṅku Ciṟappu Malar* [Second World Tamil Conference, siddha medicine seminar special souvenir], 36–38. Chennai: Second World Tamil Conference, 1968.

"Nalla Nalla Nāṭṭu Maruntukaḷ" [Very good country medicines]. *Mūlikaimaṇi* 29.9 (March 15, 2002): 41–43.

Nambi Arooran, K. *Tamil Renaissance and Dravidian Nationalism, 1905–1944.* Madurai, Tamil Nadu: Koodal, 1980.

Nandy, Ashis, and Shiv Visvanathan. "Modern Medicine and Its Non-modern Critics: A Study in Discourse." In *Dominating Knowledge: Development, Culture and Resistance,* edited by Frederique Apffel Marglin and Stephen A. Marglin, 145–184. Oxford, UK: Clarendon Press, 1990.

Naranjana Devi, R. *Teṉṉintiya Maruttuva Varalāṟu* [History of medicine in south India]. Chennai: International Institute of Tamil Studies, 2004.

Narayana Ayyar, C. *Origin and Early History of Saivism in South India*. Madras University Historical Series 6. Madras: University of Madras, 1936.

Narayanaswami, V. *Introduction to the Siddha System of Medicine*. Madras: S. S. Anandam Research Institute of Siddha Medicine, 1975.

———. "Systematic Development of Ayurveda: A Short Survey." In *The Government College of Integrated Medicine Decennial Souvenir*, 79–84. Chennai: 1957.

Natarajan, Kanchana. "'Divine Semen' and the Alchemical Conversion of Iramatevar." *The Medieval History Journal* 7.2 (2004): 255–278.

Nathan. "Cintuveḷi Nākarikam Paṟṟiya Varalāṟṟu Maṟaippu Vēlaikaḷukku Maṟuppu" [Refutation of attempts to obscure the history of the Indus Valley Civilization]. In *Kumarikkaṇṭam Maṟṟum Cintuveḷi Māṉāṭṭu Malar: Tamiḻ Aṉṉaikkum Maṟṟum Uṇmai Āyvaip Pōṟṟupavarkaḷukkum Kāṇikkai* [Kumari Kantam and the Indus Valley conference souvenir: A devotional offering to the Tamil mother and to those who treasure true research]. Madras: 1994.

Nehru, Jawaharlal. "Preface." In *The Government College of Integrated Medicine Decennial Souvenir*. Chennai: 1957.

Nichter, Mark *Anthropological Approaches to the Study of Ethnomedicine*. Philadelphia: Gordon and Breach, 1992.

Nietzsche, Friedrich. *On the Genealogy of Morality*. Edited by Keith Ansell-Pearson, translated by Carol Diethe. Cambridge Texts in the History of Political Thought. New York: Cambridge University Press, 1994.

Nijalangappa, S. "Preface." In *The Government College of Integrated Medicine Decennial Souvenir*. Chennai: 1957.

Nilakanta Sastri, K. A. *A History of South India: From Prehistoric Times to the Fall of Vijayanagar*. Fourth ed. Delhi: Oxford University Press, 1975.

Obeyesekere, Gananath. "Science, Experimentation, and Clinical Practice in Ayurveda." In *Paths to Asian Medical Knowledge*, edited by Charles Leslie and Allan Young, 160–176. New Delhi: Munshiram Manoharlal Publishers, 1993.

O'Flaherty, Wendy Doniger. *The Origins of Evil in Hindu Mythology*. Berkeley: University of California Press, 1976.

———, trans. *The Rig Veda, An Anthology*. New York: Penguin, 1981.

———. *Śiva: The Erotic Ascetic*. New York: Oxford University Press, 1973.

Ohnuki-Tierney, Emiko. *Illness and Culture in Contemporary Japan: An Anthropological View*. Cambridge: Cambridge University Press, 1984.

Palm-leaf and Other Manuscripts in Indian Languages: Proceedings of the National Seminar. Madras: Institute of Asian Studies, 1996.

Pandian, A. J. "Exhibition of Indian Medicines: Opening Address." *Journal of Indian Medicine* 1.1 (April 1935): 32–33.

"Panel to Scrutinise Tamil Film Titles." *The Hindu*, online edition, August 23, 2007. http://www.hindu.com/2007/08/23/stories/2007082353610400.htm, accessed January 14, 2008.

Parthasarathy, G. J. "Cittar Varalāṟu: Tirumūlar" [The history of the siddhars: Tirumular]. *Cittar Ulakam* [Siddhar world] 2.1 (February 2003): 8–9.

Parthasarathy, K. "Kaṭṭiḻanta Citta Maruttuvarkaḷ Orumaippāṭu" [The unification of siddha doctors who have lost their ties (to one another)]. In *Citta Maruttuva Nūl Āräycci*

Nilaiyam Mupperum Viḻā Malar [Souvenir of the conference of the Siddha Medical Literature Research Centre], 57–59. Chennai: Siddha Medical Literature Research Centre, 1983.

Parthasarathy, R. *The Tale of an Anklet: An Epic of South India*. New York: Columbia University Press, 1993.

Parvati, V. S. "Citta Vaittiyamum Makaḷir Maruttuvamum" [Siddha medicine and women's medicine]. In *Iraṇṭām Ulakattamiḻ Mānāṭu Citta Maruttuva Karuttaraṅku Ciṟappu Malar* [Second World Tamil Conference, siddha medicine seminar special souvenir], 86–89. Chennai: Second World Tamil Conference, 1968.

Pasumbonkilar, N. *Kuṟaḷ Neṟiyum Citta Neṟiyum* [The doctrine of the Tirukkural and the doctrine of the siddhars]. Pacumpon, Tamil Nadu: Sivananda Siddhaneri Payirci Kalakam, 1974.

Patiṉeṉ Cittarkaḷ Vaittiya Cillaṟaik Kōvai, Iraṇṭām Pākam [A collection of medical tidbits of the eighteen siddhars, vol. 2]. Edited by S. P. Ramachandran. Chennai: Tamarai Nulakam, 1996.

Periya Purāṇam. Translated by Alastair McGlashan in *The History of the Holy Servants of the Lord Siva, A Translation of the Periya Purāṇam of Cēkkiḻār*. Victoria, BC: Trafford Publishing, 2006.

Periya Purāṇam eṉṉum Tiruttoṇṭar Purāṇam. [The great Purana, the Purana of the holy devotees]. With commentary by C. K. Subramanya Mudaliyar. 7 vols. Coimbatur, Tamil Nadu: Kovai Tamil Sangam, 1975.

Perumal, V. "Citta Maruttuvattiṉ Māṇpu" [The greatness of siddha medicine]. In *Iraṇṭām Ulakattamiḻ Mānāṭu Citta Maruttuva Karuttaraṅku Ciṟappu Malar* [Second World Tamil Conference, siddha medicine seminar special souvenir], 69–73. Chennai: Second World Tamil Conference, 1968.

Peterson, Indira Viswanathan. *Poems to Śiva: The Hymns of the Tamil Saints*. Princeton, NJ: Princeton University Press, 1989.

———. "Śramaṇas against the Tamil Way: Jains as Others in Tamil Śaiva Literature." In *Open Boundaries: Jain Communities and Cultures in Indian History*, edited by John E. Cort, 163–85. Albany: State University of New York Press, 1998.

Pōkanāyaṉār Aruḷicceyta Pūjāviti 37 [Bhogar's 37 verses on techniques of worship]. In *Patiṉeṉ Cittarkaḷ Vaittiya Cillaṟaik Kōvai, Iraṇṭām Pākam* [A collection of medical tidbits of the eighteen siddhars, vol. 2], edited by S. P. Ramachandran, 373–381. Chennai: Tamarai Nulakam, 1996.

Pollock, Sheldon. "The Cosmopolitan Vernacular." *Journal of Asian Studies* 57.1 (February 1998): 6–37.

Pollock, Sheldon, et al. "Cosmopolitanisms." In *Cosmopolitanism*, edited by Carol A. Breckenridge et al., 1–14. Durham, NC: Duke University Press, 2002.

Prakash, Gyan. *Another Reason: Science and the Imagination of Modern India*. Princeton, NJ: Princeton University Press, 1999.

Prema, C. *Citta Maruttuva Nūlōti* [Bibliography of siddha medicine]. Thanjavur, Tamil Nadu: Tamil University Press, 1988.

Purnalingam Pillai, M. S. *Tamil Literature*. Munnirpallam, Tinnevelly District, Tamil Nadu: Bibliotheca, 1929.

Rahman, Syed Zillur. "Unani Medicine in India: Its Origin and Fundamental Concepts." In *Medicine and Life Sciences in India*, edited by B. V. Subbarayappa, 292–325. Delhi: Centre for Studies in Civilization, 2001.

Ramachandran, S. P. *Cittarkaḷ Varalāṟu* [History of the siddhars]. Chennai: Tamarai Nulakam, 2002.

Ramamurthy, Kundrathur. *Mūlikai Pēcukiṟatu* [Speaking about medicinal plants]. Chennai: Anusuya Patippagam, 1995.

Ramamurthy, Kundrathur, and R. R. Devi. *Uṭal Nalam Uṅkaḷ Kaikaḷil* [Bodily health is in your hands]. Chennai: Kundrathur Ramamurthy, n.d.

Ramana Sastri, V. V. "The Doctrinal Culture and Tradition of the Siddhas." In *The Cultural Heritage of India.* Vol. 4. *Religions*, edited by Haridas Bhattacharyya. Calcutta: Ramakrishna Mission Institute of Culture, 1956.

Ramasami, E. V. (Periyar). *Collected Works of Thanthai Periyar E. V. Ramasami.* Madras: Periyar Self-Respect Propaganda Institution, 1982.

———. *Irāmāyaṇak Kuṟippukaḷ (Ellām Ātāraṅkaḷaip Poṟuttē Tokukkappaṭṭavai)* [Notes on the Rāmāyaṇa (compiled with all the evidence)]. Trichy: Periyar Self-Respect Institute Publications, 1972.

———. *Irāmāyaṇap Pāttiraṅkaḷ* [Characters of the Rāmāyaṇa]. Trichy: Periyar Self-Respect Institute Publications, 1972 [1930].

———. *Is There a God? Selections from Periyar's Speeches and Writing.* Chennai: Emerald Publishers, 1996.

———. *The Ramayana (A True Reading).* Chennai: Dravidar Kazhagam Publications, 1998 [1959].

———. *The Revolutionary Sayings of Periyar.* Translated by R. Ganapati. Madras: Department of Information and Public Relations, Government of Tamil Nadu, 1985.

———. *Tamiḻar Tamiḻnāṭu Tamiḻarpaṇpāṭu* [The Tamil people, The Tamil country, and Tamil culture]. Chennai: Dravidian Kalaka Veliyitu, 1996.

Ramaswami Reddiar, O. P. "Hindu System of Medicine and the Spirit of Service: An Address by the Premier of Madras." *Journal of the College of Indian Medicine* 3 (April 1949): 3–6.

Ramaswamy, Sumathi. "Lemuria in Tamil Spatial Fables." *Journal of Asian Studies* 59.3 (August 2000): 575–602.

———. *The Lost Land of Lemuria: Fabulous Geographies, Catastrophic Histories.* Berkeley: University of California Press, 2004.

———. *Passions of the Tongue: Language Devotion in Tamil India, 1891–1970.* Berkeley: University of California Press, 1997.

Ranga, Rama S., et al. "Rasagenthi Lehyam (RL), a Novel Complementary and Alternative Medicine for Prostate Cancer." *Cancer Chemotherapy and Pharmacology* 54 (2004): 7–15.

Rangarajan, Malathi. "Managing a Mega Show." *The Hindu,* online edition, December 31, 2004. http://www.hindu.com/fr/2004/12/31/stories/2004123102490400.htm, accessed November 19, 2007.

Renganathan, Lakshmi. "Mutal Paricu Peṟṟa Kaṭṭuraikaḷ" [Winning essays]. In *Citta Maruttuva Nūl Ārāycci Nilaiyam Mupperum Viḻā Malar* [Souvenir of the conference of the Siddha Medical Literature Research Centre], 64–66. Chennai: Siddha Medical Literature Research Centre, 1983.

Report of the Committee on the Indigenous Systems of Medicine. Madras: Government of Madras, 1923.

Report of the Committee on Indigenous Systems of Medicine, Report, Recommendations, and Appendices. Delhi: Ministry of Health, Government of India, 1948.

Report of the Committee to Assess and Evaluate the Present Status of Ayurvedic System of Medicine. Delhi: Government of India, Ministry of Health, 1958.

Report of the Special Committee Appointed by the Joint Board of the Dravida Vaidya Mandal and the Madras Ayurveda Sabha in Reply to the Report on the Investigation into the Indigenous Drugs. Srirangam, Tamil Nadu: Sri Vani Vilas Press, 1921.

Richman, Paula. "E. V. Ramasami's Reading of the *Ramayana.*" In *Many Ramayanas: The Diversity of a Narrative Tradition in South Asia*, edited by Paula Richman, 175–201. Berkeley: University of California Press, 1991.

Ricoeur, Paul. *Lectures on Ideology and Utopia*, edited by George H. Taylor. New York: Columbia University Press, 1986.

Ryerson, Charles A. *Regionalism and Religion: The Tamil Renaissance and Popular Hinduism.* Madras: Christian Literature Society, 1988.

Said, Edward W. *Orientalism.* New York: Pantheon, 1978.

Sambasivam Pillai, T. V. *Introduction to Siddha Medicine.* Madras: Directorate of Indian Medicine and Homeopathy, 1993.

———. *Tamil-English Dictionary of Medicine, Chemistry, Botany, and Allied Sciences.* 5 vols. Madras: Research Institute of Siddhar's Science, 1991–1998.

Sami Chidambaranar. *Cittarkaḷ Kaṇṭa Viññāṉam Tattuvam* [The true science of the siddhars]. Chennai: Manivasagar Patippagam, 2001.

———. *Tamiḻar Talaivar Periyār I. Ve. Rā. Varalāṟu* [The history of Periyar E.V.R., leader of the Tamil people]. Chennai: Tamil Nul Nilaiyam, 1939.

Samuel, G. John., ed. *Citta Maruttuvac Cuvaṭikaḷ* [Siddha medical manuscripts]. Chennai: Institute of Asian Studies, 1999.

———. *Kumari Mutal Vārcā Varai: Paḻantamiḻc Cuvaṭikaḷait Tēṭi Oru Payaṇam* [From Kanya Kumari to Warsaw: A journey in search of ancient Tamil manuscripts]. Chennai: Institute of Asian Studies, 1994.

Sanguppulavar, Nelvay. *Cittarkaḷ Kaṇṭa Uṇavu Maruttuvam* [The food-medicine of the siddhars]. Chennai: Pilot Publications, 1994.

Scharfe, Hartmut. "The Doctrine of the Threee Humors in Traditional Indian Medicine and the Alleged Antiquity of Tamil Siddha Medicine." *Journal of the American Oriental Society* 119.4 (October–December 1999): 609–629.

Schomer, Karine, and W. H. McLeod, eds. *The Sants: Studies in a Devotional Tradition of India.* Berkeley: University of California Press, 1987.

Scott, Joan W. "The Evidence of Experience." *Critical Inquiry* 17.4 (Summer 1991): 773–797.

Sewell, William H., Jr. "Geertz, Cultural Systems, and History: From Synchrony to Transformation." In *The Fate of "Culture": Geertz and Beyond*, edited by Sherry B. Ortner, 35–55. Berkeley: University of California Press, 1999.

Shankar, Settu. "Tax Exemption for Shivaji." Oneindia, June 6, 2007. http://entertainment.oneindia.in/tamil/exclusive/shivaji-tamil-nadu-govt-060607.html, accessed January 14, 2008.

Shanmuga Velan, A. *Siddhar's Science of Longevity and Kalpa Medicine of India.* Madras: Sakthi Nilayam, 1963.

———. "Tirumūlar Aruḷiya Maruttuvat Tirumantiram 8000" [The 8000 verses of Tirumular's medical Tirumantiram]. In *Iraṇṭām Ulakattamiḻ Mānāṭu Citta Maruttuva Karuttaraṅku Ciṟappu Malar* [Second World Tamil Conference, siddha medicine seminar special souvenir], 49–53. Chennai: Second World Tamil Conference, 1968.

———. "Vāḻka Citta Maruttuvam" [May siddha medicine prosper!]. In *Iraṇṭām Ulakattamiḻ Mānāṭu Citta Maruttuva Karuttaraṅku Ciṟappu Malar* [Second World Tamil Conference, siddha medicine seminar special souvenir], 1. Chennai: Second World Tamil Conference, 1968.

Shanmukavelu, M. *A Study of Siddha Vaidya Muppu.* Coimbatore: Industrial Welfare Association, 1951.

Shils, Edward. *Tradition.* London: Faber and Faber, 1981.

Shulman, David Dean, trans. *Songs of the Harsh Devotee: The Tēvāram of Cuntaramūrttināyaṉār.* Philadelphia: Department of South Asia Regional Studies, University of Pennsylvania, 1990.

———. *Tamil Temple Myths.* Princeton, NJ: Princeton University Press, 1980.

Simmel, Georg. *The Sociology of Georg Simmel.* Translated, edited, and with an introduction by Kurt H. Wolff. Glencoe, IL: Free Press, 1950.

Simple Home Remedies in Indian Medicine. Madras: Directorate of Indian Medicine and Homoeopathy, 1996.

Singaravelu Vaittiyar. *Ārōkkiyam Tarum Cittarkaḷiṉ Kīraikaḷ, Mūlikaikaḷ* [The siddhars' greens and medicinal plants that bestow health]. Chennai: R. R. Nilaiyam, 1988.

Sivaraja Pillai, K. N. *Agastya in the Tamil Land.* New Delhi: Asian Educational Services, 1985 [reprint].

Sivaramakrishnan, Kavita. *Old Potions, New Bottles: Recasting Indigenous Medicine in Colonial Punjab, 1850–1945.* New Delhi: Orient Longman, 2006.

Sivathamby, Karthigesu. "The Politics of a Literary Style." *Social Scientist* 6.8 (March 1978): 16–33.

Smith, Wilfred Cantwell. *Belief and History.* Charlottesville: University of Virginia Press, 1977.

Somasundara Bharathiar, Navalar. *The Papers of Dr. Navalar Somasundara Bharathiar.* Edited by S. Sambasivan. Madurai, Tamil Nadu: Navalar Puthaka Nilayam, 1967.

Srinivasa Aiyangar, P. T. (a.k.a. P. T. Srinivas Iyengar). *Pre-Aryan Tamil Culture.* Madras: Asian Educational Services, 1995 [1929].

———. *History of the Tamils, From the Earliest Times to 600 A.D.* New Delhi: Asian Educational Services, 1982.

Srinivasalu Naidu, A. "Medical Education and Medical Relief." In *The Government College of Integrated Medicine Decennial Souvenir*, 41–47. Chennai: 1957.

Srirangam Siddhar. *Cittarkaḷiṉ Ñāṉappāṭalkaḷ* [The siddhars' verses of wisdom]. Trichy, Tamil Nadu: Shrirangam Siddhar, 1991.

———. *Siddhar's Yogic Experiences.* Trichy, Tamil Nadu: Srirangam Siddha, 1992.

———. *You Can also Become a Siddhar.* Trichy, Tamil Nadu: Srirangam Siddha, 1992.

Stein, Burton. "Circulation and the Historical Geography of Tamil Country." *Journal of Asian Studies* 36.1 (November 1977): 7–26.

———. *Peasant, State, and Society in Medieval South India*. Delhi: Oxford University Press, 1994.

Subbarayappa, B. V. "Chemical Practices and Alchemy." In *A Concise History of Science in India*, edited by D. M. Bose, 274–349. Delhi: Indian National Science Academy, 1971.

———. *Medicine and Life Sciences in India*. History of Science, Philosophy, and Culture in Indian Civilization 4.2. Delhi: Centre for Studies in Civilization, 2001.

———. "Siddha Medicine." In *Medicine and Life Sciences in India*, edited by B. V. Subbarayappa, 427–451. Delhi: Centre for Studies in Civilization, 2001.

———."Siddha Medicine: An Overview." *The Lancet* 350.9094 (December 1997): 1841–45.

Subramania Iyer, A. V. *The Poetry and Philosophy of the Tamil Siddhars*. Chidambaram, Tamil Nadu: Manivasakar Noolakam, 1969.

Subramania Pillai, G. "Introduction and History of Saiva Siddhanta." In *Collected Lectures on Saiva Siddhanta, 1946–1954*, edited by G. Subramania Pillai, 1–96. Annamalai, Tamil Nadu: Annamalai University, 1965.

Subramaniam, M. C. *Cittarkaḷ Iracavātakkalai* [The siddhars' art of alchemy]. Chennai: Tamarai Nulakam, 1985.

Subramaniam, N. *Cittavaittiyattiṉ Muṉṉēṟṟam* [The development of siddha medicine]. Dharmapuram, Tamil Nadu: Kannigaparamesvari Press, 1940.

Subramanian, K. R. *The Origin of Saivism and Its History in the Tamil Land*. New Delhi: Asian Educational Resources, 1985 [1929].

Subramanian, Narendra. *Ethnicity and Populist Mobilization: Political Parties, Citizens and Democracy in South India*. Delhi: Oxford University Press, 1999.

Subramanian, S. V., and V. R. Madhavan, eds. *Heritage of the Tamils: Siddha Medicine*. Madras: International Institute of Tamil Studies, 1983.

———, eds. *Heritage of the Tamils: Education and Vocation*. Madras: International Institute of Tamil Studies, 1986.

Subramanian, Shakti P. *Nellai Māvaṭṭac Cittarkaḷ* [The siddhars of Nellai District]. Chennai: South India Shaiva Siddhanta Works Publishing Society, 1995.

Swaminathaiyar, U. V. *The Story of My Life*. Translated by S. K. Guruswamy. Madras: Dr. U. V. Swaminathaiyer Library, 1980.

Tamiḻ (Citta) Maruttuvak Kōṭpāṭu [Tamil (siddha) medical theory]. Chennai: Tamil Nadu Government, Department of Indian and Homeopathic Medicine, 1995.

Tamil Lexicon. Madras: University of Madras, 1982.

"Tamiḻil Peyar Vaittāl Atirṣṭam Atikarikkum" [Giving Tamil names increases good fortune]. In *Mūlikaimaṇi* 29.10 (May 2002): 26–28.

Tamilpriyan. *Patiṉeṭṭu Cittarkaḷiṉ Mukkiya Pāṭalkaḷum Viḷakkaṅkaḷum* [Important verses of the eighteen siddhars, with explanations]. Chennai: Narmada Publishers, 2006.

Tangavel, M. P. "Tamiḻakamum Citta Vaittiyamum" [The Tamil land and siddha medicine]. In *Iraṇṭām Ulakattamiḻ Mānāṭu Citta Maruttuva Karuttaraṅku Ciṟappu Malar* [Second World Tamil Conference, siddha medicine seminar special souvenir], 19–25. Chennai: Second World Tamil Conference, 1968.

Taylor, Mark C., ed. *Critical Terms for Religious Studies*. Chicago: University of Chicago Press, 1998.

Thambidurai, M. "Policy Note 2001–2002." Government of Tamil Nadu, Culture and Religious Endowments Department. http://www.tn.gov.in/policynotes/archives/policy2001-2/tamil-e-2001-2.htm, accessed December 20, 2007.

Thirunarayanan, T. *An Introduction to Siddha Medicine*. Tiruchendur, Tamil Nadu: Thirukumaran Publishers, 1993.

Thottam, Paul Joseph. *Siddha Medicine: A Handbook of Traditional Remedies*. New Delhi: Penguin Books India, 2000.

Thyagarajan, R. "Key Note Address." In *Heritage of the Tamils: Siddha Medicine*, edited by S. V. Subramanian and V. R. Madhavan. Madras: International Institute of Tamil Studies, 1983.

Tieken, Herman. *Kāvya in South India: Old Tamil Caṅkam Poetry*. Groningen: Egbert Forsten, 2001.

Tiṉa Karaṉ [The sun]. Chennai.

Tiṉattanti [The daily telegraph]. Chennai.

Tirumantiram. With commentary of G. Varadarajan. 3 vols. Chennai: Palaniappa Piratars, 2006 [1978].

Tirumantiram: A Tamil Scriptural Classic. Translated by Dr. B. Natarajan. Madras: Sri Ramakrishna Math, 1991.

Tirumūlanātar Aruḷiya Tirumantiram [Tirumantiram of Tirumular]. With Explanatory Notes by Dr. Cupa Annamalai. 3 vols. Chennai: Centre for Indian Cultural Research, 1997.

Tirumūla Nāyaṉār aruḷic ceyta Tirumantiram [Tirumantiram of Tirumular Nayanar]. With commentary of P. Ramanatha Pillai. Tirunelveli, Tamil Nadu: South Indian Shaiva Siddhanta Works Publishing Society, 1994 [1942]).

Tirumūlar Karukkiṭai Vaittiyam 600 [Tirumular's 600 profound medical verses]. Chennai: Tamarai Nulakam, 1993.

Tirumūlar Vaittiyam 1000 [Tirumular's 1000 verses on medicine], edited by S. P. Ramachandran. Chennai: Tamarai Nulakam, 1993.

Tirumurti, T. S. "Presidential Address." *Journal of Indian Medicine* 1.1 (April 1935): 16–31.

Tiruttoṇṭar Tiruvantāti. In *Patiṉorām Tirumuṟai, Mūlamum Uraiyum* [The eleventh Tirumuṟai, root text and commentary]. With Commentary of P. R. Natarajan, 730–777. Chennai: Uma Pataippakam, 2005.

Tiruvaḷḷuvar Īrāyiramāṇṭu Niṟaivu Viḻā Malar [Commemorative volume of the celebration of two thousand years of Tiruvalluvar]. Kovai, Tamil Nadu: Pavendar Bharatidasan Mandram, 1970.

Tolkāppiyam. With Commentary of S. Singaravelan. Chennai: South Indian Shaiva Siddhanta Works Publishing Society, 2005.

Trautmann, Thomas R. *Aryans and British India*. Berkeley: University of California Press, 1997.

———. *Languages and Nations: The Dravidian Proof in Colonial Madras*. Berkeley: University of California Press, 2006.

Trawick, Margaret. "The Ayurvedic Physician as Scientist." *Social Science and Medicine* 24.12 (1987): 1031–50.

———. "Death and Nurturance in Indian Systems of Healing." In Charles Leslie and Allan Young, *Paths to Asian Medical Knowledge*, 129–59. New Delhi: Munshiram Manoharlal, 1993.

Urban, Hugh B. *The Economics of Ecstasy: Tantra, Secrecy, and Power in Colonial Bengal.* New York: Oxford University Press, 2001.

Uromariṣi Muppucūttiram 30 [Uromarishi's text on muppu in thirty verses]. In *Patiṉeṇ Cittarkaḷ Vaittiya Cillaṟaik Kōvai, Iraṇṭām Pākam* [A collection of medical tidbits of the eighteen siddhars, vol. 2], edited by S. P. Ramachandran, 521–527. Chennai: Tamarai Nulakam, 1996.

Uttamarayan, K. C. "Tamiḻ Maruttuvam Uyvaṭaiya Vaḻimuṟai" [The way to save Tamil medicine]. In *Citta Maruttuva Nūl Ārāycci Nilaiyam Mupperum Viḻā Malar* [Souvenir of the conference of the Siddha Medical Literature Research Centre], 42. Chennai: Siddha Medical Literature Research Centre, 1983.

———. *Tōṟṟakkirama Ārāycciyum Cittamaruttuva Varalāṟum* [Research on the natural order and the history of siddha medicine]. Chennai: Tamil Nadu Government Publications, 1992.

Vaitheespara, Ravindiran. "Caste, Hybridity and the Construction of Cultural Identity in Colonial India: Maraimalai Adigal and the Intellectual Genealogy of Dravidian Nationalism, 1800–1950." PhD dissertation, University of Toronto, 1999.

Vaiyapuripillai, S. *History of the Tamil Language and Literature.* With an introduction by Karthigesu Sivathamby. Second ed. Madras: New Century Book House, 1988 [1956].

van Hollen, Cecilia. "Nationalism, Transnationalism, and the Politics of 'Traditional' Indian Medicine for HIV/AIDS." In *Asian Medicine and Globalization*, edited by Joseph Alter, 88–106. Philadelphia: University of Pennsylvania Press, 2005.

Varadarajan, M. *A History of Tamil Literature.* Translated by E. Sa. Visswanathan. Delhi: Sahitya Akademi, 1988.

———. *Tamiḻ Ilakkiya Varalāṟu* [History of Tamil literature]. New Delhi: Sahitya Akademi, 2002.

Vellaivaranan, K. *Paṉṉirutirumuṟai Varalāṟu* [History of the twelve Tirumurai]. 2 vols. Chidambaram: Annamalai University, 1997 [1980].

Vengatasubramanian, T. P. *Tirumantiram Vaittiyappakuti* [Medical portion of the Tirumantiram]. Third ed. Thiruvavadudurai, Tamil Nadu: Thiruvavadudurai Adinam, 2003 [1957].

Venkatachalapathy, A. R. "'Enna Prayocanam?' Constructing the Canon in Colonial Tamil Nadu." *Indian Economic Social History Review* 42.4 (2005): 535–553.

———. *In Those Days There Was No Coffee: Writings in Cultural History.* New Delhi: Yoda Press, 2006.

———. "Maruttuva Akarāti Tanta Mētai: Oru Tuṉpiyal Nāṭakam" [The genius who produced a medical dictionary: A tragic drama]. In *Kālaccuvaṭu* 85 (January 2007): 72–76.

———. *Tirāviṭa Iyakkamum Vēḷāḷarum* [Vellalars and the Dravidian Movement]. Chennai: South Asia Books, 1994.

Venkatesan, K. "Alōpatiyil 'Side Effects' Atircci Rippōrṭ" [A shocking report on side effects in allopathy]. *Mūlikaimaṇi* 30.1 (November 2002): 8–12.

———. *Tamiḻ Ilakkiyattil Citta Maruttuvam* [Siddha medicine in Tamil literature]. Chennai: Shri Shakti Patippakam, 1998.

———. "Tamiḻarp Paṇpāṭṭil Ārōkkiyam" [The healthiness of Tamil culture]. *Mūlikaimaṇi* 29.9 (March 2002): 36–40.

Venkatraman, R. *A History of the Tamil Siddha Cult*. Madurai, Tamil Nadu: Ennes, 1990.

Venugopal, P. M. "Siddha System of Medicine Based on Saiva Siddhanta Doctrine." *Journal of the Government College of Indian Medicine* 4.1 (1959): 61–63.

Visswanathan, E. S. *The Political Career of E. V. Ramasami Naicker: A Study in the Politics of Tamilnadu, 1920–1949*. Madras: Ravi and Vasanth Publishers, 1983.

Waghorne, Joanne P. *Diaspora of the Gods: Modern Hindu Temples in an Urban Middle-Class World*. New York: Oxford University Press, 2004.

Weber, Max. *Economy and Society: An Outline of Interpretive Sociology*. Translated by Ephraim Fischoff, Hans Gerth, A. M. Henderson, Ferdinand Kolegar, C. Wright Mills, Talcott Parsons, et al. Berkeley: University of California Press, 1978.

Weiss, Richard. "Divorcing Ayurveda: Siddha Medicine and the Quest for Uniqueness." In *Modern and Global Ayurveda: Pluralism and Paradigms*, edited by Dagmar Wujastyk and Frederick M. Smith, 77–99. Albany: State University of New York Press, 2008.

———. "The Reformulation of a Holy Science: Siddha Medicine and Tradition in South India." PhD dissertation, University of Chicago, 2003.

Weiss, Richard, and Gregory Grieve. "Illuminating the Half-life of Tradition: Legitimation, Agency and Counter-Hegemonies." In *Historicizing "Tradition" in the Study of Religion*, edited by Steven Engler and Gregory P. Grieve, 1–15. Berlin: Walter de Gruyter, 2005.

Whicher, Ian. "Yoga and Freedom: A Reconsideration of Patanjali's Classical Yoga." *Philosophy East and West* 48.2 (April 1998): 272–322.

White, David Gordon. *The Alchemical Body: Siddha Traditions in Medieval India*. Chicago: University of Chicago Press, 1996.

Williams, Raymond. *Keywords*. New York: Oxford University Press, 1983.

Wise, Thomas. *Ayurveda, or, Hindu System of Medical Science*. Third ed. Delhi: Shri Satguru Publications, 1998.

Wujastyk, Dominik. *The Roots of Ayurveda: Selections from Sanskrit Medical Writings*. Delhi: Penguin Books, 2001.

Zimmermann, Francis. *The Jungle and the Aroma of Meats: An Ecological Theme in Hindu Medicine*. Berkeley: University of California Press, 1987.

Zizek, Slavoj. "Is It Possible to Traverse the Fantasy in Cyberspace?" In *The Zizek Reader*, edited by Elizabeth Wright and Edmond Wright, 102–124. Oxford, UK: Blackwell, 1999.

———. *The Plague of Fantasies*. New York: Verso, 1997.

———. *The Sublime Object of Ideology*. New York: Verso, 1989.

Zvelebil, Kamil V. *Lexicon of Tamil Literature*. Leiden: E. J. Brill, 1995.

———. *The Poets of the Powers*. London: Rider, 1973.

———. *The Smile of Murugan: On Tamil Literature of South India*. Leiden: E. J. Brill, 1973.

———. *Tamil Literature*. A History of Indian Literature 10. Wiesbaden: Otto Harrassowitz, 1974.

Zysk, Kenneth G. *Asceticism and Healing in Ancient India: Medicine in the Buddhist Monastery*. New York: Oxford University Press, 1991.

Index

Aryans (*continued*)
character of, 18, 97, 125, 145
corrupting influence of, 87, 116, 119, 125, 127, 131, 218n107
and Dravidians, 10, 98–100, 119, 122–123
and Hinduism, 115
and Indian nationalism, 195
and Indus Valley, 96
invasion by, 4, 79, 80, 82, 90, 91, 93, 94–98, 102–106, 204n27
and Maraimalai Adigal, 122, 123, 125, 127–128
and Orientalism, 10, 33, 90
as Other, 18, 105, 106
plagiarism by, 102–103
and Ramasami, E. V., 115, 116
and rituals, 125
and Self-Respect Movement, 122
and siddhars, 112, 119
and superstition, 18, 128, 145
and Tamil identity, 96, 97
and Theosophists, 100
and utopia, 98, 104
asceticism, 54, 60, 64, 66, 69, 113
asthma, 17, 35, 55, 61, 141, 142, 165, 192
astrology, 8, 46, 47, 48, 52, 117, 133
atheism, 111, 115, 120, 122
ātman, 54
Aurobindo, Sri, 200
autochthony
of Indian medicine, 27, 29, 31, 32, 100, 207n48
of siddha medicine, 6, 29–32, 93, 139, 144
of siddhars, 54, 56, 57, 69
of Tamil people, 57, 88, 93, 96, 99, 123, 215n31
of tradition, 39
ayurveda
and alchemy, 25, 85
as challenge to siddha medicine, 41, 72, 77, 105
and colonialism, 25, 36
as corrupting siddha, 79, 82, 83, 101–104
and education, 4, 22, 206n9, 208n62
as elitist, 166
as foreign, 55, 102, 103, 144
hegemony of, 101, 102, 147, 172
as Hindu, 72, 121
as indigenous medicine, 6, 26
limitations of, 73, 145
as national medicine, 9, 23, 24, 42, 57, 79, 95, 100, 146, 201, 204n25, 214n125
as outdated, 23, 190
as perfect, 33, 34, 35, 208n65, 216n51
popularity of, 3
and Sanskrit, 21
and secrecy, 171, 172
and siddha medicine, 30, 79, 80, 83, 84–88, 92, 95, 100–104, 118, 132, 146, 204n24
statistics of, 4
and superstition, 72, 145

Balayogi, 55
Barthes, Roland, 149
baspams. See *parpam*
belief, 43–44
Besant, Annie, 89, 100, 216n35
Bharatiar, 96–97
Bhogar
and China, 197, 198–199
and egalitarianism, 112, 158
as guru, 113
as *kāyasiddhar*, 48
as medical leader, 67
popularity of, 42
as *sanmārgasiddhar*, 47
and siddha lineage, 16, 55, 153
and siddha medicine, 68, 71, 182, 219n4
bile, 30, 31, 85, 129, 137, 143, 196, 197
biomedicine. *See* Western medicine
Blavatsky, Helena P., 89, 216n35
brahmans. *See also* Aryans
and Agastya, 81–83
as Aryans, 18, 99, 204n27
and ayurveda, 9, 24, 72, 87, 100, 127
corrupting influence of, 96, 127
critiques of, 8, 42, 47, 111, 114–116, 119, 122, 125
and Hinduism, 18, 97, 115, 116, 119, 125–126